TURNAROUND

TURNAROUND

CRISIS, LEADERSHIP, AND THE OLYMPIC GAMES

MITT ROMNEY

WITH TIMOTHY ROBINSON

Since 1947
REGNERY
PUBLISHING, INC.
An Eagle Publishing Company • Washington, DC

Cataloging-in-Publication Data on file with the Library of Congress
ISBN 978-1-59698-514-8

Published in the United States by
Regnery Publishing, Inc.
An Eagle Publishing Company
One Massachusetts Avenue, NW
Washington, DC 20001
Visit us at www.regnery.com

First paperback edition published in 2007

Manufactured in the United States of America

10 9 8 7 6 5 4 3 2 1

Books are available in quantity for promotional or premium use.
Write to Director of Special Sales, Regnery Publishing, Inc., One Massachusetts Avenue, NW, Washington, DC 20001, for information on discounts and terms or call (202) 216-0600.

*To Team 2002: the managers, staff and
volunteers who proved that dream can become reality*

TABLE OF CONTENTS

Preface to the Paperback Edition IX

Introduction and Acknowledgments. XVII

Prologue XXI

Chapter 1: SIZING UP THE OLYMPICS. 1

Chapter 2: ANATOMY OF THE CRISIS 23

Chapter 3: STRATEGIC AUDIT 39

Chapter 4: BUILDING THE TEAM 59

Chapter 5: CULTURE. 83

Chapter 6: THE BUDGET. 105

Chapter 7: UNCERTAIN REVENUES. 117

Chapter 8: NEGOTIATION AND THE IOC 141

Chapter 9: THE FACE OF SLOC 169

Chapter 10: ONGOING MARKETING EFFORTS. 195

Chapter 11: FUNDS FROM THE FEDS 225

Chapter 12: REACHING INTO THE COMMUNITY 243

Chapter 13: SLOC AND THE MORMON CHURCH. 269

Chapter 14: SECURING THE OLYMPIC GAMES. 285

Chapter 15: SEPTEMBER 11. 301

Chapter 16: HEART AND MEANING. 315

Chapter 17: THE GAMES HAVE ARRIVED 343

Epilogue. 379

Index 385

PREFACE TO THE PAPERBACK EDITION

Some years ago, my wife, Ann, and I were playing with our children. After a long day of fun and family time, all five of our boys were dressed in their pajamas and shipped upstairs for bed. As the house grew quiet, Ann turned to me and said she wished we could freeze time, to keep them—and us—just as we were then. That's not possible, of course. As we grow and age, we know that what we leave our children is our most lasting legacy.

In much the same way, many of us wish we could keep America just as it is today: prosperous, safe, free, and far from such things as the incomprehensible madness of the jihad terrorists. Some people refuse to think about the very real forces of change in the world, hoping somehow that by ignoring them, they will go away. But they will not. If we are to leave our children and grandchildren a legacy as great as that left to us, we must as a nation be fully engaged in matters of policy and politics, at home and abroad. Parents who ignore the discipline and development of their children will be shocked to see the kind of "adults" that emerge. If we as Americans were to thoughtlessly drift along, ignoring the new generation of challenges in our nation and our world, our children would inherit an America very different from that in which they grew up.

Fortunately, Americans have a long history of facing challenges head-on. Leaders have told us the truth about our problems, described what we must do to overcome them, and led the way to success. Time and again, Americans rise to the occasion. What I have learned from my association with the Olympics and then from my work with the people of Massachusetts is that the American spirit can be kindled to achieve great things. There are great challenges in front of us today, and we will have to make significant changes to overcome them, but we will do as we have always done: we will win.

My three years in Salt Lake City taught me that the qualities of the human spirit on display at the Olympics are the same qualities that make America great: determination, hard work, sacrifice, teamwork, loyalty, honor, and character. It is what inspired me to run for governor of Massachusetts when the Games concluded. Running as a Republican in a state where only 12 percent of registered voters are Republican, I beat my Democratic opponent, 50 to 45 percent. The state was in tough shape, as a national recession had dried up tax revenue and forced states to raise taxes or dramatically cut spending. The budget was in full meltdown mode. The Massachusetts economy was shedding thousands of jobs every month. Our government was hobbled with politics and patronage, making our job harder.

Today, we are adding jobs. The budget is balanced. The legislature and my administration cooperated to reform government. We replenished the rainy day fund. We streamlined and consolidated government agencies. We rescued our school building program so that we can construct hundreds of new schools. We instituted smart growth policies and environmental programs that will preserve what we love about living in New England. Tuition-free Adams scholarships are now granted to thousands of our kids every year. Taxes have been lowered, including for our seniors, and benefits for veterans and National Guardsmen have been improved. We reformed programs that were ineffective: housing, construction rules, transportation, and Medicaid, to name just a few. We insisted that our kids be taught in English. We pushed for more choice for parents through charter schools. The four years of the governorship were a whirlwind; I am proud of what was accomplished.

The change and transformation weren't easy. I didn't have a Republican majority to work with in my legislature. I was a small red dot in America's bluest state. The Massachusetts legislature is 85 percent Democratic. Our ten-member congressional delegation is all-Democrat. Our senators are named Kennedy and Kerry. I used to joke that being a conservative Republican in Massachusetts is like being a cattle rancher at a vegetarian convention. Despite the Democratic monopoly, I was able to get a good deal done in cooperation with the legislature. That's because when there are good people on both sides of the aisle, we can find a way to work together.

As a private citizen, I had always suspected there was a lot of waste in government. Boy, was I right. One example of the waste we confronted was the homeless hotel program. Amazingly, we were paying for as many as six hundred hotel rooms a night, costing over $20 million. The state's policy was to send people to a hotel at state expense if the shelters were full. I remember commenting, "Word must get around." So we changed the incentives. Now, if someone shows up at a full shelter, we send the person who's been in the shelter the longest to the hotel, and we make room in the shelter for the new arrival. With that change in policy, we got the number of hotel rooms we were renting to zero.

Waste and inefficiency is streaked throughout government like fat marbled into a piece of beef. We streamlined bureaucracies. Some departments and agencies were eliminated altogether. We merged two different park agencies, one for the urban parks, another for the non-urban parks. One commentator said we didn't go after just the sacred cows—we went after the whole herd. When I left office, we had reduced executive branch jobs by more than six hundred.

We ended up balancing our budget without raising taxes or by adding to the cost of borrowing. We took a $3 billion deficit and turned it into a string of surpluses. A lot of it was put away into our rainy day fund, which grew from $640 million when I took office to $2.2 billion when I left. I had campaigned as a fiscal conservative, someone who could take his experience at the Olympics and from a successful career in business and put the principles I had learned to work in the public sector, and the results were satisfying.

What I didn't count on was being at the center of the battlefield in some of the major social issues of our time, fighting to defend traditional values as they relate to marriage, respect for human life, and religious freedom. At the end of my first year in office, just as we were restoring fiscal balance and coming out of the depths of the recession, the Massachusetts Supreme Judicial Court struck a blow against the family by finding a right to same-sex marriage in the Massachusetts Constitution. Marriage, the court said, was an "evolving paradigm." The error of the court's decision is that it focused on adult rights, not the rights of children. The development and nurturing of children is a fundamental purpose of marriage, and the ideal setting in which to raise a child is a family with a mother and a father.

It wasn't long after this decision that my own Department of Public Health came to me with a proposal to replace "mother" and "father" on birth certificates with "parent A" and "parent B." That's not right, and I said so. The fundamental building block of American society is the family. America cannot continue to lead the family of nations if we suffer the collapse of the family at home. Not long after the gay marriage ruling, Catholic Charities announced that they were exiting their adoption practice because they would no longer be able to preferentially place children in homes with a mother and a father. These are among the reasons why I have fought so hard for a constitutional amendment that would define marriage as the union of a man and a woman. This is not about discrimination against gay people. Americans respect the right of others to live as they choose. But as a society, we should recognize that one setting is the ideal for raising the next generations, and that's a home with a mom and a dad.

Another front in the culture war opened up in my state. In 2004 researchers at Harvard and their allies in the Democratic legislature began moving legislation authorizing the cloning of human embryos for experimentation and research. As a supporter of stem cell research, I applaud medical discovery and the pursuit of cures for debilitating diseases, but I saw clearly where this legislation would take the nation: to the "brave new world" that Aldous Huxley warned about, with rows upon rows of test tubes containing human embryos grown and harvested for science. It took us across a clear ethical boundary I was not willing to cross. My veto was not upheld, and now the cloners, disappointed that the science has not been perfected, are back before my successor in the governor's office asking for something new—the right to create embryos for experimentation on a mass scale through conventional fertilization in the laboratory. It is a slippery slope indeed, once we set aside standards that respect life.

In 2005 I announced I wouldn't seek re-election. My final year in office would be the most gratifying. The stage had been set for something truly historic—the passage of a private, market-based health insurance program that would extend coverage to all our citizens. This wasn't government taking over healthcare and dictating who would get treated for what and by whom. No, it was about personal responsibility replacing government. My plan said that people who could afford insurance should either buy it or pay for their own healthcare—no more "free ride" on the taxpayers. Even the working poor were required to help pay for their insurance premiums. We moved to a system in which private insurers were encouraged to develop low-cost plans, and we took the hundreds of millions we were spending every year on "free care" and converted it into a subsidy program for the low-income uninsured. It took a lot of cajoling and shuttle diplomacy with the leaders of the House and Senate, who were at odds over different features of the bill. In the end, we came up with a good solution to an intractable problem, and we did it without a government takeover and without a massive tax increase. It was a big step forward, for Massachusetts and for the nation.

Leaving the governorship at the end of my term was difficult. I had real respect, as well as personal affection, for some of the leaders I worked with the longest, Senate president Robert Travaglini, House Speaker Tom Finneran, House Minority Leader Brad Jones and his tiny band of Republicans, and so many others. Often, they put politics aside to do the people's work. But I had begun to think about, and was encouraged by others to take a look at, running for president of the United States. I knew that we are at a critical period in our nation's history. We are under attack. Our jihadist enemy doesn't just want to set off a few car bombs; it wants to overthrow our government, kill millions of our citizens, and extinguish freedom and liberty everywhere. America also faces serious economic challenges. The growth of the Chinese and Indian economies is good news for the alleviation of poverty, but it also brings strong new players to the world market. These are no second-string competitors. They work hard. They're motivated and industrious. We have our own domestic challenges as well. We are spending too much money in Washington. We are using too much foreign oil. Our schools are below international standards. Our immigration policies are upside-down: we bar too many educated and skilled immigrants from entering the country and leave our borders open to those with neither education nor skills. And we face another challenge, a challenge to our American values and ideals. Our culture has been built on hard work, superb education, sacrifice, opportunity over dependence, family, faith, love of freedom, respect for life, and patriotism. To one degree or another, all are under attack.

But like Teddy Roosevelt and Ronald Reagan, I am optimistic about America. And I know that my love for this country and my experience in bringing change to businesses, to the Olympics, and to Massachusetts would enable me to keep America prosperous and secure. And so, in February 2006, after many conversations with Ann and my family, I returned to my native state of Michigan to announce my candidacy for president of the United States.

At the Olympics, when our athletes won a gold medal, they stood to watch the American flag being raised and listened to our national anthem. I noticed that our kids did something that those from the other countries rarely did: they held their hands over their hearts. Some even cried. Why? Because there's something very special about America.

Democrats might say that it's our government that makes us great, and it's true that we do have a great government. But that's not the source of our greatness. The source of our greatness is the American people. I know that at times the attack on American ideals and our way of life can be deeply discouraging. I love what Abigail Adams wrote to her son during troubled times. The words echo from the early founding of our country, but they are just as relevant today. She said, "It is not in the still calm of life, or the repose of a pacific station, that great characters are formed. . . . Great necessities call out great virtues." I see that happening today all around us.

I believe America will continue to fulfill its unique mission in the world, for I have seen greatness in the hearts of the American people, both in Massachusetts and in our Olympians. After the Winter Games had concluded, I talked to one of our Olympic champions, ice skater Derek Parra. Derek is a Hispanic American from Miami. After years of rollerblading, his wife convinced him to try ice skating. He was fast—real fast. So fast that he made the Olympic team—so fast that he won a silver medal and a gold medal. He was the fastest man in the world on skates. I asked Derek what had been the most memorable and the most meaningful experience of his Olympics. I imagined it would have been winning the medals. It was not. He explained that it was carrying the flag that had flown above the World Trade Center on September 11, 2001, into the Opening Ceremonies. As they started to sing the national anthem, Derek said he had barely been able to keep his emotions in check. But then the choir did something he had not expected. They sang a reprise of the last line, in higher octave and with greater orchestration: "O say does that star-spangled banner yet wave, o'er the land of the free and the home of the brave." A small gust of wind filled the flag in their hands. Derek said it was as if the millions who had fought to preserve our freedom had breathed into that flag. The tears ran down his face. I could barely contain my emotion as he told me this story. This love of freedom and respect for what America was founded to represent is what compels me to believe that America will always be the hope of the world.

Not long ago, I had the good fortune of meeting with former prime minister Margaret Thatcher. I talked with her about the many challenges faced by Britain and the United States, and I ended with an expression of my optimism for the future: "I am convinced that we will overcome all the challenges we face." Quietly, poignantly, she added: "We always have." I too am confident in the future of this great land of liberty. America faces great challenges, but "great necessities call out great virtues." As we always have before, the people of America will rise to greatness.

INTRODUCTION AND ACKNOWLEDGMENTS

"I don't test well." I've said it myself. Most kids who score a low grade say it. Tests can demand that we draw on everything we know, everything we have learned, all our skills. Further, we have to perform in a compressed time period and in a pressured setting. Because of all that, not in spite of it, we learn a lot about a person in a test.

We learn a lot about an athlete in an Olympic test. Often, the event lasts no more than a minute, but it tests years and years of training, coaching, and in-born ability. Billions of people worldwide watch the Olympics: we see humanity in a most condensed test, a test that will sometimes reveal the greatest qualities of the human spirit.

I am not an Olympic athlete. But for all of us who organized the Olympic Winter Games of 2002, the experience was as compressed, as demanding, and often as revealing as any test or competition I could imagine. I decided to share some of the life lessons and leadership lessons that emerged from the Olympic experience.

This is not the story of the Salt Lake Olympics. That would require a historian's patience. Instead, I look to Olympic experiences to showcase career choices, principles of management, and measures of leadership. Often, I will spell out what lesson I draw from the experience; often, you will have to find your own.

I write from my own perspective. Every person who joined the Salt Lake Organizing Committee had their own unique experience, just as valid and important as mine. While we each had different tasks and different challenges, we all share in the success of the whole.

Writing this book followed a convoluted process. During the three years leading up to the Games, I dictated weekly during my commute between Park City and Salt Lake City. My assistant, Donna Tillery, graciously typed my account. After the Games, I dictated further; in total, about 300 pages. Tim Robinson, a published author and editor, combined these and added material from interviews with other senior managers. He organized the topics and produced the first draft. Following his work, I edited and wrote the final draft, having asked members of the original management team to help us with factual accuracy and additional stories. For Tim and me, it was a team effort.

Cindy Gillespie, the director of federal relations and of the torch relay, drafted sections on those topics. Fraser Bullock, the COO, helped with piles of data and interviews. Kelly Flint and Brian Katz, our senior legal counsels, reviewed facts and checked for accuracy. Kelly was a source of many of the photos. Mark Lewis and Don Stirling, our marketing chiefs, Ed Eynon, our head of HR, and Caroline Shaw, our communications director all offered experiences and checked for accuracy. My wife Ann read and re-read each draft, offering critique and suggestions which helped shape the final product. Finally, Rowena Itchon at Regnery edited what we had produced, sliming it down and keeping it focused.

I am pleased with the final product. But I wish I could have written a full account of the work of each member of the management team who made a critical contribution to the success of the Games. Some senior managers, I mention only in passing; many other major contributors are not even referenced. To account for all those who produced the Games, I would have needed to write a history, and that is a different task. Nevertheless, I am fully aware that everything we accomplished, we achieved because of the commitment and dedication of the many, many people who served in the Olympics. Many great achievements are the product of great numbers of people, most of whom are unheralded. The Olympic Winter Games of 2002 are no exception.

"On a mountainside in Salt Lake City tonight, the nineteenth Olympic Winter Games will not convene with a simple ceremony of innocence, but with a ceremony of resonance,

Where nations have come together to imagine a world as we wish it could be,

Where flags fly with pride, but not prejudice,

Where men and women are not judged by the circumstances of their birth or beliefs, but only by the depth of their character and their imagination,

The snows have left behind sheets of white for the athletes of the world to write their own stories....

Since that morning without reason, we have seen the strength of ideas when they're made real.

Tonight a parade of nations has assembled on a mountain-side in Utah to make real these self-evident truths,
That what unites us can be far greater than what divides us,

And that we are beaten only when we stop believing....

The flame that is lit tonight is not like any other,

It is not the fire of destruction, but a light in the darkness."

—Bob Costas and Jim McKay,
NBC lead-in to the opening ceremonies, 2/8/02

PROLOGUE

In the early days, when I was still just considering the CEO position at the Salt Lake Organizing Committee, I held a little contest with my five sons to see who could come up with the best tag line for the Salt Lake Olympics. The winner was "It's all about sport." I felt that the scandal had brought too much attention to the administrators, the guys in suits. The Olympics is about athletic competition. The Olympian, the athlete, is what the Games are about and "It's all about sport" seemed to communicate the essence of the Olympic spirit. At least that's what I thought at the beginning.

When I moved into my new role in Utah and met with Olympic champions, I often asked them to recount the most powerful and meaningful moment of their experience. Mike Eruzione, captain of the 1980 "Miracle on Ice" hockey team, gave a surprising answer. He said that people always assume that it was when he scored the decisive goal against the Russians, but that wasn't it. Next, they guess that it must have been winning against the Finns for the gold medal. That wasn't it either. For Mike, the most powerful and meaningful moment was walking into the stadium during the opening ceremonies as part of the

American delegation, representing his country. That was the most moving moment to Mike Eruzione.

As I heard other champions say similar things, it began to impress on me that the Olympics are really about something greater than sport, but seen through sport and the Olympians themselves. Athletics are the medium, the stage on which the real drama unfolds. I have become convinced that the Olympics are a showcase of some of the great qualities of the human spirit: determination, persistence, hard work, sacrifice, dedication, faith, passion, teamwork, loyalty, honor, character. The great moments of every successful Olympics memorialize the noble qualities of humanity, qualities that receive far too little airtime in the modern world. As I had thought through the elements that made great Games, the word "inspiration" took on more focus. The Olympics inspired people. They celebrated the human spirit by revealing the Olympic athlete's unrelenting drive to push the limits of human capacity. The phrase we eventually gave as the vision of our Games was "Light the Fire Within." Those words, that vision would affect everything we did at the Salt Lake Organizing Committee.

Sport has been drenched in profit. Billions in broadcast and sponsor dollars are fought over by owners and athletes. In some cases, the story of an athlete's career could most accurately "be written with an adding machine." As the bid scandal showed, money and influence had entered Olympic management as well. A very few Olympic gold-medalists are able to parlay their renown into lucrative endorsements or professional careers. But for most Olympians, there is no money, only achievement. With very, very few exceptions, an Olympian's preparation is in obscurity and the currency of his or her sport career is character. That's what the world hungers to see every two years.

ONE OLYMPIC STORY AMONG MANY

I remember some years ago reading of a young speed skater who was a medal contender in the 1984 Winter Games. He came in fourth, one slot away from the podium.

In a culture where "if at first you don't succeed, it's time to try something else," it was remarkable to some that he was back in 1988 after four more years of intensive training. This time, he was the favorite in the 500 meters. His mother called the day of the race and told him that his sister, who suffered from leukemia, would not survive through the day. The athlete dedicated his performance to her but fell twice, failing to finish either race.

Four years later, in 1992, he was back again. Now a sure bet, he placed a disappointing fourth in the 500 and twenty-sixth in the 1000.

In his fourth Olympics, at Lillehammer, Dan Jansen slipped again in his premier event, the 500-meter sprint, and took eighth place. In the 1000, the final Olympic event of his career, he won. A look of almost perplexed wonder on his face, he skated over to the spectator stands, picked up his two-year-old daughter, named Jane after his late sister, and took a victory lap.

Dan stopped by my office soon after I joined the Games. As he was speaking, I was not paying very close attention. Instead, I was inspecting him quite carefully. Here was a gold medalist. Funny, he didn't really look that different from other people. No, what was unique about this fastest skater in the world was not his physique; it was his determination, his perseverance. Dan Jansen is a hero to me and millions of others because of the quality of his spirit.

Olympic moments are moments of remarkable courage, determination, and adherence to larger principles. Henry Kissinger wrote, "Heroes walk alone, but they become myths when they ennoble the lives and touch the hearts of all of us." The Olympians would inspire the people of the world, and we at the Salt Lake Organizing Committee would help make that possible. That was why I had signed up. That was how I would honor the memory of my mother and father.

The Salt Lake bid scandal had rocked the Olympic world and shaken the foundation of the city's preparations for the Games of 2002. But the athletes had not messed up, it was the guys in suits. But the Games weren't about the guys in suits. They were about the young people from all over the world who were pushing themselves and sacrificing in the hopes of making it to Salt Lake. Here, their athletic performances would reveal qualities that would inspire. The real absolute and enduring value that would serve to ground our efforts as an organization was a commitment to the athlete.

I was not coming to Salt Lake City to build infrastructure for Utah or to stimulate economic development. There was no way I was leaving my life in Massachusetts for that. I was coming for a higher purpose—to restore reputation, to acquit the duties of the United States toward the world, and to restore the Games for the benefit of the athletes. If Salt Lake 2002 was to be successful, the Games had to be about service to the world and to the athletes.

On the eve of the opening ceremonies, I wondered whether our Games would have great Olympic moments that would memorialize the loft of the human spirit. Seventeen days later, the world was breathless. I sat with one young American athlete during the closing ceremony. Derek Parra, a Hispanic American from Miami, came to the Games to speed skate, having "crossed over" from in-line rollerblading just a few years earlier. He would leave with both a gold and a silver medal. I asked what had been most memorable. His answer had echoes of my conversation with Mike Eruzione years before. "The flag," he said.

Derek was one of the eight American athletes elected by his teammates to carry the American flag that had flown above the World Trade Center during the attack. It would enter opening ceremonies before the national anthem. "Ladies and gentlemen, the American flag that flew above the World Trade Center on September 11, 2001 will now enter the stadium." We had anticipated cheers from the audience, as had occurred on previous event appearances. Instead, there was complete silence, profound reverence. The cortege of athletes, members of the New York Police and Fire Departments, the Port Authority, and a badly torn American flag moved past the president of the United States. The choir sang the national anthem. It was a

1930s Robert Shaw arrangement that had a climactic reprise of the final line.

Derek said he heard what he thought were the last words of the anthem and then the choir began the reprise, with higher notes and more robust voice and orchestration.

> *"Oh say, does that star-spangled banner yet wave,*
> *o'er the land of the free and the home of the brave?"*

A gust of wind filled the tattered flag and lifted it against the athlete's grip. Derek said it was as if the spirit of all those who had sacrificed for America, all the free and the brave, had breathed into the flag. That was Derek's most memorable experience.

I was standing next to President Bush during the anthem. He turned to me and said: "That was quite a moment. That was a great moment." Indeed. It was a defining moment for our Games and the culmination of our dream. That dream is the essence of the Olympics—the dream of a world united, inspired by humanity at its best.

The Olympic Games of 2002 were just as defining to those who produced them as they were to the athletes. Each of the dozen or so senior managers left higher paying jobs with superior career prospects. Scores of others likewise walked away from better professional positions to sign up with the Salt Lake Organizing Committee. For me, the decision was an inflection point in my life. That was true for many others.

Perhaps that is why executives of Olympic organizing committees write books about that experience. Peter Ueberroth did. Michael Knight of Sydney did. The Atlanta experience was chronicled by the communications director. An experience so transforming is unusual in American careers, and it is extraordinarily fulfilling, expansive, and empowering. We live "lives of quiet desperation" unless we reach for something that is as meaningful as it is unexpected. Linear, logical, focused career paths may not be so logical after all. The predictable path can be constraining, limiting, hardening. An athlete's journey to the Olympics is widely recognized as a life-changing achievement. I found that for those of us who produced the Games, they were so as well.

But the energy and power that our team experienced in Salt Lake City is not necessarily unique to Olympic organizing committees. The same principles play out in other enterprises in similar ways. Departures from the expected, refusals to conform to expectations in one's own personal life, in one's career, or in the lifecycle of an enterprise can produce immeasurable personal and organizational rewards. I believe that what was powerful in the Olympic setting can also be brought into other enterprises, even businesses. When a person finds greater meaning in what they are doing, and when they are stretched to the limits of their ability, the experience can be exhilarating and transforming. The Olympic experience I have chosen to write about displays the power of creating a vision of higher purpose and of offering challenges beyond normal expectations. That is the task of leadership.

I continue to be amazed at the difference one or a small number of people can make. My career has involved consulting to many Fortune 500 scale companies and investing in hundreds of companies of various sizes. Some of these companies had tens of thousands of employees. How can it be that leadership by so few can affect the course of so large an enterprise? But I have seen it time and again.

My leadership at SLOC would be successful to the extent that we were able to build commitment to a common vision of high purpose and adhere to that vision in every aspect of what we did together. Some enterprises are able to bump along without vision or without cohesion between their vision and their practice. This may be sustained for a time in an enterprise that has been in business for many years or when it enjoys an unusually benevolent marketplace. But in a turnaround setting like the one we faced in Salt Lake City, and with the scale and timeframe involved in organizing an Olympics, there could be no forgiveness for slack leadership. Our task was to identify a defining vision, communicate that in a compelling way, and provide the kind of focus that reinforces that vision as a living, breathing thing, not just lip service. And if we were to succeed, it would be because of the commitment to that vision by the entire team, and by the community.

Chapter 1

SIZING UP THE OLYMPICS

In the fall of 1998 I got a call asking whether I would consider taking the helm of the troubled Salt Lake Organizing Committee for the 2002 Olympic Games. I dismissed the notion out of hand.

It was a preposterous idea. I had no background in sports administration. The notion of leaving Massachusetts where my wife, Ann, and I had spent our entire careers and raised all five of our sons made no sense. We had built our home there. I was involved in Church and civic activities. I had a son still in high school.

The firm I had founded was performing extremely well. After years of nurturing and investment, Bain Capital was paying ever more spectacular dividends. When I started out in 1984, we had $37 million in assets under management; we now had billions. And we had just added a new billion-dollar-plus fund.

Moreover, though I was always a fan of the Olympics—at least the televised version of the Games—I had never supported the Olympic bid movement in Utah. Or perhaps it is more accurate to say I had always been indifferent to it. The announcement that Salt Lake City had landed the 2002 Games was certainly no big moment in my life.

I don't recall watching it on TV. I don't even remember having a conversation about it. For me, it was no big deal.

I do, however, have family ties to the state of Utah. In a sense, Utah is my family's historic center. My ancestors were Mormon pioneers who made the arduous journey across what was then Indian Country to the Salt Lake Valley. The precipitous mountain pass that led the pioneers down into the Salt Lake Valley and still is the route of access from the east on Interstate 80, was first explored by my great-great-grandfather, Parley P. Pratt. He had worked a road up along "Big Canyon Creek" as an act of speculation when his crop failed in the summer of 1849. He charged tolls to prospectors making their way to California at the height of the Gold Rush and even had a Pony Express station commissioned along his pass.

As an undergraduate I had attended Brigham Young University just south of Salt Lake City in the town of Provo. Two of my own children were then attending BYU. Our church is headquartered in Salt Lake City and, twice a year, words of general counsel and religious instruction are broadcast from there. But the cultural and economic development of the state had never been a concern of mine. My home was Boston where Ann and I had lived for over thirty years.

I remember thinking, "Why would anyone want to bring the Olympics to Salt Lake?" Even if the Games were successful, the net effect would only be to bring more people to the area. More people would bring more development, more demand on water resources, and more pollution to a state known for its small town communities and pristine natural beauty. It seemed to be too high a price to pay.

What's more, in 1995 I had had a personal brush with the Olympic committee that left me with a bad taste.

DINNER WITH TOM

That was the year that Ann began looking for property for a family house in Deer Valley, just next to Park City in the Wasatch Mountains above Salt Lake City. In fact, it was just south of the mountain pass that my great-great-grandfather had cleared. But family ties aside, it was the spectacular snow that had drawn us. Utah boasts some of the finest skiing powder on the planet. We were hoping to build a retreat where our adult children could gather with us for years to come, and where we could take our grandchildren onto the slopes.

In one visit to look over property, I was invited to dinner by a close friend. Kem Gardner had served with me in Church assignments back in Boston and was then living in Utah where he managed a real estate development business. He was active in state and city affairs and had always had a knack for knowing the right people. "I've got this friend who I want you to meet," he said on the way to dinner, "his name is Tom Welch."

Tom was, of course, the head of SLOC at the time. SLOC was the unfortunate acronym for the Salt Lake Organizing Committee for the 2002 Winter Games, a mouthful. After thirty years of trying, he and Dave Johnson, his number two at the bid committee, had managed a successful Salt Lake City bid for the Games. Later they would be implicated in the influence peddling allegations that would bring on the scandal, but at the time they were high in the saddle. Kem took us to an exclusive French restaurant. The restaurant was over-the-top, the perfect setting for a man like Tom Welch. After sitting down with us briefly and placing his order, Tom excused himself to work the crowd. We watched him from afar as he glad-handed guests and played cutesy with the waitresses, who were dressed in period costumes with low-cut bustiers. Tom drew focus like a magnet. He seemed larger than life.

After dinner, Tom graciously invited us up to his house. He had purchased a sculpture of an eagle that he was anxious for us to see. When we pulled up to Tom's house, he took me in to show me the eagle. It was in his front window and had spotlights trained on it. Tom's house was perched high on a mountain bench overlooking the Salt Lake Valley. So his claim that you could see it from miles away was no exaggeration. It was lovely, but it seemed a little ostentatious, propped at the window, under a spotlight. Everything about Tom seemed made for show. I suppose I attributed the same motives to the Utah Olympic effort, an opportunity to put on a show. I couldn't help but reflect back on that dinner when, much later, I first heard word of the ensuing scandal.

SCANDAL FROM UTAH

Of course, I was sickened by the news of the bid scandal. Given the straight-laced, public face that the state of Utah seems naturally to exude, the media couldn't resist jumping on the suggestion that this had all been a false front. There seemed to be an implied association of the scandal with the standing and character of the state and, further, with the Mormon Church. Those who thought us Mormons to be too goody-two-shoes felt confirmed in their suspicions. I remember thinking what a shame it was that the entire community was being given a black eye by the seemingly unscrupulous actions of a flamboyant few.

I was convinced that the vast majority of the players had been above reproach. The integrity of the whole community had been called into question by the poor judgment of a small number of people. And yet, charges of disingenuous grandstanding didn't seem to be very far afield from my limited personal vantage point. Bringing the Games to Utah had been ill advised from the start. All the more reason for me not to carpetbag to Utah and take up the Olympic banner.

The friend who called with the invitation was Kem Gardner, the same friend who had introduced me to Tom Welch years before. SLOC had just lost their chief executive due to the scandal and had put together a team of leading civic and business leaders in an effort to identify a replacement. Somehow my name had come up.

SLOC's chairman, Robert Garff, had recently been in my office at Bain Capital to talk about financing for a new car dealership concept he had in mind. Steve Coltrin, the New York public relations executive bidding for work at SLOC, had met me at a New York event. Utah

Senators Orrin Hatch and Bob Bennett were acquaintances familiar with my background. All have since taken a piece of the credit, or blame, for thinking me up. But it was Kem who made the call.

Would I consider taking the helm of the troubled Olympic committee? Could I restore the public credibility of the organization, overcome the growing political resistance, and work with a hobbled International Olympic Committee, United States Olympic Committee, and other partners to stage successful Games? Would I allow my name to be considered?

If Kem had put these questions to me directly, I would have shut him down on the spot. But Kem knows that. He knows I don't suffer foolishness well. So he deployed a flanking maneuver—he called Ann instead.

Kem laid out for her why I was the right person for the job. SLOC was looking for someone with managerial expertise, ties to the area, preferably high profile, and no hint of any skeletons in the closet. Board chairman Bob Garff had said to the press that, "the candidate I'm looking for is a white knight who is universally loved." Kem joked that they could overlook that one requirement.

Ann must have fallen for his appeal, because after hanging up with Kem, she called me at the office. Before I could get beyond hello she put me on notice, "Now, whatever you do, don't just say no out of hand. Hear me out on this before you dismiss it...." She proceeded tentatively, "I talked to Kem. He thinks that you ought to consider running the Olympics...." But before she could say another word, I immediately blurted out: "Why in the world would I ever consider going to Utah to run the Olympics?" I couldn't help myself.

PERSUASIVE ARGUMENTS

Ann let me bluster a bit and then quietly made some pretty good points. She continued the lobbying when I got home that evening. She said that while I may not have been gung-ho about Salt Lake's

Olympic bid, now that the Games had been awarded and Utah had signed on, the reputation of Utah and America were on the line. She said that the entire Olympic movement could be damaged by the scandal and that the Games might have to be moved to another country or possibly even called off. Athletes who had been training for years for the 2002 Games, especially American athletes who had hoped for a home field advantage, would bear the brunt of the misdeeds of a few people in Salt Lake.

But it was the last thing she said that got to me, and it would be something that I would come to deeply believe. She said that the Olympics are not just a sporting event or a grand celebration; there is a lot more to them than that. They are different than watching the Super Bowl—the Olympians themselves are different. The feeling you get is different. They are inspiring, not in a religious sense, but in the sense of pride you feel for the athletes and their accomplishments. Ann reasoned that if the Olympics were in jeopardy, if Utah was in trouble and our country embarrassed, that these were compelling reasons for leading a turnaround.

My response was, "Yeah, but why me?" I could think of a dozen individuals with more relevant sport management experience.

Ann replied, "Just think about it. If there's any one person ideally suited for this job, it's you." She referenced my business experience in turnaround situations. At Bain Capital, we had frequently worked to invigorate underperforming enterprises by utilizing bold and creative maneuvers. I had also been CEO of a consulting firm that had successfully navigated a turnaround. I had the chance to start a business from scratch and to build it into a prosperous enterprise. In every business setting, I had to sell myself and my company. I had contacts galore.

And she brought up the campaign. In 1994 I had made an unsuccessful bid for a Senate seat in Massachusetts. "You know what it's like to be in the public eye. This is a public job. This is a job where interactions with the media will be critical to restoring public support in Utah and in America and around the world."

Then there was our new house in Deer Valley. "We have a house out there, a place to stay. This is made to order. It couldn't be more perfect. You have just the right skills, all the right resources. There's no one else who can do it."

I came back with names—prominent managers, some from the world of sports. One by one, she deflated them, arguing that each lacked the full mix of skills that were necessary—lack of turnaround experience, unfamiliarity with the community, absence of media experience—important elements that would each be at play.

I argued that it was terrible timing. After fifteen years of effort, Bain Capital had become extraordinarily lucrative. How could I walk away from the golden goose, especially now that it was laying even more golden eggs? She countered: "We have all we need, more than we ever dreamed of having. You can afford to take this job when others can't." The more I protested, the less crazy the idea seemed. The more thought I gave it, the more I softened to the idea. Within two weeks, I would make a complete about-face. I would leave friends and family behind and move to Utah. I would walk away from my leadership at Bain Capital at the height of its profitability and take a position without compensation.

I later joked with the press that it was due to an overdeveloped community service gene. And that wasn't far from the truth. Ann's arguments had resonance, but they had resonance because she knows my core beliefs and my life aspirations. She knows that somewhere deep inside, I hoped to commit myself to things greater than making a living or building a fortune. It was the spirit of service in one form or another—a family poltergeist that has haunted my ancestors for generations. It was the legacy of my heritage, and of my youth.

BACKING UP A WAYS

Romneys are, by nature, an adventurous breed. In 1837 my great-great-grandfather, Miles Romney, was convinced by Mormon missionaries that the church of God had been restored to the earth by a young prophet in New York State. Taking it on faith, Miles left behind an established practice as an architect in England and took his family over the sea to New Orleans and then, by steamer, up the Mississippi where they joined with the "saints" in Nauvoo, Illinois. Miles plied his trade and helped design and construct churches and tabernacles for the community. Later, when Joseph Smith and his brother were killed, the family followed the Mormons west across the plains to Utah. Miles's son, my great-grandfather Miles Park Romney, was seven at the time of the exodus and, like his future wife, Hannah Hood Hill, walked almost the whole way to the Salt Lake Valley.

The Romneys were later sent by Brigham Young to settle southern Utah for the cause. Carpenters and architects all, they built a temple in St. George and established a comfortable homestead before Miles Senior was killed by a fall from some scaffolding and Miles Junior was asked to move again, this time to build a settlement in St. Johns, Arizona. To every request, Romneys were obedient. And leaving behind all they had worked to establish, they yet again pitched themselves against the arid terrain, the cactus, alkali, quicksand, and rattlesnakes. They built schools and libraries. Miles Junior was the founder of a theatrical society on the frontier. He dug irrigation trenches and plowed up the desert soil.

Eventually Miles was called upon to settle in northern Mexico, where his son, my grandfather Gaskell, would wed and my father George would be born. My great-grandmother, Hannah, would follow her husband down to Mexico later in the year. I have the account that she dictated of that voyage. She couldn't find any men to travel with her because the great Indian chief, Geronimo, was on the warpath. She put her kids in a covered wagon and made her way on her own. At night, she would keep sentry next to the campfire while her children slept. At one point along the way, she came across freshly slaughtered U.S. Cavalry horses. She paused only long enough to pry the shoes from the wasted horses, re-shod her own wagon horses and journey on. When she arrived at the border of Mexico, she was asked to pay an entry toll. Having no money, she was forced to leave behind the iron stove that she had carried across the wilderness as collateral.

Theirs was a life of toil and sacrifice, of complete devotion to a cause. They were persecuted for their religious beliefs but they went forward undaunted. Despite emigrating, my great-grandfather never lost his love of country. He had an abiding loyalty to America and a deep interest in politics. He left behind writings insisting that it was the duty of all citizens to ensure that good men were elected to positions in government, men who would faithfully administer the affairs of the people. He was a staunch Democrat, an ardent admirer of Grover Cleveland and had kept abreast of developments in his administration while living in Mexico. His biographer wrote of him, "Few men in his generation sense more fully than he the advantages of living in a democratic country, and at the same time the responsibilities attendant upon citizenship under a government of the people.... Loyalty to country and to his church was a cardinal virtue with Miles P. Romney, a loyalty based on sanity and not on fanaticism. His was the assumption that men should be students of both state and church government in order that they might intelligently carry on in harmony with the fundamental law and discipline of each and not be like 'dumb driven cattle,' exercising no mind of their own."[1]

These were the same values and commitments that animated my grandfather and my father and mother. They were the same values that were passed along to me.

"IF NOT ME, WHO? IF NOT NOW, WHEN?"

I grew up in a home where a great deal was expected of the children. My mother had these great phrases though I didn't always know

---

[1.] Thomas C. Romney, *The Life Story of Miles P. Romney*, pp. 217-9.

what they meant. Nothing Mom said made a lot of sense to me. And yet as I've gone back and read the things she said, she was actually quite eloquent.

One of her favorite quotes was something she was fond of saying when confronted with an opportunity to serve: "If not me, who? If not now, when? If not here, where?" She held to this philosophy. I saw her serving in various ways growing up, whether it was in the Church or on charitable boards or for political causes. While my friends attended beautiful churches with steeples, gothic archways and carillons in Bloomfield Hills, we went to a little branch of the Mormon Church in Pontiac, Michigan. My family attended Sunday meetings in a little house in Pontiac where we had to set up folding chairs and tables. For Mom, it was all about serving, building, and making a real difference in the lives of other people. I heard that all the time. And when the Michigan Republican party needed someone to run against a popular incumbent U.S. Senator from the other party, my mother said, "If not me, who? If not now, when?" She ran a vigorous campaign. She won the primary, but lost the general election to the popular incumbent. There was no shame in losing. She would pull out a familiar quote: "I aspired, and though I achieved not, I was satisfied."

SAVING AMERICAN MOTORS

If at times I didn't fully grasp my mother, my father made perfect sense to me. I grew up idolizing him. I thought everything he said was interesting. I argued incessantly with him but respected his views implicitly. Both he and my mother had an underlying belief that the purpose of life was to make a difference in the lives of others—to serve God and country.

When I was ten years old I saw my father grab the reins of a failing car company. It was one of the most powerful experiences of my childhood watching him turn American Motors around. He had been offered the presidency of Studebaker-Packard, a bigger, better-known, more profitable company. He turned it down to be vice president at American Motors for less money. Why? Because he believed in American Motors. He thought it had a better vision of the future and offered more chance for growth.

A few years after taking the job, the company's president, George Mason, died. My dad became chief executive. The stock collapsed and the banks were considering calling their loans. The company was on the verge of insolvency, but he was going to turn it around.

We had just sold our home in anticipation of building a new one. We were living in a rental house while we were getting ready to build. He took the money from the sale of the house and bought stock in the company. He literally risked his net worth on his ability to turn things around.

He started by getting the workers on board. He would go out on to the factory floors and gather them around him. "We're going to make this company great," he would say with flinty resolve. "Together."

He introduced a new automobile design, the Rambler. Actually it was an old automobile design that had been retired earlier, but Dad was going to resurrect it and it was going to save the company. It was what he called a "compact" car—a family sedan built on a smaller frame to be more fuel-efficient. Fuel-efficient cars would be popular because they would save money, he told his employees. The company's customers would also save fuel and put an end to the pollution and excesses of the "gas-guzzling dinosaurs." It was progress. They were ahead of the curve.

Listening to him, he was not like a businessman speaking about business. It was more like he was on a great mission with American Motors to build innovative cars so that people could save money and fuel, and have better lives. Work was never just a way to make a buck to my dad. There was a calling and purpose to it. It was about making life better for people.

In 1962, when I was fifteen years old, my father ran for governor. He walked away from success at American Motors—from an increased salary and options and a new generous pension program—to devote himself to public service. His pension under the old program would total $67 dollars a month.

I went to work on his campaign. I was the switchboard operator for a while, using electric cords to connect the internal phone lines to the calls coming in. Then I was a road warrior and a stump speaker at county fairs. I believe I visited all eighty-three Michigan counties over two campaigns. We took a little Ford microvan around the state and set up "Romney for Governor" booths. I would introduce myself and shout out to people walking past, "You should vote for my father for governor. He's a truly great person. You've got to support him. He's going to help make things better...." And I really believed it. We all did. It was true.

There was always a sense of doing something important with Dad. It never occurred to me that it was just a political race so that Dad could get a better job. We were engaged in something bigger than that. As governor, he approached his work with a sense of nobility. At least in my eyes—in the eyes of a boy—he was doing important work.

In the last thirty years of his life, he was a tireless advocate of volunteerism. Arguably the country's most vocal supporter of volunteers, he secured the support of the White House and Congress. Every Sunday he and Mom would call each of their children on the phone to talk about the week. We would end up laughing because Dad would inevitably start intoning about volunteerism. "People problems can only be solved by people!" he would say, as if my wife and I were the Department of Health and Human Services.

I remember someone once asked my father why he was never a top leader in his church, like his cousin Marion G. Romney who became one of the three highest ranking, as counselor in our church's First Presidency. Dad said that Marion was called to that course, but that he was called to a different course. He said that his mission was different from his cousin's, but no less significant in its own way. He believed that his life had a purpose ordained by providence and that his duty was to government, to improving the lot of fellow citizens, to the principle of liberty. For Dad, his most profound convictions found expression in the preservation of constitutional freedoms. And with those freedoms, came certain responsibilities.

In the back of my mind, and I know in the back of my brother's and my sisters' minds, there was always an innate sense that if the opportunity presented itself, there had to be something greater to life than just earning a living. We would have to make some contribution—and the greater the contribution, the more meaningful and fulfilling the life.

STORMING THE CASTLE

Fast forward to late summer 1993. My life to that point had been filled with challenges, but of the more homegrown variety. I had successfully wooed my high school sweetheart. We had wed and had five sons. I had sought degrees in English literature from Brigham Young University and then in business and law from Harvard. In 1978, I joined a young, up-and-coming consulting firm, Bain & Company and had worked up the ladder. After six years, I left Bain & Company to start a sister company venture capital fund. Bain Capital had been successful and, apart from a stint back at Bain & Company in 1991 when the firm was in trouble, we had led a fairly peaceful existence. We worked hard. We raised our boys and were active in our community and in our church.

But in 1993, something almost irrational happened. I began thinking about making a run against Senator Ted Kennedy. Ann and I believed that there needed to be a different course offered to the people of Massachusetts. It seemed clear to us the policies of the liberal Democrats of the '50s and '60s, though well intentioned, were wrong. We felt that someone needed to stand up, to offer a different vision from the one Kennedy and his colleagues had been pitching for decades. I wondered if that someone ought not be me. I began to think "If not me, who?"

We recognized that there was no way I was going to beat him. A Republican, white, male, Mormon millionaire in Massachusetts had no credible chance. Even when the campaign was riding high, I never put our odds better than one out of ten. I went to see Governor William Weld when I was thinking of running. He was very positive and encouraging and suggested I get together with a political consultant in the area by the name of Charlie Manning. Charlie said flat out, "There's just no way you can win. You probably can't win the primary but you certainly can't win the general election. I know what you're thinking about. I would be happy to help you. But realize this is just not going to happen." We still felt compelled to try.

I had been very fortunate in my business career. The company that I had helped build from the ground up was then one of the most successful private equity firms in the country. But I kept asking myself, "Do I really want to stay at Bain Capital for the rest of my life? Do I want to make it even more successful, make even more money? Why?" The people that I had hired to work with me were every bit as good at the business as I was—in some cases better. I thought of my dad.

My dad always said that if he'd have spent his whole life working at an automobile company as chief executive, accruing more and more stock options and making more and more money, that he'd have been enormously bored. His life would have been unfulfilling and uninteresting. He felt strongly that the course he took in public service meant that he had great new vistas and opportunities. It was a thrilling experience for him.

I also knew from my father that you didn't have to win to do something meaningful. My dad had run for president in 1968 and lost. Yet he felt real purpose in the fact that he had spoken out and helped direct the national conversation in ways he thought were important.

So I ran. I worked harder than I had ever worked in my life. We found some enormously talented people who joined with us. And it was amazing, because we did much better than I would ever have imagined. For a moment, just after I won the primary election, I was even tied or slightly ahead in the polls. But then Kennedy came back strong and did what good politicians do, he swept me up and off the floor.

Kennedy launched a particularly effective attack campaign. His ads reinforced people's misperceptions about me as a money-grubbing businessman. He injected my Mormonism into the campaign in a highly visible way. Our polls showed that my faith was a significant negative in largely Catholic Massachusetts. Ideas I brought forward were dissected and distorted to their illogical extreme. When it was all said and done, he beat me soundly.

I learned a great deal from the experience. But after it was over, neither Ann nor I felt like we had accomplished what we set out to do. We felt that there was a greater purpose to our campaign than winning. We wanted to raise new ideas for government, help rebuild a disappearing second party, and stand for something bigger than self-interest. We knew all along that we would ultimately lose, but the loss felt worse than we had imagined. For several months we would say to ourselves, "Why did we do that?"

Kennedy ran a great campaign. I had a lot to learn. I didn't harbor any ill will. Yet, I didn't feel that we had made the kind of contribution we had envisioned. The campaign had been about charges and misperceptions, not ideas and ideals. I kept asking myself what had I really accomplished with all the effort. I wondered if anything lasting for the community, even for political dialog, had really come of it. Those questions remained unanswered for years.

THE ROARING '90s

The morning after the election, I showed up at Bain Capital and called a meeting. I gave people assignments and reviewed upcoming deals. People looked at each other with wide eyes. They must have been thinking, "He's baaaaaaaack." I'm sure I ruffled a lot of feathers. I had been gone for a year, and they were getting along fine without me. But Bain Capital was my baby and I was back in town. I owned 100 percent of the voting stock. I basically went back to doing what I had done before, without a day's rest.

Business was picking up. The stock market roared. The next five years at Bain Capital were very profitable. Bain had some of the best investments in the history of private equity. Most of them were companies that no one has heard of—TRW's credit services, the Yellow Pages of Italy. We pursued what is called a "value investment strategy." It was not the standard investment banker approach of snatching up companies with high, sustained growth, hanging on for six months, and then flipping them for a profit. Instead we were looking for troubled companies, businesses that were not performing as well as we think they could. We would invest in these underperforming companies, using the equivalent of a mortgage to leverage up our investment. Then we would go to work to help management make their business more successful. I never actually ran one of our investments; that was left to management. But my years as a consultant at Bain & Company, my turnaround experience at my former firm, and the extraordinary talent of the team at Bain Capital gave me confidence we could succeed with our approach. Did we ever.

Yet I found myself unsatisfied. Impressions I had formed on the campaign trail stayed with me. The experience of walking into diners and onto construction sites and hearing people tell me their problems was not easily put aside. I had the bug of wanting to be more involved. I wanted to make more of a difference in people's lives.

So when the opportunity to work with the Olympics came along, I couldn't help wondering if it was the doorway I had been looking for—the doorway from contribution to commitment.

JANUARY SKI TRIP

Kem's call came in December 1998, and it happened that Ann and I had been planning a January ski vacation for months. Kem got wind of the fact and asked if he could make some introductions while we were in Utah. I consented. I went on vacation consumed by two opposing impulses—one was that this was the greater purpose I had been looking for, the other was that it was completely crazy and I should flee.

We arrived in Utah and Kem went right to work. He took me around to meet members of SLOC's board of directors. Looking back I realize he was operating on two levels at once. He puts on this country hick facade, but he's as wily as a coyote. Kem recognized that there would not be an immediate "Oh, let's hire Mitt Romney" reaction from the selection committee. There would have to be some selling.

Kem found us at our new house. He said, "Mitt, you've got to come down to Salt Lake with me." We drove the forty-five minutes to have breakfast with two board members of SLOC at the Alta Club—Spence Eccles from First Security Bank and Verl Topham of Utah Power. We talked about the scandal and what it would take to get SLOC back on track.

Kem also introduced me to Don Cash, CEO of Questar and other prominent members of the SLOC board. During these meetings, we had no prior appointments. Kem would just bust into people's offices and say, "You've got to meet Mitt Romney, he's a friend of mine. Maybe we ought to get someone like him to run the Olympics." We would sit down and chat for a few minutes. All the while he was getting them vested in me. The informal visits, his broad congeniality— it wasn't as if he were making an official recommendation, it was more like the board members were baking the idea themselves.

Later in the week, Kem arranged for me to meet SLOC Chairman Robert Garff. We met on the second floor lobby of the Marriott hotel for a couple of hours. It went well and at the end of the conversation, Bob deferred, "I want you to meet with the person who is currently running the Games, Frank Joklik, the outgoing CEO." I agreed to meet with Frank.

Frank was very skeptical about me from the start. It was clear from our first few minutes together that there was no way he thought some investor from Boston would have the moxie to pull off an Olympics. I asked him what he thought the most important characteristic would be for whoever took the position. He said he thought that project management skills were the most critical. Of course, Frank's background was in engineering. He looked at me and saw someone who had never engineered or constructed anything in his entire life.

We had a good chat nevertheless. He asked about my experience at Bain Capital and Bain & Company. We talked about the Kennedy campaign. At the end of the conversation he said, "You know, you would do really well here...." I protested, "I don't have any project management experience." And he replied, "Well, you could get that. You'd have people on your team who would have that." He seemed to have changed his thinking about me over the course of one conversation.

FINALIZING

Ann and I returned home not having skied nearly as much as we had hoped. I kept things quiet at work, but I was on a plane back to Utah a week later to meet with the governor. Governor Mike Leavitt was making a trip to Los Angeles to give a speech to technology companies on Utah's favorable business climate. He asked if I would accompany him. Apparently, reports from the members of the board had been favorable. We talked all the way there. There were a few members of the search committee on the plane and while the governor gave his speech, we had breakfast. Then we flew back together. We talked about my background and my approach to management. I allowed myself to express my interest and we agreed to set a formal meeting with the entire search committee over dinner at the Governor's Mansion.

The search committee had some concerns. Certain prominent members of the community had expressed a strong interest in the job. The board was anxious to make sure that they had been very deliberate in their selection process. Yet they had held only preliminary talks with some of the local candidates. I had no interest whatsoever in being a candidate in an extended process; I was ready for them to make an offer. We discussed terms over dinner. I told them I didn't care much about compensation and would be happy to accept whatever Frank had been given.

I left with what I thought was an offer in hand. There was a bit of confusion when the governor continued to accept visits from other prominent applicants. I had to call and explain that, all appearances of due diligence aside, I was not one to have my name bandied about—with all that that would mean for my relationship with Bain Capital—only to be passed over for the job. They either wanted me or they didn't. If they didn't, they should say so outright. If they did, I would accept.

LEADING FROM COMMITMENT

There is no question that I approached circumstances in Salt Lake City at the end of January 1999 in an atypical way. My appointment was not the culmination of a career in sports administration. I was not being promoted from within. I had no aspirations for further appointments with the International Olympic Committee (IOC). And despite suspicions to the contrary, I had no plans to parlay the experience into political advantage.

There was almost nothing about the road after the Olympics that was clear. When I talked to my partners at Bain Capital, I opined that it wouldn't make sense for me to come back to the company at the end of my tenure at SLOC as I had following my campaign. Three years is a long time and the firm would have changed. It wouldn't be fair to them.

Who knew where it could lead? I gave very little thought at all to what I would do afterwards. Many people can't believe that. They think that I had calculated the political benefits. But honestly, I had no idea. I saw no political connection at all. The idea of going to Utah as a way of helping me run in Massachusetts was nuts. If I wanted to run, I would have stayed in Massachusetts. And I had no appetite for staying in Utah for a political career. There were plenty of people who had lived there all their lives, who were prepared and qualified. I was going to Utah to run the Olympics. Ann and I felt it was the right thing to do. We felt it brought greater meaning to what we had already done. I wanted to serve the community, not run for office.

It was the spirit of public service that attracted me. The only way SLOC and the community in Utah would turn things around in the wake of the scandal was for people to recognize the higher purpose of the Games. Great enterprises are driven by great values. Leaders establish vision and values that motivate and create unity of purpose.

THE WORST OF TIMES, THE BEST OF TIMES

Looking back, it was more difficult and more demanding than I had ever imagined. Had I known the level of effort that would be needed, it might have frightened me away. By the same token, it was more exhilarating, more fulfilling, and more rewarding than any professional experience I have ever known. Coming to know the athletes and experiencing firsthand the Games, the ceremonies, and the drama of the Olympics was beyond a dream. I would never have imagined that I would be a part of bringing to life such remarkable stories as those of Jimmy Shea and Vonetta Flowers and Janica Kostelic.

As we were working hard, we wondered, would our Games rise to the level of prior Olympics? And then to have such unforgettable Games, lauded in almost every media. They helped heal the nation. The spirit of patriotism flowed unrestrained in the wake of the attacks of September 11. They helped bring the world together. I'll never forget the French coming into the opening ceremonies with specially crafted flags: French flags on one side and American flags on the other.

Quotes came in calling it the best Olympics ever. Those of us who worked on the 2002 Games have to look at it as a high point in our careers. While in my professional life I've done things that are very interesting and challenging and rewarding, and I may do so in the future, I cannot imagine how anything could surpass the Olympic experience. Trite but true, once in a lifetime.

Chapter 2

ANATOMY OF THE CRISIS

I don't pretend to have first-hand knowledge about who is to blame for the Salt Lake Olympic scandal. I was not there at the time nor did I carry out an independent investigation into the wrongdoing. Most of what I know came from reading the newspapers, although I often came into contact with people involved with the bid committee. I don't recall hearing any primary information, just opinions. Only a few people really know who knew what, and who did what.

The federal government spent a great deal of time investigating the case. It indicted Tom Welch, the bid committee CEO, and Dave Johnson, his number two man. Neither was ultimately convicted, a result widely circulated as vindication. Of course, not being convicted of a crime isn't vindication of wrongdoing, and not all unethical behavior is criminal. Even when criminal conduct occurs, it may be difficult to prove—and that's with effective prosecutors. I believe those who pursued Welch and Johnson were inept.

What is clear is that the allegations had a seismic impact on the community, the Olympic movement, and the people who made up the Salt Lake Organizing Committee.

The story broke with the leak of a drafted letter from Dave Johnson to Sonia Essomba, daughter of Rene Essomba, then president of the National Olympic Committee in Cameroon. The letter was leaked by an undisclosed source to KTVX Channel 4, the ABC affiliate in Salt Lake City, and discussed a final lump sum tuition reimbursement of over $10,000 to Ms. Essomba. The letter was unsigned and the lump sum payment was never made. But further investigation revealed that Ms. Essomba's tuition at American University in Washington, D.C. had been reimbursed by the bid committee.

As secretary general of an association of African Olympic committees, Rene Essomba was presumably in a position to sway the votes of certain African members of the IOC. Africa was second only to Europe in the number of IOC members. And Rene Essomba himself had a vote. Tom and Dave wanted every vote possible for Salt Lake City to make sure that it didn't lose the bid for the Winter Games, again. It didn't take long for the obvious to be said: "if it looks like, walks like, and quacks like a bribe.... "

The tuition payments had been made under the auspices of a "National Olympic Committee Assistance Program," set up in the bid committee budget to provide tuition, travel, and lodging expenses to athletes and coaches from third-world nations—a sanctioned form of "humanitarian" aid. Ms. Essomba was not an athlete, and even if she had been, such open generosity towards a relative of an influential official would have to be viewed with suspicion. With a public relations crisis looming, SLOC's legal counsel and its finance director sequestered themselves in the sixth floor conference room of the headquarters, hastily convening a comprehensive review of all assistance program expenditures.

What they found was nearly $400,000 in payments for education and "athletic training" made to thirteen people, six of whom appeared to be relatives of voting IOC members. They delivered their findings directly to president Juan Antonio Samaranch at a regularly scheduled IOC executive board meeting in Lausanne, Switzerland, the following week. Samaranch promptly announced the appointment of an IOC "Juridical Commission." He put his first vice president, Dick Pound of Canada, in charge of the investigation. Governor Leavitt announced Utah's own review by an independent board of ethics, headed by the former chief judge of the Utah Supreme Court.

With the scent of blood in the water and investigative reporters circling Lausanne, IOC Olympic elder statesman Marc Hodler found a willing gallery for his offhand comments describing the payments as "outright bribes." On the eve of several IOC meetings—the perfect hothouse for the story to gain international status—Hodler further speculated about a written list naming IOC members whose votes could be bought and about dedicated agents who took payments to secure voting blocks, up to 7 percent of the total voting body. The claims were widely reported but never substantiated and in the prevailing climate, they seemed more than credible. A subsequent study found that stories of the IOC in the international papers peaked at over three hundred articles per day that week—six times the number during previous periods of high interest such as existed during the 1998 Nagano Winter Games.

MORE ALLEGATIONS

FBI agents converged on Salt Lake City. The Justice Department announced its investigation into criminal wrongdoing. Before long, the USOC would appoint former Senator George Mitchell who had helped negotiate a cease-fire in Northern Ireland to conduct an independent inquiry. The USOC would also begin its own internal investigation. The U.S. Senate would hold hearings on the allegations. And a steady stream of revelations would continue to appear in the papers.

In addition to tuition reimbursements for the children of voting IOC members from Mali, Libya, Cameroon, and Swaziland, other improprieties soon surfaced.

Jung Hoon ("John") Kim, son of Un Young Kim, an IOC member from South Korea and chairman of the IOC's Radio and Television Commission, had been employed by a local Salt Lake City communications company through the efforts of the bid committee. When the communications company demurred on more than commission for payment, the bid committee itself paid for Mr. Kim's $45,000 salary from its "humanitarian" fund.

The bid committee had also sought employment for Bjarne Häggman as a consultant to a forestry engineering company. He was husband to Finnish IOC member Pirjo Häggman. Allegedly, it paid $33,000 for a consulting analysis that was never used by the engineering company.

There was reportedly $28,000 worth of free health care for Jean-Claude Ganga, an IOC member from the Republic of Congo, and for members of his family at local Salt Lake City hospitals.

Most damaging of all were allegations of direct payments: $60,000 to Rene Essomba, $70,000 to Jean-Claude Ganga, $35,000 to Charles Mukora, all IOC members. These payments were ostensibly to defray the costs of official Olympic business but there appeared to be no confirming documentation. The money was paid into personal accounts.

To the IOC and to Utah, it was disgraceful and humiliating. Jay Leno was pulling "money bags" punch lines on the *Tonight Show*. World leaders were making critical comments about Salt Lake City. It was a bitter pill for a community that had only recently been celebrating their new prominence on the world stage.

THE GOVERNOR TAKES ACTION

With the New Year, Governor Leavitt took further action. He asked for the resignation of David Johnson and put two SLOC employees who were party to the bid committee on paid administrative leave. Tom Welch had previously resigned in 1997 amid allegations and no contest pleadings regarding spousal abuse. Following his resignation, Welch had been retained by SLOC as a consultant for which he was scheduled to be paid an astonishing $1 million. With the scandal revelation, Welch's "consulting" was terminated. The governor also asked SLOC CEO Frank Joklik to step down. Joklik had been chairman of the board during the period of alleged wrongdoing and later had been appointed president and CEO after Welch's resignation. Joklik was not accused of knowing or participating in the payments, but some felt that he had not come forward when the irregularities were brought to his attention. And, as one of the visible leaders both at the time of the alleged wrongdoing and in the years following, Governor Leavitt had to restore SLOC's credibility.

The resignations and departures led to the formation of a SLOC search committee, a collection of Utah and USOC officials tasked with interviewing candidates for CEO. But even as I met with members of the search committee, scandal developments continued to pour out. Dick Pound's IOC commission issued its report. Focused mostly on the actions of IOC members, it accepted the resignations of three implicated members and urged the expulsion of six more. The IOC passed new regulations on the selection of host cities, limiting bid committee contacts with individual voting members.

With so many bodies flying around, I approached my assignment with some trepidation. My wife and I joked that I was committing professional suicide. But we knew that as the process ran its course and as those implicated of wrongdoing stepped aside, the crisis would ultimately pass. The team would move on in a new direction.

As I flew to Salt Lake City in February 1999, I knew that the first thing I needed to do was to draw a clear, bright, heavy line between what had happened before and what was going to happen in the future. In almost every way I could think of, the SLOC I would lead was going to be different from the SLOC led by Frank Joklik, Tom Welch, and Dave Johnson.

Peter Ueberroth, who took over the Los Angeles Games at another time of crisis in Olympic history, wrote that 20 percent of executive authority is appointed and the other 80 percent is asserted through decisive action. The most important steps I would take in my first hours on the job would be to establish as much distance as possible between me and the old SLOC.

The board of ethics report was due to be released two days before the public announcement of my appointment. It confirmed many of the allegations that had already been discovered by or leaked to the press; there were no stunning revelations.

The report painted a picture of deep disappointment in the wake of Salt Lake City's narrow defeat to Nagano in 1991. Salt Lake had been the clear front-runner to win the bid. But it did not. Bid committee members alleged that Nagano had given IOC members free laptop computers, which were quite expensive at the time. Leading Japanese companies had reportedly donated millions of dollars to the IOC museum in Lausanne—President Samaranch's pet project. Nagano was believed to be a far inferior site for the Winter Games than Salt Lake, but Nagano had made some apparently wise investments in "IOC causes."

The ethics report depicted an all out, heedless effort by Welch and Johnson, following the loss to Nagano, to secure the loyalties of key voting members from Africa, South America, and the Pacific Rim for the next Winter Games selection. The fund that had been established by the SLOC board to provide academic scholarships to athletes and coaches had been expanded ten-fold over the course of four years and used to make unspecified payments to IOC members and their families. What had transpired was unethical. Clearly it was deeply embarrassing. But the ethics panel stopped short of accusing anyone of criminal conduct. There simply did not seem to be a law that made what Tom and Dave did illegal.

It has always been Tom's and Dave's assertion that other members of the board knew of the suspect payments they made from the fund, including the governor. Every board member surely knew of airline tickets, trips to Salt Lake, and hospitality gifts for visiting IOC members. Those things are not unusual in a business setting. But what the bid committee did went far beyond normal business gifts and hospitality. And as of this writing, neither Tom nor Dave has offered any evidence that anyone but themselves knew of the hundreds of thousands in cash and tuition payments for IOC members.

HERE WE GO

With the announcement of my appointment scheduled to occur at the February 11 board meeting, there was little time to prepare for a move. I hastily made arrangements to move into the ski home Ann and I had just recently completed in Park City, Utah. I said my good-byes in Massachusetts, asked my lawyer to negotiate a departure agreement with my partners at Bain Capital, threw a few suits, shirts, and socks in a suitcase, and headed for Salt Lake. On the night before the official announcement of my appointment, I was scheduled to meet with the governor, then with each of the members of the SLOC board of directors. It was a chance for them to ask final questions and for me to make final arrangements.

I was particularly anxious to finalize the other announcements that would be made at the board meeting where I would be introduced. As it would garner world media attention, it would be our first opportunity to publicly lay out the new direction. I wanted to make sure nothing else would detract from our message. I knew that the structure of the board itself was going to be a major issue at the meeting. Governor Leavitt had been an advocate of restructuring the board. I too was insistent that any lingering association with the bid scandal be eliminated. As important, I felt it was critical that we establish strict conflict of interest policies, stricter than any I knew that existed elsewhere. While other organizations might be able to weather an ethical storm, SLOC could not. It had already exceeded its quota.

CHANGES TO THE BOARD

When the board of directors was originally formed in 1991, part of their mandate was to provide oversight that would "build public confidence" in the Olympic bid by "shar[ing] the blame if things go wrong." While no evidence had arisen to suggest their complicity with wrongdoing, the board had failed to provide adequate oversight. We needed to take action that would re-engage the board members in active oversight of the organization.

The Governor's office suggested expanding the board to allow more representation. A newly formed Management Committee of twenty board members would have the lead responsibility. A rule was proposed to make 75 percent attendance at all SLOC board meetings mandatory. This would address the chronic absenteeism of some of the board's most prominent members. Most important, all SLOC board meetings would be open to the public and the media. The public could also request copies of any SLOC documents. There were some limitations, of course. Personnel identifying information like credit card numbers and medical histories would be kept private, as would contractual terms with SLOC employees or Olympic sponsorship agreements that were subject to confidentiality clauses. Basically, I would be running an organization with complete transparency to the public and, more significantly, the media.

In the mind of the public, there was another major issue related to conflicts of interest for certain board members. It had been widely reported that Earl Holding, a member of the board, was to receive $13.8 million in rent from SLOC as the owner of Snowbasin Resort, one of our alpine skiing venues. He also was constructing a hotel that would presumably house IOC delegations during the Games. Another member, Nick Badami, was part owner of Park City Mountain Resort, another Olympic venue. And Alan Layton, a longstanding board member, owned a construction company that had won the bid to build the speed skating oval. The media charged: "conflict of interest." This was accurate but it did not mean that any of them had done anything inappropriate.

In the business world, the reality is that so-called "conflicts of interest" occur with some frequency. A conflict of interest just means that by virtue of various assignments, people face situations where they have conflicting responsibilities. When that happens, they simply disclose their conflict to both parties and step away from the table. If they're not involved in any decisions relating to the conflicted issues, they can't be accused of favoring one interest over another. There's nothing morally ambiguous about *having* a conflict of interest, only in not disclosing it and recusing oneself from the discussion.

From the public's viewpoint, however, the mere *presence* of a conflict of interest somehow seems incriminatory. It creates headlines. The truth of the matter was that Earl Holding, Nick Badami, and Alan Layton had done nothing wrong. It made perfect sense to have business leaders from the community on the board and, as long as they recused themselves on matters concerning their personal interests, their perspectives and expertise were extremely valuable. That said, there was no question in my mind that they had to leave the board. I was insistent upon it. I wanted to have the strictest conflict standards in the country. It wouldn't be enough for a board member to withdraw from discussion on a matter affecting his personal interest; the public would always suspect that influence flowed behind closed doors. While the details of my responsibilities at SLOC were still unclear to me, one thing was clear: we had to restore the ethical credibility to the organization without delay. Asking them to resign would in no way harm their personal or corporate interests and SLOC would surely be able to replace their expertise with others in the community. We had fifty-three board members!

I asked Charlie Manning, my friend and the former communications director from my senatorial campaign to fly with me to Utah for my announcement. I knew he would have helpful suggestions about what I should say. He might also be able to guide my first few days of interaction with the media if SLOC didn't have the requisite skills on hand. We discussed enumerating certain "absolutes" in my comments to the board and to the public. My first absolute was that SLOC would abide by the highest standards of ethical conduct.

If I were asked about bid committee wrongdoing, I wanted to be able to truthfully reply that we had taken every action to rectify mistakes. We were now looking forward. I was not going to answer questions about the scandal. Any time I was talking scandal, I would be linking myself to it. Just talking about something connects you to it in people's minds. And we couldn't afford that at SLOC. Not anymore. It drove the media nuts: every question about the scandal got the same answer, "I'm looking forward, not backwards."

The governor would announce the new policies and board restructuring. He would deal with any issues relating to the scandal and leave me to articulate a vision for the future. He also offered to speak with the three board members who would be affected. That was important to me, in part, because one of the three, Alan Layton, happened to be one of my good friends. The governor said, "I will do it. This will be on my watch. I'll take care of it before you step in." It was big of him. These were people who were important to Utah. I'm sure they had helped to support his campaigns. But the governor was gracious to step forward so the issue would be behind us when attention turned to me.

Unfortunately that was not precisely how it played out. John Fowler, the governor's official liaison with the Olympic committee, apparently didn't know our plan. When Alan Layton showed up for his final due diligence meeting with me, Fowler said, "Mitt has asked that you be taken off the board, Alan." When Alan came in to see me, he looked terribly hurt. He felt like his friend had betrayed him. I explained the reasoning behind the decision. I talked about how important it was to put the Olympics back on secure footing. But it was very painful for him.

I felt terrible too, and I admit that I hadn't properly calculated how high the personal cost would be for Alan and the others. Because of the timing of the announcement, the public tended to associate the three departing board members with the SLOC executives who had been asked to step down due to the scandal. Of course, these guys had absolutely nothing to do with that affair. But because of the timing and the reports of conflicts of interest, it seemed to some that they had done something wrong. That was wrong. They had been heroes.

Over the course of my three years at SLOC, I would meet with Earl Holding several times in conjunction with developments at his Snowbasin resort. I don't think there was ever a time we met that he didn't rehearse for me again the injustice of that day and the lack of gratitude SLOC had showed him. And by SLOC, I knew he meant me. And he was right. To have asked him to build a hotel for the Games and to expand Snowbasin to the tune of over a $100 million and then to embarrass him by asking him to resign was a bitter pill.

I never met with Nick Badami, but I learned subsequently something about the price he had paid for the Games. Nick's son, Craig, had worked very hard to bring the Olympics to Utah as well. Together, they had hosted some international skiing competitions at the Park City Mountain Resort in an effort to raise the credibility of Utah venues. Following one of these races, Nick's son boarded a helicopter that suffered mechanical failures and crashed. All aboard were killed. It was a devastating loss. It had been incurred on behalf of the Games.

I made every effort at SLOC to include Alan Layton, Earl Holding, and Nick Badami in all our Olympic family functions during the Games. We made sure tickets and accreditations were available. We recognized them publicly for their contributions. Mr. Badami's grandson was asked to lead one of the teams into the stadium during the parade of nations. They had already given a great deal in voluntary service but perhaps their greatest contribution was in stepping away when doing so helped restore public confidence. It allowed us to put critical voices aside and move forward. It helped to draw the line between past and future.

ARTICULATING THE VISION

It was necessary but insufficient to correct the failures that permitted the scandalous conduct by the bid committee. It was just as important to articulate a new vision. We could no longer spend our time and energy looking back into the past; we had to look forward. These too would be included in my enumeration of absolutes. At the board meeting, the national and international press corps was there in force. We had convened in a hotel conference room, draped in blue for the occasion. There were dozens of reporters near the back. At least fifteen television cameras were on a stage.

The Governor spoke. The new structure of the board was presented. The resignations of Earl Holding and Alan Layton were announced—Nick Badami was not in attendance; his would come later. I was formally nominated, seconded, and approved as the new CEO. It all happened very quickly and before I knew it, Chairman Garff made a ceremonious introduction and turned the time over to me. In reference to the unanimous and speedy voting, I quipped, "Where were you when I needed you back in 1994?" There was laughter. The room loosened a bit. It was time for me to articulate my "absolutes." It was time to draw a picture of the future.

"The Olympics is about sport, not business," I said. "The Olympics is about the athletes—young people aspiring for greatness, not the managers. The managers, those are the guys like us who hold the stopwatches and clean the equipment after the event. And sure the managers have messed up big time, but the athletes haven't...."

I committed to do four things without compromise. I made four promises that would give shape to our work in the future.

First, I pledged that from that time forward, preparations for the Olympics would be held to the highest standards of ethical conduct. We would not "accept as an answer for failure 'everybody else does it.'" I called for the resignation, not just the disclosure, of any board or staff members with conflicting business interests. I promised to review my own investments and responsibilities with an eye towards eliminating any potential conflicts.

Second, I pledged fiscal discipline. "We will not ask for money from Utah taxpayers." SLOC would spend no more money than it took in. I vowed to begin reviewing the budget immediately. There was a real fear that they might eventually need to be bailed out by the state. Utah is staunchly conservative and anti-tax, but for that matter, no Olympics could be seen as successful that did not cover its costs. Financial assiduousness would become our primary concern and our greatest burden. It was an absolute commitment. No shortfall was acceptable. No debts would be left for the taxpayers.

Third, I vowed to protect Utah's environment, to feature the spectacular scenery Utah afforded without damaging its legacy.

And fourth, I promised that Utahns would share in the Olympic experience. Those who would live through the agony of construction delays and diverted tax revenues leading up to 2002 deserved to participate in the spectacle.

I closed by inviting scrutiny. "Anytime there has been a breach of trust by people at the top, that organization is going to be placed under a microscope, and that is appropriate. We will be viewed much more carefully than any other organizing committee perhaps in the history of the Olympics, and we deserve to be so viewed. I believe we will come through with flying colors."

It seemed to go well. A brief question and answer period followed. "Mr. Romney, do you feel that the integrity of Mr. Samaranch's leadership has been compromised?" There were many questions regarding the causes of the scandal and on potential reforms within the IOC, but I was stalwart in my refusal to speculate. I said I had enough on my hands not to get tied up in matters that were out of my control and unrelated to my mission. "I am looking forward...."

It was clear that the people of Salt Lake, and even the local media, were as interested in putting the past behind as I was. The media gushed that I was a "torch-bearer of the new hope" with "politics and entrepreneurial talent...wired into the Romney DNA," even "savior of the Games" and the proverbial "white knight." This was vainglorious praise for a guy who had done precisely nothing up to that point, but it was welcome nonetheless.

After the press conference, I met with Shelley Thomas, the senior vice president of communications, and Steve Coltrin. Coltrin & Associates was a New York public relations firm that had been awarded a contract just prior to my arrival—in part due to Steve's willingness to donate much of his time. Both gave me decent marks on the day's performance. We sat down to further map out SLOC's media strategy.

I immediately clicked with Steve Coltrin. He had known my father during his days of political activity. Steve is an immensely likeable fellow. He is somewhat diminutive of stature with pugnacious features. Raised on a farm in Idaho, he built his career in Manhattan, and needs no more than three or four hours of sleep a night. His hardboiled straightforwardness allowed him to be equally at ease among farmhands and Fortune 500 CEOs. Some of his clients had included 3Com, 3M, Palm, Del Monte, British Petroleum, Marriott, BASF, and U.S. Robotics.

Back when the allegations against the bid committee had first surfaced, Steve had sent an urgent message to then President Frank Joklik. He told Joklik he had forty-eight hours to maintain the viability of his leadership by doing three things: calling for an independent investigation, putting anyone implicated by the scandal on administrative leave, and holding a news conference to admit openly that something had gone terribly wrong and that SLOC was committed to getting to the bottom of it.

Joklik initially demurred for his own reasons, but to Coltrin, the basic strategy remained the same: admission of fault, commitment to rectify the situation, and boundless visibility. Openness, integrity, and media, media, media, Coltrin insisted, were the only way to restore the confidence of potential sponsors and recapture the good graces of the public. He didn't need to elaborate. We had the same vision. My own experience with the media had taught me the importance of visibility and of promptness in responding to criticism.

Indeed, there was a lot to counter. The bid scandal was further enhanced by the stories of luxurious accommodations, lavish junkets, and influence bartering that had hung over the IOC for decades. Peter Ueberroth had suggested that free airplane tickets, easily transferable for cash, had been key in securing the Seoul, Korea bid in 1982. There was the uncomfortable fact that Samaranch insisted that he be called "His Excellency." There were five-star hotels in Lausanne, extravagant budgets for flowers, and personal drivers.

We had to find a way to pick up a new storyline. Coltrin was convinced that visibility was the key. Though we weren't exactly sure of the message at that early stage, we knew we needed to deliver one. He and Shelley were anxious to get me on the road while the honeymoon effect of my arrival persisted. I told them I would go anywhere they told me to and would focus on the absolutes that would drive the future course.

Chapter 3

STRATEGIC AUDIT

The principle of triage is not lost on me. I was involved in a terrible car accident when I was about twenty years old serving a volunteer assignment in France. I was at the wheel of a full-size Citroën on my way from Bordeaux to Paris. I came over the top of a hill to find a Mercedes coming directly at me, passing a truck on a curve, on a tree-lined road. The Mercedes was traveling at about seventy miles an hour; I later learned that the driver had been drinking. We literally did not see each other until we were about thirty feet apart.

Tragically, there was a fatality; one of my passengers and a close associate was pronounced dead at the scene. I was also pronounced dead. One of the gendarmes at the scene found me lying unconscious on the side of the road and wrote, *"il est mort"* on my passport before moving on.

The erroneous accident report was picked up by a news service that broadcast the report in the United States. My parents and Ann, my then-girlfriend and future wife, learned I had expired. They didn't believe the story. I guess no family initially believes that kind of report. My father called a friend of his, Sargent Shriver, who was then the U.S.

ambassador at the American embassy in Paris. Ambassador Shriver assured them I was very much alive.

At the small hospital where we were taken, the doctor's triage led him to focus on another of my colleagues. Broken ribs, wrists, facial lacerations, and bleeding were more threatening than my broken arm and swollen forehead.

My first few days at SLOC felt something like a collision, although in quite a different way. So many problems came at me, so quickly, that it was hard to process what was happening. I knew that the organization was in serious trouble. In fact, that was one of the reasons I took the job—the opportunity to tackle a challenging situation in a worthy cause. Ann had told the *Boston Globe* that I would never have considered doing it "if it wasn't a big mess...He loves emergencies and catastrophes." That was probably true, but from my vantage point in Boston, I hadn't fully grasped the extent of the problems. To sort it all out and to be able to make headway required a kind of triage. I have come to call it a strategic audit.

THE MAP

In business turnaround settings, the first thing we had learned is that you should begin with a strategic audit. In a large business, the process could last as long as three months or more.

Our strategic audit took us to customers, to board members, to Wall Street analysts, to bankers, to suppliers, to former employees, and where possible, to competitors. We also got copies of every report that the company produced. We analyzed the numbers according to the tools that had been proven to work before in other diagnostics. Every conceivable way of interpreting market shares, segmentation, business definition, cash flow, investment policy, competitive position, product quality, customer satisfaction, technology position and countless other measures were employed. At the end of the strategic audit, we had a pretty good map of what was right and wrong in the business, of what had to be fixed, and which things were urgent and which were long term. We had hypotheses on which actions would have the greatest impact.

The strategic audit at SLOC would not be easy. But I was anxious to get underway with a full diagnosis so that I would know what other problems existed and what resources were at our disposal. I went right to work by interviewing my function directors, the senior managers. And there were an awful lot of them. Most businesses have ten or fifteen functions: manufacturing, marketing, distribution, accounting, etc. The Olympics had forty-two functions. There were the athletic functions: sport, medical services, doping control, and event scheduling. There were operational functions: transportation, venue development, environment, etc. There were the hosting functions such as accommodations, food services, and ticketing. There were technology functions: information services, telecommunications, timing, scoring and results. There were creative services and ceremonies. There was the torch relay. And, of course, there were the support functions: human resources, accounting, legal affairs, federal relations, and on and on. Forty-two functions—that fact alone was daunting. But the stories the function directors were telling were even more disturbing.

I had to catalog the problems. It seemed there was a fire at every turn. With each director interview came another problem. I started writing down the most pressing problems on a piece of notepaper to keep track of them all. I called it "The Map." It grew almost daily. The phrase, "deer in the headlights" was mentioned again and again by the management team. The entire organization had been shell shocked by the revelations of scandal. Their senior management had been fired or put on leave. The media characterized SLOC as the bums, not the heroes. My most urgent and important job was to get the team going again, motivated, and driving toward the same destination.

TROUBLES IN WASHINGTON, PART ONE

SLOC was subject to an ongoing criminal investigation. Our attorneys were spending a lot of time responding to requests for information by the Justice Department. Even worse, Brian Katz, our associate general counsel, explained that SLOC itself could be held criminally liable for the activities of its former executives if it could be shown that they were acting on behalf of SLOC or in the due course of business when they allegedly made inappropriate payments to IOC members. As evidenced by the plight of Arthur Andersen, the auditing firm, SLOC could not now insulate itself from legal action simply by firing those who would be accused of wrongdoing.

Perhaps it goes without saying, but if SLOC was indicted as an organization, the Games in Salt Lake City were probably over. Potential sponsors would disappear for good. Committed sponsors could insist that they be released and given back any proceeds we had received. The federal government and Congress in particular, would never think of appropriating money to an indicted organization. Indictment meant we were toast; conviction wasn't necessary to put us out of business.

So our legal strategy was given high priority on my triage scale. I had been trained as a lawyer, and while this matter was beyond my experience, my background meant I could converse knowledgeably on strategy, risks, and the consequences of different courses of action. I would need to work closely with Brian Katz, Jim Jardine, the senior partner at our Salt Lake law firm, and Barry Sanders and Beth Wilkinson, our client leads at Latham & Watkins, our criminal defense counsel in Washington D.C. All were top drawer. Jim had been on law review at Harvard when I was there. Barry had been counsel to the Los Angeles Olympics. Beth had previously been a federal prosecutor and had prosecuted Timothy McVeigh, the Oklahoma City bombing monster.

TROUBLES IN WASHINGTON, PART TWO

SLOC needed a lot of help from Washington if we were going to have Olympics in Salt Lake City. I found that the budget blithely assumed that SLOC would get more from the federal government than any other Games in history, more by a wide margin. No authorized agency had made a commitment to provide what we needed, nor had Congress. We would have to get the support from literally scores of departments and congressional committees. The lobbying task would be monumental. And it would face resistance.

It didn't take long to understand the need. We needed help on critical transportation infrastructure projects like Interstate exit ramps and overpasses, highway widening, and new access routes. We would need the State Department to develop an entirely new visa system to accommodate traveling athletes and coaches. Customs would also have to build systems to deal with athletic equipment coming in to the Games—we could hardly charge duty to visiting athletes for their skis and bobsleds. Of course, there would be big dollars involved with security. Thousands of law enforcement and National Guard personnel would have to be brought to Utah, all housed, transported, fed, and clothed for extreme outdoor conditions. The cost would be in the hundreds of millions for security alone. SLOC had just assumed we would get it all. Of course if we didn't, if the federal government said that it was the Olympics' responsibility to pay for Olympic security, we were sunk. There was no way to fill a hole that big.

In the face of needs which grew more daunting the longer I listened, I was informed that the mood on Capitol Hill towards SLOC was not friendly. The scandal, with its intense media focus and ballooning allegations, had made Salt Lake City's Olympics a hot potato. Congress was so upset they were talking about public hearings on the scandal. There was even a proposal to remove the tax-deductibility of an Olympic sponsorship—that would have killed us right then and there.

There were other problems in Washington. The prior Games in Atlanta were believed to have abused their federal support. Senator McCain had pushed through legislation following Atlanta to strictly limit inappropriate military support for the Olympics due to the abuses. An investigation by the General Accounting Office had found irregularities. And a Justice investigation of compliance with the

Americans with Disabilities Act at the Atlanta Games had been costly and time consuming. These Olympics weren't looking so good to legislators.

Finally, the award of the Olympics had been quite freely cited by some from Utah as the reason a particular project should be funded by the federal government. Cities and towns used the Olympics to bolster grant proposals with some success. Even the state got into the act, linking the massive Interstate reconstruction project with the Olympics in the minds of some legislators. On one of my first visits to Washington, Cindy Gillespie, our head of federal relations, introduced me to her old friend, Senator Richard Shelby. He said, "I don't know why you're coming to Washington; I've already given you a billion dollars for your Olympic highway." What highway? That wasn't an Olympic highway: it was the state's project. SLOC hadn't asked for it and didn't need it for the Games. Our needs hadn't even been surfaced yet.

Cindy explained that we had only three appropriation cycles left; the next one began in the spring just ahead. We'd have to move immediately or potentially be left out of essential funding. Okay, government relations made the triage cut as well. I would be spending a lot of time in D.C.

A FINANCIAL MORASS

It took at least two weeks to begin to comprehend just how bad our financial picture looked. There was a reason it took so long: SLOC's were no ordinary financials, and I had seen a lot of financials in my day.

First was the confusion of VIK. "Value in Kind" was goods or services provided to us by sponsor companies. Let's use McDonald's as an example. I won't use the actual numbers because they're subject to confidentiality agreements, but I'll give the real flavor. First off, McDonald's was one of our best sponsors. We loved the company as much as I loved their burgers. And that's saying something. But like most of the other sponsors, they presented VIK problems.

Let's say that they had agreed to provide $2 million of free hamburgers to athletes at the Olympic Village. The SLOC accounts would show $2 million in revenue. That $2 million couldn't be used to pay for venue construction or salaries. It was on the books as sponsorship revenue, but I couldn't use it for anything I needed to spend. It didn't even save me any money for food in the Olympic Village; there, menus were prescribed by the relevant sport organizations. McDonald's burgers enhanced the experience for the athletes, but they didn't reduce our budget needs. We called VIK like this "budget enhancing." In contrast, when VIK met a budgeted need, say donated fuel from Texaco for our cars, we called it "budget relieving." It relieved an item on our budget.

It gets more complicated. Say that our sponsorship agreement with McDonald's provided that SLOC would be responsible for building the McDonald's "stores" at the Olympic Village where the $2 million in "free" meals will be served. SLOC would then have to bring in the electric power, provide the ventilation, supply the tenting, and so forth. Assume these things would cost SLOC something like $2.5 million. Of course, when the agreements were signed, nobody really knew what the cost would be. So this VIK from McDonald's could actually end up costing SLOC. Here it was on my books as $2 million of revenue but in one sense, it was really a liability, not an asset. Of course, other parts of the McDonald's deal might provide tens of millions of dollars of benefits; but that's not the point. The point is that the financial accounts could be highly misleading and unreliable, especially where VIK was involved. And it was always involved, usually in a big way.

One of my favorite budget enhancing VIK stories involved Budweiser. They gave us a certain amount of VIK beer as part of their sponsorship, except you can't sell or even serve alcohol products that have not been purchased from authorized dealers and distributors in Utah. That meant the Bud VIK had no value to us. And because we owed the IOC a 5 percent royalty on all revenue, it actually cost us money. How do you reflect that on the books? You don't, at least it wasn't reflected on the books when I came in. What looked okay to the board and the public was actually not okay at all. Incidentally, before the Games began, we assigned a person full-time to figure out how to get some value, any value, from VIK that we hadn't been able to use. We had thousands of kitchen and laundry appliances from Sears, for example, that we traded to an apartment developer for his project in another state in exchange for partial payment of rent we would owe him on his building in Utah. In total, VIK was listed on our books as having hundreds of millions of dollars in value, but there was no reliable way to know its true value. The true gap between revenues and costs was blurred by the fact that VIK was such a large part of the equation.

There was another problem with SLOC accounting. There were three different budgets. Originally, the Utah public had been told that the Games budget would be less than $1 billion. Just before I arrived, Frank Joklik had hired Bechtel engineers to do a soup to nuts analysis of what the real figure would be. It was $1.9 billion, including federal support. What the public had been told was off by about 100 percent. There were good reasons for the discrepancy, inflation being one of them. But a public and political storm was likely.

The senior managers told me that when management saw the new figure, a decision was made to recast the budget in three sections to make the total seem smaller and to reduce some of the political heat. The basic SLOC budget would not include either federal support or "matching costs." Matching costs were expenses that would be presumably matched with revenue. If there were no revenue, there wouldn't be any cost, or so went the logic. For example, the torch relay budget of $25 million was put in the matching account because management presumed they would spend on the torch only what a sponsor gave them to spend. The torch presented no risk to SLOC and thus it wasn't put in SLOC's base budget. Same for hotel rooms. SLOC had an obligation to contract for and secure all rooms for sponsors, broadcasters, officials, and so forth. SLOC's matching account for these hotels was $81 million. Frank reasoned that the companies and broadcasters that were gong to stay in those rooms would be paying SLOC back for them, hence, there was no risk for SLOC and the figure wouldn't go on SLOC's base books. There was a logic to all this, but some problems as well. For example, while we would be contracting for hotels well ahead of the Games, if people didn't show or didn't pay, we were on the hook. That's what happened in France's Albertville Games: the organizing committee was left holding the bag for $40 million in room costs. So in fact, there was risk in matching costs. How much, no one had calculated.

The same was obviously the case with the federal account. By putting all costs that were presumed to ultimately be picked up by the feds, SLOC was seriously underestimating its potential obligation. If the feds didn't come through on an item, then SLOC would have to pay.

So SLOC had three budgets: the official base budget of $1.5 billion, the matching budget of $0.2 billion, and the federal budget of $0.2 billion (the actual federal support we would need turned out to be much larger, closer to $0.6 billion). And when I calculated the financial gap I was facing, I looked only to the first of these. But I knew the other two had inherent risks as well. You just had to close your eyes and wish real hard, as one manager told me. Three budgets had led to errors as well. Kelly Flint, our legal counsel, explained that they had found a $41 million error arising for costs that didn't appear in the correct account. The mistake hadn't been disclosed to either the board or the public.

So as I performed my strategic audit, I had unreliable figures to look at: VIK, the matching account, and the federal account made the extent of our problem unclear. But when I got it reasonably sorted out, one thing was sure: SLOC was in a deep hole. A very deep hole. No one told me that before I joined up. And no one had told the public, the legislature or the governor.

The night I had finally put it together, I remarked to Kelly, "By my reckoning, we're hundreds of millions of dollars in the hole!"

Kelly laughed, "Yeah, now you get it. You're right. We're in deep trouble."

A DRY PIPELINE

When a budget is out of balance, there are two possible remedies: cut expenses and raise revenues. I knew from experience that I would find ways to cut costs—I had done that before. But how much I could cut was unclear. I knew that every day, contracts and commitments were being made that locked in spending levels. I would need to take a quick swipe at staunching the spending immediately, then launch a detailed cost containment process that I knew would probably take months. A preliminary review of the cost numbers, however, showed that there would be no way to fill the budget hole solely through cost cutting: too much was already committed or spent, and the Bechtel budget-builders had been pretty conservative. As I said to the local media, it didn't look like the budget had been "all larded up."

So the answer to our budget problem would have to be new revenues—marketing and sales. The good news was that companies had already signed on as sponsors, most of them at higher support levels than in prior Olympics. But that was also the bad news: the usual suspects had already been rounded up. Companies that had traditionally sponsored the Games had virtually all signed on and we were still hundreds of millions short. That meant we would have to find new sponsors, companies that had never been Olympic sponsors. And that's not easy; nor is it as predictable. While it would probably be relatively easy to get a company like American Express to sign up, they were not a potential target because their competitor, Visa, was already a sponsor. We were not permitted to sign more than one company in a given business. I would need to get a quick read on marketing prospects, but the initial indicators pointed to trouble. No new sponsor had been signed in six months and my marketing director predicted it would be at least that long until we added another. Marketing and sales jumped to high priority status.

NERVOUS BANKERS

During my first week on the job, Bank of America, SLOC's bankers, came to town for a check-up. Because SLOC spent money on building venues and hiring people well before the bulk of our revenues from sponsors and broadcasters came in, SLOC needed a loan from the bank to bridge our cash needs until we were going to get paid. Our internal projections put that gap as high as $190 million. Bank of America had agreed to loan the money. But any working capital loan like that is subject to the bank's continuing conviction, and the borrower's honest, good faith representation that he would be able to repay. The bank has no obligation to loan money if they think there's any significant risk that they won't be repaid.

Now what I was seeing during my first days at SLOC, the guys from Bank of America were also seeing. They saw the budget gap. They knew the feds were being counted on to provide heroic levels of support. They knew about the drought in new sponsors. And they surmised that the scandal would possibly dry up our support. So Bank of America was understandably wary. They came to take my temperature.

Jim Nash led the bank team in our meeting. Our finance team delivered a thorough, but decidedly optimistic presentation. He asked questions, pointed to our most obviously generous assumptions, and smiled. The smile was not for happy, it was for forbearance. He wasn't there to argue or embarrass. He hadn't lent the money yet, so he held all the cards. He asked me for my read of the situation at SLOC. I told him the truth. We were in a deep hole financially. I was going to evaluate how serious our problems were. Then I would go to work to fix things. I would keep him fully informed. He smiled.

I decided that I needed to spend time with the bankers, even making a trip to bank headquarters in North Carolina to meet with their CEO.

If they pulled the plug, we would be lights out. And from what I was told by the board, they would be almost impossible to replace.

THERE'S TROUBLE IN WHO-VILLE

The people of Salt Lake City didn't know who was to blame for the scandal, but they knew that their community looked real bad, in America and around the world. They were not happy. They were ashamed. People in Salt Lake City aspire to live by the highest standards of ethical conduct. We Mormons are sometimes accused of wearing our righteousness on our sleeves. And people of other faiths in Utah sure don't want to be left behind on the ethics meter. So it came as a shock to everyone that the community had become the international poster child for bribery and unethical conduct.

The attitude of the community toward the Games and SLOC was more important to me than just a standard public relations matter. If people in America, Utah, and around the world felt bad about the Salt Lake Games, then no company would want to sponsor them. The federal government wouldn't send resources to help us. Ticket sales would be lackluster. Volunteers would be few. Changing the public attitude about the Games of 2002 was very high priority. I wondered if it was even possible.

OPERATIONS TARDINESS

With all those problems crying out for immediate attention, I may have understated the challenges in just pulling off an event as massive as the Olympics. A number of the operations and planning functions were on track, but a number were behind schedule, even problematic.

Security planning had been a huge issue in Atlanta. For our security program to be successful, we would require unprecedented levels of coordination among local, state, and federal agencies. Yet the key players had not yet been clearly identified and, at that late date, had not held their first meeting to organize the planning process.

IBM had decided to drop out as the sole Olympic technology sponsor and provider. After forty years of uninterrupted Olympic sponsorships providing computers, architecture, systems integration, timing, scoring, and broadcast and information networks to the Games, we would have to lead an entirely new and as yet unidentified team of providers. That meant replacing IBM in multiple categories of technology. It meant overcoming compatibility issues and getting systems and hardware from different companies to work together in one integrated structure. It had never been done before at an Olympics. Many on the board saw this as the greatest risk to the Games. And on this, I was a fish on dry land.

Our transportation plan relied almost exclusively on public transportation to move people to our mountain venues. Tiny mountain roads were ill equipped for the kind of volumes that would come with Olympic spectators. In some cases we had identified the need for new roads, new overpasses, expansions, and repair. We needed to build park-and-ride facilities but we didn't even own the land where the parking lots were drawn on our operational maps.

ALL IS NOT LOST

Fortunately, there was a lot that was in good condition at SLOC. On the plus side of the ledger, there was the published budget itself. It was as comprehensive and detailed as anything I had ever seen. Frank Joklik had engaged Bechtel in a multiple month project to create a bottom-up analysis. It was twenty-four volumes of material. That gave us the ability to go through line-by-line and find savings. It gave us a huge leg up to know our costs.

A great deal of work and planning had gone into venues, transportation, and other operations. Some have argued that had it not been for the disruptive shock of the scandal, SLOC may well have been able to proceed without a turnaround. Others insist that the scandal provided the opportunity to get SLOC on track. Whichever, the tsunami of financial, banking, legal, government, morale, and sponsor problems following the revelation of the bid scandal swamped the organization. It was the most troubled turnaround I had ever seen.

The good news was the quality of the SLOC team already in place. Frank Joklik, and Tom Welch before him, had put together a pretty darn good group of people. One of the best personnel moves that Frank made occurred only days before I arrived: he selected Donna Tillery to be his, then my, personal assistant. She was off the charts organized, professional, and willing to take initiative. There could not have been a better fit for what I needed.

Looking at the notes I had jotted down on my map, there were several things that jumped out. First, we had a lot of problems, and big ones. Second, I had penciled in myself to take a personal lead on quite a few fronts. And third, I couldn't possibly do this by myself. Even with the good team that had been assembled, I needed more management at SLOC, and I needed it motivated and working hard.

I also needed Ann, my wife. She had stayed in Boston to be with our youngest son Craig until he graduated in June, four months hence. But I really had to have her support and counsel. For the past thirty years, at the end of every day, I had unloaded all my worries and concerns on Ann, and she had done the same to me. We'd give each other advice and perspective, not only on how to deal with a particular issue, but also on what was most important to us. Keeping life in perspective goes a long way to being able to confront problems with a calm head and sound judgment. Ann is my most trusted advisor; her judgment on the widest range of business, organizational, and human resources matters was more sound than any other I know. I simply could not turnaround the Olympics without her daily counsel. I called Ann and we agreed. Our older son Matt and his wife Laurie would move into our home in Belmont, Massachusetts to be with Craig until his graduation. Ann would fly out to join me as soon as possible.

THE TURNAROUND FORMULA

This wasn't my first turnaround. In my years at Bain Capital, the venture capital firm, we had invested in several companies that were losing money. In some cases, my partners and I had played very active roles in helping them get back on track. When Bain & Company, the consulting firm we had left to found Bain Capital, got in some financial distress, I was asked to return to it as its CEO to lead a turnaround, which I did. And even as a young consultant years earlier, I had a seat at the table of companies that were in turnaround mode.

Over the years, I had followed a straightforward turnaround formula. First came the strategic audit, a complete review of every aspect of the business. Then came building the team, both in terms of selecting the right people and building unity and motivation. Finally, it was time to "focus, focus, focus." Turnarounds that failed did so because management tried to do too many things rather than focus on what was critical. I would follow the same formula at SLOC. We would kick off the strategic audit first; that would take a month or two. Simultaneously, I would start building the team. I knew at least one or two positions that I would want to fill immediately. The "focus" stage was going to be hard largely because there were so many things that had to be repaired.

Some problems required immediate decisions. Money was being spent every day. I needed to slow down the pace until I could sort out spending priorities. And like it or not, it is during the first few days that people form their impressions of a new leader. There's no time for strategizing: what you do right away speaks volumes. What you do later isn't being watched as intensely. My speech to the board on accepting the job was more closely followed than any I would give again. So I knew what I did right away would have substantive value, like getting spending down. But it would also have symbolic value.

With the budget one of my highest priorities, I wanted to immediately create a new culture of spending. We were going to be frugal. Everybody. From now on. I called a series of all-day meetings with senior management to review the budget and find savings. Function directors were invited as needed. My first official meeting with the board of trustees was scheduled one month to the day from my arrival. My hope was to announce a $200 million budget cut.

To help me, I called on my friend and former colleague from Bain Capital, Bob White. Bob cut through budgets "with the greatest of ease." He generously flew to Salt Lake City on three separate occasions, staying several days at a time. Most of our cuts reflected our decisions to reduce the scope of the Olympic experience. For instance, we would reduce the signage and decoration in our various venue cities, and instead look to localities to decorate their own downtowns. We decided that volunteers would have to bring their own lunches rather than be served from cafeterias. The savings would be almost $20 million. We replaced color brochures with black and white, and booklets with photocopies. We eliminated portions of the opening and closing ceremonies. We even revisited architectural designs of certain Olympic venues to see if we could eliminate some permanent bathrooms and replace them with port-a-potties. And I announced a hiring freeze.

I knew that the symbolic cost savings would be almost as important as the first budget cuts. I remember once when Bill Marriott, Jr., the chief executive of Marriott Corp. and a family friend, came to Boston. I gave him a ride to the Marriott hotel about fifteen miles away from the airport so we'd have a chance to catch up with each other. At the Newton exit, the toll was 35 cents and I didn't have exact change. I said, "Bill, do you have 35 cents?" He did. As we were pulling away from the tollbooth, he asked, "Could you get me a receipt." This was a billionaire and he wanted a receipt for 35 cents! Later, I related the incident to my boss, Bill Bain. He explained, "The reason he asked for that receipt is that he will attach it to his expense report. And everyone back at headquarters who hears about it will know that Bill Marriott cares about 35 cents. He is careful with money." It was a symbolic statement that was consistent with everything at Marriott—the details are important.

I had a few of my own "symbolic cuts." I announced that SLOC would no longer rent conference rooms at hotels for board meetings nor provide free meals and beverages to the directors. Board members would be asked to contribute one dollar for a Coke and one dollar for a slice of pizza. This would save $250,000 from our budget. The papers picked up the story. Formerly freewheeling with bribery money, SLOC was now penurious. "No More Free Lunches" ran a local headline.

My regularly scheduled trips to Lausanne, Switzerland, to report to the IOC would no longer be done with a large entourage of support staff, as had been the custom. I would travel alone. And I would only stay the day, rather than the extended visits that were the norm. On my first visit to Lausanne, I complained publicly about the IOC's arrangement for me to stay at the Beau-Rivage, a five-star hotel. Staying across town at the economy Movenpick Hotel would save a few hundred dollars each trip. Again, the press noted the change. And so did everyone at SLOC.

I announced that I would not seek a severance package at the end of my term, as the prior Olympic CEO Tom Welch had required for himself. I would also work without compensation until the Games were over and proven financially successful. It is a luxury to be able to work for an extended period without salary, to be sure. But my personal finances were such that I could afford it, and I wanted to make it entirely clear that I was at the Games to serve, not to make a bundle. I also zeroed out over $1.5 million that had been budgeted to the CEO for outside consulting and support services.

All in all, after a few weeks of effort, we came up with a total of $98 million in budget cuts. It was well short of the $200 million goal, but a fair chunk of change nonetheless.

DEALING WITH THE EX-PATS

One of my early decisions would have a big impact on how the organization viewed my leadership. Frankly, I didn't weigh that fact in my
decision. Think about it: when you take a job to perform a service,
not to earn a paycheck or win a jackpot, you don't really care a lot
about how people think of you. You have the absolute luxury to do
exactly what you think is right. Ann kept reminding me that this was
about serving. It was a great relief and it freed my anxious mind to
really do what I thought was right.

The decision I faced was what to do about the men who had been
out on administrative leave pending the ethics investigation and
report. Rod Hamson had been licensing director and Kelly Flint had
been senior vice president and chief legal counsel. Both had also
worked for the bid committee that preceded SLOC.

The bid committee had been quite small. With Tom and David
Johnson frequently traveling, Kelly and Rod had been the ones to
countersign checks. This meant that the checks for the bribe-like
expenditures for tuition for IOC relatives had Kelly's or Rod's signature on them. Some in the media believed that Kelly and Rod had
therefore known of the wrongdoing. The ethics panel found that Rod
had indeed made an ethical misstep. The panel recommended that no
disciplinary action be taken as Rod was young and inexperienced. People at SLOC also liked Rod. He was by all accounts a good guy who
had been blindsided by Tom and Dave into thinking what they were
doing was standard practice. Some people, by the way, believe that no
one in Salt Lake did anything wrong at all. But I agreed with the ethics
panel. Because Rod had made an ethical mistake, I decided that he
should move to another organization. There was simply no way I
could assert that SLOC was dedicated to the highest standards of ethical conduct and simultaneously retain Rod. I asked Ed Eynon to offer
him the chance to resign. He may have beaten him to the punch.

Kelly Flint's situation was very different from Rod's. The ethics
panel noted the circumstances of checks co-signed by Kelly, but they

found no evidence that he was aware that the recipients were IOC relatives. There was no evidence that he had been aware of wrongdoing. Before I would make a decision, I wanted to meet Kelly and form my own impression.

To be frank, I don't remember exactly what I said to Kelly. Kelly's recollection is that I never even mentioned the scandal. I asked him about his family and his appraisal of various other people at SLOC. We talked about the problems facing SLOC. I asked him about his decision to join. Kelly had worked for the law firm that did pro bono work for the bid committee. It was the premier firm in Salt Lake. After the Games were awarded, the firm stood to make a great deal of money in billings to SLOC. Kelly had taken the laudable step of leaving the firm to work directly for SLOC in order to avoid any conflict of interest. The decision would surely cost Kelly a lot of money and a career at the firm. By having him on-board, in-house, we would probably save a million or more. I listened and watched and I came to trust that Kelly was an honest person who had not knowingly participated in the scandal.

My old boss, Bill Bain, had often said there is a scientific basis for trusting your gut instincts. He reasoned that there are all kinds of signals, body language signals that your subconscious brain detects without you even being aware of it. The reading of these subtle indicators can form your impressions of someone. And those impressions may thus be just as reasonable as your other inputs. Whether or not that is so, I've tended to listen to what I feel in my heart about people. I offered Kelly his job back and he accepted.

It would have been better from a public relations point of view to drop Kelly. *The Salt Lake Tribune* was going to rag on Kelly without end. They had a bit in their mouth about Kelly Flint and Jim Jardine and the other associates at Ray, Quinney & Nebeker and they were never going to let their suspicions die. I spoke with Jay Shelledy, the paper's editor-in-chief. He fundamentally believed that Kelly and his firm had done something wrong. I realized my decision on Kelly Flint would hurt us in the public relations arena. But to throw him over would be unfair to Kelly and wrong. Each time the *Tribune* ran another story attacking Kelly, he'd come see me and ask whether I wanted his resignation. I think that happened at least twice. The answer was always the same.

Chapter 4

BUILDING THE TEAM

"Location, location, location" are to real estate as "people, people, people" are to an enterprise, be it a business, a charity, or an endeavor like the Olympics. And while some organizations can muddle through with a mediocre team, a successful turnaround can only happen with top people. Turnarounds require a lot of strong arms, all pulling in the same direction.

By the time I took the reins at the turnaround of Bain & Company in 1990, I had learned that lesson. Bain & Company was short of cash and short of new clients. My first step was neither to call on the bank for a loan, nor was it to hit the road to sell new customers. It was to meet face to face with the firm's thousand plus employees. And because the firm was international, that meant flying to Munich, Tokyo, London, San Francisco, and more. It meant speeches and dinners and meetings. But the key task was to commit the people, the team, to stay with the firm during the turnaround and to work in lockstep together to get the company back on track.

After a worldwide swing, I came home to the Boston headquarters where I had called a meeting of the company's fifty or so top officers.

These would be the leaders, without them, there would be no turn-around, and no company. These guys had career options. Other firms would be delighted to hire away our top officers and rainmakers, but if they left, the rest of the team would be out of luck. So when I met with them, I asked that each make a personal commitment to me and to the group to stay with the firm for one full year. Each one did. While the turnaround would eventually take two years to achieve, it was all in the cards when those commitments were made. Top qual-ity people, pulling together. That was the essential ingredient.

Actually, top people, pulling together are two ingredients. There are plenty of organizations with excellent people who don't "pull together." Just as hard as recruiting and retaining people is commit-ting them to a shared vision. At Bain & Company, the top people were already in the firm but they had begun to pull apart. Departures, uncertainty, and more than a hint of fear about the future had led an excellent company to lose its edge. My job over the two years leading the turnaround at Bain & Company would contain a large compo-nent of time and energy devoted to creating the vision, culture, and passion that would make a good team great.

What was true for Bain & Company was even more so for the Olympics. When I glanced at my "map," I was a bit overwhelmed by the task ahead. One thing I knew. The task would only be mastered if we had a top team, all pulling hard in the same direction. Pulling hard meant that we would need a heroic level of output from every-one. We would need them to become so committed to the greater vision of what the Games could represent that they would go through walls to achieve that vision. The team I inherited at the Olympics was the good news; the spirit of that team was the bad news.

A TEAM THAT WILL GO THROUGH WALLS

In fact, the people were superb. My predecessor, Frank Joklik, had put together a solid team. His years as CEO of one of the largest corporations in the country had undoubtedly taught him the same lesson I had learned about the importance of good people.

Our head of sport, Cathy Priestner-Allinger, was extraordinary. She knew sport and the Olympics inside out. She had managed the speed skating venue at the Calgary Winter Games and was herself an Olympic silver medalist, having represented Canada. As impressive as her experience was her straight talking, no nonsense approach to management.

Cathy's job, sport, requires a bit of description as one might think that the whole of the Olympics is sport. The managing director of sport had the responsibility to make sure that the competition sites, field of play, and arrangements for athletes were both excellent and in conformity with highly exacting international standards. Those standards are established and enforced not by the International Olympic Committee but by sport specific International Federations (IF). There is a federation for hockey, another for biathalon, another for bobsled, and so forth. They could virtually dictate to an organizing committee, like us, all matters relating to the sport.

Cathy Priestner-Allinger's Olympic history is not terribly unusual among Olympians. But it explains a lot about her success as a leader. A Canadian, Cathy moved to Winnepeg, not far from a speed skating oval. At eleven years old, she was invited by a friend to go to the rink to try a few laps around the track. Cathy had tried hockey skates, but they were different. Hockey skates have short blades and the skating is fast but only in very short bursts. Speed skating skates have long blades that extend well in front of the toe. The skating stroke requires a very different motion. And, of course, the object of speed skating isn't short bursts of speed but instead, long stamina-testing exertion.

Cathy strapped on the ungainly skates and made a few runs around the track. She was fast enough to beat her friend who had skated many times before. Impressive. She raced the young people at the oval and beat them all. Very impressive. Thirty days later, she won a junior championship. More than impressive; seriously gifted. From that young, pre-teenage girl would come a life decision. She would leave her country, family, friends and school to spend her

Problems dealing with the various IFs and National Governing Bodies (NGB's are the national entities that oversee sport, such as the U.S. Figure Skating Federation) had been a huge problem for Peter Ueberroth in Los Angeles and more recently for Michael Knight in Atlanta.

Most Games organizers remember their sport department as one of their biggest headaches. Not me. I never had to worry about sport. That doesn't mean we didn't have to sustain a high level of effort to appease the various federations. Our problems with the various IFs were legion, but Cathy was so respected by the federation leaders and so solid in her management of the department that the problems were consistently overcome. And if one function is the most critical in an Olympics, it has to be sport. Having Cathy there was a great start for a new CEO like me.

Our senior vice president of human resources and international relations, Ed Eynon, was fabulous. Prior to the Games, Ed had run human resources at a large customer services company based in Ohio. Ed decided to take a break from a successful corporate career. From my first days on the job, it was clear that he would dedicate himself completely to making these Games a success.

Ed and I focused on how to get our management and our entire staff on a unified course. Ed knew that it would take more than e-mails from the CEO or occasional pep rallies to turn hundreds and then thousands

Continued from 61

adolescent years in training in Europe. Coaches would drive her to the edge of her endurance, day after day. One coach drove her to the point of near death from which months of rehabilitation were the only rescue. Competition after competition, sometimes winning, sometimes not. No real chance for a "normal" adolescence with friends. Family time only in the summer on a return home. And she got the silver when it was all over, not the gold. Three-tenths of a second was the difference between first and second place. I asked her if it was hard giving her young life to speed skating and then come in second. Her answer: "Not compared to the hundreds of girls who give just as much as I did but don't place at all." Cathy was driven, and focused. And she knew how to go through walls.

of employees into a team. Under his guidance, our management team learned to reinforce unity and commitment in every action, whether in one-on-one meetings or company-wide sessions.

Ed also recognized the need to create our own culture at SLOC. Because the team had been assembled from many other companies and brought together in an entirely new organization, each person had brought with them the culture and norms of those different places. We didn't have a culture, we had confusion. Ed and I went to work on a project that would make SLOC more informal, collegial, and united.

Ed not only built culture and commitment, he established and managed a program that would hire thousands of people and recruit tens of thousands of volunteers. Compensation, training, benefits, performance reviews, retention, education, international relations, and even terminations were all his. I know of no human resources management task in corporate America that compares with what Ed had to do. And he did it all, masterfully.

Cindy Gillespie led federal relations. An old colleague from my class at Harvard Law School, Jim Jardine, called me when I took the job to say that there were two people I absolutely had to keep. Cindy Gillespie was one of them. He explained that she had quit once and was probably going to leave and that I should do everything in my power to get her to stay. As a first step, I told the entire group of managers in my first meeting what Jim had said. I wanted Cindy to know that even though I didn't know her yet, she was critically important to me.

Cindy had run federal relations for Atlanta's Olympics. She not only knew all the ins and outs of the Olympics, she knew Washington like nobody I had seen before or since. And she is smart, real smart. Smart enough for it to be obvious real fast. I like smart people, a lot. Bill Bain, my old boss, used to joke that most things can be fixed, but smart—or dumb—is forever. Cindy's longtime personal relationships with senior staff in Congress and in federal departments meant that we would have access and a friendly hearing. Her best friends were on the appropriations committees of Congress. No wonder Jim Jardine said I had to keep Cindy Gillespie.

I was at risk of losing Cindy because SLOC was a nightmare. The scandal had sickened the entire team. Management had been entirely preoccupied, and the vision of the Games was almost lost. For Cindy, her job was less about the paycheck and more about the personal and emotional rewards. It's a bit like family. And the SLOC family had become dysfunctional. Much to my benefit, Cindy would agree to stay.

The information technology hires that Joklik had made were excellent. Dave Busser, chief technology officer, was responsible for all systems, telecommunications, Internet, timing, scoring, and hardware and software. His budget was almost equal to the construction of all our Olympic venues: literally hundreds of million of dollars. I hadn't met anyone like Dave Busser before. He had an unusual combination of technical ability and business sense. When it was crunch time and we were desperate to find a computer sponsor, Dave took to the road and was a highly effective marketer and salesman. I had met great technology people before, but never one with Dave's combination of business acumen, management skills, and personal savvy.

Sharon Kingman was responsible for a telecommunications budget that totaled more than $100 million. It was much more than phones. She was responsible for the hundreds of miles of wiring that would connect the thousands of computers, cameras, and TV screens in the Olympic grid. Among many other tasks, she worked to install high bandwidth databus highways called "SONET rings" that connected Park City with Salt Lake City and the venues in Ogden and Utah Valley. We needed redundancy so that any terrorist activity that cut one area wouldn't bring down the communications systems of the entire Games. Utah now has three SONET rings, more than any single European country. Samsung, Qwest, Lucent Technologies, and AT&T were all sponsors. Sharon's ability to manage four fierce competitors into working as a team, for at least the three years while I was there, was legendary in the industry. She had that quintessential southern thing going for her: exceptionally good looks, bless your heart charm, and the strength of iron. Those who thought they could slack off or blow something by her learned that you don't mess with Sharon Kingman. Soft on the outside, hard as nails on the inside. What a manager.

Alice Mahmood, our head of information systems, was charged with pulling off an Olympic miracle. IBM had been the longstanding systems provider for the Olympics. Their relationship was part supplier and part sponsor. Over time, the sponsor side of the relationship seemed to be giving way to the supplier role. In addition to the value of contributed services as the official systems sponsor, IBM increasingly wanted to also be paid very large sums to build the Games systems. The IOC finally had enough and awarded the sponsorship to a European company, SchlumburgerSema. It had never done an Olympics and had agreed to assume only limited systems responsibilities. Alice would integrate the hardware, software, and timing systems of a whole team of providers (including Sema)—the whole ball of wax. No nonsense, unflappable, and superbly experienced. Bless Alice Mahmood.

Grant Thomas, our head of venues, was responsible for building all of our facilities. These could be permanent, like our speed skating building and ski jumps, or temporary, like the tangle of tents and bleachers that would be set up at ski resorts. Grant was on loan from Bechtel where he was a senior project manager. He and his team were professional and capable. But Grant was reporting first to Bechtel and second to me at SLOC. The conflict could be a problem. Moreover, Bechtel insisted that in exchange for Grant's services, we employ ten other Bechtel engineers, and that we pay Bechtel a handsome fee for their work with us. Frank Joklik had agreed to the arrangement. I could not. If I were going to build a committed, unified team, and if I were to get our costs under control, I couldn't have the person responsible for venue construction reporting to a company that had different priorities. I called Bechtel's CEO. We talked several times and met in person. When we were finished, Grant had left Bechtel and our obligation to use Bechtel engineers was nearly cut in half. We now had a world-class venue head on our team. His two lead managers, Jerry Anderson and Ranch Kimball, were just as strong and committed.

These managers are only a sample of the talent at SLOC. More than just the talent, I found a core group that would go through walls if guided in a shared vision. I expanded and changed their responsibilities to draw more from their talents. Now it was time to begin filling in the holes.

THE HOLE NEAR THE TOP

Olympic organizing committees begin as very small bid committees and over the course of five years or so, grow at a fast rate. In February 1999, I was the 237th employee on SLOC's records. When the Games began in February 2002, there were 7,438 employees on staff and 50,000 if you include consultants, private contractors, and volunteers under our direction.

The $98 million in budget cuts that Bob White and our management team had identified during my first weeks at SLOC were half the figure we would eventually need. In addition, our cuts had been based on the assessments of managers, not a line by line, "bottom-up" analysis of our detailed budget. We knew our figures were directionally right, but not entirely reliable. We needed someone to lead a truly comprehensive effort to cut unnecessary costs.

A thorough bottom-up analysis would take more time and attention than I could possibly make in light of our other challenges. As I looked at the map, it was clear that we needed more management at the top of SLOC. And the person we needed would have to be a truly extraordinary manager, someone who could cut costs, oversee operations, and guide a wide range of internal functions. In some companies, the title for such a manager is chief operating officer, or COO. My guess is that most companies in the U.S. have a COO. My consulting and investing years had taught me that while most companies had COOs, many also experienced conflicts between that officer and the CEO. In some, the conflict is so debilitating that one or the other has to move on. But before that exit, the entire organization often becomes embroiled in the political battles that surround their conflict. We needed a COO, but we couldn't endure conflict and division. The SLOC team had already endured too much.

Bob White had been by my side during my first weeks at SLOC and helped me cut an initial $98 million from the budget. Bob had saved my bacon time and again in my career. He helped me found Bain Capital. He joined my losing senatorial campaign in its final weeks to improve my showing and to keep me upbeat and strong. I asked Bob if he'd be willing to do it again: come to the Olympics as COO. Bob couldn't see leaving Bain Capital. But he volunteered to help me scout for a COO. Bob's advice would prove invaluable.

Ed and I had worked through a handful of credible candidates through the formal search process. The board had also assembled a long list of potential candidates. By this time, six weeks had passed. I was no closer to finding my COO.

Bob asked if I had spoken with Fraser Bullock. Of course not, I replied, there was no way Fraser would come to SLOC. Fraser had been a colleague of Bob's and mine at Bain Capital. We both had a high opinion of him and Bob assumed that I had already spoken with him. He was even living in the area. Fraser had moved to Salt Lake City a few years earlier to start his own venture capital enterprise. But I knew Fraser would be deeply invested in launching his own business. Fraser Bullock was started on the path to fortune, and perhaps fame, by organizing what *Forbes* magazine called "poof companies." Fraser would take small, private companies, get them to agree to merge, and take them public on the day of their merger. This was working like a charm. Fraser told me that in addition to making good money, he found he could take five months off each year for time with his family. It made no sense at all that at the critical launch of his new company he would consider coming to work at SLOC. Bob insisted I give him a call. Certainly no harm in that, if only to see if he knew any viable candidates for the job.

I began the conversation by asking Fraser if he knew anyone who might be interested in the COO position at SLOC. Fraser deadpanned, "So you're looking for someone with suicidal tendencies?" It was only partly in jest. Fraser had watched the bid scandal erupt and knew that during my first weeks in office, I had been vocal about SLOC's shaky financial footing. Fraser continued: "You want someone with a death wish. . . . I'll give it some thought and see if anyone comes to mind." Then I pushed the issue and asked if Fraser himself might consider the position. There was a pause on the line. I think he was a little taken aback, but he didn't say no right away. He said he would give it some thought and get back to me. Be still my heart, was there hope?

Being convinced that Fraser was the right guy was one thing, convincing Fraser of that fact was another. How do you ask someone to walk away from a business that earns him over $1 million a year and instead take up an almost impossible task that will pay $200,000? One thing is certain, you don't talk about the money. You also don't talk about perks. Fraser would be entitled to drive a new Chevy Blazer, but he would have to put his new Dodge Viper in the garage. And then there was the vacation time. Five months of free time would be replaced by working 24/7, fifty-two weeks a year. It would of course be a challenge, an opportunity to test one's skills at the highest level and under the scrutiny of international attention. But there are other challenges that are far more financially rewarding.

Fraser came to see me at the SLOC offices. At the heart of my pitch was the opportunity to make an important difference to the world through the Olympic Games. Fraser didn't give us a definitive answer that day and, in fact, later told me that he had been leaning away from taking the position. His sense of personal direction didn't allow for "suicidal tendencies." He felt content to let me tilt at windmills with some other Sancho Panza by my side. But while Fraser was with his family one Saturday morning, his father listened patiently to his many reasons for declining the position, then quietly intoned, "It's a good time to be of service, Fraser. It's a good time to be of service." Don't you just love parents!

That changed his thinking. Like me, Fraser must have recognized that his skills were exactly what was needed for SLOC to be successful. If there ever was a guy who understood finance, technology, and how to operate and manage an organization, it was Fraser. He knew he was the best fit for the job. Perhaps if he could have thought of someone else who could have done the job better, he might have felt like he was off the hook. He couldn't. He was needed and he had been raised to answer the call of service. He phoned to accept.

That was my best day at SLOC. We had a strong manager. We also had someone who was there for the right reason, to serve. And I knew the two of us wouldn't be pulling in opposite directions because of different personal agendas.

Knowing Fraser was on board, I felt a burst of energy. He would need until May to be able to join us, some four months after my arrival, but he was worth the wait.

The announcement drew predictable criticism about Fraser being another white, male, Mormon businessman and a former colleague of mine from Bain. I was charged with "cronyism." But given our precarious financial position, lack of public credibility, and the very real possibility that we would not be able to meet our financial obligations, I could not have cared less about criticism. I knew Fraser could deliver budget reductions. I trusted that his attention to detail could make up for lost time on the operational front, even without prior knowledge of Olympic information, security, or transportation systems. And frankly, the fact that we shared a common background, could speak in a sort of shorthand, and trusted each other's motives and capabilities, had huge advantages.

But besides sharing some history, Fraser and I have different skill sets. Fraser has an immense capacity for detail. He loves to drill into the most mundane issue and spend hours going deeper and deeper into each facet and layer. I enjoy wallowing in the detail when I feel the issue is critical, but I quickly tire when I face row after row of numbers on what seems like minutia. If we were going to create a new budget, bottom-up, it would require Fraser's type of attention.

Fraser also had unusual people skills. He was open and direct with people. He was honest and did not hesitate to give critical feedback, on the spot. I had learned that his brand of open, direct communication didn't engender defensiveness from the people he managed. That, indeed, was a valuable skill.

We needed a great deal from Fraser, but job number one was cost reduction. Our team's initial review of the books with Bob White had proven that the numbers were pretty tight. There weren't obvious over-allocations. If anything, the numbers were optimistic. And in addition to the imbalance on the books, we knew that budget surprises were a distinct probability. The nature of complex operations is such that unidentified costs crop up all the time. The Sydney organizing committee had required an $84 million bailout by the state government four months before their Games. We would never get that from Utah or from the federal government. If we got in trouble, there was the possibility that the Games could not go forward.

Fraser's tasks were finance and operations, and both needed help. In operations like logistics, security, systems and technology, complete plans were not in place, necessary resources had not been identified, and management was stretched thin. Because the scope of our operations was so vast, and because Fraser and I had no Olympic experience, we felt we needed to find seasoned sporting event experts to join the team. Cathy and Ed began to recruit and over the next few months, they put together a team of managers who were also world-class athletes. It was one of the most impressive sports management teams ever assembled.

We also had a new financial planning officer in Brett Hopkins, who eventually became our CFO. We brought in an operations team with

Doug Arnot—the veteran from the Atlanta Games. John Bennion, a former colleague at Bain & Company, took charge of the enormous array of functions in Games services. And as the Games drew closer, we hired Jim Brown, an alumnus from Sydney and a master at events management.

MORE TOP TALENT

The sales function in the Olympics is misnamed marketing. Olympic marketing includes selling sponsorships, licensing merchandise, and, in our case, finding donors. The USOC was responsible for marketing and they received a handsome cut of the proceeds. Marketing to Utah companies was SLOC's job, and it had been very ably managed by Don Stirling.

Don had a long history in sport. He'd been with the National Basketball Association and with the Ladies Professional Golf Association. He had deep roots in the community. Most important, everyone who knows Don loves him. He was as close a friend and confidant as I would know at SLOC. We talked daily on the widest range of topics. He'd joke and cajole and kibitz. He'd tell me when I messed up.

Don's personality meant he had a lot of friends in Utah and that had opened doors. He was on the verge of signing several deals when the scandal broke. That had put everything on hold.

When I had taken a look at the books, and after the meetings with the USOC which I'll get into later, it was clear that in addition to Utah marketing, we needed to take over all U.S. marketing. That meant additional talent. Hard to find talent: Olympic experience and sales savvy.

I first turned to SLOC's legal counsel, Kelly Flint. Kelly was smart, very smart. I figured he could do anything I asked of him. He willingly took on the responsibility, but we both knew there was no way he could do both jobs for long. One afternoon, one of the top marketing people at Meridian, the company that does all of the marketing for the IOC, came by to chat with Kelly and Don. His name was Mark

Lewis. Mark asked Kelly if SLOC might want him to move to Salt Lake and work for us. Kelly knew a great thing when he saw it. He practically had signed Mark up even before I got to meet him.

Mark was the best salesman we could imagine. A letterman linebacker at the University of Georgia, he had lived and understood sports and competition. He was also smart—a Rhodes finalist. In the last round of his interview, he was asked by an officious German interviewer, "Who is your greatest living hero?" Mark's answer, "Ronald Reagan." A short burst of horror followed from the German. He protested that any young person who isn't a liberal has no heart. Mark rejoined with the rest of the saying: any mature person who isn't conservative has no brain, and he, Mark went on, had matured early. As far as I was concerned, Mark had won that round.

Mark had been an attorney at Atlanta's prestigious law firm, King & Spaulding, where he had worked on the Atlanta Olympics account. From there, he had joined Meridian Management where he drafted and negotiated key IOC agreements, many of which we at SLOC would also enter with the IOC. Mark Lewis: smart, Olympic experience, and thoroughly enjoyable to be around.

Mark took the lead for national sponsors, Don Stirling for Utah companies and donors. They worked together hand and glove. What could have been an uncomfortable, political situation was smooth as silk.

Besides the budget and the quality of our sport program, I cared most about the opening and closing ceremonies. The opening would set the tone of the entire Games. Even with money tight, I wanted our opening ceremony to touch the heart of everyone who saw it. Our Games would be emotional and inspirational. I wanted feeling and emotion.

When I met with SLOC's creative team, I was convinced that we didn't have what it was going to take. Obviously, I'm no pro at Olympic ceremonies. But as an old English major and a frustrated creative type, I wanted to keep a direct hand on what we would produce.

Shelley Thomas had chosen a fellow named Scott Givens to produce the unveiling of our Olympic mascots. It was a big affair, complete with staging, big music, lights, and fireworks. When it was over, she suggested that Scott join the team as head of creative. That was a great call.

Scott was creative with a capital "C." And unlike many creative types, he was good with numbers and had a practical bent. An engineering major at Purdue University, for a big football game, he had used his computer to design and carry out an elaborate card stunt for the grandstands. There hadn't been anything like it before. After graduation, major sporting events hired him to design bigger and better stunts. Suddenly he was a producer in the entertainment business. While I admit to having limited experience in this arena, I have never met someone of Scott's equal. Nor can I imagine anyone better. Scott's creative genius, management ability, and practical sense were key to the spirit of the Olympic Games of 2002.

THE COMMUNICATIONS TEAM

Shelley Thomas is something of an institution in Utah. A longtime reporter and anchorwoman for the most popular local news station in the state, she had a great deal of visibility in the community and was widely respected. Shelley had navigated SLOC through the media storm following the revelation of scandal. Given the severity of the charges, there was no way she could have put a positive spin on the stories. Rather, she had done her best to show that SLOC management was responding responsibly. Her resources were the personal integrity of Frank Joklik and SLOC Chairman, Bob Garff. Bob had a heart of gold and was known throughout Utah as the former Speaker of the House. But he was even better known as the owner of Utah's premier auto dealer network. Neither Frank nor Bob were ready for the onslaught; there was nothing in their backgrounds that could have prepared them for the crush of the worldwide press. Shelley frenetically corralled the media and coached Frank and Bob with as fast a download as they could absorb. No one would grade SLOC's public relations during the scandal storm as a home run, but Shelley did a remarkable job, considering the circumstances.

When I showed up, I relied heavily on Shelley's advice. She knew the reporters, the politics, and the history. She also had a well-tuned aptitude for handling the widest array of topics. Day one, she set me up with the reporters who would write the local articles that would in turn, shape the coverage of the national and international press.

About a year into my tenure, Shelley decided to leave us for a position at the Huntsman Cancer Center.

For the key communications and media task, we promoted Caroline Shaw, previously director of media relations under Shelley. Caroline didn't have Shelley's history and visibility in the community, but she had developed trust and goodwill with the local media. In fact, the editor of Salt Lake's largest daily took me aside after her appointment and said that she was one of the best media people he had ever known. She also took the lead in building relationships with the regular Olympic beat reporters in the national media. Like the locals, they came to respect her enormously.

A New Yorker, Caroline was open and direct with people, in and out of the organization. She made no pretenses: what you saw was real and unvarnished. A few people found her too blunt and impolitic; I loved that about her.

Before coming to SLOC, Caroline had been the public relations officer for the U.S. United Nations delegation in New York. She turned out to be as good a media person as I have ever known. Her instincts, counsel, and relations with the media were top-notch. And I liked working with her.

ALL TOGETHER NOW

If capable people, pulling in the same direction are the key to the success of a turnaround, SLOC was now on very good footing. But getting the team to actually pull together can be as hard as finding the good people in the first place. And the task never ends: conflict, dissension, politics, and defensiveness have crept in to almost every human institution I have known. The two most critical jobs of leadership are building a good team and keeping the teammates highly motivated and working collaboratively to achieve the organization's mission.

Getting a team to pull together starts with organization structure. It sounds boring, but it's absolutely critical. I had seen good organizations, and bad. In Fraser and my days at Bain & Company, our case team organizations had come to look like what we called "I" formations. The client manager reported to the junior VP who reported to a slightly more senior VP who reported to one or two more senior VPs. The structures hadn't been planned that way, they just seemed to grow of their own. And for the case manager, responsible for most of the work at ground level, the structure meant that he or she was far removed from the people who had the most experience, insight and responsibility. It drove managers and case teams nuts; it made middle VPs feel redundant, which they were; and it stretched the senior VPs across too many cases for them to be truly effective. Ultimately, we blew up the "I" formations, putting VPs in charge of their own cases. That separated the high performers from the hangers-on, and it juiced the company's growth.

SLOC seemed to have a bit of the "I" formation feel to it. Officers reported to more senior officers who reported to Frank Joklik. That meant that what Frank saw and what the front line officers saw of Frank was filtered by those senior officers in the middle. Fraser and I wanted to get rid of the middle hierarchy structure and have all the key officers report to one of us directly. But that would violate a longstanding organizational design rule that no more than five or six people should report to a single boss. The heck with that rule. Even though we had so many functions at SLOC, we would have them almost all report to either Fraser or me. We would flatten the "I" formations.

Ed Eynon championed the change. But he wanted to make sure that SLOC didn't evolve into two cultures and two visions, one led by Fraser and the other by me. He insisted that I take personal responsibility for resolving major conflicts, solving cross-company issues, and establishing the vision and culture. He arranged for me to meet at least once a week with the entire management team. We also instituted a quarterly review schedule: each function presented key accomplishments from the previous quarter, sought counsel on continuing challenges, and set goals for performance for the following quarter. Fraser and I weren't the only managers in these meetings: the entire senior management participated with their functions. It increased the flow of knowledge between departments. When changes in scope or schedule were presented, the affected managers were there to ask questions, raise objections, or make commitments.

It wasn't hard dividing the functions between Fraser and myself. There were two primary considerations: which function would most benefit from either his or my skill set and which did we enjoy. I guess that latter factor was why I took ceremonies, "look of the Games," the cultural Olympiad and the torch relay. There was also another consideration. I was the person who had been given the ultimate responsibility for the success of the Games. I would retain those functions I thought were most critical, not just because of their importance, but also because of their state of disrepair. When we had completed the reorganization, I had most of the functions that interacted with the world outside SLOC: marketing and sales, federal and state government, media and communications, volunteers and donors, legal, and the IOC and USOC. To retain management oversight of the internal organization, I also had Ed Eynon, the head of human resources and of course Fraser report to me directly. And I had our new CFO report to both Fraser and me directly; unorthodox, but I wanted a first hand report and I needed Fraser's experience and attention to the financial detail. I assigned Fraser most of the internal and operating functions: venues, sport, IT, transportation, games services, operations planning, security, accreditation, accommodations and the like.

Ultimately, regardless of who had the direct report, Fraser and I came together on the big issues. He jumped in on a number of occasions to deal with municipalities and to look at ceremonies. And when ticketing sales were underway, he and I met for several hours each week with the ticketing management to keep things on track. Ticket scandals had plagued virtually every organizing committee before us, so we wanted to avoid the pitfalls. We were counting on $180 million in ticket sales, more than double that of any prior Olympic Winter Games. We also came together after September 11 to work on our security program and contingency planning. Big issues brought both brains into the action.

Getting the organization structure right was a critical first step. Building the team's commitment to each other and to the Games was an ongoing effort. From the start, we had our hearts in the right place. Every member of the senior management team was making significantly less at SLOC than they would have made in private sector jobs. Ed once did the math: all but one had taken a very big cut to accept the SLOC job. We hadn't come for the money. We had come because we felt that we were doing something important, something meaningful. If we could keep that sense of purpose, and if it were well enough defined, this team would move mountains, literally as well as figuratively. In fact, it did.

I remember my first meeting with management, the day after I came on board. Frank Joklik was there to graciously introduce me. My speech was short and the vision I offered was right, but not well developed. I said that the Games were all about sport and that sport and the athletes should come first in everything we did. Cathy beamed throughout. As the months rolled on, I saw a great deal more in the Games that came through the sport. I saw the athletes as examples of the best qualities of humanity—perseverance, determination, faith, sacrifice, friendship, and teamwork. I knew that the Games could be an opportunity for service, bringing the community closer together. Ultimately, I realized that they could help heal the nation following the attack of terror. And as my vision expanded, I shared it with my management team.

Ed also made sure that the entire team understood what we were undertaking, in the most expansive sense. He organized regular "All-SLOC" meetings where members of management spoke, with passion, to the entire staff. There was plenty of humor too. Beth White, head of the press center, had done some time as a stand up comic. She got plenty of material by watching our mistakes. And she roasted the management, person by person, with more and more gusto as the meetings progressed. And there was no defensiveness: members of the team heaped deprecation on themselves in large doses, to the delight and approbation of the audience. These meetings ultimately got quite big, numbering in the thousands.

We bundled our vision messages with laughter, food, and gifts. We had a policy that if anyone in management at SLOC got an outside gift, we would bring it to those meetings to be given away in a random drawing. Giving away the gifts underscored the point that we didn't think our jobs made us more important than anybody else by keeping the goodies to ourselves.

THE EXCEPTION PROVES THE RULE

You can't put on an Olympics by yourself. You need outside contractors and consultants, too. Some of them had the same sense of purpose that SLOC had. Our broadcaster, Manolo Romero, had produced the Games for the world numerous times. I had presumed that NBC and the other worldwide stations placed their own cameras at the venues and managed all the switching and such that goes into a TV show. But I was wrong. It was SLOC's responsibility to produce the electronic video images of all the events and provide them to all the broadcasters. With scores of broadcasters, you would have camera chaos on the slopes if it were any other way. Manolo was hired to place the cameras, manage the operators, build out the control center (complete with hundreds of miles of cabling) and give each broadcaster a perfect shot of every event. He performed flawlessly. And he made virtually every decision with an eye toward showcasing the Olympic athletes in ways that would thrill and inspire the audience. Of course, there were conflicts now and then; budgets were always too tight. But fundamentally, we worked things out smoothly because we had the same vision.

Another massive project was the torch relay. To most people, the process of bringing a torch across the country doesn't seem terribly complex. Mark Lewis opined that he and twelve fraternity brothers could do it. In fact, it would require almost three hundred people and a budget over $25 million. Shelley Thomas, then director of communications, correctly concluded that we would be wise to hire a company that had expertise in such events. We selected ALEM. Its owner and CEO, Steve McCarthy had by far the most experience: he had participated in the Atlanta torch program. But he operated with a very different agenda than the rest of us. And his management methods were from another planet, at least that's how it seemed to me. My thoughts about Steve, below, are my own opinions, but they serve to show how the senior executive deals—or doesn't deal—with matters he perceives as problematic.

Steve loved the torch more than anything else. To him the torch was more important than our budget problems, keeping sponsors happy, or making sure the Games were on track. The fact that he was working for SLOC was lost on Steve: he felt that he was the protector of the integrity and prominence of the torch relay. He didn't want to be part of a team. And he resisted taking direction.

In Nagano, the Games organizers had found that the best way to expose the largest number of Japanese citizens to the torch relay was to have several runners carrying the flame from different corners of the country to a single final destination. But Steve felt that this "diminished the purity of the flame." I felt that this took the torch to more people, expanded the Olympic experience to people who couldn't afford to come to Salt Lake City or to one single route in Utah. So I directed Steve to map out plans to bring the torch when it reached Utah to three or four corners of the state and run each to Salt Lake City. Steve agreed to implement my directions, at least to my face.

Because the start of the flame would come from Olympia in Greece, the Hellenic Society exercised contract controls over the relay, even in the United States. Kelly Flint had checked the previous contract with Nagano and Sydney. There was nothing in the contract to prevent "splitting the flame" into three relays, as had been done in Nagano. But when Steve McCarthy came back from meetings in Greece, he informed us that the Hellenic Society had insisted on inserting a provision in our contract that prevented us from splitting the flame. In my view, he had gone from irritating to disloyal. Perhaps worse, we found that he was bidding to get the torch relay business for Greece's Games in 2004. And he got that business.

So why did I stay with Steve McCarthy? He was one of a handful of people on the planet who had actually run a torch relay before. He had dealt with the permits, the accommodations, the food, the sponsor services, the ceremonies, and the protocol involved. We had hired him to produce a successful relay. That he did. Despite his peculiarities, he produced results. So I hung with him and experimented with different management structures to get the most out of him. We put him under people with a knack for no-nonsense, straightforward pragmatism. In the end, the torch relay succeeded beyond our expectations. The attacks of September 11 had a lot to do with that, as did our prescient choice of "heroes" as the criteria for selecting our torch runners. But Steve's logistical production went off virtually without a hitch.

ROUNDING THE FLAT SPOTS

The idea of countering one person's weaknesses with the strengths of someone else on the team was something we called "rounding the flat spots." Back in my early business days, I gave people I managed feedback on their weaknesses, drafted action plans with them to correct those weaknesses, and then followed up on their progress. That is what had been done with me by my bosses over the years too. But I found that almost no one actually got rid of their shortcomings. Come to think of it, neither had I.

One day I was talking to Tom Stemberg, founder and CEO of Staples, about his management team. We at Bain Capital had been first-round investors in the start-up of the company and I was still on his board. Tom started talking about flat sides and how he was rounding them. Flat sides? He explained that he had found it a lot more productive to get a great talent to focus on his or her strengths than to struggle with their weaknesses. "Get someone else to do what they don't do well: you hired them for what they do better than anybody else."

That guided my hiring and personnel management from then on. At Bain Capital, I recruited for big brains, big talent, rainmakers and super managers. I didn't worry about the weaknesses. If one partner was a rainmaker but didn't like managing a company after it was acquired, we hired a great manager to take over for him. I did my best to bring out their strengths and find others to complement their weaknesses.

SLOC's managers had weaknesses too. Even if we had had time for personal reconstruction, which we didn't, I never spent time trying to fix people's flat sides.

We had an Olympic transportation expert in Tom Halleran. Tom was head of his own transportation consulting firm before coming to SLOC. There probably isn't another person in the country with as much experience and expertise in scheduling a fleet of busses and cars and moving them around. But the transportation needs of the Olympics are huge. In Olympic history, transportation had been a disaster time and again. There are so many groups to move: spectators, media, athletes, sponsors, IOC members, government officials and dignitaries. And there are so many places to move them, at the same time. The IOC sent a team of transportation experts to assess our state of readiness; they delivered a negative report.

Fraser wanted a detailed transportation plan that included blueprints of loading areas, tables predicting how many busses could load how many people in a given span of time. This was not a natural exercise for a down and dirty bus guy like Tom. So instead of trying to push Tom to do what didn't come naturally, Fraser brought in a fellow he had worked with before. Matt Lehman knew nothing about transportation but knew a lot about planning. Matt I'm sure made many mistakes, obvious to experts like Tom. But together in collaboration, Tom and Matt built a detailed transportation plan that exceeded everyone's expectations. And it worked marvelously.

With six months to go before the Games, we identified another need in transportation: a public "demand management plan." We needed to inform the public how to avoid traffic problems, where to park, times to depart, etc. One of our former federal relations team members, Mike Huerta, had taken a senior and lucrative job at Affiliated Computer Services (ACS) in Washington. Our SLOC transportation guys asked if we could try to get him to come back for six months to put it together. Cindy approached him; it made no sense for him to leave a great job, but his heart was with the Olympics. His immediate boss said that if he left, he couldn't return. He scheduled a meeting with the ACS president, John Brophy.

Brophy related the experience of a young executive who signed on to the Olympics in Los Angeles in the '80s. He left his job and career to make a difference. He eventually started his own company with the mission to help government serve people better. That young executive was John Brophy. He told Mike, "When I look in your eyes, I see the same commitment I had. Go help SLOC; we'll pay your salary and benefits. Come back when it's over; I want people with commitment like you in my company."

The SLOC organization wasn't without flaws and weaknesses and flat spots. But good people, working together with a shared vision, created a very strong team.

Chapter 5

CULTURE

I know what it's like to work at a place where the culture doesn't fit the vision. It doesn't feel very good. It's the mission that suffers most. The culture overpowers the most noble mission statement. A few years into the life of Bain Capital, a number of my partners and I began to feel that something was wrong. Our financial results were spectacular, so that wasn't it. We had extraordinary people, as well. But the personal conflicts and tension between us were wearing. The consulting firm from which we had emerged had only recently gone through a "team building" exercise with psychologists in California. The firm that led the program was called Human Factors. The whole thing sounded way too la-la for me to take seriously until some people who attended the sessions came back with rave reviews about the experience. Even then, I resisted taking my team and myself through the process. But my partners convinced me it was worth a try. In fact, I really did learn a lot. One of the more revealing observations was that our firm's culture was inconsistent with our stated mission. It was even more out of line with our personal values. The guys from Human

Factors said that when an organization's practices weren't aligned with its aspirations, stress and dissonance would be the result.

At Bain Capital, we aspired to have a firm that put our investors' interests first, even before our own. We would respect others, enjoy a team spirit, and endeavor to develop the capabilities of each member. But our culture had begun to take on a very different cast. Self-interest had occasionally figured quite prominently in decision-making. It was commonplace to criticize one another quite stridently, but always behind the other's back. Alliances and competition were increasingly the norm, not teamwork and cooperation. My partners even suspected that I wanted to foster competition to drive people to higher performance. We did indeed have the performance, but the competition didn't make it very enjoyable. We were experiencing the stress that Human Factors had predicted.

We went to work to change our culture, to make it more consistent with our personal values and with the objectives we had for our firm. We made progress, and it felt better. With time, I'll admit that we slipped back into some old habits. But the struggle for integrity between mission and culture was never abandoned. And that made Bain Capital a better place to work.

Getting SLOC to be the organization that would rescue the Winter Games also meant aligning our culture with our mission. From my first meeting with the managers, it was clear that morale was in the basement. Months of accusations, devastating revelations of misconduct, and disciplinary actions against senior officers had left a shell-shocked team. Kelly characterized the time following the scandal bombshell: "Management spent weeks huddled in the board room of the SLOC office complex monitoring media reports and exchanging doomsday scenarios."

Framing our mission as clearly as possible had been the first step. But now we needed to realign our culture. Ed Eynon and I met at some length during my first few weeks to discuss morale and culture. It was clear that as the CEO and the new guy on the team, people would be watching me like a dog looks at a bone. I would have a huge impact on the culture.

I started out by speechifying, both to the senior people and to the entire staff. I talked about values and culture, about having fun, working as a team, and to abide by the highest standards of integrity. After what I thought was one of my most eloquent speeches, I asked Don Stirling what he thought about it. He said, "Talk's cheap." They had heard it all before from guys that had done some pretty bad stuff. Truly establishing a culture that fit the lofty purposes we espoused would require a lot more of me and the senior managers than good speeches.

Building a new culture at SLOC would mean first, that I would have to become exhibit one. I would need to be seen and heard from on a frequent basis. I charged Ed with finding ways to get me in front of people. From All-SLOC meetings to management meetings, from articles in our in-house newspaper to media interviews, Ed made sure that our team saw a lot of me in those formative weeks.

If I were to be the culture mascot, I wanted to break down the distinctions. I instituted a casual dress policy. We had chambray shirts made up with the SLOC team insignia; I wore them religiously, almost every day. To my delight, other senior staffers did too. Several times every day, I roamed the halls and sought one-on-one interaction with members of the staff. If I were lucky, we would find something to laugh about, usually something funny they had taped to their wall or displayed on their desk. Not surprisingly, humorous photos and such multiplied. And as people learned that I particularly enjoyed having fun poked at me, the photos now and then included a caricature of Fraser or me or other managers. We broke up the little clot of senior management offices, spreading us around the floor. When we moved to our new space on Main Street, senior offices were distributed almost entirely evenly throughout our multi-floor space. We would be seen and heard.

Ed said something that should have been obvious to me. Because SLOC was an entirely new organization, assembled with people who would each come from different organizations, its culture would be a hodgepodge of all the cultures of those individuals' prior companies. If we were going to successfully build a distinct culture, it should come from all of us. And so we formed several culture task forces, each discussing and drafting what would form the backbone of the culture we hoped to create. Our Guiding Principles would be codified, printed, and placed on every SLOC desk. Many of the principles speak for themselves, a few deserve elaboration.

SLOC'S GUIDING PRINCIPLES

Teamwork
- Involve all appropriate stakeholders in each project/issue.
- Think horizontally, not vertically, within SLOC's structure.
- Consider other viewpoints and find win-win solutions.
- Emphasize and recognize team success.
- Be helpful to others.

Passion and Pride
- Seek "Gold Medal" performances in your own job.
- Love what you do.
- Relish each small victory and achievement.
- Realize your impact on history while at SLOC.

Communication
- Be honest, direct and respectful in all your communication.
- Accept feedback, avoid defensiveness.
- Seek prompt resolution to issues with others in a personal and professional manner.
- Listen more, talk a little less.

Integrity
- Be loyal to those not present.

➤ Do what you say you will do.

➤ Don't have hidden agendas.

➤ Respect and value diversity in others.

Fun and Celebration

➤ Take your work seriously, not yourself.

➤ Encourage laughter at all meetings.

➤ Don't sweat the small stuff.

➤ Look for opportunities to include others.

➤ Celebrate those who demonstrate SLOC's Guiding Principles.

PASSION AND PRIDE: GETTING GOLD MEDAL PERFORMANCES

Given what we faced, average performance wasn't going to cut it. Great talent, teamwork and commitment to a shared vision were indispensable. We would need gold medal performances from every member of the senior team and from many of the middle and junior staff members.

I really didn't understand what winning a gold medal meant until I came to SLOC and met some gold medalists. I was told that a few of them had such extraordinary physical prowess that getting to the top step of the medals platform hadn't been a daunting struggle. But I never actually met one of those "naturals." Every gold medalist I met had worked harder, sacrificed more, and persevered longer than normal humans would believe possible. And then they had to be terribly lucky as well, lucky to not have an injury, to have the right conditions on the field of play, to know the right coaches, and to have total focus at the time of their event. If we were going to succeed as we hoped, we needed those kinds of performances from our people. We would need to go for the gold.

It may be counter-intuitive, but talented people actually like to be asked to do something very, very difficult. They prefer, for example, to be asked to increase their productivity by 200 percent than to go for 20 percent. Perhaps it comes from an innate desire to rise to the occasion, to stretch to the limit of ability. It seems particularly so in a crisis, where the need for dramatic improvement is authentic and not manufactured.

At SLOC, we were flush with crises and thus with opportunities for gold medal performances. I set Fraser off to work scouring the budget, line by line, to come up with $200 million in cost savings. I asked Cindy Gillespie, our federal relations chief, to bring in more federal funding than had ever been appropriated for any Olympics, summer or winter. I told Ray Grant, our director of the cultural Olympiad and Diane Conrad, our director of environment that we needed to produce the best cultural and environmental programs in the history of the Olympics. I also explained that I had cut their budgets to zero; they would have to raise all the money for these programs themselves. There are three Olympic "pillars" for an Olympic organizing committee: sport, culture, and environment, but we could only afford to pay for the first of these. Neither person had marketing or sales in their job descriptions, but Ray and Diane went to work without complaint to set up their own marketing plans to attract sponsorships and donations. When Ray reached his goal, I added that he should raise enough to help fund other aspects of the Olympics as well. He did. And Diane raised a good deal more than was called for in her original budget. Gold medal work was everywhere at SLOC.

UTAH HEROES

I asked Don Stirling, our man in charge of Utah sponsorships to raise his sights high, very high. When I had first met with the USOC's marketing director, John Krimsky, he had said that the USOC had planned that Utah would generate Fifty million in local sponsorship revenues. I used that figure in my budget projections for one of our early board meetings. The room erupted in laughter. Fifty million dollars was pie-in-the-sky. The state had only one Fortune 500 scale company, and an out-of-state parent owned it. That kind of money just wasn't realistic for a small state like Utah.

I doubled the target to $100 million. That's what we really needed. He had already been laboring with Utah companies on sponsorships. Even though hoped-for commitments had fallen through after the scandal erupted, Don figured we could get them back on track plus add several more companies. But to reach the new target, we would have to do something that had never been done before: we would put together a massive donor program to raise big bucks. The donor program was high-octane money for us because we didn't have to share any of the proceeds with the USOC or IOC. Sponsor dollars were shared about 50 percent with the USOC and 5 percent with the IOC. But donations were all ours.

We went to work designing a donor package of benefits. Don and I turned to the guy who had talked me into taking the SLOC job in the first place, Kem Gardner. We made him the chairman of our donor program. Together, we fashioned a program unprecedented in Olympic history. Our bronze level cost $100,000 and entitled the donor to four tickets to each of several prime events over the seventeen days of the Games. Silver was $500,000 and brought eight ticket packages as well as merchandise, special parking, and the like. A cool million included twelve ticketing packages, a dedicated vehicle and driver during the Games, and special recognition on our wall of honor, a special granite tribute at the Gateway Mall. There were all sorts of other benefits as well, like Olympic donor uniforms and venue passes. But the donations were really charity, through and through. Our benefits could mostly have been bought later when tickets were sold for a fraction of the cost of our programs. So the people who donated were heroes to us, and to the Games.

Because no good deed goes uncriticized, the donor program attracted its fair share of naysayers. Rich people were going to get special deals. Yes, and we would get an even more special deal because these rich people would be helping us pay for Games that were in financial crisis.

After we had been at it awhile, we decided to raise our sights again: we created the platinum level. This was available for $8 million or so. And we had three sign up: the George S. and Dolores Dore Eccles Foundation, the business holding group of the Mormon Church, and Intermountain Health Care or IHC. IHC would provide $9 million in free health care to athletes and visitors during the Games. Kem had helped sign IHC before I came on board; we awarded them the platinum package later. The donors gave us the margin we needed to dig out of our financial hole.

There is nothing harder than asking friends for money, but Kem, Don and I were emboldened by the cause. I called my old partners at Bain Capital: they generously agreed to contribute $1 million. I had several meetings with Jon and Karen Huntsman; they too contributed $1 million, directed to help the Paralympic Games that SLOC also managed and funded. Kem and his partner Roger Boyer also kicked in a million dollars each. They knew that the cost of friendship had gone up, by $1 million. Board members Jim Swartz, Spence Eccles, and John Price signed on as well. Because my job as SLOC CEO was pretty widely publicized, I quite often received calls from friends from out of town asking how they might get great tickets. It wasn't what they were hoping to hear from me, I'm sure, but they came through time and again. Kevin Rollins, an old colleague from my consulting days and now President and CEO of Dell, agreed to a donor package.

Don knew quite a few other folks from Utah who we visited together. The founders of Nu Skin, Blake Roney and Steve Lund, each contributed at the gold level. Of course, there were a lot more rejections than there were contributors. We made the rounds, calling personally on every billionaire and multimillionaire we knew or had heard about. Some drove us nuts with long and frequent meetings but no juice in the end. Our sales pitch fell flat more than it worked. But in truth, we were surprised at the level of success we were having. I had been in politics where I had to screw up my courage to ask for $1,000. Now I was asking for $1 million. And you know what, it's actually no harder. Next time, I told myself, remember that because it's always hard asking for money no matter what amount, I might as well ask for a very big amount.

Dollar by dollar, million by million, Don climbed toward the $100 million goal. We enlisted 105 donors, 20 at the gold $1 million level. O.C. Tanner, Marker, Nu Skin, Utah Power, Questar, KSL, Smith's and other Utah companies became sponsors. Combined with Kem's donor program, Don helped secure over $100 million. It was a gold medal performance.

FOOD FOR THE SOUL

Our food services team also took the gold. Our revised budget to feed the athletes, coaches, dignitaries, volunteers, spectators, media and sponsors totaled $18 million. In some cases we would be able to charge for the meals, as with our concessions. The $18 million was net out-of-pocket cost. Our director of food services, Don Pritchard, was a Teddy Roosevelt kind of guy: big enthusiasm, big voice, big appetite, and big on a bully challenge. We asked Don to get his net cost down to zero. And that's just about what he did.

He made a trip to see the folks that managed the Certified Angus Beef brand at the Iowa Beef Corporation. He talked them into providing us $3 million of free beef products. Of course, selling steaks is pretty tough at a mountain venue, so he ordered Certified Angus Beef hotdogs. Our concession stands featured hot dogs as their number one, and sometimes only menu item, because they were free. Oh, Don had variety: chili dogs, jumbo dogs, etc. And of course the chili was made with ground Certified Angus Beef, too.

People weren't used to hot dogs being so good. They were very popular and in a few days we sold out. People ate as many hot dogs in those few days as had been forecasted for the entire Games. We made an emergency call to get more. Their return to our concession stands was greeted with cheers.

Don got other food folks to also chip in. PowerBar helped us with our athlete nutrition program. Campbell's Soup sent cups of their soup. General Mills sent us Wahoo! snack chips. We thought we were getting twenty-eight cases of chips, but instead, we got twenty-eight truckloads. We had so many Wahoo! chips that we were still handing them out to our volunteers at the one-year anniversary of the Games. But they were all free. One company sent truckloads of breakfast items and we passed along three trailers to the Salt Lake Food Bank to help the poor. To be designated as an official supplier to the Games required a $3 million commitment of product and Don, on his own initiative, found six different companies willing to reach that level. This food guy, this chef, became one of our best marketers.

TEAMWORK

Most of this book is about teamwork in one sense or another. Our guiding principles put special emphasis on one aspect of teamwork: involving all shareholders. That made quite a difference to us, right up until the final days of our preparations.

With only a few weeks to go before the Games, we staged a cross-functional rehearsal. There actually are professional firms that specialize in conducting these mock rehearsals. The one we selected put together various contingency scenarios and worked out detailed time-lines. We stationed several hundred of our people at several of the key venues—the stadium where the opening and closing ceremonies would be held, the figure skating arena, the speed skating oval, etc. We also had representatives from the police, the fire department, the FBI, and the Secret Service in our main operations center. The idea was to simulate as nearly as possible the actual communication patterns, radio contacts, and decision-making processes that would govern our response to a real security threat.

In one scenario a bomb threat was called in along with reports of smoke coming from our figure skating venue. Our cell phone capability had reached capacity due to people calling 911 or family and friends, so we were forced to rely on police radios. The security people at the center confirmed that there was smoke in the venue. We asked them again: were they sure there was smoke in the venue where the bomb threat had been received? Yes. It didn't take Fraser and me long to make the decision to direct the evacuation of the venue. In fact, we didn't have a great deal of time on our hands: the rehearsal had already posited an exploded bomb that morning at one of our hockey venues. We were juggling statements to the media with medical reports and security briefings. So yes, immediately evacuate the 16,000 spectators at the figure skating venue.

We learned later that the law enforcement reports were misleading. The smoke was actually coming from *outside* the skating venue. This was a detail we hadn't asked. There had been a fire in the parking area and it was belching thick smoke. Our evacuation had sent 16,000 people into harm's way.

Fortunately, these scenarios never materialized in real life. Most of us grumbled that they were a bit far-fetched. But on reflection, we realized that they identified what we had been talking about from the first day we wrote the guiding principles: involve all appropriate stakeholders in an issue. We hadn't. Fraser and I should have spoken with the venue manager before we made the call. In fact, we should not have made the call at all. It should have been made by law enforcement at the scene or by our venue manager. We got so caught up in the exercise that we jumped over our own protocols.

The performance review that followed the exercises focused on this and other mistakes, and determined that most of us at the main operations center were making many decisions that should have been made locally. The venues were kicking decisions to senior management that they needed to make themselves on scene where they had greater access to information and greater flexibility to respond to changing circumstances. A couple of weeks later, we tried new mock exercises, although on a more local basis. This time we did a good deal better, sticking to our guiding principles.

NO ONE-MAN TEAMS

If decision-making is unilateral, without the active participation of others with perspective on the issue, there really isn't teamwork. In most organizations, there are those who reserve the important decisions to themselves. Some managers are happy to ask others, including subordinates, for their views, but they really want a consensus view, preferably their own. Not me. I like debate, unless, of course, there is genuine consensus. When I'm presented with a single viewpoint, I invariably take an opposing view. I've been told I'm prone to push it vehemently. Some call it arguing. I don't. I call it debating the issue.

There are some benefits from my "devil's advocacy," but the truth is that I'm not thinking of the benefits of the approach when I begin the debate. It just comes naturally, probably from a stubborn determination to find at least one other viable option. But the debate does have merits. First, it usually produces additional insights. Second, it nails down all the logic for each option. Third, occasionally, it comes up with a better answer. But most of the time, I end up agreeing with the answer that has been brought by the team. If they've agreed, it's probably the result of pretty good thinking. And fourth, when the team knows I want to hear different views on an important issue, members feel comfortable advancing their own. They don't feel that they have to go along when they don't agree. I don't give a hoot who's view "wins" in the end; I care only that people bring strong views and strong arguments for their position.

SLOC had its share of contentious issues: how many premium tickets to sell and at what prices; what role should we take in driving security planning; how confrontational should we be with the IOC; how hard should we fight in the scandal-related legal battles; which officer would be given which responsibilities; who's budgets would be cut the most. There was no end to issues that seemed critical, at least as we confronted them. We got used to debate. And all in all, we made some pretty good decisions.

HORIZONTAL, NOT VERTICAL

Management consultants have made a living in this country helping businesses organize and re-organize time and again. Sometimes, they'll design a vertical structure. Then, when communication fails, they'll move to a matrix. Usually they settle in on a design that seems to work best for them, but it can take a number of years and a number of consulting dollars. We didn't have the luxury of either.

Vertical structures have people grouped by function: production, sales, finance, marketing. The function manager serves as their link to the rest of the company. Matrix structures also have individuals report to a function manager, but in addition, the individuals report to a team leader who supervises people from different functions. Vertical structures fail because of poor communication. The manufacturing guys, for example, don't hear what the marketing guys want to sell next year until it's too late for manufacturing to get the right equipment to make it. Vertical structures rely on the person at the top to keep everyone informed. At SLOC, we had opted for vertical functions: sport, finance, transportation, venues, marketing, etc. And because Fraser and I had such a large number of function heads reporting to each of us, the task of keeping each one informed about the work of the others was almost impossible.

Our answer was to overlay as many horizontal communications vehicles as possible. Ed took charge, but almost every senior manager volunteered suggestions to increase horizontal communication. Of course, there were the Monday morning senior management meetings: every manager reported on what they were doing that week, what issues they faced, and what matters might affect other functions.

They didn't need to rely on Fraser or me to bring them up to date. They heard it directly from one another.

SLOC was vertical for almost my entire three years there. But with months to go before the Games began, we took the step every organizing committee takes: we reassigned almost the entire organization to venue teams. Their new boss was, for example, the head of the ski jump venue. To him or her reported a volunteer manager, a human resources manager, a finance manager, a facility or venue construction manager, a ticketing person, a food person, a medical director, an accreditation person, and so forth. We went from function teams to venue teams; from vertical to horizontal. During Games time, all the action would be at the venue. And that was also true in the months leading up to the Games as equipment, tents, bleachers, phones and radios, sport equipment, and systems were being installed, a process we called "fit up."

After spending years building communications, cementing personal relationships among vertical team members, and establishing practices that foster teamwork, everything would have to be thrown up in the air. Remarkably, the transition went quite well. The old ties and connections that had existed within functions now facilitated cooperation between venues where that was needed, and communication to Fraser and me at the top. The caps and t-shirts that read "SLOC Food Services Team" were slowly replaced with ones that read "Salt Lake Ice Center team." The team spirit remained.

OPEN, HONEST, AND DIRECT

When my partners and I at Bain Capital had made our trip to Human Factors in California, we decided that one of our guiding principles would be to be "open, honest, and direct" in our communications with one another. We had endured a culture where private criticism was only surpassed by public denials. The commitment to change helped.

So when I came to SLOC, "open, honest, and direct" was a must. I also knew that it was easier said than done. I had some personal experience. I found that it's not terribly hard to stop criticizing people behind their backs, particularly when everyone you talk with knows that you've mutually agreed to do so. No, the hard part is telling people honestly and directly when you have a problem with them or with something they're doing.

I met my friend Kem Gardner when he moved to Boston in 1990. One of the things I admired most about him was his ability to be what he called "sweetly bold." He'd give criticism straight out. Remarkably, people didn't seem to be offended. It was quite a talent. Somehow, when I tried, it just didn't always work out that way. I figured that Kem's Wyoming, aw-shucks, manner and way of talking made people just that less defensive. I had seen heavily accented Southerners dish out tough medicine with such a smile that people said thanks. Maybe it was my midwestern earnestness and lack of disarming charms that put me at a disadvantage. But Fraser looked and sounded like I did, and he had learned to be a master.

On one occasion we were having difficulties integrating our medical service plans with our chief medical sponsor, Intermountain Health Care. There was a lot of money involved and figuring out which things SLOC would be responsible for paying and which would be donated by IHC was complicated and potentially contentious. Further complicating matters was the fact that our chief medical officer was part-time and had come on loan from IHC. Dr. Charles Rich's loyalties surely flowed from his many years of association with that organization. Reporting to Dr. Rich was our full-time director, Ginny Borncamp, who also was on loan from IHC. Ginny and Dr. Rich were having difficulty seeing eye to eye on the IHC matters. It's not unusual when people first come together and have to figure out how to divide up duties that there would be clashes. We heard that IHC may have been unhappy with Ginny. It was rumored that they felt she had been disloyal to their interests, favoring those of SLOC. Fraser and I felt instead that she had been entirely fair to both organizations; further, she had been an extremely competent and effective manager. She was one of the very best at SLOC. We presumed that IHC's concerns were the result of reports from Dr. Rich. I asked Fraser to speak with Dr. Rich about the problem, as Fraser was his boss, and I thanked my lucky stars it was Fraser who had the job.

Dr. Charles Rich was a man of a respectable age with an impressive resume. In fact, he was a brain surgeon and one of the most noted and respected doctors in the entire state. He was also a close friend of almost half of the movers and shakers that Don Stirling and I were approaching for donations. We wanted him on our side, but we also wanted things to change—a delicate operation, in medical parlance. Fraser's tack was direct. He laid out the concerns and the changes we expected him to make. Dr. Rich listened attentively. Fraser said the meeting went well but he didn't know how Dr. Rich was going to take the direction.

Dr. Rich called me the following day. I braced myself for an earful. Dr. Rich observed that Fraser was a most capable leader and that I was lucky to have him at SLOC. He raved about his forthright manner and keen observation. Dr. Rich was one of our most enthusiastic and dedicated team members. His unique medical experience and community renown led to heroic levels of contribution by the medical community to the Games. There really could never have been a better medical chief than Dr. Rich. Had we let the conflict smolder and the misunderstanding fester, there could have been a very different outcome. A bad one. It's not easy being direct but it's awfully valuable.

One more place where open, honest and direct helps. It's when you know you've fallen short, made a mistake, or failed to deliver. It feels awful to let others down. And even when you know in your heart that you're somewhat to blame, you also know that it isn't entirely your fault. In fact, the more you think about it, the more you become convinced that it mostly was others fault. It was really out of your control.

Honesty and directness produce a response that is a great deal more salutary than what greets disingenuousness and deflection. That had been my guide at SLOC in dealing with the media and the public. At the same time, I knew that how I dealt with the public had to be consistent with how I wanted people to deal with each other in the organization. Same face outside the organization as what I wanted inside.

One of the building projects that our venues team was most proud of was the speed skating oval at Oquirrh Park. Rather than employ standard steel beam construction, our engineers had used a design that was infrequently employed. The roof was held up by a series of cables that were stretched between opposing piers. The building was enormous: it would have held almost five football fields. The design meant less steel was necessary, the ceiling could be lower, and there would be no internal columns that would limit camera and spectator views. And, it was less expensive. About a year out from the Games, the shell of the building, including the roof, was almost complete. Only one cable and roof section of the twelve needed to be attached. Grant Thomas, our managing director for venues, called to report that the final cable had detached during construction. The section of roofing had collapsed. The forces unleashed had been tremendous. The cable, about five inches in diameter and three hundred feet long, had fishtailed across the floor, crushing a trailer and taking out a cinder block wall. Miraculously, no one was killed or seriously hurt.

Grant and his team had to be devastated, but he was as cool as a September morning. He told us everything he knew and accompanied me at the site. His focus was on action, not blame. Of course, his team hadn't designed the building, done the engineering, or done the construction. But he accepted responsibility anyway. Ultimately, the buck stopped with Grant and venues management. Grant's forthrightness carried over to our contractor and to the engineering firms. They went right to work to understand what had failed. Grant brought in two independent engineering firms to evaluate the causes and how we could recover. After several days, it was determined that the bolts that fastened the cables to the piers were significantly undersized. Apparently, the top brain power in the lead engineering firm had focused on the tough challenges relating to the cable such as the forces involved, vectors and load capacity. A junior employee had done the specification engineering for the mundane bolts that would fasten the cable to its anchors. What was straightforward had been assumed to be routine and was overlooked. The contractor had potentially exacerbated the weakness by substituting a similar bolt on the last cabled pier that failed. Fortunately, the last section failed when it did. If it had held until the building was filled with spectators and if weather or wind caused a collapse, the results could have been catastrophic. We all knew how lucky we were. There was no need for recrimination or berating. Grant and our team met with all the parties; each was open and honest. The lawyers were kept at bay. The responsible parties paid for the disruption, delay and reconstruction of the entire roofing system.

LET THE GOOD TIMES ROLL

"Fun and Celebration" may seem like an odd guiding principle for an enterprise. But I had long before decided that if you don't enjoy your time at work, life could be pretty miserable. We instituted a rule at Bain Capital that every meeting had to begin with a joke. I love jokes and I love laughing. The humor spread through the entire meeting: people were always on the lookout for a laugh. When Ed began the process of having task forces determine which should be our guiding principles, I directed that "fun" needed to be one of them. It was. And I always tried to begin meetings with a joke, just to keep things in their proper perspective.

The tone of the organization was set in large measure at the All-SLOC meetings I described in the previous chapter. Beth White's shtick kept us pretty darn loose. On one occasion, she skewered Bill Clinton's sex-capades only to learn that a member of the White House staff was attending the meeting as our guest. So instead of laying off, she dug in deeper to the delight of the SLOC crowd.

TEAM-BUILDING ACTIVITIES

Mark Lewis came by my office one day and suggested that each function be given a budget to spend on group activities and fun. Now that went against my Yankee grain. I believed in fun, but I hated the thought of spending money wastefully. But Mark argued me down. He was right, a budget meant that managers would actually take the time to plan and carry out activities that would bring the team together and be enjoyable at the same time. We allocated about $25 per employee per quarter. It was enough that by waiting a quarter or two and saving up, some of the departments could do some pretty big things. The marketing department went skiing for the day. The communications team went river rafting down the Green River. Legal joined with federal relations for fancy dinners as well as outings.

We scheduled All-SLOC activity days as well. Twice we enjoyed Park City Mountain Resort's generous offer to deeply discount lift tickets and food to take the entire thousand-person-plus staff for a day on the slopes. Lunch was together. Ed's team had a stage set up for a speech from me, awards for outrageous outfits, free gifts and plenty of Beth's humor.

When successes and milestones were attained, we celebrated them. Ed Eynon had "FITCaP" pins made up to publicly recognize good corporate citizenship (FITCaP being an acronym of our five guiding principles). He instituted the "lima bean" award, complete with an acrylic encased lima bean, which he presented at All-SLOC meetings. Recipients of the lima bean award were nominated by their peers for having accepted an unappealing task and pursuing it to completion (I had once mentioned that I would eat a plate of lima beans with a sponsor if it would help close a deal). He also put other mementos in Lucite for tombstones and trophies—like a tiny copy of the letter from the Justice Department informing us that we were no longer the subject of indictment proceedings. We took fun quite seriously.

There was quite a lot of inter-departmental hi-jinx that went on informally as well. Our creative department lived up to its name when it came to humor. Scott Givens, its managing director, kept a notori-ous little book of SLOC quotes. It was something of a competition to make it into the book each week. Most of the winning entries were spontaneous expressions that reflected the day-to-day pressures of try-ing to pull things off that had never been done before. After enduring yet another budget review, our director of the "look of the Games," Bob Finley, noted: "All this begging for money will be valuable in my next career as a homeless person."

On a particularly stressful Monday—only weeks out from the Games when Scott Givens was under tremendous pressure—a couple of his colleagues had t-shirts imprinted with choice quotes surrepti-tiously taken from Scott's quote book. Throughout the day, as Scott sat down to meetings with various colleagues inside and outside of his department, people would nonchalantly unbutton their shirts to reveal a quote. His administrative assistant, Joyce Long, donned a shirt with one of her best lines: "Your schedule is so booked, there's no time for a potty break. Wear your Depends...." One of his editors took off his work shirt to reveal a quip from an outsourced transla-tion company who had translated the word "biathalon" into Russian as "There's a gunfight between competitors." On and on this went throughout the day, culminating in an afternoon meeting with me.

I am prone to the occasional tangential story when in meetings. Unbeknown to me, Scott would lean over to his colleagues when he thought I was getting a little off topic and whisper, "Buckle up. He's about to make a left turn." But Scott was way too polite to let me see his irritation; he just hid his remark in his little quote book. That after-noon, while Scott and I were reviewing milestones and budget figures, I casually reached up and loosened my tie. I kept talking as I unbut-toned my shirt and opened to reveal Scott's words. Scott laughed ner-vously, incredulous that I was in on the gag. "I didn't even know you knew about that quote," he confessed. "Well, I do now." With that, Scott's editorial director made it into the quote book one more time. While patting a slightly embarrassed Scott on the back he assured him, "We'll always make time to make fun of you, Scott."

ROMEO AND JULIET

As the Games approached, the time for fun seemed to be getting short shrift. I asked our federal relations team to step up to the task of restoring humor. Cindy Gillespie went to a thrift store and purchased a woman's wig, a pageboy wig, a princess dress and a man's tunic. She turned up Monday morning with her costumes, a video camera, and photocopies of both the balcony scene and the suicide scene from Shakespeare's *Romeo and Juliet*.

She wandered the floor at SLOC getting different pairings from different departments to don the costumes and perform a scene on video. Some of the pairings were hilarious. Kelly Flint, our senior VP of legal, was about as dry and straightforward as you would think a chief legal counsel would be. But he donned the pageboy wig and did the balcony scene with a colleague who was at least eight months pregnant at the time.

We held a screening of all the videos that Wednesday at lunch. It was a huge hit. The screening concluded with me playing Romeo to our human resource chief's Juliet. Ed Eynon is about six-foot-four. He had on the long curly wig and the princess dress and was lying on a conference room table, having drunk the potion. I was reading the lines of Shakespeare, but I also threw in some of my own: "Juliet, you're ugly as sin, and you need a shave to boot." Ed would contort with painful faces, feigning death, at every insult. It took everyone a while to figure out who was playing Juliet. When they realized it was Ed, they roared.

What we at SLOC were working to create at the Olympics mattered a good deal, but so did having fun while we were doing it.

PASSION AND PRIDE

Perhaps the biggest leap for SLOC when I walked in the door was to think of our jobs in terms of passion and pride. The scandal, the press, and the reality of how the SLOC team had been betrayed had lowered spirits and deadened enthusiasm.

Shortly after I arrived at SLOC, as the true scope of the crisis and the problems we were facing became clear to me, I felt pretty low myself. Worry came easy, sleep didn't. I wondered whether I had taken on a hopeless cause.

There were other concerns, bigger ones. My wife Ann had been diagnosed the year before with MS. I was at the office for long, long hours. I loved the challenge of a daunting task, but I missed the recharging I knew at home, with Ann.

What gave me energy was the passion I felt for the Games, for what they meant to America and our athletes, for the people who had sacrificed to come to SLOC, and for the thrill of taking on a turn-around project of such magnitude. I sure wasn't alone in the way I felt. I learned that the people I was working with had made sacrifices themselves.

I don't think there was a meeting I spoke in during my first six months when I didn't repeat, quite honestly, that this was the best management team I had ever had the opportunity to work with. It was not because their skills were above all others I had seen, but because they were sacrificing more, giving more, and caring more. And they were very, very effective because of it.

Chapter 6

THE BUDGET

My ten years in consulting and my sixteen years in venture capital and private equity taught me that there are answers in numbers—gold in numbers. Pile the budgets on my desk and let me wallow. Numbers can help solve a mystery. I discover trends, form hypotheses, most of which fail but lead to others that are more fruitful. Almost without exception, I learn something that is key to the success of the enterprise.

When I arrived at SLOC, we had wonderfully detailed budget numbers that Frank had contracted to be developed by Bechtel. Gordon Crabtree had gathered every figure he could find from prior Games. Much to my amazement, and great disappointment, there was no standard for accounting from past Olympic Games. Each organizing committee presented their numbers in the most favorable political light, often ignoring whole expense categories, like what it had cost to build the Olympic venues. Figures were also lumped together in non-comparable categories. The gold from the numbers piles would be a lot harder to mine.

Our first budget review was helped enormously by the observations and insights from the SLOC managers. By and large, they knew where the excess was buried. Bob White and I would push into the most promising veins and take core samplings where our instincts told us more could be found. We came up with the $98 million described before.

I did not feel there was any need to keep our newly budgeted cost reductions a secret. The media was listening at SLOC's door for any indication of crisis. In fact, budget progress might help slow stories of impending financial doom and "bills" for Utah taxpayers. Shelley and I spoke with the press about our early progress on the $98 million and some of the substantive as well as symbolic changes that would be required to hit the new figures.

The openness seemed to have the desired effect. Both the local and the national media were abuzz with stories about the new frugality at SLOC. "Romney Keeps It Simple and Frugal" read the headline in the *Boston Globe*. An editorial cartoon in one of the Salt Lake City papers depicted me standing in front of a McDonald's-like store labeled "MittFrugals." Another featured a large sign announcing: "Get your Olympics... Cheap!" I liked the new angle, especially for the cost cutting ethic it would bring to our organization. Of course, there are always those who see the bad news in everything: "Won't these cheaper Games make us look bad compared with other Olympic cities?" The media had a new angle for criticism. I felt like answering, "Not as bad as if we go bankrupt and can't hold the Games at all, dummy." I saved that answer for a few board members who called to complain about the new frugality, although I left off the "dummy" part.

Even with the sense of relief that came from our preliminary "top down" budget cuts, I knew there was no substitute for a protracted, line by line, bottom-up analysis of every budget volume, and there were over twenty volumes ready to be dissected. And the more I studied our overall financial picture, the more I saw risk and uncertainty. By the end of my first month, we had been able to aggregate the various accounts to recognize that our true budget was approximately $1.9 billion, including federal programs and matching costs. The fig-

THE BUDGET · 107

ure was a good deal more than we had been telling the public and ourselves. The largest cost categories would be $328 million for venues, $282 million for technology and telecommunications, and over $250 million for people and office space. We owed $99 million to the state of Utah to reimburse them for diverted tax revenues and to fulfill an obligation to set money aside for ongoing operations at the venues after the Games were over. Our largest spending, however, would be for security. It would total hundreds of millions, most of which we were planning on coming from the federal government. And most was not included in any of our budgeting. Hence my worry about the attitude in Washington about the Salt Lake Games; there was no legal obligation for the federal government to pick up security costs, but if they didn't, we were toast. Burnt toast.

On the other side of the balance sheet we had $409 million in cash revenues (mostly from broadcast payments and sponsors) and, as best as we could determine, about $190 million in sponsor donated goods and services.

How big was the financial work ahead of us? Technically, we had more than a billion in revenues to raise before we reached breakeven. But we knew that number overstated our problem. We were quite confident we would be selling tickets and receiving payments from broadcasters and the IOC sponsorships. So we decided to calculate an official budget gap. We would estimate all the revenues we had solid prospects to receive, subtract that total from our total cost, and have a figure that would indicate the size of our problem. Our fiscal hole.

For purposes of this calculation, we assumed we would sell all the tickets that we planned in our budget, we would get every matching dollar, we would receive all the money we needed from Washington, we would sell all the licensing deals we needed, and so forth. With all those optimistic assumptions made, we still were $379 million short as of March 1999, about a month after I joined. That was our official budget gap. It felt more like a gulf than a gap.

There were two reasons for concern: one, we were making awfully optimistic assumptions about things like ticketing, licensing, and federal support. The federal government was particularly squishy given the scandal and the fact that no one had ever told or committed the many federal agencies and committees to do what we were expecting from them. And second, even with our optimistic assumptions, a very large gap remained. It would have to be closed by cutting more costs or by acquiring more sponsors. And virtually every company and industry category that had been previously sold an Olympic sponsorship had already been signed up.

HEADS-UP FOR THE GOVERNOR

As the financial picture became clear and my nights became more fitful, I decided it was time to let Governor Leavitt in on the full financial picture. I wanted to make sure there was no doubt that he fully grasped the risks.

Despite having a large and capable board, I felt Mike Leavitt was my real boss. It was he who made the decision to hire me. He appointed half the members of the board as well and they served at his pleasure. He was without question the power in Utah. As head of the dominant political party, as governor, he was the man. The meeting would give him everything he needed to know about what we faced. I never wanted him to be surprised.

We sat down in the Governor's Mansion on South Temple Street, in a turn of the century victorian parlor. Together, we turned through my copy of the facts and figures.

"I have to level with you," I said "We're way behind. The reality is that we haven't sold any new sponsors in over six months. Budgeted costs currently exceed contributions by about $379 million. We'll surely receive some amount of federal support but the budget assumes we'll get more than our government has ever given, by a lot. I can't tell you today what level of costs we'll be able to cut or where the additional dollars will come from. There is some possibility, I hope not a large one, that the Games might run out of money before they begin."

The governor knew what I meant. If we ran out of money, there was virtually no bailout imaginable. We could be liquidated by our creditors, and shamed. I went on to show him, for academic purposes only, what would happen financially if we pulled the plug on the Games that very day. This I compared with all the risks of going forward. By my calculation, it made better financial sense, even by just looking at the cold hard numbers, to proceed. And of course, considering all the non-financial features, proceeding was a no-brainer. But I wanted the governor to know the whole story.

Regardless of the risks, the only way to have any hope of recovering the $59 million investment the state had made was to stage the Games. There would be no revenue at all without Games. Even if we signed no new sponsors, we would still be financially better off holding them. "It seems to me we have no choice but to carry on," I said. "I'll do my very best to turn things around, but I want you to know the risks up front. Ultimately, it is your decision."

The governor didn't hesitate an instant. "I have full confidence. Carry on." Riding home, I rehearsed what we would need to do:

- ➣ cut costs;
- ➣ sell new sponsors;
- ➣ sell the feds;
- ➣ get donors;
- ➣ pray.

We did all five.

PUBLICIZING OUR SHORTFALL

Almost immediately we went public with our financial situation. Our first budget revision took the budget total and the gap higher, given the identification of new expenses. These more than engulfed my $98 million in cuts, a potentially controversial point. Some executives blanche at the prospect of announcing weaknesses and shortfalls before they occur or before reporting is legally required. But we had received $59 million in public funding. Community support would be critical to our success and so we viewed the public as one of our key stakeholders. With public transparency in board meetings and public access to our records, there was little prospect of keeping such gaping deficits secret for very long anyway.

The higher budget and financial shortfall drew a great deal of media attention. So much so that USOC marketing executive, John Krimsky, publicly denounced us for giving it so much focus. "We seem to be pre-occupied with the budget at the moment...I am calling for an end to political rhetoric...We can't chill the sales and marketing agreements and drive sponsors away because they feel these will not be the best Games ever—for whatever reason."

Krimsky's was the alternative approach: no matter how bad things are, just smile and act like everything's going great. No one wants to board a sinking ship. From his view, I was giving even the rats a chance to stay clear of the ship. There's a lot to be said for Krimsky's viewpoint. It is probably not a good marketing tool to point out problems. But I felt this was not a normal situation. Everyone in the sport world knew SLOC was in trouble. And if there was a company out there somewhere that hadn't heard about the scandal and the resulting financial challenges we faced, their consultants would tell them.

Our employees also needed to hear the truth. I knew that the doomsday scenarios they were imagining were a lot worse than the reality. When people hear the truth, they can deal with it. When they have to guess, it can be frightening and paralyzing. I was anxious to shift the focus of attention away from speculation about the extent of our troubles to the progress we would soon be making towards their resolution. No one likes joining a loser, but they like rooting for, and helping, a comeback kid. And that's what SLOC had to become, soon.

TAKING THINGS APART

Fraser's arrival on the scene was an extraordinarily happy day for me. He'd do what I was dying to get at: he'd take the definitive whack at the SLOC budget. Fraser took sixty days to get the lay of the land, spending half that time personally interviewing managers and directors—debriefing and assessing. Fraser asked each director to divide their entire budget, line by line, into those items that were "Must-Haves" and those that were "Nice-to-Haves." The former were strictly defined as items without which the Games could not proceed. The remaining "Nice-to-Have" items were further assigned to three levels of priority—first tier, second tier, and third tier.

Fraser's approach was all encompassing. In most budget meetings and cost-cutting exercises I have seen in corporate America, managers bring in their recommendations for reductions. There are a number of problems with that approach. First, its very hard for the senior executive to know just how much excess there is in each and every department. One department might have tons of cost reduction opportunity; another only ounces. An overall 15 percent cost reduction goal is too easy for the one, too hard for the other. The approach is also subject to the age-old ploy of a manager putting an item that is obviously critical on the list of things to be cut. The senior executive quickly restores the critical item and is thereby convinced his subordinate has no fat whatsoever left in his budget. As governor of Massachusetts, I see some municipal officials announce drastic cuts needed in police, fire, and teachers. Predictably, the public is appalled. But what about patronage jobs, less essential functions, excessive pay contracts? From them, the attention has been deflected.

When Fraser's first budget was complete, he'd identified most of what we needed. Some of it would be very painful to cut and would affect some of our higher priorities. We spent several days reviewing the cuts and the tier assignments. In a number of cases, I restored items or assigned them to different tiers. In others, I took deeper cuts. Ultimately, we would decide to strictly limit all hiring, and we would remove the inflation factor from everything we were to purchase, effectively reducing our budget on these items by several percent across the board. These were the largest sources of savings. In addition, we had a long list of Nice-to-Have items that would be cut if they could not be funded by donor or sponsor funds. Some of the items that went on the Nice-to-Have list included: top quality uniforms for volunteers and staff, hot meals for staff and volunteers during the Games, enhanced elements for opening and closing ceremonies, funding to pay for the broadcast of the Paralympics, a nationwide journey for the Olympic torch in addition to its Utah route, and so forth. We would only have these features if we raised the money that was needed.

SMART MONEY

It is easy to cut costs. It is a lot harder to do it smart. To the SLOC team, the budget management process would only make sense if we preserved our highest priorities. Below this page is a side bar that enumerates the priorities I presented to the board of directors. They adopted them unanimously. Besides fiscal responsibility, our primary objective was to stage great Games for the athletes and to provide a great experience for spectators, television viewers, and for those all around the world. If we succeeded, our legacy objectives would take care of themselves, our reputation as a host city would be restored.

Our Objectives
1. Great sport, shared by people all over the world.
2. Fiscal Responsibility: leave no debts behind.
3. The Olympic Experience, shared with the community.
4. A Lasting Legacy, with a reputation for hospitality and friendliness.
5. Games with Heart and Meaning, Lighting the Fire Within.

OH THOSE NICE-TO-HAVES

Some of the first costs we targeted were IOC accommodations. The budget prepared for SLOC by Bechtel called for spending more than $4.5 million on the IOC for hotel rooms, transportation, meals, and other services. During my second trip to the IOC headquarters in Lausanne, I proposed to cut that figure nearly in half. In particular, we asked to be relieved of our obligation to pay a $1.2 million subsidy for hotel rooms at the new Grand America Hotel. Our contract with the IOC called for us to provide the IOC with rooms at the guaranteed price of no more than $200. But, given their decision to stay in the brand new, five-star Grand America Hotel in Salt Lake, we would need to subsidize in order to meet that price. I offered instead that the IOC stay not in the new five-star location, but in its older sister across the street. Little America was a fine hotel to be sure, but it was not luxury accommodations. My guess is that it was built forty or more years ago. Much to my amazement, President Samaranch quickly agreed. Cha-ching: $1.2 million for the good guys, thanks to the IOC's good will.

Fraser saw a line item for flowers for meetings with international guests. Nope. We went through the HR budget and found $10,000 allocated for guest speakers for All-SLOC meetings once every quarter. When asked what this was for, the response was: "Well, we're going to have outside speakers come to the organization to motivate the troops." Fraser and I would have to do. Gone.

We further cut our travel budget by eliminating entourages, minimizing stays, and staying in economy hotels. And, with AT&T as a telecommunications sponsor, we were able to use videoconferencing to eliminate traveling to several IOC meetings. Each time we spoke with the IOC via videoconference link, we saved roughly $10,000 and three days of travel. I don't know that it was particularly well received by the IOC to have me and our officers report via video, but it saved time and money.

We pulled money from our fireworks budget (which broke my heart), from entertainment budgets for the athletes at the Olympic

Village, at venues, and at the downtown celebration sites. Flush from the initial $6 million in savings from my February hiring freeze, Fraser performed an extensive staffing survey in every department looking to identify redundancies and over-allocations. We determined to hire 15 percent fewer people and fill some of the tier two and tier three jobs with volunteers.

We cut the "look of the Games" budget for decorating Salt Lake City by more than half, and we took a similar cut in publications. Fortunately, in Bob Finley and Libby Hyland, we had two superstars running these functions: they did not raise their creative hackles. They went to work on prioritizing. We also took more than half the funding out of opening and closing ceremonies. Funding for the cultural Olympiad was cut to zero. Our environment budget was cut to zero.

I knew we couldn't afford to allocate resources to lower priority functions. You could have great Games without decorations or cultural performances, without educational and environmental programs. But you couldn't have great Games without world-class field of play, athlete accommodations and transportation. Certain support functions were just as essential: computing and timing systems, security, broadcasting. For the Olympics to touch the hearts of the people of the world, the Games had to be seen as well on TV as in person.

I was impressed at how well our entire team coalesced behind the budget process and its outcome. Those whose budgets were slashed simply began figuring out how to do more with less. We all knew that our job was to produce great Olympics, not make our own jobs easier. We would succeed or fail together.

At the end of the first bottom-up analysis, Fraser and the management team had identified $97 million in further cuts above those we had identified during our initial top-down review. They had placed an additional $72 million into three Nice-to-Have tiers of enhancements that would be held back until or unless revenues became available. At the same time, they identified another $56 million in previously unbudgeted expenses. The net savings from the bottom-up exercise was $113 million. The official "deficit-o-meter" in the local papers put our revised gap at $187 million by the late summer of 2000.

We certainly weren't there yet, and we knew unexpected expenditures would keep rolling in. We committed our finance team to performing a new bottom-up analysis every quarter, which coincided with quarterly function-by-function reviews. Another $16.5 million in cuts came in September along with $6.4 million in newly identified costs. We saved $3.5 million by reducing the number of buses and drivers allocated to transporting journalists.

It was late in 1999 that we decided to blow up a big portion of our inflation factor. Each line item of the Bechtel budget projected a 3 percent increase per year to keep up with inflation. All together, the inflation adjustments totaled more than $52 million spread across our direct budget. We told our people they would just have to make due with 1999 dollars and either buy early or find a better deal. Each department had to scale down across the board. By Games time we had taken all inflation out of the budget.

And thus it went—identifying more costs, identifying further savings. Eventually our marketing efforts began to produce on the other side of the equation. The money from new sponsors and donors permitted us to restore some of the tier one and tier two items. My priority candidate for reclamation was opening ceremonies. I believed that they would set the tone for our Games.

We also put greater funding in our contingency account. It reached $140 million before we began to dip into it in the spring of 2001. The seemingly constant string of unanticipated costs made me cautious, as did reports from prior organizer CEOs about last minute and Games-time surprises. I did not want to be out of money, begging, when the athletes arrived.

At the end of Fraser's first year, I knew how fortunate we were to have him looking over finance and operations. His brand of unrelenting, hard-nosed discipline produced a financial roadmap that would take us all the way to the Games.

Chapter 7

UNCERTAIN REVENUES

You can only get so far by cutting costs. In my business life, the fastest way to improve the bottom line was to pare back expenses. But it is never the complete answer. In the long term, the bottom line will only look good if the top line looks good too. In business, the top line is sales or revenues; it's the ultimate vote of the customer. If revenues are failing, there's no amount of cost cutting that will make the business successful.

SLOC wasn't a business, but some of the same principles applied: we would never get out of our financial hole unless we grew the top line revenues. There are three primary sources of private revenue for an Olympic organizing committee: corporate sponsorships, broadcasting rights, and ticket sales. We had decided to add a fourth, the Olympic donor program. While it would be an unprecedented success, the big numbers would have to come from the big three.

We had high hopes for strong ticket sales. But the budget called for more than just strong sales. It depended on a miraculous level of sales. Nagano held the prior ticket sales record for Olympic Winter Games:

they sold $80 million. The SLOC budget called for $162 million, a figure we later raised to $180 million. For purposes of calculating our financial hole, I just took the ticket budget as if it was money in the bank. It was far from it. I knew it would take another heroic effort to reach that figure.

Broadcasting rights are sold directly by the IOC, with about two-thirds of the entire worldwide revenue coming from the United States broadcaster alone. There were several mouths to be fed at the broadcast revenue trough: the IOC, the national Olympic committees like the USOC, and the Summer and Winter organizing committees, like us.

NBC and ABC had traded off Olympic coverage in the U.S. for a number of years, with CBS making a dark horse entry for Nagano. In late 1995, rights for the 2000 Summer Games in Sydney would go on the market. NBC approached the IOC with a preemptive bid. They offered a billion dollar package deal for rights to the next five Games. The IOC jumped at the offer. That did two things. It linked the Sydney and the Salt Lake Games in the U.S. market since we would be covered by the same network. It also meant that SLOC's broadcasting revenues were largely determined three years before I even got there. Broadcast and ticket revenues weren't going to be the source of the additional revenues to close our financial gap. We would have to look to new sponsors.

A BRIEF HISTORY OF OLYMPIC SPONSORSHIPS

For all intents and purposes, modern sports marketing was invented by Peter Ueberroth and his Los Angeles Olympic organizing committee. Los Angeles took the Games after Montreal's fiscal catastrophe, where the city swallowed over $200 million in losses. There just weren't any other viable cities willing to host the 1984 Olympics. Given that bargaining position, and his own exceptional skill, Ueberroth negotiated a very favorable marketing deal for Los Angeles with the IOC. Then he set out to raise the bulk of his revenue through the sale of Olympic sponsorships. To say that he did very well is an understatement. He did so well, in fact, that long before the start of the 1984 Games, the United States Olympic Committee (USOC) took note and started selling sponsorships of their own.

This bears a little explaining. The Games organizer is called the organizing committee. It builds the venues, puts together the computers and systems, feeds the athletes, etc. All of it costs a good deal of money; in SLOC's case, about $1.5 billion. But there is also an entity called the United States Olympic Committee. It is what is referred to as a National Olympic Committee, an NOC. There's one of these in every country that sends athletes to the Olympics. Their primary job is to recruit, train, and field teams of athletes for the Olympics. For an NOC like the USOC, that task also costs a lot of money, many millions of dollars a year.

Ueberroth's success in selling sponsors was not lost on the USOC. They wanted to get in on some of the action. They sent out their own marketing people to sell sponsorships. Ueberroth sold a company the right to be a sponsor of the *LA Games*; the USOC sold the right to be a sponsor of the *U.S. Team*. Unfortunately for the sponsors, that meant that the Olympic rings were attached to competing companies and competing products. Kodak was a sponsor of the U.S Olympic Team and Fuji was a sponsor of the LA Games. Time and again, competing companies came face to face as sponsors at the same event. There were some very unhappy executives. And unhappy sponsors could mean hurting the value of Olympic sponsorships down the road.

A SHOTGUN MARRIAGE

The IOC recognized that it needed to set rules to keep the LA problem from happening again. From now on, when they awarded a city the right to organize the Games, they would add to the contract with that city specific language requiring that the organizing committee that puts on the Games (the OCOG) and the organization that fields the team (the NOC) enter into a joint venture to coordinate their marketing programs. This would prevent competing sponsorships. SLOC and the USOC had done this before I had arrived. The USOC held all the cards.

In most countries the NOC is weak when it comes to marketing. It's typically a government ministry that has never sold a single sponsorship. For a modest percentage of profits, these NOCs are often happy to let the OCOG market the Games and keep most of the proceeds. Things are different in the United States. The U.S. government does not fund athlete training or Olympic teams. Instead Congress adopted a statute granting exclusive use of the Olympic rings for marketing purposes to the USOC. So the USOC has the law on its side.

The USOC and SLOC had agreed that the cash raised in sponsorships would be split roughly 50-50. VIK went to the organization that could actually use the donated goods and services, or 50-50 if both could. So when my budget hole was $379 million in May 1999, I knew that for every dollar that would come from sponsors, we would have to sell two dollars of sponsorship. We had an even bigger job than people were thinking.

The deal also granted to the USOC the responsibility and the right to do all the marketing. The exception was for marketing in Utah; they left the local crumbs to SLOC. So filling my budget gap was largely up to the USOC.

Olympic marketing gets even more complicated. The IOC also wants to sell sponsorships for its budget and to support teams from developing countries. So it reserves to itself 11 categories or industries that it alone can sell. Neither the USOC nor SLOC can market to these companies or their competitors. In return for our forbearance, SLOC is entitled to about 15 percent of what the IOC gets from them. They're called TOP Sponsors, TOP standing for "The Olympic Partners." They include McDonald's, Coca-Cola, John Hancock, Kodak, Panasonic, Visa, Xerox, Samsung, SchlumbergerSema, and *Sports Illustrated*. Their sponsorship, for four years and a Winter and Summer Olympics, sold for $55 million each. The IOC had its 11 categories, the USOC had signed up the usual U.S. sponsors, and we were still hundreds of millions short. Time to talk to the USOC about marketing.

KRIMSKY AND THE USOC

The head of marketing for the USOC was a much-celebrated figure who held court in his own building with his own dedicated staff. John Krimsky was heralded as a marketing wiz in the press. By the time I arrived, he had already successfully re-signed all but one of the significant sponsors from the Atlanta Games and had also found companies to replace regional Georgia players like Bell South. Even more impressive, he had signed the companies at markups from their Atlanta sponsorship levels. It was really quite an accomplishment.

But his efforts to secure new relationships had gone cold, very cold. When I arrived in Salt Lake City, there had only been one small marketing deal and no official sponsorships in over six months—a drought that actually preceded the bid scandal by four months. It would end up lasting a year before it broke.

When I was first introduced to the leadership at the USOC, I asked Krimsky if we could meet together for a moment alone. Would he meet the sales target? The budget called for $859 million in sponsorship revenues to cover costs. We were far short of that figure. Krimsky responded that there was no question about it. He was highly confident that the entire marketing budget would be achieved. USOC President Bill Hybyl and Executive Director Dick Schultz gave me the same assurance.

A TRIP TO COLORADO SPRINGS

Nine days after my hiring, I was invited to speak to the USOC executive board meeting at their national headquarters in Colorado

Springs. Having spent a week with the numbers, I was anxious to meet with Krimsky to pin him down on specific prospects for new sponsorships. I wanted the names of the targets, the dates they would be ready to sign, and how much we would receive. I scheduled a meeting with him to precede the board meeting by one hour. But when I arrived at the USOC headquarters at 8:00 am that Saturday, he was nowhere to be found.

When the board meeting began an hour later I was asked to make some remarks. I said that I was very concerned that the Olympic committees did not have accurate, comparable, and detailed financial statements from prior Games. Midway through my remarks, I noticed John Krimsky slip in the door and sit near the back of the room. After my comments, he was asked to give an update on marketing prospects for Salt Lake City. He assured the executive board that he was "highly confident" all the forecasted funds would be raised.

Following his comments, I walked over to John and asked to meet for a few minutes after the meeting. It was clearly not what he had planned. He had no notes, no figures, and it was pretty clear, no interest in being grilled for specifics. I asked for two things. First, the amount of money that had been raised in Atlanta. Atlanta is, of course, a much bigger metro area than Salt Lake City and the Summer Games are a much bigger draw than Winter Games. By comparing our marketing budget to Atlanta's actual sponsor dollars, I would be able to gauge whether our forecast was reasonable. Second, I wanted the names of the top ten companies in the pipeline. Was the pipeline full or just a pipe dream?

John said he could not recollect what the total marketing number was for Atlanta, not even a rough estimate. I wondered if that were possible from the head of marketing. And, when pressed for the names of the next likely sponsors, he danced. He talked about percentages of money raised vs. his targets and so forth, but he gave me no names of targeted new deals on the horizon. This time I figured he might just be proprietary with his leads; he didn't want some new-comer interfering. I left the meeting very concerned. I couldn't be sure "the emperor had no clothes," but I was pretty suspicious.

Krimsky and his team in Colorado Springs were my marketing arm and they were just not getting the job done. I had asked to join in sales calls and they had been enthusiastic about having me help, but I got no calls from them. Either they thought I couldn't be of help or they had no sales calls.

JOHNSON & JOHNSON

Our marketing prospects weren't helped when Johnson & Johnson backed out of an intended Olympic sponsorship. While technically not rescinding an offer since they had never signed the letter of intent, Johnson & Johnson's decision not to proceed felt like a defection. *Brandweek* magazine listed Johnson & Johnson's concerns about coordinating the sponsorship among their many brands. But it also mentioned being "spooked" by the allegations of bribes and impro-prieties at SLOC and at the IOC.

The deal was worth about $30 million and even though marketing was Krimsky's, I was not about to let it go without giving it my best shot. I called Mark Dowley. He had originally introduced the Olympic opportunity to Johnson & Johnson and worked with them to help put the deal together. He was kind enough to set up a meeting with the head of Johnson & Johnson marketing.

We had breakfast at the Warwick Hotel in New York City. I out-lined the dramatic changes that had taken place at SLOC. These would be great Games, held in the U.S., and broadcast to a record audience. I pitched as well as I knew how, but there was not a glim-mer of encouragement. Johnson & Johnson did not want to be asso-ciated with scandal.

We had lost the Johnson & Johnson sponsorship the old fashioned way: we had earned it.

It felt pretty awful. And at about the same time, David d'Alessandro, CEO of the John Hancock Company and one of the IOC's TOP sponsors, was making his own highly visible retreat from the Games.

TENTATIVE EXECUTIVES

On February 11, 1999, the very day that I was announced as the new chief executive at SLOC, representatives from the eleven international sponsors of the IOC were meeting in New York City to discuss the impact of the Salt Lake City bribery allegations. For the most part, they had been very quiet about the scandal. The exception was d'Alessandro. He had been quite outspoken in his criticism of the IOC, calling Olympic sponsorships "radioactive." He wrote an op-ed piece in the *New York Times* demanding specific reforms and threatening that his company would abandon the Olympic movement if action were not taken.

Back at Hancock, he had ordered the Olympic rings taken off of company stationery, advertising, the annual report, and Hancock buildings. And in a departure from the other Olympic sponsors, they pulled $20 million in advertising from NBC that had been scheduled for the Sydney broadcast.

Dick Ebersol at NBC had fired back, calling d'Alessandro a "bully," but NBC itself had removed the Olympic rings from its own logo during news broadcasts. Just one year earlier at the 1997 Super Bowl, it had advertised its Olympic deal through 2008 with a promotional campaign featuring the tagline "10 years, 5 Olympics, 1 network." But now NBC investigative reporters were all over the story, all over the air.

Only three international IOC TOP sponsors had renewed their sponsorships for the Salt Lake 2002 and Athens 2004 Games. SchlumbergerSema signed for a portion of the information technology category that had been vacated by IBM. Eight others had yet to renew: Hancock, Xerox, UPS, Samsung, Panasonic, Kodak, McDonald's, and Visa.

The renewal program coincided with a rise in the price the IOC charged for a sponsorship, from $50 million to $55 million. The program had increased in price ten-fold since the Los Angeles Games in 1984. But even the managing director of Meridian Management, the sports marketing firm that handled TOP sponsor recruitment, was quoted in the *Wall Street Journal* admitting that, "if the Olympic movement loses its attachment with idealism...we won't be able to command the prices we are getting."

TAKING THE FIRST STEP

I went to see d'Alessandro personally. His now oft-quoted remark, "any CEO who signs on as an Olympic sponsor should be fired" was pretty difficult to overcome in the marketplace. Even the companies I had visited in Utah were anxious about what he had said. I also wanted to see if there was a prospect of getting Hancock back on board. If there was something that needed to be done at the IOC, maybe I could push that as well. Perhaps he was concerned about us at SLOC too. And there was another reason for my visit: if Hancock re-signed as an IOC TOP sponsor, for $55 million, SLOC would get its share of that sponsorship, about $8 million.

D'Alessandro also hails from Boston. While he had been a visible supporter of Senator Kennedy's successful re-election campaign over my challenge, I had come to like and respect him. I knew him to be a smart, straight shooter. I figured that he would tell me where we stood in the clearest of terms.

We met in March 1999. His office is a bit overwhelming. Located on the top floor, fifty-four stories above the street, it has magnificent floor-to-ceiling views of the Boston skyline and waterfront. And there's a collection of American memorabilia that rivals any museum's that I have seen. After I said my oohs and aahs, I asked what the Olympics needed to do to get his support again. He didn't hold back. D'Alessandro wanted the IOC members off the reform committee. He wanted IOC voting members barred from visiting bid cities. He wanted a "morality clause" inserted into his sponsorship agreement releasing Hancock from obligations if the IOC failed to live up to standards of integrity. They struck me as reasonable requests. Eventually, he would press the IOC to accomplish many of them.

D'Alessandro had been an IOC TOP sponsor. I wondered why he had not signed instead as a USOC sponsor where I presumed he could get sponsorship rights for a lower price. There were three reasons. First, he wasn't so sure the price would be less. Second, he didn't trust the people at the USOC, particularly John Krimsky, and third, he liked the logo he got from the IOC sponsorship better than the one he'd get from the USOC. One more bit of Olympic marketing lore. Depending on what you pay and who you pay, the IOC or the USOC, you get different Olympic trademarks. If you pay $55 million to be an IOC TOP sponsor, you can use the Olympic rings, plain and simple. But if you are a USOC sponsor, the rings must be accompanied by the letters "USA" beneath them. So Hancock, as an international financial services company, needed a trademark that wasn't so U.S. specific. Further, if you can't or won't pay for the highest level of USOC sponsorship, the trademark changes again. Now, you can use a graphic that says "Official 2002 Supplier." The rings are almost invisible on this logo. No surprise: you get more if you pay more. And Hancock wanted the best logo for their company.

D'Alessandro was not the only sponsor making noise. U.S. West had delayed a scheduled $5 million payment to the USOC and us. It was clear to all that they were sending a not-too-subtle signal about what they thought about the scandal. I knew that USOC and SLOC sponsors were busy conferring with their lawyers to see if they could get out of the sponsorship agreements. Kelly Flint assured me that whatever your view might be about John Krimsky's marketing prowess, he was a master at making sure the contracts with sponsors were unbreakable. Kelly had high praise for the USOC lawyering.

"The contracts are steel traps." I figured he had to be exaggerating. But no sponsor ever defected or even suggested trying.

BANKING ON THE BRAND

My pitch to Hancock and Johnson & Johnson was more than sales talk: I had come to believe that the Olympics were something a lot larger than a story about scandal. Otherwise, I would never have signed on. The scandal involved old guys and administrators, not athletes, not Olympians. I had evidence that the scandal had not and would not harm the Olympic brand. The USOC had engaged a polling firm to survey attitudes about the Olympics and about other sport events. Despite all the talk of scandal, the interest in and respect for the Olympics were virtually unchanged and exceptionally high. All across America, in demographic after demographic, more people listed themselves as "fans" of the Olympics than of NASCAR, the NBA, or even the NFL. People continued to associate the Olympics with friendship, peace, cultural exchange, and honor as well as competitive values such as determination, courage, striving, and fair play. The values people saw in the Olympics were unlike any other sport or event. It is what made the Olympics such a powerful draw for companies like Coca-Cola: by linking Coke to the Olympics, the Olympic values were associated in consumers' minds with their products. So our marketing offering was real, not just a pitch. And the meaning I had found in the Games was also keenly understood by the people of America. I just needed to convince more sponsors of that.

REVIVING THE MARKETING EFFORT

My meeting with Krimsky had left me uneasy. The more confidence he exuded, the less confidence I felt. I asked him to send me an example of his most recent sales presentation. What I had expected to see was an analysis of the target company leading to a targeted sales pitch. Every company would have different reasons for possibly considering an Olympic sponsorship. An effective marketing proposal would be tied to those attributes. And, of course, there would be a calculation of the economic value that would be derived from becoming an Olympic sponsor. Companies don't pay millions of dollars to sponsor an event unless they are convinced they will get a good return on their money, at least they shouldn't.

What I got from Krimsky was a stack of color Kodak slides showing the different Olympic logos that were available, and prices. Other than a cover sheet naming the target, there was no link to the customer, no analysis of their needs, no calculation to compare our sponsorship with other alternatives. It was simply a generic sales brochure. I was sick. No wonder the USOC guys were only able to sell prior sponsors: they had nothing to convince new accounts why they should sign. We had a long, long way to go.

While there are many diverse reasons why different companies decide to sponsor the Olympics, most are drawn to the potential for the Olympics to positively impact their brand. Branding has become a big buzzword these days. The idea is straightforward: I think back to the time when I couldn't care whether I got a Coke, a Pepsi, or an RC Cola. They were all the same to me: sweet, delicious, and, because my Mom frowned on caffeine drinks, rare. At the soda machine, I would have selected whichever was closer to my pointer finger. Over the years, I began to associate Coke with all sorts of things I like: smiling young people, sports, music, the Olympics, and recently, polar bears. Those associations make me "feel good" about Coke, a lot better than I do about RC Cola (are you still out there RC?). So when I pick up a twelve-pack at the grocery store or step up to a soft drink machine, I'll push the Coke button (of course caffeine free, Mom) even if it costs a little more. It costs hundreds of millions a year to build and maintain the kind of brand Coke has.

So reason number one for sponsoring the Olympics is branding, particularly for companies like Coke, Budweiser, AT&T, Delta Airlines, and McDonald's, but also for Xerox and Panasonic.

The John Hancock Company had one most unusual benefit they got from the Games. Every Olympic year, the sales agents who reach a certain target, I believe it's called the President's Club, are invited to attend the Games with their spouse, all expenses paid by Hancock. The Company finds that in an Olympic year, the number of agents who reach the target expands dramatically, and then stays at the higher level thereafter. The Olympic trip jumps their sales production, permanently. The increase is quite large; it pays for their Olympic sponsorship many times over.

Some companies become Olympic sponsors to put their products on display, either to the spectators and corporate chieftains who come to the Games, or to the folks at home. In Salt Lake, York International surely considered the opportunity to show off its heating and cooling equipment to executives who came to the Games. By giving SLOC their equipment as VIK, it was installed in virtually every venue. York marketing folks were free to take prospective customers on tours of our massive installed systems, all of which were performing flawlessly. Certified Angus Beef was quite literally putting out a platter of their product every day to hundreds of thousands of people. Of course, showcasing product is what brought IBM to the Olympics for so many years. People knew that IBM computers and systems were powering the Olympics; if IBM could do that job, they could do any job. The IBM relationship began to fall apart in Atlanta. Billy Paine, my counterpart in Atlanta, was so proud of what had been assembled by IBM and his team at the central systems command center that he announced to arriving media that it was the most advanced and sophisticated in the world. He did tours himself in the days leading up to the Games. But then the system encountered some start-up glitches: scoring sheets, comparative times from races, even the finish order of athletes could not be produced. The sponsorship was an effective showcase, but in this case, IBM didn't like what it was showing.

IBM would make sure that the Atlanta debacle never happened again. So when Nagano preparations began, IBM loaded the job with literally thousands of their people. Of course, the cost ballooned, and IBM insisted that Nagano pay for the amount of resources they had contributed that were above their sponsorship VIK figure. By the time our Games rolled around, IBM was estimating that SLOC would have to pay well above $100 million that we would get from them in sponsor VIK. My predecessors concluded that the figure was way high and urged the IOC to drop IBM and find another technology sponsor or consortium of sponsors. I wasn't there at the time, but either IBM was dropped or it quit, depending on which side you believe. But the deal was over. Now the Olympic movement would have to find new sponsors to take IBM's place, and SLOC would have to guide the integration of all the products. Both were huge tasks. But what we had going for us in our marketing pitch was the fact that whoever provided technology to us could brag to the world that they had done what IBM couldn't. And as it turned out, they did it without flaw and at a fraction of IBM's price.

There were a number of companies who derived much of their sponsorship value from showing off their products: Visa, Panasonic (giant video boards), Samsung (cell phones), General Motors, Nu Skin (facial products used by spectators), Sensormatic (security systems and equipment), Lucent Technologies (telecommunication equipment), and a host of others.

It seemed that each company had its own unique mix of benefits from Olympic sponsorship. One of the most unusual was Smith's Food and Drug Stores. In exchange for becoming a sponsor, Smith's would be the place where we would distribute free tickets to our Medals Plaza concerts and sell event tickets. That meant that literally hundreds of thousands of people in Utah would have to go to Smith's. And while they were there, they would probably grocery shop, potentially forming new shopping patterns and loyalty. For this benefit, SLOC would get millions.

Usually, these benefits didn't immediately come to the mind of a target sponsor. Our marketing job was to fashion a series of features that would match the target's unique mix of interests and then make that very clear to the company. At Smith's, for example, the idea of linking their sponsorship to the distribution of tickets, especially our free concert series, was what inked the deal. And it was our job to do the creative thinking because we knew the Games as they could not, especially if they had never been sponsors before. That's why I was so distressed to see the Krimsky pitch materials (and later to see a live pitch to a prospect). There was almost no crafting of benefits and features that matched the target's needs. Good salesmanship isn't fast, glib talk. The best salesmanship is about research, creative engineering of benefits and features to match the target's needs, preparation of effective communications, and finally delivering the proposal itself, in person. If we were ever going to come close to our marketing target, I would have to revamp marketing.

Of course, SLOC had not built its own marketing organization. Don Stirling had been brought on to sell to Utah companies and to represent our interests with the USOC. According to an agreement signed at the creation of the Salt Lake Olympic Committee, the USOC had sole custody of the marketing process. Yet SLOC was going to have to work within the confines of the joint venture agreement to take a more direct role in marketing. Within the first one hundred days we had hired our own Olympic marketing specialist, a very capable fellow named Mark Lewis. One of the things he was able to tell me was how much money had been raised in Atlanta.

SALT LAKE VS. ATLANTA

I was happy to finally have real numbers to compare, but the picture they painted was bleak. The total amount Atlanta had raised in sponsorship revenues was only $480 million. How could that be? Our budget required $859 million, 80 percent more than Atlanta! Summer Games are more expensive than Winter Games. How could it be possible that we had to raise more money in order to break even?

The fact was that the Atlanta Summer Games were more expensive to host than our Winter Games. But Summer Games had other sources of revenue which more than made up for the difference. Atlanta's non-sponsorship revenues were way larger than ours could be, so we had to make up the difference with sponsor dollars.

Here's where Atlanta had an advantage: 1) Summer Games were allocated twice as much broadcast revenue by the IOC as we were; 2) they were given twice the share of IOC TOP sponsor revenue as we were; 3) USOC was taking a much bigger share of the U.S. sponsorship revenues from our Games than they did from Atlanta; and 4) Atlanta would get three times as much ticket revenue as we could.

The ticketing disparity deserves some explanation. Events for the Summer Games are held in arenas that hold up to 80,000 people. For top track and field events, Atlanta was able to sell 80,000 tickets. Our top events for winter events could only be held in much smaller venues: mountain sites and ice rinks are only so big. Freestyle aerials accommodated only 11,000 ticket-holders. Women's figure skating, our marquis event, was held in the Delta Center, home of the Utah Jazz NBA basketball team. But an Olympic-sized ice rink is so much bigger than a basketball court; we had to take out the front rows to meet Olympic specifications. With all the "seat kills," we could only fit 15,000 seats in the arena.

Atlanta had close to $600 million dollars in ticket sales. Nagano came in at barely $80 million. We were hoping to get $180 million, more than double the high mark for Winter Games but hardly in a league with Atlanta's take.

The Summer Games cost 1.4 times as much to produce as the Winter Games, but they got as much as two to three times the revenue from sources other than sponsorships. Of course, the analysis led me to the IOC to increase our share of TOP sponsors and broadcast, and then to the USOC to re-cut the marketing deal.

I went to the IOC with my analysis, complete with a detailed cost comparison of Summer and Winter Games. They almost threw me out of the room. What I was saying threatened the age-old maxim that Summer Games deserved twice the revenue share as Winter Games. There was no willingness whatsoever to consider my findings or to look at numbers. Being right was irrelevant; the deal was set and it had been agreed to by Salt Lake long before I got there. All true.

The USOC was just as helpful. The deal had been signed in 1997 by Tom Welch and there was no going back now. They needed and wanted the money, too. Of course, the deal had been signed by Tom when he had no option: the USOC rights to the Olympic brand in the U.S. put SLOC over a barrel. True, but irrelevant at this point.

When I was able to get someone to listen to my arguments, they usually had a problem believing that Summer Games only cost 1.4 times as much as Winter Games. That's what the Atlanta and Salt Lake numbers showed, but was it really true? Aren't there many more events and people in the Summer Games than just 1.4 times as many?

The reason Summer and Winter Games are as close in cost is that there are many Olympic costs that don't depend on size. One of our biggest direct expenses was for information technology—systems, computers, telecommunications, etc. And most of our IT cost would be the same whether we had ten venues and ten events or twenty. It was the same with security, our other huge expense. Security on the side of a mountain for 10,000 people actually costs a lot more than security in a stadium for 80,000 people: the stadium has only a few fixed entrances; the mountain needs a massive perimeter, manned day and night.

I was like an old man with a bad knee: I was telling everyone I could about my problem. It didn't help with the IOC, the USOC, or my friends. It did help convince a few folks in Congress that we really did need their continued help. But most of all, it told us to get off our derrieres and get selling.

BAD NEWS AND GOOD NEWS

Mark Lewis had brought me the figures on Atlanta. John Krimsky finally came through with his top ten prospects list. It read like a Who's Who in corporate America. I breathed a sigh of relief. If these companies were ready to sign, if they were ready to go, we had a fighting chance. I noticed that some of the companies were familiar: I had worked as a consultant at one and knew executives at a few of the others. Not content to wait for Krimsky to tell me when they would be actually signing, I called them. Gary Crittenden, a fellow I had tried to recruit for Fraser's job, was CFO at Monsanto, and Monsanto was on the list. He was my first call. Gary checked with his marketing folks. No one he could find had ever heard from the USOC, never seen a presentation or a proposal. I flushed. The next calls reported the same thing. Krimsky's top ten prospects list hadn't even been contacted. This was a wish list, looked up in a directory.

Mark, Don Stirling, and I met with Kelly Flint to find out whether we had a legal right to go around the USOC directly to prospective sponsors. It was clear they were not on the job; if we waited for them, we would risk going bankrupt. Kelly had drafted the joint marketing agreement between SLOC and the USOC. He advised that we could hire additional sales people for our SLOC office but that we would have to have the USOC salesmen tag along if we went outside Utah. That was fine. We also decided to insist that the USOC put more people and more responsibility in their local Salt Lake office. I had met the local USOC rep, Chris Sullivan, and found him approachable, honest and capable.

We had Mark and Don, we would hire more salesmen, we would push the USOC locally, and I would hit the road as well. But we needed more than that. With the size of the budget gap, the ongoing allegations of bribery, and the absence of any real pipeline, we knew we needed more. Mark's suggestion: hire a top sports marketing company to supplement the USOC.

We figured that would be a battle. Krimsky's reputation as a marketing guru was so well publicized, and cultivated, that the likelihood of his agreeing to hire an outside marketing firm had to be nil. SLOC had no authority to retain marketing help on our own. While Schulz and Hybil were technically the top guys at the USOC, in reality they were completely deferential to Krimsky's wishes.

Out of the blue, I got a call from Krimsky. He said he wanted to hire a sports marketing firm to help get new sponsors. He hoped we would be willing to go along with his request for help. He had selected a company called the International Management Group (IMG). Talk about speechless!

As it turns out, there was method to his madness. Krimsky had been preparing to leave the USOC for months. United Airlines was creating a new position at a key contractor just for him. So by hiring IMG, he was preventing a charge that he was leaving us in the lurch. The less charitable among us were of the view that he was leaving to avoid being blamed for failing to meet the marketing budget he was so confident we would reach. The more charitable felt he was offered a better job. But one thing was sure: when he was expressing his confidence he would deliver the budgeted sponsorships, he had to know he was not going to be the one who had to do it.

Fortunately, Krimsky had chosen well with IMG. The firm's senior VP, Rob Prazmark, was a gifted sports marketer with Olympic experience. Years earlier, he had helped craft the TOP program for the IOC. He also proved to be an indefatigable workhorse on the road. And best of all, he was an eternal optimist. In Rob's view, there was no company that shouldn't be an Olympic sponsor; he'd go anywhere to get a first meeting with a prospect. Rob also convinced his colleagues at IMG to assign ten or twelve other sales personnel to the Olympic project.

Mark, Don, Kelly, new SLOC salespersons, and IMG—by April 1999, we had the right stuff.

PULLING OUT ALL THE STOPS

The SLOC team started on the phone. I called every business contact I knew. Mark and Don were doing the same. Rob at IMG went to work to put together a first-class marketing presentation, one that could be modified to match the needs of any given prospect. Combined with a mail campaign he would launch, he was ready to put some leads into the national pipeline. But the pump had to be primed; we needed some success to dispel the "damaged goods" moniker that had been stuck to us since the scandal.

There's an old salesman's adage: *if you're going hunting, start in the zoo.* That saying had already taken Krimsky to the companies that had previously been Olympic sponsors. For us now, we felt that the best zoo to hunt was probably Utah. Don Stirling had been working with Utah companies for months. In fact, he had had a pretty good pipeline of companies until the scandal had spooked them.

With a list of all Utah companies with revenues of at least $50 million, Don Stirling assigned those of us with personal contacts to get to work on the phones. But our first priority was to revive the leads that had gone cold.

THREE UTAH HEROES

Don had been working on O.C. Tanner for over a year. It was America's leading "recognition" company, manufacturing and marketing lapel pins that recognize an employee's years of service in his or her company. Because it was a private concern, we didn't know how big it was, but it had showed interest and that was all we were looking for. O.C. Tanner's CEO and I were friends: a mutual friend had introduced me to Kent Murdock years before. We went on a vacation in the Caribbean together and regularly exchanged Christmas greetings. One of O.C. Tanner's board members was also a friend: Chase Petersen had been an officer at Harvard where we had grown close. Don set up a meeting with the CEO. He and I delivered as strong a pitch as we could muster. He was sufficiently persuaded that he scheduled a meeting with his board of directors.

Our proposal to O.C. Tanner was that they make and contribute the more than three hundred Olympic medals: gold, silver, and bronze. Officially, they would be called a supplier to the Games. There were three attractions for O.C. Tanner. First, as the folks who produced the medals, they would be seen as the undisputed champion in their industry. Second, they would be heroes in the Utah community. The founder's daughter, now chairperson of the board, was the Episcopalian bishop for Utah. This company had deep roots in the community. Finally, an Olympic sponsorship would build even more loyalty and goodwill with their employees. This last feature was an important element of the O.C. Tanner culture. Quarterly, they had all-company meetings where products and people were recognized and celebrated. They were, after all, a recognition company; they practiced what they preached. Critical to their decision was whether SLOC would make them proud or ashamed. The financial commitment, nearly $3 million, was much, much larger than anything they had ever done.

The board meeting was cordial, but not effusive. They asked probing questions, geared to assess where we were heading as an organizing committee. Fundamentally, were we going to be a success or a disappointment? I sat in the front lobby afterward to await their decision. CEO Murdock stepped out of the meeting following their discussion; he said it went well. Days later, he called to announce that it was official.

Questar, the local natural gas company, was another one of those companies that Don Stirling had been working with for a long time. Here again, we were looking for several million dollars of support, this time in natural gas for our venues. Utilities don't have wide margins or fat profits, so giving away free natural gas was not an easy thing. What we were asking for was unlike anything they had ever even considered before. Questar's Chairman Don Cash was on my board at SLOC. We spoke time and again about the sponsorship. It was clear that he was particularly concerned that if they went ahead, they would be given as good a deal as any other sponsor. Don Cash knew that sometimes in business, it pays to wait until the last minute, when desperation drives a better bargain. But getting a new sponsor signed up right away was critical to re-igniting our sales effort. It was critical to him and President Nick Rose, the point person on the deal, that we commit to a true "most favored nation" policy. That way, they would be promised, in writing, that if we gave a better deal to anybody else, we would retroactively apply it to them. We would get the momentum up front, and he'd get the best deal. Agreed. We were ready to go with Questar.

A third Utah company marketed ski outerwear: coats, sweaters, gloves, etc. Our proposal to the Marker company was that they provide the outerwear that would be worn by the 23,000 volunteers, 2000 staff and 1000 officials; about $20 million worth of gear. It was Ed Eynon, our head of human resources, and in charge of our volunteer program, who would drive Mark, Don and me to ink this deal. He knew that one of the biggest attractions to becoming and staying a volunteer was a great uniform. In my effort to trim the budget, I had decided that we would have only as good a uniform as we could get contributed to us. So Ed, knowing how important it would be to our volunteer program, was relentless.

Mark, Don and I met with CEO Darryl Santos and his management team time and again. His financial backers came to town as well. Mark fashioned a most creative deal. We put on our best show, but we knew it was a hard sell. Our friends at the USOC had just made it a good deal harder for us.

The USOC announced that they had signed a sponsor to provide the uniforms that the American athletes would be wearing in opening ceremonies. Roots—of Canada (!)—would get the honor. But the deal they had agreed to did not provide anything for us, not one single uniform for our volunteers. Of course, the uniforms that everyone would see on TV would be the U.S. Olympic Team uniforms. Roots only had to clothe a few hundred athletes compared to the 26,000 uniforms we would need. Yet Roots would reap the plum marketing prize. This wasn't lost on the folks at Marker. And the nature of our partnership with the USOC wasn't lost on me either.

I can't say why Marker came through, but they did. Frankly, I can't think of a more critical and beneficial sponsorship, coming when it did.

Don managed to corral all three companies for a combined announcement on the weekend of May 14, 1999, timed to coincide with the unveiling of our Olympic mascots. We bundled everything together in the hope of breaking through the regular news clutter to send the message to corporate America: "we're back." It was a big production; fireworks, music, and the entire SLOC staff and community were invited. We were putting "a new face on the Games." Nick Rose from Questar spoke about his company being motivated to step up and support SLOC in the wake of scandal, to support the people of Utah. "It heightened our resolve," he was quoted as saying. The Reverend Carolyn Tanner Irish, chairwoman of O.C. Tanner and an Episcopal bishop in Utah, spoke of moving forward. And Daryl Santos, president of Marker, paid us the high compliment of saying that it was the "greedy capitalist" in him that motivated the deal. That's what we wanted companies all over to hear: the Olympics were still very good business, not just a charity case.

We had broken the sponsor drought. And it was significant that the corporate community in Utah had stepped up. Everywhere I went, from new sponsorship calls to meetings with federal officials and legislators in Washington, D.C., people would ask what the state of Utah was doing to support the Games. I could answer with numbers, not just platitudes. We were bankable again and there was no time to lose.

Chapter 8

NEGOTIATION
AND THE IOC

The IOC was key to getting straight with the bank. Jim Nash at Bank of America was nervous about his commitment to provide a working capital line of up to $190 million for us. Olympic contracts are structured in such a way that almost half of SLOC's broadcasting and sponsorship revenues would come in lump sums *after* the Games. Some payments extended beyond 2004 to as long as five years. Most of our ticketing revenue would come in the months just prior to the Games. Yet the lion's share of our $1.5 billion direct operating expenses would be incurred years in advance. As a matter of course, we tried deferring payments for goods or services until after March 2002. We had some luck getting partners to postpone invoicing SLOC until our broadcasting, sponsorship, and ticketing revenues had hit. But the contractors building our venues, the lawyers staving off a potential indictment, the employees receiving weekly paychecks at SLOC; none of these groups could accept postponement of payment. We also had ongoing obligations to the IOC and the USOC, and our contract with the state called for a $98 million payment in January 2002, one month *before* the

Games. A cash flow analysis, projecting scheduled expenditures and revenue disbursements over time, indicated that we might need the full $190 million in short-term working capital loans to make it through.

Bank of America had extended a line of credit to SLOC in 1998. Around the same time, they signed on as an Olympic sponsor, donating over $50 million in cash and services. But the lending arrangements were independent of the sponsorship deal. The line of credit had to be renewed annually and was subject to adjustment every March. Depending on our financial prospects, Jim Nash could decide to sharply reduce our line of credit or pull the plug. Exploratory inquiries with other banks were anything but encouraging. We needed to keep our account with Bank of America.

In March 1999, the bank renewed our line. But they lowered the amount we could borrow by $40 million. Publicly, the comment was that this was standard procedure; that credit amounts were often adjusted and, indeed, had been adjusted down for the Atlanta Games. "Lines of credit fluctuate all the time as a general rule" was the statement. But in private consultations, Jim Nash expressed concern about SLOC's ability to meet its financial obligations. In particular, he complained about payments to the IOC, USOC and to the state of Utah that were scheduled to precede our repayments to them. Banks never, never like to be paid last.

Over the course of ten years, $59 million of state sales tax revenues that otherwise would have gone to Utah cities and towns went to build sport venues that were promised to go to SLOC if Salt Lake were successful in winning the Games bid. When the Games were awarded and SLOC was created, a contract was signed making SLOC responsible for paying $1 million back to Utah cities and towns upon the completion of the venues and the other $58 million a month before the Games were to begin, plus an additional $40 million endowment for future operating expenses. Though it might seem odd to require full reimbursement of a cash advance the month before the Games, the whole point was to guarantee that no matter what contingencies came into play during the Games themselves, Utah taxpayers would get their money.

This did not sit well with Jim Nash. Neither did the fact that SLOC was required to make regular royalty payments to the IOC and USOC on sponsorship, licensing, and ticket revenues as they came in. By the bank's calculation, that put them fourth in line. Our loan with Bank of America would not come to full maturity until March 31, 2002, and by that time, many of SLOC's obligations to the state and the Olympic organizations would already have been met.

In Nash's view, the state of Utah, the IOC, and the USOC were all stakeholders in the 2002 Winter Games. They were all in a position to directly benefit from their investment. Stakeholders get their money out at the end of a deal, not at the beginning. Banks come first.

Nash let me know that this arrangement was unacceptable. Though he did not explicitly tie the bank's position to the impact of the scandal, the bank was "no longer confident" of its credit position "given recent developments." Some on the SLOC board protested that Bank of America was using the scandal as an excuse to change the deal, but that was really beside the point. They had the money, and we needed it. Nash said that unless we were able to delay payment to our other creditors and settle the bank's account first, he would not renew our line of credit. There was nothing to do but approach the IOC, the USOC, and the state of Utah to ask for forbearance.

I knew it wouldn't be easy. The whole point of the state payment schedule was to guarantee that Utah taxpayers would get their money out first. I knew that politicians could demagogue the change as "putting a private bank ahead of the public." But if we didn't keep the bank line of credit, we wouldn't have Games and if we didn't have Games, the cities and towns would get precisely zero. Give the forbearance and the cities and towns had a shot at the whole $99 million. Despite the compelling logic, at least in my mind, Bill Shaw and our government relations folks didn't rate our chances as high as I had hoped.

I knew the debate in the legislature would be the most contentious. Since concessions from the IOC and USOC were also required, we determined to secure their cooperation first. The hope was to approach the state with royalty payment concessions from the IOC and the USOC already in hand. If everyone else had given, they'd feel the pressure to go along as well.

I put a trip to the IOC first even though I knew less about them than I did about the USOC. But I figured they couldn't be any worse. In almost every interaction we had had, the USOC had been indecisive, internally confused and political, and resistant to any change that might affect in the slightest their self-interest. I knew that the bank concessions I wanted from the IOC would just be the beginning of the special help I would want from it; I might as well get started.

THE IOC

The IOC is ostensibly a democratic institution. Voting members on the IOC are asked to decide everything from leadership, to the site of each Olympics, to changes and amendments to the Olympic charter. But, at least at the time, it was also something of an authoritarian regime. The same man, His Excellency, Juan Antonio Samaranch, had been re-elected to power again and again and had, it is fair to say, almost single-handedly shaped the modern Olympic movement. Samaranch was the focus of a great deal of media skepticism, particularly here in the United States. During the scandal, there were frequent and repeated calls for his resignation. He, more than anyone, seemed to typify the cronyism, ostentation, and abuse that plagued the public image of the Olympic movement. Much of the criticism was likely well-founded. Whatever the Olympics had become, Samaranch had to claim responsibility. And yet, in my personal dealings with the man, I found him reasonable and decisive.

Within my first month on the job, just prior to my meetings with Jim Nash, President Samaranch wrote requesting a meeting with me at IOC headquarters to report my progress. I wrote back thanking him for his interest and support but explained that, with only a few weeks under my belt, I did not want to leave Salt Lake City for a trip abroad. I could hardly be expected to deliver a report on progress. Mr. Samaranch's gracious assistant, Madame Zweifel, called me to explain that my appearance in Lausanne was not negotiable. The IOC Executive Committee was anxious to get acquainted with me and I would put other interests aside. I was, in effect, being summoned to Lausanne.

So I went. In order to save money and to make it clear that my efforts in the future would be devoted to putting on the Games, not fulfilling protocol responsibilities, I went alone and I went only for one day. The executive board of the IOC was scheduled to meet on Monday and Tuesday, with a full convention of IOC meetings and business scheduled for the rest of the week and weekend. Standard procedure for Olympic organizing committee executives was apparently to arrive early in the week with a full entourage of support staff and stay throughout the week. I was being asked to deliver a status report on our transition on Tuesday, but my formal involvement with proceedings would end there. I made arrangements to fly into Lausanne on an all-night flight, arriving Tuesday morning. I made my way over to IOC headquarters—a stately campus near the banks of Lake Geneva.

THE EPICENTER

Things were still very much in commotion due to the ongoing investigations of the scandal. Dick Pound, the powerful IOC executive committee member from Canada, had not yet released the full findings of the IOC's own investigation and the hallways were filled with rumors as to who would be implicated and what punishments would be imposed. Salt Lake City's ethics board report in February had been followed by that from the USOC's investigative commission headed by former Senate Majority Leader George Mitchell of Maine. His assessment was that the IOC was chiefly to blame for the mistakes made by the Salt Lake City bid committee. "We do not excuse or condone those from Salt Lake City who did the giving. What they did was wrong. But, as we have noted, they did not invent this culture; they joined one that was already flourishing."

In the week leading up to the March IOC convention in Lausanne, Pound had added another half-dozen or so names to the list of IOC members under investigation and subject to corrective action, bringing the total to nearly a third of the organization's membership. A vote on expulsions and amendments to IOC policies was expected later in the week. Four IOC members had already resigned and another implicated in wrongdoing had passed away.

Prior to my official report, I met privately with President Samaranch and Anita DeFrantz, the only American on the IOC's prestigious executive board. We had a pleasant first encounter. Mr. Samaranch asked about my family and told me something about his own. I found him to be quite friendly and cordial, not stiff or overly formal. It was clear that he was amazed at the degree of media interest in the scandal. He expressed dismay at the growing publicity and the calls for reform. But he believed that most of the outrage was being manufactured by the press and did not represent the true feelings of the public.

My presentation to the IOC Executive Board was to be made in the conference room on the second floor. I waited in the lobby outside. On the agenda ahead of me was a delegation from Nagano, presenting the IOC with a copy of their final Games Report. A group of ten to fifteen Japanese exited the conference room, smiles beaming. It was astonishing to me that so many people would fly so far merely to present a bound volume. I would learn that I was the real anomaly: I had come alone to deliver SLOC's report. The executive board did not seem at all offended, at least publicly. Kevin Gosper, an IOC executive board member from Australia, later remarked in the press that it was the first time in his experience "that a report has been done by one man." He added, "It's a good thing he's not looking back over his shoulder. He's a man to look forward. We were very, very pleased to meet him for the first time and eye him up as he eyed us up."

After the Nagano delegation left, I waited briefly while the IOC met in a closed session. Fifteen or twenty minutes later the heavy doors swung open and Ms. DeFrantz and some of her colleagues on the executive committee came out to greet me. And as we were making our way back into the boardroom, I heard someone shouting. I recognized Mr. Kim, the powerful chairman of the media sub-committee. He was yelling at Mr. Pound and was gesticulating wildly in his direction. Mr. Samaranch left me to go over and quiet Mr. Kim. This was not the diplomatic, quiet decorum that characterized the century-old congregation of international diplomats. Later that evening, I got a call from a member of the press asking if I had witnessed Mr. Kim assuming the Taekwando stance. I guessed that I had, but had not recognized it as such. He had reportedly shouted "What do you want from me?" in Korean. Clearly he was feeling the pressure of behind-the-scenes negotiations preceding the release of the ethics panel report.

PRESENTING TO THE IOC

I chose to be complimentary and diplomatic in my remarks. After all, I would soon be asking for favors. I made no reference to our pressing need for royalty deferrals. Instead, I quoted President Samaranch from a speech he had made to the U.N. on a prior occasion. I spoke of the purpose and ideals of the Olympic movement, and expressed the hope that I would be able to fulfill that spirit in the work we would do in Salt Lake. I meant every word.

A number of the IOC executive board members expressed their support. I recognized that I would need a lot of help from the IOC, including voluntarily giving up certain privileges and financial considerations.

I did not want to aggravate a relationship that would be so important to us.

There were several factors that would assure constant tension between SLOC and the IOC. The most obvious was the recent history of the scandal itself. Things had gone terribly awry for the IOC on Salt Lake City's watch. The scandal was directly responsible for the expulsion of six IOC members and the public reprimand of many others. Atlanta, Nagano, and, most notably, Sydney would all be implicated along with SLOC and the IOC, but the story had been broken on a Salt Lake City news program and pursued by Salt Lake City newspapers. The incriminating documents were Salt Lake City documents. And there was definitely a palpable feeling among the members of the IOC that Salt Lake City and SLOC had not suffered as much as the IOC.

I urged the members in my presentations not to confuse the current administration of the Salt Lake Organizing Committee with the bid committee, but with only limited success. I represented Salt Lake. I also represented the United States and I would be made to feel the salience of that fact.

Since the scandal had broken in Salt Lake City, U.S. agencies were taking the lead on the criminal investigation. The threat of subpoenas and other Congressional action against key members of the IOC constantly hung over their heads. I hoped the IOC would not confuse SLOC with the FBI or U.S. Government, but in many countries, there was no wall between government prosecutors and the Olympic committee. Why didn't I just make the investigation go away? In this setting, securing forbearance and favors would be difficult, to say the least.

Added to this context was the fact that my requests of the IOC were frequently at odds with their tradition, protocol, and conservatism. Over the years, I would need three things from the IOC: financial assistance including the forbearance on scheduled royalty payments; authorization for changes to be made to Olympic protocol; and approval to reduce services and benefits for IOC members during the Games. I was going to be about as popular at IOC meetings as a mink coat at a PETA convention.

SEOUL

My June 1999 presentation to the IOC was to be held in Korea. I was finally ready to give the executive board a full picture of our budget needs. I had pre-wired all of my requests with IOC staff, Marc Hodler, chairman of the coordination committee, Jean-Claude Killy who headed the organizing committee in Albertville and was an Olympic gold medalist, and other key board members. I had learned that most of what happens in these meetings has to be agreed to by the board before the meeting begins, with me outside the room. The give and take I was used to in American meetings was foreign in IOC settings. Agreements were worked out before the meetings; the meetings were a formality.

I outlined in detail our initial budget assessments and standing deficits. Our initial efforts to find cost reductions in the SLOC operating budget had led us to reduce the amount allocated for Games-time accommodations and services to IOC members by over a million dollars. The cuts were mostly in personnel, like reducing the number of drivers traditionally provided to IOC members during the Olympics. Further, I proposed that we would host the IOC and Olympic Family at the Little America Hotel rather than the five-star Grand America across the street. Finally, I broached the subject of deferral of all payments that were to be made by SLOC to the IOC. I reviewed the bank's ultimatum and its implications. I acknowledged that such forbearance by the IOC placed their payments at higher risk: they would be getting their money only after the Games were over. Any financial shortfall would mean they might not be paid at all. It also meant SLOC would save several million dollars in interest costs; it would cost the IOC the same.

I had expected intense questioning and concern, mixed with a bit of anger. There could also be insistence that I get the State of Utah and the USOC to agree first, or at least simultaneously—a task that would be hard to achieve. But that's not what happened. Samaranch seized the microphone as soon as I had finished speaking. "The IOC will work with you to help solve your financial problems. I would like you to meet with a small working group to work out the details of the arrangements before you leave, if that is acceptable." Unlike the other meetings I would attend, in this case President Samaranch left no room for other board members to speak. The matter was closed, and closed in my favor. My response was simple: "Thank you, Mr. President."

The next morning, Marc Hodler, Michael Payne, Dick Pound, François Carrard and I sat down together. Payne was the IOC's head of marketing, Carrard was the staff equivalent of what we would call the COO. We worked out the outline of the forbearance agreement. It deferred until the month after the Games all royalties due the IOC on sponsorships, licensed merchandise sales, and ticket sales. It was contingent, however, on the USOC and the state of Utah ultimately agreeing to the forbearance that was required of them. I surmised that this was designed to both protect the IOC's interests and to give me the ammunition I would need with Utah and the USOC.

And that, as they say, was that. I was amazed at how businesslike and expeditious the IOC had been. Even more, it was clear that despite the anger expressed by the IOC membership at large, the executive board, or more particularly President Samaranch, wanted to see us produce successful Games and they were willing to help us even if that meant cutting back IOC perks and payments. It was a very different result than I had been led to believe I would get from the IOC. It was a good sign.

ASKING FOR A LARGER TOP SHARE FOR SLOC

My other request at the meeting in Seoul was not so well received. As it was, the Winter Games were entitled to one share of aggregated international TOP sponsorship revenues, roughly 16 2/3 percent. Summer Games received twice as much despite the fact that their comparative costs were less than 50 percent. I laid out my analysis.

But my presentation touched on the third rail of IOC relations: the disproportionate role of the U.S. in financing the IOC and the Olympic movement. The relevance was that SLOC was unable to secure these U.S.-based companies as sponsors; they were reserved for the IOC. Eight of the eleven existing TOP partners were headquartered in the United States. Because we received no direct funds from our government, we needed a larger portion of the financial support from these companies.

This time, I got the intense reaction I had expected from my prior request. It was clear, vehement, and passionate. Dr. Thomas Bach asserted that while eight IOC TOP sponsors were American based, they were international in their scope, deriving 90 percent of their revenues from international sources. I checked that out later: the point was fair but the percentage was not. Dr. Rogge pointed out that the USOC was already taking a lion's share of the TOP pie, and that giving any more to a U.S. entity would be terribly inappropriate. This was also true. Of the TOP proceeds, the majority goes to the national Olympic Committees for their operation, and the USOC received fully one half of that total, a share equal to all the other countries combined. Giving any more to SLOC, another U.S. entity, would add insult to injury. My numbers on the costs of Summer versus Winter were good, but his point was undeniable. Marc Hodler made the sole comment in my favor, but as the universally recognized and biased advocate of the Winter Games, the others did not give his support much weight. I left Seoul with what I needed: forbearance for our bank financing. I didn't fret about what had been turned down; if I never heard them say no, I wouldn't know if I had left money on the table.

USOC AND STATE APPROVAL

With the IOC's agreement to defer royalty payments until March 2002, we were in position to pursue our case with the USOC. Far more modest concessions were needed from the USOC, yet the process of securing their approval was more cumbersome, time consuming and frustrating. My argument was that things had changed since the Games were awarded and we needed to recognize that. We had suffered from the scandal—Salt Lake's fault. We had been misled by John Krimsky's marketing budget—the USOC's fault. We were all in the hole together and together we would have to get out. Both sides should give.

The final deal did just that. The USOC gave SLOC the payment concessions we needed to satisfy the bank. SLOC agreed to give the USOC special hotel accommodations as well as accreditation advantages. We agreed to donate $1 million of VIK advertising space in *Sports Illustrated* and *Time* magazine to the USOC in exchange for $2 million in cash to help fund pre-Games training operations, which we further reduced in scale and schedule. The USOC used the advertising VIK to launch an add campaign promoting their image in the wake of the scandal, something we had previously declined to participate in. The whole exchange was punctuated by terse letters from lawyers, an "inadvertent" leak of confidential documents to the press, maddening delays, and high levels of frustration on both sides: a typical negotiation.

State approval was a noisy affair. There was no avoiding the fact that the deferral of money to be paid to the public in favor of accelerating a payment to a private bank would be the occasion for grandstanding. Legislators were quick to point out that when Bank of America had granted the line of credit, they expressly acknowledged the prior payment to Utah as a feature of their proposal. I had the same point to make as with the USOC: that was then, and this is now. Things had changed. One of the most important was that Utah had already put its money in and the bank had not. Point to self: remember, last in, first out.

Again, there were two payments that were to be made to Utah: $59 million in repayment for venues constructed by Utah in contemplation of winning the Games, and $40 million for an endowment. Deferral of the $40 million endowment was quickly agreed. But delaying repayment of the $59 million was another matter. "They're playing hardball," complained one state representative. "We don't want to be a stumbling block, but we also don't want to be a scapegoat," asserted the Senate majority leader. SLOC should seek concessions from its corporate sponsors. "Why does it have to be public money at risk rather than the beneficiaries of the Games?"

Quite understandably, state officials didn't want public money to be at risk. But truth be told, it was probably at risk no matter what they did. It would be practically inconceivable that if Utah took out its $59 million first and the bank couldn't be repaid in full, that the bank wouldn't come after the state to make up any shortfall.

But politics and public perception were at play. We came up with an idea to place a $229 million payment from NBC that was due to SLOC two weeks after the Games in escrow until the full $99 million had been repaid to Utah. We would pay interest on the deferred amount between the original January repayment date and the newly scheduled repayment of March 8th. The proposal was good enough for everyone to claim victory. The legislature eventually approved the deferral measure with no time to spare. The time and work and energy that had been invested to get the parties to do what was actually in their own best interest was a precursor of what we would see again and again.

DOCUMENT DISCLOSURE PROBLEMS WITH THE IOC

A constant source of tension between SLOC and the IOC was our commitment to public disclosure and transparency. An integral part of our new culture in the wake of the scandal was the invitation to the public to attend SLOC board meetings and to inspect SLOC files and documents.

Almost immediately after our announcement of transparency, we were bombarded with requests for documents by the local newspapers and by journalists from national and international media outlets. Most of the requests pertained to the scandal and inappropriate dealings between the Salt Lake bid committee and various members of the IOC. Both SLOC's ethics panel report and the IOC Judicial Commission report alluded to SLOC documents they had reviewed that were not yet public; we were flooded with requests to see them.

One of the early requests came from an Australian journalist interested in reports that an Australian IOC member had accepted lavish vacations for himself and family members to resorts in Utah and to the 1995 Super Bowl in Miami, Florida. A request was made for all documents relating to or naming IOC member Phillip Coles. We made sure that Mr. Coles was not a part of the federal probe, collected a stack of receipts and correspondence associated with Mr. Coles, about an inch thick, and released them according to our policy.

The documents included within them information about Mr. Coles' countryman, Kevan Gosper, the powerful and friendly IOC vice president and executive board member. The files were not incriminating—Mr. Gosper appeared to have paid his own way when coming to Salt Lake City to meet with city officials—but they did give a glimpse of the extent to which the bid committee had solicited his allegiance. They also "fed the beast," allowing the media to keep writing stories, filled with guilt by mention. Long personal letters were reproduced from Tom Welch to Mr. Gosper and his wife, inviting them to all-expense-paid river rafting trips, skiing adventures, private dinners with the governor, unsolicited airplane tickets purchased and forwarded. They looked like something you'd get in an email spam. "You have been identified as one of the four key individuals who must see our city if we are to win." These documents were not incriminating to any degree beyond that which had already been discovered. Mr. Coles already had been reprimanded by the IOC and Mr. Gosper had resisted the entreaties from Tom Welch. But the public release of the data continued to stir coals we were all hoping would die down. And the fact that releases came piecemeal, months and years after the ethics panels had concluded their reports, kept the story alive. And our influential friend, Mr. Gosper, was dragged through another indignity.

Given that reality, there were more than a few who viewed our policy of transparency and the resulting water-torture releases of documents as self-defeating. The scandal kept generating headlines. We never were able to put the scandal securely behind us. We kept waiting for the media appetite to diminish. It never did. But our commitment to transparency and public scrutiny was not up for discussion.

Ironically, our only hope of distinguishing ourselves from the bid committee and the abuses of the past was in fully complying with the media requests which in turn had the effect of perpetuating the story of the abuses. Of course, any effort on our part to interrupt the free flow of information or limit access to documents would make us complicit with past mistakes. I wanted to make dead sure that the argument could never be made that SLOC had something to hide, that we had participated in a cover-up of any kind. If we were to err, I wanted to err on the side of too much disclosure. This did not sit well with the IOC, since so many of the names included in such documents were still active members intent on rebuilding the IOC reputation for integrity and fair play. All of this came to a head in Rio de Janeiro at a general meeting of the IOC membership.

GELD

There was a single document in the SLOC archives that achieved something of mythic status in the month leading up to our June 2000 meeting in Brazil. The existence of the so-called "geld memo" was first reported on KTVX Channel 4, the same news station that broke the bid scandal. The memo was not addressed to anyone in particular and had apparently never been delivered to any addressee.

It was an internal working document. But it had been discovered by SLOC's attorneys on a disc believed to have come from former Vice President David Johnson's bid committee computer. It was dated to 1991, shortly after Salt Lake had lost its bid for the 1998 Games to Nagano. The word *geld* means money in several languages, including Flemish, the second language spoken by David Johnson. As it was described in the press, the memo was essentially a list of IOC voting members with notes next to some of their names listing gifts given or intended to be given. Some of the names reportedly had the word *geld* next to them. It was a cryptic notation but more than evocative.

With several allegations of inappropriate payoffs already reported and the feeling in the air that there must still be more to be found, it took about a millisecond for several news organizations to jointly request the memo. I wanted to get it out as fast as possible. It was anticipated by the media like a page out of the *Maltese Falcon* screenplay—a holy grail or a smoking gun. The truth was somewhat more prosaic. I took a look at the document that had become such a target of speculation. It was a list of IOC member names. The word *geld* did appear next to some of them, without further explanation. Information about likes, dislikes and special interests of individual members was listed. There was nothing more than what had been covered already in the previously released files. The word *geld* was interesting, but it appeared next to some names that otherwise had no bearing in the case and it did not appear next to names that had already been determined to have accepted cash payments. Other words like "cookies" and *jonge*—apparently a Flemish term for bachelor—also appeared in the document. And most of the names on the list had no notations at all.

I was very, very anxious to release it and be done with the speculation and hype, but our attorneys in Washington held us back. With SLOC still potentially the subject of federal investigation and indictment, the last thing we should do was release something that might be viewed by Justice as compromising their investigation. Their concern was that the government could intend to use the document to corroborate or contradict Johnson's or others' grand jury testimony; releasing it could potentially compromise their prosecution.

Critics, including attorneys for KTVX, protested that the government had had plenty of time to make use of the document and that SLOC should not feel bound. I myself argued that we should give the government a 60-day waiting period and grant the document's release after that. I took the matter to SLOC's management committee. By a 12-5 decision, the management committee trustees voted to refuse the media's data request until the government could give SLOC assurance that our release would not be found to interfere with their investigation. That assurance came while I was with the IOC in Rio.

The document hung like a gargoyle over my presentations to the IOC. We depended on IOC meetings to secure required approvals for a wide range of elements in our Games. At this meeting, we needed approval for our venue construction and specifications, for our ceremonies and other creative elements, for transportation, technology, scheduling, ticket pricing, accreditations and accommodations. We were seeking approval for seven new sport events including women's bobsled and men's and women's skeleton.

But with the issue of the geld memo not resolved, members of the IOC were not anxious to focus on our problems, if we were not focused on theirs.' The IOC had requested to see the document, but we declined. Journalists in Rio peppered me with questions. They were sure that the reason we had not released geld was that it was highly incriminating and embarrassing. Little did they know; I was dying to make it public. It was generating much more ink while withheld than it would when it was public.

I reiterated that we would not be releasing the document until we were given the go-ahead by the Justice Department. Then, when I was checking in at the Rio airport for my return flight, I got an urgent call from Brian Katz, our attorney at SLOC. Word had come that Justice was poised to release the *geld* document to the press. The action was right but the release coming from Justice would make it look like we were the party trying to cover up. I had no choice but to have Brian immediately release the geld document to the media. I then jumped on my flight and headed home.

The release of the document caused something of a whirlwind. Those IOC members who had the word *geld* next to them were quick to make statements in the press asserting their innocence. President Samaranch announced that the document would be reviewed by the IOC's newly formed ethics panel with an eye towards appropriate action. But anger among the membership of the IOC continued to burn.

At the next IOC congress three and a half months later, they were calling for my head. "Perhaps it's time for us to condemn people who continue to call into question our personal dignity, who question our honesty," said one member from Italy. "I think we have defended ourselves, and perhaps now it's time to attack."

"Perhaps we should see if we can do something legally to defend our dignity," said another in a public session. "It's really very irritating and regretful that we should be treated as bribed and bribers and totally corrupted." No actions were taken against individual members of the IOC as a result of the memo. Instead, the IOC Ethics Commission, which had been tasked with reviewing the document, reserved its reprimands for me. The suggestion was made by the head of the ethics commission, former World Court judge Keba Mbaye, an IOC member from Senegal, that members would be justified in suing SLOC for libel—either as individuals or in a class action suit.

During the time allotted for my update of SLOC's progress I was asked to put an end to the "lies and slurs" coming out about the bid committee's dealings with the IOC. I expressed regret for the consternation and confusion felt by certain members of the IOC. I was quick to stress that I was certain not everything written in bid committee documents was fair or even accurate. I shared their anger that the documents were even written at all. But I warned them that they should steel themselves against the pain such releases caused, because the federal probe had produced some 400 boxes of scandal-related documents and I was committed to giving the public access to them once they were de-classified. In the United States, the Games belonged to the public and the public had a right to the information.

Nothing substantive ever came of the heated words. Neither did the IOC's threats of litigation against us prove to be earnest. Threatening legal action is a pretty good way to underscore innocence. But the ongoing release of documents continued to play an unfortunate roll in our relationship with our partners at the IOC.

BUCKING PROTOCOL

On several occasions over the course of my three years dealing with the IOC, I sought exception to rules and procedures stipulated by the Olympic charter or practiced in conformity with longstanding tradition. In each instance, I felt our requests met the criteria of being common sense adjustments that would improve the Games or our ability to stage them. Our record of success in securing the changes was mixed, and seemed largely dependent upon whether or not President Samaranch himself was willing to move our issues forward or whether we would be subject to the deliberation of the executive board or, even worse, to the General Assembly.

For all that is critically written about Mr. Samaranch in the American media, I found him to be fair, practical and refreshingly decisive. The language barrier made it difficult to engage in elaborate arguments of persuasion, although I suspected he feigned less fluency with English than he actually possessed, in part to forestall my entreaties. If he agreed with the point I raised, he understood it quite well and moved ahead.

This process works particularly well one-on-one with the president, but also is the standard operation at an executive board meeting.

While these meetings often have twenty or more executive board members and senior staff executives who ask numerous questions and provide unabashed opinions, it is Samaranch who decides. He doesn't justify his conclusion to anyone. He just makes the decision. Given the variety of interests among the executive board meeting attendees which include International Federation members, Olympic associations of various flavors, staff aspiring for greater recognition, and IOC contestants for the upcoming presidential and officer elections, his decisiveness and leadership were what allowed the process to work.

DAKAR

The 5th of February, 2001 took me again to an IOC executive board meeting, this time in Dakar. There were several important decisions that I had brought for review that turned out to be issues subject to repeated deliberation.

One of the most contentious involved the Games-time doping laboratory where the athletes blood samples would be tested for various banned substances. It could remain at UCLA, where it was already a permanent installation, or it could be duplicated and moved to a temporary location in Salt Lake City during the Games. The cost of such a move was approximately $1 million. The benefit was that the members of the IOC Medical Commission would be able to attend athletic events and subsequently observe conditions at the lab without having to make a trip to Los Angeles. As the host city contract did not specifically call for such extravagance, we were insistent that the lab remain in Los Angeles. Tradition and protocol were against us. Although it was not specified in the contract, virtually every previous host city had been required to build doping facilities in the venue city.

We had originally negotiated a deal with the University of Indiana to bring a lab to Salt Lake City. They were one of only two IOC approved labs in the United States, the other being at UCLA. Then the director of the Indiana lab left to take a position with the United States Anti-Doping Agency, leaving us UCLA as our sole U.S. alternative. For backup, we initiated conversations with Montreal and a lab in Lausanne, but in January 2001, the IOC Medical Commission said that in addition to requiring a lab to be IOC certified, it must also be ISO 9000 certified. Neither Montreal nor Lausanne met that test. As a result, UCLA was our one and only option.

The director of the lab, Dr. Don Catlin, was both a perfectionist and a professional. He felt moving the lab could impact its quality and add to risk. Instruments would have to be re-calibrated, technicians would need to be recruited from Los Angeles and conditions would be unfamiliar to the team. None of these arguments phased the Prince de Merode, the IOC member who chaired the medical commission. He insisted the lab be moved and offered virtually no compelling reasons for doing so; it was his decision to make and he needed to justify it to no one, especially me. Dr. Patrick Schamasch, Merode's right hand staff person at the IOC, explained that the lab needed to be close to the members of the medical commission so that it could be controlled. I remarked that no one was going to control Dr. Catlin and that the perception of IOC controlling doping results was the last thing that anyone needed. In a telephone conversation with President Samaranch prior to the Dakar meeting, he had confided that he would support my request to keep the lab at UCLA. But given his absence in Dakar, I wondered how the matter would play out.

Upon returning home to Salt Lake City, Caroline Shaw informed me that the Prince de Merode told the *Salt Lake Tribune* that the location of the lab in Salt Lake City was a done deal. It seemed the final decision had been made. And we weren't even in the room. It was a battle we were pretty resigned to losing, but we hated to have to spend the extra money for what some of us thought was the Prince's convenience.

In the category of less important but still worthy of consideration was our proposal to have one night of professional figure skating as part of our Cultural Olympiad. The idea was to have something like the Ice Capades or Disney on Ice on the night prior to closing ceremonies. This would draw a large TV audience for NBC on an otherwise quiet Olympics evening and could keep spectators in Salt Lake City over the weekend, encouraging them to also buy tickets for closing ceremonies which were far from fully subscribed. This idea lasted about as long as a worm in a chicken coop. Member after member jumped on the idea. Their argument was that it was not fair to let professional athletes who had sold themselves out for money detract from the heroic performances of the Olympians. The animosity towards the professionals, many of whom I had met and had found to be loyal ambassadors of the Olympic movement, was a surprise. I couldn't understand how anyone could be critical of athletes who sacrificed so enormously to compete in the Games who then ultimately decided to make a living.

We also recommended that athletes entering the stadium for opening ceremonies during what is called the parade of nations select one person from each team to offer a verbal greeting to the world as he or she passed the dignitary stand. This athlete would be handed a cordless microphone as they walked past the viewing stand. Spoken both in their native language and English, the words for their greeting would be provided in advance in writing to our broadcaster. If any athlete strayed from the text that had been provided, the delayed mike would be turned off to prevent embarrassment. Our objective was to make the march more interesting to the audience, both at home and in the stadium. I personally had found the march in Sydney to be pretty slow; I had gone out for refreshments during the hour-plus segment.

But our innovation was not well received. One IOC staffer intoned at length on the raucous and untrustworthy nature of athletes coming to the Games. "You have several chefs de mission in attendance at this meeting," he explained, "and you should listen to their concerns about the antics of the athletes." Wait a second, was he really disparaging the athletes? Just who did he think the Games were about? Of course, I realized that it was conceivable that an incident of some kind might follow from an athlete's vocal greeting. But in my view, even if something outrageous were broadcast, it would just make the ceremonies more interesting. I wanted the athletes of the Olympics to be seen *and* heard. But tradition and caution prevailed; it's hard to argue too vehemently when you may well be in the wrong on a matter that doesn't make much of a difference anyway.

But that's just what I did on the medal awards protocol. I became convinced by Scott Givens and his creative team that we should award the Olympic medals in the order of bronze first, then silver, then gold. That order would allow us to reach a climax of celebration for the gold medal winner, leading directly into the national anthem of the winner. But the IOC's tradition had always been to give gold first, then silver, then bronze, and then return to the national anthem of the winner. Totally anticlimactic. We had taken the idea to the Athletes Commission, an elected board of Olympians, which endorsed our recommendation. So did NBC. But the IOC Executive Board had discussed it at great length prior to my presentation on the matter and then again following. It had been unable to reach a conclusion. Again, the passion on our proposal ran high. Months later, President Samaranch agreed to our medal order request, but noted that it was a demonstration project that would not carry to future Olympics. Here again, Samaranch had apparently engineered a compromise that satisfied our request without reversing tradition or overruling colleagues.

"PHANTOM VIK"

Another haggling point with the IOC concerned our request not to pay, ever, a 5 percent IOC royalty on sponsor donated goods and services which could not be used in the Games and thus had no value to us. In some cases, the USOC or SLOC entered a sponsorship relationship in which we would agree to accept VIK product or services which we recognized would have little if any value to us. We labeled this relatively valueless provision "Phantom VIK." Technically, it qualified as VIK, but its value was ephemeral. Our royalty agreement with the IOC specifically contemplated this kind of circumstance and provided that our 5 percent royalty could be waived; however, decisions on forgiveness of the royalty on Phantom VIK would be considered on a case-by-case basis, generally decided after the Games were over.

As of the Dakar meeting, our Phantom VIK totaled over $125 million. That meant we were obligated to pay the IOC 5 percent or $6 million as a royalty for VIK we would not use. We were entitled to millions of dollars in beer we could not sell or use, phones that didn't work in the U.S., body lotions that made skin soft and young but didn't help our budget.

As the Games drew near, it became important to know how much money we could spend on items we had put in Nice-to-Have tiers in our budget: fireworks, ceremonies, decoration and other growing budget categories. We wanted to know whether all or part of the $6 million we had budgeted to pay the IOC could instead be spent on Game's features. We originally thought this was a topic for the IOC Executive Board meeting in Dakar. We thought it would be helpful to put our request in context: by our calculations SLOC was going to be paying more in royalty to the IOC than any Games in history. Unlike Games like those in Sydney, our Games had to be financed primarily by sponsors, and sponsors meant royalty for the IOC. Sydney, Nagano and Athens received money from their governments and there was no royalty on that. Even if we paid no royalty on Phantom VIK, we would still end up paying more in royalty than any other Games. Moreover, Sydney and Athens received twice the broadcast and TOP revenue as Salt Lake. We got less from the IOC but paid more in royalty. Perhaps the numbers would lead President Samaranch and the executive board to approve a waiver of royalty on Phantom VIK. But President Samaranch became ill and was unable to lead the Dakar meetings; my request would have to wait.

WINNING SAMARANCH

Following Dakar, I redoubled my efforts to receive support from the president. By phone and fax, I raised with him the issues of the drug testing laboratory, adjustments to ceremonies, and Phantom VIK. Of course, in the overall picture, it was funding support that was most critical.

In May 2001, I journeyed to Lausanne to take up once again these issues with Samaranch and his team. Our financial request was, in my view, more than reasonable. He was personally amenable to working something out, but he deferred to his staff on the particulars. And here, François Carrard and Michael Payne refused to budge when it came to total forgiveness for royalty on the Phantom VIK. They insisted that if the Games in Salt Lake City were profitable, the royalty payment be made. But they did finally agree to make the royalty due only in the event that Games were profitable. In other words, we could spend money as if we didn't have to pay a royalty. If there was a profit left over in the end, they wanted to be paid on the Phantom VIK. That seemed more than fair. It would allow us to spend funds for the Olympics rather than preserve them to meet IOC obligations. The Phantom VIK and a similarly contested royalty on certain technology VIK were effectively transformed from a liability to a contingent liability, meaning that we would have almost $10 million more to spend on the Games. The IOC staff insisted that these additional funds be directed towards "look of the Games" and ceremonies elements; they wanted to make sure that any parochial interests on the part of SLOC board members would not receive funding by virtue of IOC forbearance. François Carrard prepared a letter of agreement reflecting the new deal. The outcome was a home run for SLOC. There really is no harm in asking.

Samaranch was also supportive when it came to the Los Angeles location for our doping lab. He recognized the waste inherent in relocating a lab in Salt Lake City. He was also concerned about legal challenges from athletes by virtue of lab certification uncertainties. He asked that I put together a strong presentation on the matter for the executive board.

Samaranch also asked that I personally appear before the executive board at their May 13, 2001 meeting. Of course, I had hoped instead to make my agreements with Samaranch and his staff. But he felt that his imminent departure from the IOC top job made it important to get the participation of the executive board members, including each candidate for IOC president, on any deal we had reached together.

My return trip to Lausanne on May 13 was another one day special. My presentation touched on non-controversial matters and only tangentially mentioned that we had resolved financial uncertainties through work with the IOC staff. No questions on the topic were raised. Following the meeting, I met with Thierry Sprunger, Michael Payne, and François Carrard and hammered out the final agreement that would be reflected in François' letter.

I included in my executive board presentation a carefully crafted pitch to retain the Los Angeles location of the doping lab. I knew Samaranch and his staff fully supported our position. Prince de Merode virtually dozed during my entire presentation, but when the time for questions arrived, he flatly inserted that there was no way that the lab would be located anywhere but in Salt Lake City. Literally no response or comment was made by President Samaranch or any other executive board member. How in the world did Prince de Merode have such unilateral power? Ultimately, I recognized that President Samaranch abhorred conflict: when weighing the pain from an intermittent Mitt Romney with the ever-present Prince de Merode, I was sure to lose. But when the Games were over, the IOC quietly picked up the incremental cost of moving the lab.

CONCLUSION

In the final analysis, our relationship with the IOC was productive. Despite the dramatics of ongoing investigations and the accompanying distractions of face-saving maneuvers and the politics of resentment, both SLOC and the IOC were committed to the same thing, making the Salt Lake 2002 Winter Games as successful as they could be. While the culture of opulence that had grown up around the Games and allegations of influence peddling had damaged the IOC's public image, it cannot be said that the organization had lost the vision of the purpose of the Olympics. While the same could not always be said of the USOC leadership during my tenure, President Samaranch and President Jacques Rogge after him, had a deep and abiding commitment to the athletes, recognizing their sacrifices to prepare and to compete. They understood the role the Olympics can play in the world to promote peace and understanding. In fact, despite the intrigue and excess on the part of some, the mission of the Olympics is strong enough to keep the organization from becoming permanently derailed. Most observers trash the IOC but I can't go there in good faith. The presidents, the executive board and the coordination commission were good to us and quite effective. I do not believe they are part of the Olympic movement for money, fame or glory. I can't say the same thing for all the IOC members; a few had long ago forgotten that the Games were about people other than themselves.

President Rogge would bring a different style of management and a more open and less opulent culture to the Games. He would be very involved in the decision making process, relying less on the staff. From what I would see of him, I believed he would be an important addition to the Olympic legacy, even for an administrator. Remember, the Games are about the athletes.

Chapter 9

THE FACE OF SLOC

My job came with a plate pretty full of surprises, but the public relations mess was not one of them. Even as far away as Boston, it took no genius to know that public support for the Olympics was in the tank. People in Salt Lake wanted nothing to do with us, while across the country people just shook their heads. Executives I met told me that no matter where they traveled around the globe, their meetings always began with expressions of incredulity about the Salt Lake scandal, as it was called. One large international corporation CEO even said that Salt Lake's reputation had seriously affected the reputation of his Utah-based company. It is funny how bad news travels fast, and far.

SLOC's reputation mattered for a lot of reasons. A persistently poor public perception would hurt not only marketing, but ticket sales, donations, volunteering, and the sorely needed government financial support. A positive cast could propel us in each endeavor. My year-long battle with Ted Kennedy for a Senate seat from Massachusetts had taught me more than a few lessons about dealing with the media. If it is true that you learn more from your mistakes than from your successes, some would have figured that I qualified for a PhD. But in fact, there was still an enormous amount I did not know. It is one thing to be in a campaign for political office; it is quite another to launch a long and steady effort to rebuild the reputation of an enterprise.

At SLOC, I had several pros I could turn to. In Salt Lake, Shelley Thomas put me on the right track and Caroline Shaw kept me there. Steve Coltrin was the strategist. He looked long term, set the course, helped craft the message, and coordinated the work of the overall media team. Steve flew into Salt Lake every few weeks and for major media events. I cannot possibly describe all of Steve's principles of public and media relations—he had built up his strategy over an entire career—but there were some pointers that stood out, even to an amateur.

First, the media were not all the same. Of course, there was a big difference between broadcast media and print, but there was also a divide between the local folks and the national. And with the national, there were journalists that followed the Games as part of their assignment and others who came to the Olympics only when there was "news" of some kind. Steve looked at each segment of the media and planned our approach. The local media came first, quite literally; immediately after my acceptance speech to the board, they were waiting for an interview. Steve's philosophy with the local press was to be entirely forthright and fully accessible. I couldn't have agreed more. In fact, that's all I knew.

FIRST MEETINGS

When I returned to the SLOC office after my speech, I invited the top Olympic reporters from the two Salt Lake City daily papers into my office. Mike Gorrell of the *Salt Lake Tribune* and Lisa Riley Roche of the *Deseret Morning News* had been on the Olympic beat for some time. I knew they were both more conversant with the history and issues surrounding the Olympic Games than I was. Shelley expected to come into the interview with me, but I felt that looked like she was there to make sure that I didn't get in trouble. I asked her to wait in her office. Now, that's usually not a good idea. Having a pro there to hear what you say makes sure that if you miss something or get a fact wrong, they can clear it up, either on the spot or later. It avoids a bad story. But I wanted to make it clear that I had nothing to hide. So, it was just the three of us. Without any interference from handlers, I answered every question they could throw at me as directly as I could. Roche's lead in the *Deseret Morning News* picked up on the signal: "The first thing Mitt Romney does as he greets two reporters for an interview as the new boss of the 2002 Winter Games is to kindly but firmly dismiss a public relations person who wants to sit in. "They want to make sure I don't say anything I shouldn't, but whatever I say, I've said it," he explains. Shelley must have shaken her head.

I remember the story, probably apocryphal, about a friend of the late Senator Sam Erwin. He asked the senator if he could give him any advice as he was preparing to appear before a Congressional investigating committee. The senator's supposed response: "Don't try to be funny. Don't lie. And whatever you do, don't blurt out the truth." Well, I was committed to that very same treacherous course. And it actually worked out quite well in the end.

Our policy of open and accessible relations with the Salt Lake media fit nicely with SLOC's open meetings and open document policy. We believed that both were essential to restore credibility in the wake of the scandal. We committed to provide any document on file at SLOC to anyone in the public or in the media upon request—something of a daunting task. We charged a fee for document preparation, more to ensure intent on the part of the requesting party than anything else. We could imagine all kinds of outlandish requests coming in at once and crippling our staff as we rushed to fulfill them. It did not really stop the rush, particularly during the first weeks that the policy was in effect. Perhaps as a means of testing our resolve, almost every news organization sent in requests. Most requests had to do with the ongoing scandal investigations. Receipts, itineraries, correspondence, and other documents pertaining to the bid committee's interaction with voting IOC members were particularly popular.

It bears mentioning that Salt Lake City's two dailies have very different roots. The *Salt Lake Tribune* says on its masthead that it is Salt Lake City's "independent newspaper." That is referring to the fact that the other daily, the *Deseret Morning News*, is owned by the Mormon Church. Over the years, the *Tribune* has gained market share from the *Deseret Morning News*, now placing it solidly in first place. It prides itself on more critical reporting, but that was actually not my experience. My review of the articles from the preceding months showed that Lisa Riley Roche had the most hostile pen. In fact, the *Deseret Morning News* editor-in-chief was a former journalist with the *Christian Science Monitor* and was not himself Mormon. Both papers seemed quite willing to take us to task for our mistakes. Neither was willing to shill for SLOC in the interest of community spirit; they reported and called it like they saw it. My predecessors reportedly complained to the Church about articles by Lisa Riley Roche and were informed that they had no influence over the reporting of the news. Editorials could be reviewed, but not the news coverage: that was the deal with the editor they had recruited.

The *Tribune* had two reporters following us. Mike Gorrell was the consummate reporter. In three years, I only recall one error in any one of his hundreds of articles. For which, by the way, he called to apologize. He had an uncanny ability to get all the facts straight, and to report them that way. He was not always on our side, however, and was just as willing to accurately report the charges of our critics. But he was looking to get the news right, not to win the Pulitzer for "uncovering" the inside scandal.

Linda Fantin was the other *Tribune* reporter on the Olympics beat. She was looking to find that new scandal that she knew must "be in there somewhere." After all, it was a TV reporter that broke the bid scandal, right under the nose of the print media. Over three years, she would frequently call, minutes to go before her deadline, insisting we get back immediately because she had found such and such a scandalous thing about us. Generally, there was a misunderstanding that had to be cleared up. But the 5:00 pm fire drills didn't go away, until I did.

The editor-in-chief was Jay Shelledy. He was fair minded, very critical of anyone around at the time of the bid scandal, and with perspective on the community I found to be most helpful. We would meet once or twice a year. But true to the Coltrin model, Shelley and Caroline had solid relationships of trust with Jay and with his team. For Steve Coltrin, media is about relationships of trust. I likewise met with the *Deseret Morning News* editor-in-chief, John Hughes. Years living in the East gave him a sympathetic view on my adjustment to the Salt Lake City community.

Lisa Riley Roche was both the news and investigative reporter for the *Deseret Morning News*. She gave us no slack at all, nor did she try to twist or distort. I liked dealing with someone who was tough, honest, and even unforgiving. We made enough mistakes for her articles to be interesting without her having to invent more. Looking back, I have to admit that I respected both papers. They didn't write puff pieces like I would have liked, but they were fair, and interesting to read. If it's not interesting, no one will read it anyway.

TRANSPARENCY

Our open documents policy led to an avalanche of requests. The *Salt Lake Tribune* was particularly interested in SLOC's correspondence with members of the Latter-day Saints (LDS) Church. Dr. George Van Komen of the Alcohol Policy Coalition—an anti-alcohol advocacy group in Utah—put in an immediate request to see SLOC's contract with Budweiser, an official sponsor of the Olympics. There were some documents that we could not share—personnel documents, and those contracts that were protected by confidentiality clauses. We also had to be careful not to undermine the ongoing investigation by the Department of Justice and the FBI. But apart from those few exceptions, we handed over everything that was requested. We appointed one of our attorneys, Brian Katz, as our disclosure officer with independent authority and instituted a process of appeal that was adjudicated by the SLOC board of directors.

It is fair to say that SLOC was the most transparent organizing committee in Olympic history—perhaps among the most publicly accessible organizations in America. The public and the media were in attendance at every SLOC board and management committee meeting. We built a reading room at our own expense where members of the media or the public could come to examine core documents and submit their document requests. Our correspondence, our files, our financial records—everything was available to the public. For all intents and purposes, we were naked.

I don't know that I would recommend such transparency for every organization. But given where we had come from, and given the scandal that apparently grew out of obfuscation, the only way I believe we could have restored confidence was with disclosure. And as long as there was suspicion and cynicism about SLOC, it would have been impossible to convince the public, the government, and even our own people that we were now operating by the highest standards of integrity. So we let the media in. It's not fun having them poke around, asking probing questions, jumping to unsavory conclusions. But it had to be done. Coltrin was right on.

ELECTRONIC FOOTPRINTS

The local media were important to us, very important. Steve explained that the hundreds of media outlets around the world would follow the papers in Salt Lake every single day to see what they were reporting about us. If there was a big story, they would follow up, perhaps with their own reporter. So the *Tribune* and the *Deseret Morning News* were creating the electronic footprint that would characterize us. Beyond the press, any executive considering a sponsorship or licensing deal would first run a quick search on us. When they put "SLOC" or "Olympics" into LexisNexis or Google, what were they going to find? How many articles on ethical lapses and how many articles on progress? In our campaign to restore credibility, every article is a vote of confidence or no-confidence.

Our life would have been a lot easier if they would just print what we fed them. Heaven knows we sent out enough press releases. Every major development in venue construction was cause for a press release. Every new executive brought in warranted one. Every new sponsor or contributor justified a press release. Every time we determined an element of our creative program we released it to the press. We held press conferences almost every week at SLOC headquarters. The message was clear: Brick by brick, we were building a successful Games. Sometimes reporters started with what we offered, but to give the story interest they needed to uncover conflict. That they were sure to find from our detractors who, thereby, provided a valuable service to us, hard as it is to admit. They kept us interesting to write about. Then there were the stories we had no role in originating. I would cringe when I opened the papers in the morning, and I knew I didn't have to go looking in the back pages. Because these guys knew their material was being followed by their colleagues around the world, it got great billing. I saved the copy I got daily of each story and piled them in the corner to see how much media we had generated. In my three years, the pile reached over six feet tall, just from the local Salt Lake City papers. Trying to steer all those stories away from the cliff was a huge job for us all, but especially Caroline Shaw. She was the one, year after year, who took our side of the stories to the media, in Salt Lake and across the country.

THE FACE

When you run for U.S. Senate, you are essentially the only person in your campaign that gets media attention. It was all about Mitt Romney and Ted Kennedy and nobody else. But in an organization like SLOC, there were tons of people doing important things, not just me. It made sense to me that Mark Lewis make the marketing announcements, John Bennion do the ticketing announcements, etc. But Coltrin said no. He explained that the media and the public associate one person, one face, with an organization. When they think of Ford, they think of Bill Ford. Michael Eisner was Disney; Jack Welch was GE; Lou Gerstner was IBM; and Auggie Busch was Budweiser.

Now that I'm a governor, I have found just how right Coltrin is. Like it or not, everything that comes from my administration comes with my face, my label. What has been most surprising is that even when I know nothing whatsoever about a certain matter, it is still said to be "Romney's plan" or "Romney said." Our local Boston transit authority, which is independent and does not report to me, recently decided that it would not remove an unsightly overpass prior to the Democratic National Convention that is coming to town; the paper attributed the decision to me. In fact, the first time I even heard of the matter is when I picked up the paper and read about what I had supposedly decided. There is nothing terribly surprising in this to someone who has been in front of the media a good bit. It is simply a fact that people associate things with the person at the head, for good or bad.

Coltrin said the same was true at SLOC. I was the face of the organization. As such, it was important that I present the right message and the right image. SLOC would have credibility and integrity if I did. SLOC would be seen as being open, responsive, and accessible if I was. But any time someone at SLOC came across as confused, evasive, or contradictory, that would be associated with me and with the entire organization. He also pointed out that a story would be given better placement, better visibility, if I were the one who was telling it.

My photo was that much more recognizable to the public. So for a whole host of reasons, Steve was insistent that I be front and center with the media. All major announcements, all major controversy, I was to be the spokesperson. And I should speak only when I had all the facts clear: "Don't go out to the press and speculate on something and have to come back later with a different answer. That is how you lose credibility." Steve called his approach "single voice messaging." Multiple voices and multiple messages were confusing, possibly contradictory, and led to a loss of credibility.

Of course, routine matters were released and discussed by Caroline. And occasionally, the directors of a function led a discussion of a matter under their purview, but not often. I must admit to feeling sheepish about Steve's directive: it sure looked like I was taking all the credit for the work of the thousands of people who were really doing it. And, it often put Caroline in a position of having to tell a director or other officer, often a peer in the organization, that they were not to take a matter to the press themselves. Instead, it would be thoroughly researched by the media staff, then announced by me. That didn't always make Caroline popular: everyone wants to be on TV or in the paper. Of course, almost everyone knows that he who has been on TV will soon be forgotten by the public. "Fame, if you win it, comes and goes in a minute."

THE NATIONAL MEDIA

While the national and international media would be following what we were doing at SLOC largely from afar and through the eyes of the local print media, Steve was not content to sit back and see what developed. He had two basic approaches, one for the national journalists who followed the Olympics as a regular part of their assignment, and another for those who tuned in only to report on a news development. With the former, Steve wanted Caroline and me to build personal relationships of understanding and trust. They should have as much time with me as they wanted, to get to know me on both a personal and professional basis. That was fine with me: they were interesting people. Caroline Shaw took the lead here as well. Of course, if they hated me, I could only blame myself.

It's a pretty small group: it includes Alan Abrahamson of the *Los Angeles Times*, Kristine Bremmer and Vicki Michaelis of *USA Today*, and John Powers of the *Boston Globe*. These were the people who wrote about the Games as they were being developed; they wrote the expansive pieces about Olympic developments. They traveled around the world to IOC meetings, followed the USOC, and watched closely what we were doing in Salt Lake. They might write a story about SLOC every two or three months, but because they were so well known and respected, what they said had an enormous impact on the perceptions of the media around the world. I might have thought I really didn't need to worry about what was written in, say, the *Los Angeles Times* by Alan Abrahamson, but Steve knew that what Alan wrote was gospel to many, many others.

Charlie Manning, my Boston communications director, had the same instinct on this as Coltrin. The day I came to Salt Lake to accept my new job, he had me call John Powers ahead of time and give him an exclusive interview. Charlie knew that there were people who really mattered in the Olympic world and John was one of them. Caroline arranged meetings with Kristine or Vicki whenever we were in the same city at the same time, sometimes over a meal. Alan went right to the point himself: he asked for and got my home and cell phone numbers.

Coltrin had a different but similar approach to the other national media. Their interest in the organizing committee would come suddenly on the eve of the Games, if at all, or if there were another major news development like the bid scandal. Here, Steve wanted to establish relationships of trust as well, even though they would not be writing about us for months or years. His plan was to have me visit these media in regular, extensive interview sessions, and generally with their editorial boards. In an editorial board session, editors and reporters typically are invited to spend as much as an hour with you, discussing as wide an array of questions as they choose. Shortly after becoming SLOC CEO, Steve organized a national media tour with folks like ESPN, *USA Today, The New York Times, The Chicago Tribune, The Washington Post, Sports Illustrated, Newsweek, Time,* CNN, NBC, and others. I assumed that he planned for these folks to write articles about SLOC after my interview, helping me to get things back on track ASAP. But that wasn't what he planned. Sure, he would try to spin a story out of the meetings, but his real intent was to build credibility and trust for the long term.

I balked at Steve's tours. He wanted a lot more than I felt I had time to do. And I would argue that if it didn't help me with stories today, when I was trying to sell sponsors and such, what was the purpose? He would counter that having the confidence of members of the media was essential to fair and complete reporting when things developed in the future. Coltrin was insistent. "Trust me," he would say, "trust me. You've got to see these people. They've got to come to know you." Despite my arguments, I did trust Steve, and I made the media tours. By my count, I made eleven trips to the East Coast with Steve.

Steve's formula for building credibility was a great deal more extensive than just meeting reporters. He explained that I should make clear statements of our objectives and milestones and then return in the future and measure ourselves against those milestones. You built credibility by demonstrating it, not by having a big smile and a funny line.

Steve turned out to be right. Those relationships were eventually critical. Establishing my accessibility and investing in relationships with the editors and reporters of key media outlets meant that, by and large, we were treated fairly when the big stories were eventually written. Especially on breaking stories like the impact of 9/11 on the Games or the flap about the World Trade Center flag, where we did not control the pacing of the information.

AN APPARENT CONFLICT

Steve and Caroline said they wanted me to be open and direct with the media and they wanted me to stay on message. I wondered if those were not contradictory instructions. Staying on message was something I had heard a good deal in politics. In the storefront campaign office of a presidential candidate, there was a sign written in bold letters just above the door, "You have the right to remain on message." In a much different context, I had heard of a press interview of the president of the Church of Jesus Christ of Latter-day Saints. He had a very "on message" way of handling the press. At one point he was gently taken to task for "not answering the question" he was asked. He smiled and replied, "You get to ask whatever questions you want. I get to give whatever answers I want. That's the deal."

Staying on message is particularly critical with the television media. I find that it is actually very hard to do. When someone asks you a direct question in a high pressure situation, with the camera rolling, it takes a good deal of practice and skill to acknowledge the question, dispose of it quickly, and find a way to bring the focus to the points you want to make. If you do not get to your own message, the tape will only include topics you do not think are the most important or the most helpful.

There was an interview I did with Lou Dobbs on CNN that Coltrin set up for us early on. Lou kept asking different questions, and I kept answering with my same answer: "People don't care about the managers, they don't care about guys like me in suits and ties, they care about the athletes. That's why the Games will be successful." Afterwards, Lou came up to me and said, "Boy, were you on message!"

Of course, staying "on message" only works with broadcast journalism, where it's all about the video clip. With the print media, I went wherever they took me with their questions. The last thing I wanted to do was to be evasive. We used to joke that the best way to guide a story with the print media was to be scintillating and quotable on the good stuff and thoroughly bland on the bad. There was a corollary: let the communications people get out in front of the bad story. Give me the good news, give Caroline the bad. If I was the more quotable, the one who got the better placement, do not put me in front of something we did not like. The TV news does not want to have the press secretary— "And now we have a comment from the press secretary." They want number one. You can see this with the White House: good news comes from the president. Bad news comes from the press secretary.

UNDERSTANDING THE MEDIA

I thought I had pretty good media instincts, but I also made mistakes. At one of the early meetings of the newly established SLOC management committee, the subset of board members with voting power, we discussed the fact that confidential information was being leaked to the press by an unknown member of the board. One of the new board members protested that he got more information from the newspaper reports than he did from the board meetings. In particular, he was upset about the reporting of legal matters relating to the ongoing investigations stemming from the bid scandal. This information should be held confidential. In fact, that was only the tip of the iceberg; someone had consistently leaked confidential data, beginning well before I arrived. A board member proposed an amendment to our bylaws that would require the resignation of any board member who willfully made public any information that had been officially determined to be confidential. This included legal briefings, contract terms with sponsors, and the like. I was sympathetic with his concern. While I abstained from commenting or voting on the issue, it passed without opposition. I should have known better.

Good political instincts should have reminded me that that action was not likely to be reported at face value. The press would not write that the board was opposing the release of confidential data by members who were violating their duty of loyalty to the board and to the organization. With our new openness policies in place, there were reporters in the room when the vote was taken. I didn't have to wait very long to see how it would be played by the press. Our vote was in a morning session, and before lunch was over, there was already a headline on the *Deseret Morning News* website. "Games Committee Votes to Resurrect 'Gag Order'" read the headline. So much for our effort to restore credibility, encourage openness, and separate ourselves from the sins of the past.

When we reconvened for our afternoon business, I addressed the committee. I read the website headline and the lead paragraph: "Despite promises that the 2002 Winter Games would be more open after the bid-buying scandal, the newly formed oversight committee voted Thursday to oust members who make confidential information public...." I asked the board members if that was really the message they wanted to send to the world in light of our recent woes. We overturned the bylaw on the spot by a unanimous vote. Even the committee member who had proposed the action earlier that morning voted to repeal it. The next day's headline read, "SLOC Does an About Face on 'Gag Order:' Committee Rescinds New Policy Just Hours After Approving It."

We did indeed look like the gang that couldn't shoot straight, reversing ourselves like we did. But my political instincts told me that that was a lot better than the stories that would come out if we had dug in. Both papers would have put it on page one. The critics would bring out all the old claims of cover up and secrecy. We would never have enough time to recover. If you make a mistake, fix it as fast as you can. Admit, fix, and move on.

FEED THE BEAST

I had not heard that phrase until I came back to run for office in Massachusetts. The governor and I had a meeting and after it was over, she said it was time to go out to the door and "feed the beast."

At the doorway, a gaggle of reporters and cameras were gathered, ready for a statement and a host of questions.

I learned what should have been obvious. Reporters assigned to the Olympics have to write a story every few days. If we did not have anything for them to write about, they would have to find something on their own from somewhere else, like from our critics or the board member fond of leaking stories. So part of Caroline's job was to make sure we had stories almost every day. She would line up releases with the calendar, spacing things out in sequence so there was enough to keep them writing. She was doing all of us a favor. She was feeding. Sometimes they took our story, often they passed on it and went a different direction. But Caroline was doing her best to keep us on message, rebuilding trust and confidence with the public.

We knew that the world media would arrive in Salt Lake City ten to twenty days before the Games were to begin on February 8. Organizers from other Olympics predicted that they would move in and start driving around Utah asking people questions and visiting the venues. They would form their impression of Utah and how well we were prepared by what they learned before the Games had even begun. In Sydney, complaints about media transportation arose because it wasn't in operation until immediately before opening. Likewise in Atlanta. So part of getting ready for the media was to have things working well before the Games started.

We also recognized that we had to be prepared to "feed the beast" before the Games began. Caroline outlined a schedule of what stories we could provide every day before the Games. There were the venues, the security arrangements, and food service and accommodations for the athletes. We took them to our main operations center, our volunteer center, the communications and information centers, and explained how we were approaching transportation planning. We knew they would want the Mormon story as well; when we spoke to the Church about the early arrivals of the media, we found that they were way ahead of us, having prepared videos and other materials dealing with every possible story, positive and negative.

DEFUSING THE BOMB

There were some stories we knew were ripe with potential to hurt our credibility and reputation. Of course, the best antidote would be to fix the problem in the first place. But some circumstances can't be fixed. They approach like a fuse burning on a stick of dynamite. Steve and Caroline were insistent that we tell the story rather than have it "discovered" and served up to the public like some secret we were hiding. We tried to stay ahead of potentially damaging stories by disclosing problems up front. The three "Ts," ticketing, technology, and transportation, are perennial bugaboos for organizing committees. When we failed to fully staff for the demand for tickets on the first day of sales, our website and phone sales center were both incapacitated by excess traffic. We were quick to make this public and bring in more resources to address the problem. When sight lines were obstructed, we worked hard to disclose it fast. We wanted to inoculate ourselves against charges that we were hiding the truth.

At the Delta Center, virtually none of the views were superb for figure skating. That is because the Delta Center was built as a basketball arena and not an Olympic figure skating arena. We were selling tickets for a lot of money ($475 per ticket for the better seats). The most sought after series of events were going to be at the Delta Center. Therefore, we took every measure conceivable to inform the public of the problem. I acknowledged the matter up front to the media. The managers of the Delta Center were actually quite disturbed that I was so critical of their venue, so I tried to make it clear there was nothing wrong with the building, just something unusual about Olympic-size ice. Controversy surrounded the issue of who had chosen the Delta Center for figure skating in the first place,

SLOC or the International Federation. It helped draw more attention to the problem: exactly what we wanted.

In our ticketing brochure we described the fact that the Delta Center had sight line problems. On our website, a person buying a seat at the Delta Center would see a pop-up window that said "All seats at the Delta Center have partially obstructed views. Do you want to proceed with your purchase anyway?" The person would have to click "Yes, I accept that my seat will have a partially obstructed view." And the person went to pay at the end of the ticketing order, there was another window that popped up. "You have selected seats at the Delta Center. All our seats have partially obstructed views...." We told the public the bad news ourselves, rather than have the media and others think we had pulled a fast one. It would have been just the kind of story the media loves: we are not the open and honest people we pretend to be. We are trying to get people to pay money for bad seats. We covered up; we hid the truth. What a great story.

I never saw a story saying we had been unfair with our Delta Center seating or ticketing. Sure, there were a few public complaints about sight lines, but nothing that implicated anyone for doing something wrong. Tell the bad news first. It won't go away, but it won't have the sting.

GOTCHA

One part of journalism that I am not terribly fond of is what I call the gotcha reflex. A writer wants a big story, a surprise, a shocking development. Sometimes if they can get you to say a certain word or acknowledge a certain fact, it can be turned into a blockbuster story and headline, even if it is not at all what was intended. Even the most reputable reporters can't resist a gotcha if you give it to them.

Let's say a reporter asks whether the Games could possibly go bankrupt. Now we all know that any organization can go bankrupt, SLOC included. In fact, SLOC's position was a lot less stable than most. Let's say I answered directly: "It is very unlikely. In fact, I would give it less than a 1 percent chance. But it is conceivable that the Games could go bankrupt. Not at all likely, but conceivable." The evening news and headline the next day will read: "Romney Says Games May Go Bankrupt!" What would follow would be quotes from the critics saying they had been right all along. Our financial gap would be described in detail. My quote on TV would show only the words "...it is conceivable that the Games could go bankrupt..." That's a gotcha. I would have been accurately quoted, the story would be correct. But it would be terribly misleading or as one frequently hears from us politicians, "distorted and out of context."

Reporters sometimes serve up questions that have to be answered with a gotcha; they know it, you know it. I committed a gotcha that almost got us into trouble. When you get in trouble with the media, that is when it pays to have a terrific communications staff on board, people who have the media's respect and confidence.

On one occasion I sat down with the Utah state transportation people. They were mad at me because we were getting money for roads we needed for the Olympics and they were not getting what they needed. I felt that they just didn't appreciate how tenuous our condition was, how desperately we needed the federal government support, immediately. So I met with the transportation commissioners and I said, look, let me tell you the kinds of things that I am worried about. Let us put this in context. You guys might be thinking that there is a scorecard as to who is winning the federal appropriations, but I'm really just trying to keep these Games alive. I'm not trying to come out on top here. I'm trying to keep things going in the face of financial difficulties that could cancel the Games. That phrase, "cancel the Games" was a gotcha, but I had said it in private, to people I thought were our allies. Wrong.

One of the transportation commissioners went straight to the *Tribune* after our meeting and told them: Mitt Romney said he is afraid the Games won't happen, I have a direct quote. You can say things in context about trying to keep things afloat and needing all the help and understanding you can get, but if it gets boiled down to "The head of the Olympics is afraid the Games might be cancelled" we had a problem. The national media would pick up on it. What would sponsors think about it all? They were giving us millions of dollars in support for Games that, according to reports, might not happen. And yet, that was what they could legitimately write. They called us and said, we are quoting you as saying this, do you have a comment?

Shelley Thomas had a good relationship with the editor of the *Tribune* and called him in with the writer and said, "That is just not the intent of what Mitt was saying. It would be unfair and wrong to leave that impression." They spoke with other commissioners who were at the meeting; they confirmed Shelley's account. The paper did not run the story. They could have run with the gotcha. But in part because of Shelley's relationships with the writer and editor, and in part because of the paper's journalistic sense of fair play, they did not go with the story. It happens that way, too.

THE MOTHER GOTCHA OF THEM ALL

September 11 was also quite understandably the basis for renewed, intensified media interest in provisions made for Olympic security. With the press understandably anxious for any quotes about our public safety plan, it was only a matter of time until they would be able to extract some real pearls from one of the many of us who felt qualified to talk about security and the Olympics. Salt Lake City's sheriff, Sheriff Aaron Kennard, remarked that it would surely be possible for a plane to crash into opening ceremony at Rice Eccles Stadium. Less on target but more horrific was the comment from the IOC's Executive Director, François Carrard: "Our catastrophe scenario has always been a passenger jet, loaded with fuel, crashing into opening ceremony on worldwide television." These were not exactly the messages we had hoped to communicate. They had all the earmarks and all the play of gotcha quotes. I hoped to have the opportunity to urge more discretion to the members of the IOC.

A few weeks after the Septermber 11 tragedy, a reporter in Norway had questioned Gerhard Heiberg, the president of the Games in Lillehammer, regarding the concerns of some Norwegian athletes about attending the Games in Salt Lake City. Heiberg was quoted to have said that if the current conditions, with the U.S. leading a war on terrorism, were still in existence at the time of the February 2002 Games, he believed the Games might have to be cancelled. Media worldwide jumped on the story. CBS even interrupted their evening news with the breaking report that a leading IOC official had said the Games might be cancelled.

I was in New York getting ready to board a plane back to Salt Lake City when I received a call from my administrative assistant telling me that Ina Grennes, our director of national Olympic committee relations and a native of Norway, had translated the original article from a Norwegian newspaper. Of course, we recognized that Heiberg's comments would create the headline the media had been seeking for several days: the Games could be cancelled. We had gone to great lengths so far to avoid ever mentioning the "C" word.

From the outset following the attack of September 11, the media peppered me and other members of the Olympic movement with questions regarding cancellation. Would we ever consider canceling the Games? What kind of conditions would have to exist in the world to cancel the Games? Would all out war lead to cancellation of the Games? Every possible combination was offered in the hope that one of us would acknowledge any circumstance whatsoever that could involve cancellation. I recognized the gotcha, as did President Rogge. The media tried every trick to get me to use the "C" word. After awhile, they focused on whether we were making contingency plans in the event the Games might be cancelled. Of course, if I were to say yes, they would have a chance to put cancellation in the headlines.

It's difficult not to respond to a question when asked. I found refuge in an answer I gave time and again. "I'm just not willing to consider unthinkable circumstances; the Games will go on." I wouldn't elaborate. The media smiled; they knew what they were doing and they knew what I had to do. They get to ask the questions they want, I get to give the answers I want.

So when I heard of the Heiberg comment, I called François Carrard at his home. Despite his own comment to the press about a plane crashing into the opening ceremonies stadium, he was, like me, amazed by the severity of the Heiberg quote. He felt that it had to be an inaccurate report. His knowledge of Gerhad Heiberg suggested that it would be impossible for him to do something which could be so damaging to our Games.

I was able to reach Heiberg when I returned to Salt Lake City. He by now had recognized that he had caused a worldwide media storm. He said that he would do anything to calm the waters. I asked if he would accept a call from the *Deseret Morning News*, as they were the next paper in Salt Lake City that would go to print. He told Lisa Riley Roche that he was 100 percent certain that the Games would go forward, and that in no circumstances would it make sense to cancel them. Over the next several days, Heiberg insisted to any media representative that would listen that he was fully convinced that the Games must go forward. Generally, the press treated his comment as an apology. And, of course, the apology and retraction received far less press than the original headline. In the minds of most people I spoke with, there was still the belief that IOC leadership was calling for a cancellation of the Games. Even the assurances of President Jacques Rogge and François Carrard that the Games would proceed was given far less visibility than Gerhard's original comment.

A few days later, I encountered the reporter from Norway that had interviewed Heiberg. He insisted that Heiberg was not at all misquoted, and offered to produce a tape recording and transcript of their interview. At this point, what was or was not said was not relevant;

what was important was the impression that had been left in the minds of the public.

During the coordination commission meeting itself, Hodler, Carrard, and Heiberg kept to the script that the Games were going forward. The famous statement by President Roosevelt that the only thing we had to fear was fear itself had some applicability to our circumstance. If the media were to blare a headline that the Games might be cancelled, it could potentially become a self fulfilling prophesy, or at least have very serious financial and personal implications.

TRUSTING JOURNALISTS AS PEOPLE

Late in fall of 2001 we learned that the popular news magazine show *60 Minutes* was preparing a segment featuring an exclusive, in-depth interview with Tom Welch and Dave Johnson, sharing their side of the scandal story. This could be the perfect "cat bites dog" story the media loves: Tom and Dave were the good guys and everyone else, they were the bad guys. That would not help our effort to rebuild confidence in SLOC. It was clear that Tom and Dave felt unfairly vilified by the media and by community leaders. I presume they may also have had no love loss for me, the purported "white knight" that had "saved the community" from the legacy of their misdeeds. From their perspective, I had inherited an organization that was on solid financial ground, the Games were largely organized before my arrival, and I was unfairly given credit for their work in making the Games successful. They may have simply chosen to ignore the devastating impact of the bid scandal.

Everyone told me to stay away from it. Calling Mike Wallace, they said, would only associate me with a story that was bound to be filled with allegations and scandal. I remembered that my father had respect for Mike Wallace. If Dad respected him, and if the story was not already in the can, meeting with him personally might make a difference. I called Mike Wallace and he agreed to meet in New York City.

He asked me all kinds of questions about the scandal, but I told him I had no better sources than he—I had been in Massachusetts at the time. Never mind whether or not the bid committee had done anything criminally wrong; I could not understand why Tom and Dave had never apologized to the community for what it had endured. Even if they were not the only ones complicit, the scandal had occurred on their watch. I expressed disappointment that they had not stepped forward to admit their accountability at least on that level. He raised their assertion that I was profiteering from their hard work. I agreed. They were 99 percent responsible for winning the Games, albeit through questionable tactics. They also had successfully worked to design venues and to sign sponsors for big dollars. That still left the fact that there was a good deal of work that had to be done by Fraser and me and the team in the three years leading up to the Games. And it was far from easy.

The segment aired without me in it, which was as I hoped. I was not a formal part of the story but had been able to express my views and have them be represented in the analysis of the segment's producers. I came to share my father's respect for Mike Wallace, the person and the professional.

MY EXCELLENT ADVENTURE

Our first big piece on the *Today* show was two years out from the Games. Caroline and Steve saw the appearance as potentially *the* piece that could transition national attention away from the allegations of wrongdoing toward the excitement of the Games. They needed more than just an interview with me to capture the imagination of the public, and also the imagination of Katie Couric who would be conducting the interview.

Jamie Rupert, one of Coltrin's top executives, came up with an idea for me to wear a TV camera on my back as I went down the skeleton track. Skeleton was one of the new sports for which we had received IOC approval. An athlete lays on a steel sled, a little larger than a cookie sheet, head first, arms at the side, and shoots down the bobsled ice track. He or she reaches speeds between 70 and 80 mph. Going down the bobsled run head first, without the protection of a bobsled, was something you had to stop and think about. Ever since taking the job at SLOC, I had done my best to try a wide range of Winter Olympic sports. Kristi Yamaguchi took me skating. I had skied the men's downhill, curled, played hockey, taken the bobsled, and so forth. With an interview with Katie Couric in the balance, I decided to give skeleton a go. Jimmy Shea, who would later become the sport's gold medalist, took me up to ride the skeleton. We started working weeks ahead of my *Today* interview so I could be ready for prime time, not just as one of the "suits" watching from the sidelines, but as a participant.

Jimmy loaned me his sled. I would eventually make eighteen runs before I became good enough to go from the top for national TV. On my first run, I began on the bottom 40 percent of the track. Jimmy let me borrow his special cleated shoes to walk on the ice.

I was terrified. The ice came so fast with my face two or three inches from it, and with my head scraping on the ice as I went through turns due to the G-force, that my brain couldn't process fast enough to know what was going on, and therefore to steer a safe course. I was only going about 40 or 45 miles per hour that first run, but think about being dragged behind a car on something two inches off the ground at 45 miles per hour. You can't believe how fast the ground is coming at you. The natural inclination is to drag your feet to slow yourself down. I was digging my feet into that ice without even knowing it. At the end of the run I stood up somewhat dazed and said, "Wow, that was really scary." I looked down at Jimmy's new shoes; the tops were gone. I saw my socks. I had totally worn away the tops of Jimmy Shea's special training shoes. I took them off: "Here are your shoes back, Jimmy."

We did two or three runs a day and gradually I moved up the starting position as I grew more confident. Interestingly, your brain learns how to deal with it. I got to the point where I could see and anticipate each curve. I had memorized when I was going to go right or left and could lean the right way. The piece was a huge success on TV. Katie began the interview by asking if I was "completely nuts," to which I had to reply, "Maybe a little."

Chapter 10

ONGOING MARKETING EFFORTS

From my first days at SLOC, I knew that I would have to be a salesman. I know there must be people out there who love to sell, but it is far from my favorite thing. But, contrary to popular perception, it is probably one of the most critical components of work in senior management in corporate America. At Bain & Company, the consulting firm, we had to sell new case studies and new clients. At Bain Capital, the investment firm, we had to sell business owners on why they should sell their business to us. We had to sell banks to lend us money, and we had to sell folks on giving us their money to manage.

SLOC would also be a sales job. We were hundreds of millions of dollars in the hole. Things we had cut to help narrow the gap were things we hoped to eventually restore, if we could find the money and sponsors. With the Marker deal, we would get the volunteer uniforms I had pared back, but I knew that cuts to opening ceremonies could hurt the Olympic experience and perception of our success. And every time Fraser and his team went through the budget to identify more areas for savings, they also found hidden costs, overruns, and overstatement of the value to us of VIK we had already been promised. In fact, the total value of proceeds from our first new corporate sponsors—Marker, O.C. Tanner, Questar, and KSL—was almost entirely offset by updated assessments of our true costs and revenues.

Every resurgence of the scandal into the headlines seemed to have something of a chilling effect on our ongoing marketing calls. We wanted potential sponsors to focus on the athletes and the coming competition. But the federal probe and its drip-drip-drip progress made that difficult. "There are things that make your job easier and things that make it harder," I explained to the press. "Warm weather in the mountains: I can't do much about that so I don't worry about it. In the same category, I put the whole scandal crisis."

When you sell a product you sell the whole organization. No executive was going to make a multimillion dollar marketing deal without seeing what had been written about us in the press. If most of what they saw was about scandal, cover-up, and extravagance, it would be a pretty tough sell. We worked hard with the media to reestablish a positive "electronic footprint" for SLOC and the Olympic movement in general. We tried to fill between the intermittent peaks of scandal news with stories of progress. The IOC's efforts to set its own house in order helped. The USOC was a different story: its infighting and lack of leadership made it hard to rise above itself.

TROUBLES IN COLORADO SPRINGS

At the time of my appointment, the USOC was a kingdom divided. Three separate executives were effectively running their own staffs from remote locations. John Krimsky held court in his own well-appointed office complex across town from USOC headquarters. Executive Director Dick Schultz ruled headquarters while volunteer, part-time President Bill Hybil had his base of operations in an office suite connected to a nearby hotel. Three chiefs, all in the same city, all in separate buildings. I had never seen anything so bizarre, or unproductive. Based on my meetings with them, they would have been even more comfortable in different cities...or states. At the top of this triangle, the executive committee of the USOC Board of Directors held tightly to decision-making authority. It was next to impossible to get a decision or secure a commitment.

I had seen how ineffective the USOC sales team had been in drumming up new sponsors. I suspected that the rest of the organization was also ineffective. Given the financial advantage which the USOC enjoyed relative to other National Olympic Committees, their preparation of the American Olympic team was unimpressive. U.S. medal counts from Summer and Winter Olympics were adequate, not exceptional. So little seemed to be happening to bring young people into Olympic sports. It seemed to me that SLOC's Bob Bills, our director of youth programs, generated more interest and recruits for Olympic winter sport in Utah than the USOC.

In addition to my disappointment over their effort to get more American kids into sport, I chafed at the dollars going to the USOC as part of our joint marketing agreement. They got about 50 cents of every sponsorship dollar. More specifically, according to our contract, the USOC was entitled to $23 million for their marketing expenses, 25 percent of all sponsorship revenues and an additional $50 million to go to the various national governing bodies of sports in the U.S. This latter amount was justified as a compensatory payment because we were selling sponsors that supposedly they otherwise could have sold themselves, to support their own sport. A subsequent USOC president, Sandy Baldwin, would later admit that the money was just relieving USOC obligations and had little to do with marketing rights. The USOC was taking about 50 percent.

Given how hard we were working for every sponsorship dollar, the thought drove me nuts. In private meetings with Hybl and Schultz, and in our joint marketing meetings, I pushed time and again for the USOC to trim its staff, eliminate dead wood, and reduce its budget, but to no avail.

FAMILY PROBLEMS

The national and international media loved to write about the excesses of the IOC. The arrogance of certain IOC members made them an easy, and sometimes worthy, target. But from my view, it looked like the IOC was relatively restrained compared to the USOC. Schultz made a salary of $600,000, whereas Samaranch took no compensation. USOC executives each drove a Cadillac Seville. In fact, Krimsky had ordered a fleet of them delivered to the Nagano Winter Games for the USOC executives. Each was colored gold, with U.S. Olympic flags installed on their front bumpers. I will bet that went a long way to building ties of friendship and understanding between the USOC and the Olympic officials from other countries, to say nothing of the local Japanese. Krimsky occupied an office about twice the size of that enjoyed by American corporate CEOs. All the players at the USOC had massive, elegantly appointed offices in Salt Lake City and in Colorado Springs, despite the fact that they visited us no more than one to two days per month. The waste was disheartening. The USOC enjoyed protection from competition: that was guaranteed by federal legislation. There was little oversight: Congress had far more important matters to attend to and the USOC board was packed with people who were looking for USOC favors and deals. The combination was a Petri dish for waste and excess.

Senator McCain and his Senate hearings into the scandal correctly focused on the IOC because of the reported $1 million in gifts and inappropriate consideration given to its members by the Salt Lake City bid committee. But one had to wonder whether anyone would take a good enough look at the USOC to evaluate how well it was doing its job and how well it spent its money. I remember flying over the mountains near San Diego and having someone point out the USOC training camp below, complete with its own golf course. Golf course? Did they actually need their own golf course to train American athletes? Or was it another boondoggle for USOC officials and friends?

To add to the other strains within the marketing partnership, Schultz and other USOC executives were suspicious of our every motive. I aimed to build my own marketing team to put our future into our own hands. But USOC officials complained that we had been overly critical of them, damaging their reputation. It was true that our feelings were hard to keep entirely below the surface. As I have been writing this book, I told David d'Alessandro that I had not quoted his criticisms of the USOC and Krimsky: "Oh please do!" he injected.

Bill Hybl remarked to NBC Olympic Sports chief executive Dick Ebersol that his number one objective was to establish a better relationship with me. To me, he acknowledged that the USOC simply had to spend much more time marketing out in the field. I told him, in as diplomatic way as I could, that the more time the USOC sales force spent on the road, the worse things would be. I frankly was convinced that they did not have as strong a sales team as IMG or our own people at SLOC. Krimsky was a proven commodity, but his replacement and his sales force were not there yet.

USOC GETS AND LOSES A CEO

In 1999, the USOC took a big step. A study by the well known consulting firm, McKinsey & Company, had concluded that they should be run by a full-time chief executive officer, hardly a novel management conclusion. Bill Hybl, the volunteer part-time president officer at the time would be kicked upstairs. Dick Schultz would retire and a search would be put in place for a new president.

The result of the USOC search was Norm Blake. A successful chief executive of several corporations including USF&G and Promus Hotel, Blake was reputed to be a no-nonsense, take-charge manager. I was hopeful that there would be real change in the organization. Eight months later, he was out of a job.

Norm's first mistake was failing to understand how the media could interpret and distort his initiatives. Perhaps Norm's most important initiative would be to find a better way to direct USOC money to the national governing bodies. It was his intention to evaluate the effectiveness of every NGB to decide how much money to allocate to each. It would have been hard to argue with that. But that's not how Norm explained his initiative to the media. Instead, he said that money would go to the NGBs that produced the most Olympic medals. Money for medals. Kind of reminiscent of guns for hostages. No one liked the way that sounded, particularly in light of the SLOC bid scandal. The media loved it. More scandal.

Norm's second mistake was his failure to recognize that with a board of 120 people, including representatives of very disparate groups, he could not expect the kind of autonomy he had enjoyed in corporate life.

His third failing was that he did not build a base of power with virtually any constituency. As a result, there were no strong voices insisting on his continued leadership. The one group Norm really loved and spent time with was the athletes. He cheered them on at every event in Sydney and attended their coaching sessions. But Norm and I and other business managers of the Games had to remember that to young athletes, we were a collection of old fogies, has-beens, and never-weres. They had little loyalty to administrators like us; we were almost invisible to them. When an inevitable move was made on Norm, there was virtually no one behind him. The move came following embarrassing allegations of a USOC doping cover-up at the Sydney Games. But it was merely pretext.

I got a call from Bill Hybl informing me of Norm's departure. Scott Blackmun, the very able and bright attorney for the USOC was selected to lead on an interim basis. The hope was that by the sheer dint of his intelligence, youth, and energy, he would succeed. Perhaps he could emerge as the permanent CEO as well.

Another exhaustive search was performed, but it did not take place until the summer of 2001. Blackmun had by that time served as "acting-CEO" for a full year. In October, the USOC board of directors named Lloyd Ward as the new chief executive. Ward, the former chairman of Maytag Corp., had been voted one of *Business Week's* "Top 25 Executives." He was a charismatic speaker with good management credentials. But with only three months to go until our opening ceremonies, it was far, far too late for him to have any impact on our preparations.

Ward too had a short shelf life at the USOC. Following our Games, Congress had had enough. It took a close look at the USOC and didn't like what it saw. It put things in order. Today, there's a new board, new management, and new oversight.

SUCCESS

Despite the challenges presented by our USOC partnership, our marketing effort went forward at a steady pace. Our initial trio of Utah partners was followed by support from the local NBC affiliate, KSL, the business holding company of the Mormon Church, and the Herman Miller Corporation. Another Utah corporation, Nu Skin, announced a major sponsorship in the fall, slated for $20 million in value. In addition to being a large scale deal, Nu Skin promoted the Games heavily, both in the state and through their distributors. We owe a lot to the fact that its founders, Blake Roney and Steve Lund, believed in the Olympics and cared deeply about the community's reputation. By the New Year, we were finally hitting stride.

IMG brought us Monster.com, the first online Olympic sponsor, followed shortly by Tickets.com to help us take online ticket orders and fulfill them. Marriott Hotels and Certified Angus Beef were also announced in January, both products of the SLOC marketing effort. IMG brought us Sears and Kellogg's about the same time. Weeks later the SLOC team scored with a human resources training company called Achieve Global and the local power company, Utah Power.

At that point the international sponsors finally started coming back into the fold for the IOC: Visa, Xerox, McDonald's, and Eastman

Kodak, capped by John Hancock and its outspoken CEO, David d'Alessandro. Because these were American-based companies and because we got a share of every dollar they committed, Mark Lewis and I called on IOC TOP prospects as well as our own. We made numerous trips to Atlanta for UPS and Coke. We worked with executives at Xerox, McDonald's, and Kodak. And we pitched a number who would say no, including UPS. Without a doubt, selling took as much of my time as CEO as anything else. Strategizing with our team, preparing the pitch, flying to meetings; money was the lifeblood we needed. Mark Lewis and Don Stirling and their team did the lion's share of the work. But the top guy can't abdicate that responsibility either.

One of the biggest moments was the announcement of Gateway as our sponsor in the computer hardware category in November 1999. Apart from the much publicized $379 million shortfall, there were other holes that needed filling. One of the biggest was in information technology.

Without IBM, we would need to get computers from one company, timing and scoring equipment from another, software and systems integration from another, and, if we could afford it, Internet services and hosting from another.

BREAKING APART THE DYNASTY

The IOC had found SclumbergerSema to fill the TOP sponsor category, but SchlumbergerSema agreed to do only systems integration and software. That left timing, results, hardware, and Internet services still unaccounted for.

Seiko, a sponsor inherited from Atlanta, stepped in to provide the timing equipment. We decided that the risk of problems with the results systems was great enough that we could not afford any further delay. Each sport had intricate and different scoring and results requirements; any mistakes would be potentially devastating to the competing athletes, and to our reputation as well. We would step up to pay for product and services. We contracted a German technology company known as WIGE MIC that executed further contracts with sport-specific suppliers and integrated the systems. And they guaranteed their work.

We had decided to cut the Internet from our plans. Our IT staff was incredulous that I would eliminate it but we could have Games without our own website. Fortunately, we never had to put that to the test. It would eventually resurface and be supplied magnificently by MSNBC.

Computer hardware had us stumped. It was a huge budget item and we felt it had great marketing value for a potential sponsor, but we hadn't sold it. We had worked to pry the hardware category loose from the IOC. Their preference would have been to sell a hardware company at their level; in that case, we would get only 16 2/3 percent of the proceeds and they would get the big share. But because they hadn't sold the category yet and because our Games were getting close, they finally agreed to let us try the sale on our own. It was another example of the IOC giving something up to help us. If we gained a sponsor, they would get a deal that would include Athens as well as Salt Lake Games.

Plan A was that we would get Digital Equipment Corporation. If we could not get DEC, we felt confident Compaq would step up. If we could not get Compaq, we could surely get Dell. I had former dealings with Michael Dell when I was at Bain Capital.

Dave Busser, our director of information technology, was out talking to these companies. He was one of the overachievers at SLOC. Here was our technical guy out working on sponsorship deals, pitching the Olympics, and negotiating terms.

After months of discussion, DEC did not come through. He contacted Compaq. Busser worked out a great deal with Compaq. They negotiated all the details. It was an enormous effort. With only about an inch to the goal line, Compaq pulled out. It was completely out of the blue. After careful deliberation, they felt that Salt Lake would work for them but they were concerned about having to supply Athens as well. And we were asking for a pretty big sum: a full $20 million sponsor level commitment. And for most personal computer companies at the time, that was quite a big bite. We then contacted Dell, HP and Gateway. Discussions led nowhere.

THE GATE TO GATEWAY

At this point we were about thirty days out from our September 30, 1999 drop dead date. If we didn't have a computer sponsor by then, we would have to start buying them at retail. We simply had to start programming the thousands of machines we would need at Games time. Given the number of rejections, we were feeling a little desperate. Did anyone know anything about computer companies in Asia or Europe? And as of the fall of 1999, we had only been able to secure two sponsor level deals in other categories, and both of those had been local Utah corporations; we were not real confident.

And we needed 4,200 computers! They had to be at every venue so each of the 160 international broadcasters could key in and see all the other events and scores. We needed computers in the security centers, operations centers, everywhere. And they all needed to be of the same vintage (year and model) for the network to integrate seamlessly. Time was running out.

Hardware companies were reluctant because they had seen how tough the job had been for IBM. If the system as a whole didn't work—if SchlumbergerSema couldn't get the systems to work or our team couldn't integrate things properly—the less visible software and systems players weren't likely to get too much of the blame. But whoever provided the computers would get the black eye—it was their name on the machines. It was a huge risk. Just as surely as a successful Games could enhance a company's reputation in the marketplace, a negative experience could hurt it.

I was in New York City with Mark Lewis one morning. We were making sales calls on financial services companies but our schedule had a one hour gap. Mark suggested we visit Mark Dowley, head of sports marketing for an international marketing company. Mark Lewis had known Dowley for years; I had come to know him through a mutual friend. Dowley was one of the people I talked to about the Olympic job before I took it. We didn't have an appointment and we really didn't have an agenda. Mark just thought it was a good idea to touch base. You never know.

We exchanged stories in Dowley's office. There is all sorts of banter surrounding sport marketing: athlete deals, sponsorships, trades, and the like. At one point, Mark Lewis had a brainstorm: he said flat out, "Mark, we need a deal with Gateway. We'll do whatever it takes. Help us get a deal with Gateway."

Dowley thought for a moment then shot back, "How serious are you guys?"

I employed the worst sales strategy known to man: the honest, unvarnished truth. "Mark, we're desperate. Everyone else has turned us down. We have nowhere else to turn. You get whatever deal you ask for. Whatever deal Gateway wants, they can have it . . . because we have no one else! We won't blow any smoke that we've got other people lined up and we've got a special deal for you. We're telling you the story straight. Gateway is the only company left. And we're desperate."

Dowley thought Gateway would be interested. Really?

MANO A MANO IN SAN DIEGO

There was a new CEO at Gateway named Jeff Weitzen. He had formerly been an executive with AT&T, a longtime Olympic sponsor. He was experienced with the value of Olympic sponsorships—AT&T had paid tens of millions over the years to be a U.S. partner. He knew what companies typically paid, how sponsorships could be used to propel a brand and promote product sales. And maybe with our desperation there was an opportunity to become a sponsor at a bargain.

Weitzen agreed to meet with me, but he insisted we meet alone. The overwhelming majority of marketing meetings were done by Mark Lewis and his team. But Weitzen wanted to do it *mano a mano*, CEO to CEO...." Come on in and cut the deal: we don't want this to be done by our underlings because it will be negotiated forever." I said, okay. I figured that he suspected that I was the only person who could agree to a bargain. In truth, Mark Lewis had 100 percent authority to do what he felt best. But we were not going to argue with the customer.

I flew to their headquarters in San Diego. Most people think Gateway is headquartered in Iowa given all those cow splotches on their boxes. The building was nondescript, without even an identifying logo or nameplate. I checked the address a couple of times before parking in the lot. Was this really Gateway headquarters?

Gateway's consulting agent, Mark Dowley, also flew in from New York. As I walked in Dowley advised: "Tell it to him straight, tell him what you need." Weitzen was about to go on vacation that afternoon, if the deal didn't get done today, it probably never would.

The pitch that Mark Lewis and I had worked out was as compelling as we could make it: 1) you get an extraordinary opportunity to get a good deal because we're desperate and 2) if we all pull off the technical challenges and have Games systems that work, Gateway will be the company that did what IBM could not: pull off flawless Games. The dark side of being the hardware supplier is that you get blamed for any problems. The bright side is that if the systems work as planned, you will get most of the credit. Hundreds of millions will be spent on systems, but Gateway could walk away with the bragging rights. Further, people's last recollection of Olympic computer systems was in Atlanta, with big IBM mainframes that could not get the job done. You'll have the cow-spotted computers from Iowa that powered the Games and did it successfully.

Mark Lewis and his team had done a bang-up job of preparing the pitch. He had a presentation on DVD showing all of the perks and privileges of Olympic membership. He had storyboards drawn up for me unveiling an ad campaign dramatizing how the biggest information technology project in the world needed help. "And where did they go? They went to Iowa!" We showed Gateway trucks pulling up to the Olympics, saving the Games from the big computers in the blue boxes.

Weitzen loved it. He said that they would think about it. He asked what precisely we needed.

I said, "I just need computers. I don't need your money. Just your computers."

"How many?"

"5,000. 4,200 for us and 800 for the USOC." And I added, "We have to know right away. We have to start buying computers or get them from you. One or the other. We have no time to lose."

He said, "Okay, we'll get back to you this week." He called within a few days. "It's a deal."

RIVALRY BREEDS INTEREST

Gateway proved that even the worst sales strategy can work in the right situation. The tried and true strategy of lining up competing bidders is much more effective—and enjoyable for the salesperson. But in at least one situation, I wished that it had not occurred.

One of the categories we hoped to sell was office supplies. Like any other large organization, SLOC had a significant monthly budget for items such as stationery, pens, file folders, paper clips, and paper. In the interest of making every penny count, I was anxious to sell the category and get our office materials donated as VIK. The CEO of Staples, Tom Stemberg, was a friend of mine, so I mentioned to him that we had an opening in his category. He laughed. If you can sell that category to someone, be my guest," he said. "I have no interest in it at all."

For a while, it looked as if his dismissive appraisal of our chances was basically on the nose. We contacted Office Depot—no interest. We pitched OfficeMax—same result.

We took one more swing at Staples. This time Mark Lewis cooked up a deal that he thought they could not refuse. If Staples would become an official supplier of the Games, we would calculate the amount of their contribution as a percentage of how much their sales increased in the Salt Lake City market. Then we would get to work lobbying SLOC board members and other corporate contacts to switch their office supply contracts to Staples. Stemberg showed interest, but his VP of marketing was stalling. Mark's phone conversations with the VP went nowhere.

About this time, a call came in from Rob Prazmark over at IMG. He was checking on our availability to meet with the newly appointed CEO at Office Depot. Their prior CEO had said no to a deal, but IMG had sparked interest from the new guy. Mark explained to Rob that we were a stone's throw away from cementing a deal with Staples. Rob insisted that there is nothing like a little competition to close a sale. He also was entitled to a commission if Office Depot signed. Our agreement with IMG said they could pursue any category not yet signed by us or the USOC. So technically, he was entitled to proceed. Mark sent Don Stirling to join Prazmark at the Office Depot meeting.

Next thing you know, Don is calling Mark from Florida with a much richer deal on the table than we were working on with Staples. It was mostly cash, not just office supplies. Their only condition was that we had to finalize the deal with them on the spot. They did not want SLOC going back to Staples and shopping for a better deal.

Mark did what he felt was the right thing. Even though he was extremely close to signing a deal with Staples, a better deal was in front of him. He had a duty to IMG and to SLOC to do what was in the best interest of the Games. He authorized Don Stirling to sign the deal with Office Depot. Mark called Staples to give them the news directly.

Well, when Staples learned that one of their chief competitors had "stolen" the sponsorship category right from under their noses, they were not happy, to say the least. And from Staples' perspective, we had not done the right thing, either. Putting that aside, they said they would meet all the terms of the Office Depot deal and up it by a million dollars.

Mark felt terrible. He even asked Office Depot if they would entertain the idea of being bought out: SLOC would pay them a million dollars to back out of the deal, everything Staples was going to pay us above their deal, but they refused. Think of it, Office Depot would get a $1 million profit for a day's work. But they said no! So here was a category no one wanted, that is until there was a little competition. And suddenly it was red hot. Mark did his best to provide ticketing and other benefits to Staples given their work on the deal. Mark personally felt pretty bad. But sponsor dollars were coming in, and from places we would have never expected—office supplies.

NEVER UNDERESTIMATE THE VALUE OF YOUR PRODUCT

Rob Prazmark of IMG was always calling me to help sell deals with him. He was tireless. I was committed to help him and made countless trips to meet with potential sponsors. I had a lot of other demands on my time, though, and at times it was difficult for me to find room in my schedule for yet another pitch meeting, especially if I thought the deal was a long shot. I have mentioned Monster.com earlier. When Prazmark called to say he wanted me to pitch an online job posting company in Massachusetts, I thought, how in the world is a dot com going to come up with $20 million. But Prazmark insisted. I probably would not have gone, but one of my sons had actually worked at the company as a consultant for about six months. And besides, a trip to Boston was a trip home.

Prazmark, Mark Lewis, and I met with a room full people at Monster.com. They came through. They made a requisite cash commitment and donated job posting capacity on their site. They became the official sponsor for job listings for the Olympics—and as the Games drew near, we had a lot of recruiting and hiring to do. We had tremendous response to our postings. Thousands of resumes poured in from all around the world. The people at Monster.com recognized an opportunity to establish their site as the premier place for job listings. They promoted "Olympic job opportunities" heavily. Everyone knew to look on Monster.com if you wanted to work for the Olympics.

It is very, very hard in marketing to know who is going to buy and who is not—it's almost impossible to predict. As Yogi Berra says, forecasting is hard, especially when the future is involved. You know your product so well. You do your homework and careful analysis of each potential client. You would think that you would be able to predict who would be motivated to buy. So often we were wrong. There were also disappointments.

BMW AND MORGAN STANLEY

The automotive categories are typically among the most sought after. The values and characteristics typically associated with the Olympic brand: competitiveness, excellence, performance, fitness, distinction. They all play very well in the car market. While it may be debatable whether an Angus Beef hot dog will be associated with distinction and competitive performance, it is easy to see how a car can. Mercedes was a sponsor in Europe. General Motors was an early sponsor of ours, and they were a fantastic partner to work with. The Chevrolet Division of GM stepped up with Coca-Cola as cosponsors of the torch relay, in addition to their sponsorship of the Games. Time and time again they came through for us. But the domestic car sponsor was only one of two available slots. We also had the right to sell a foreign car category in the U.S. BMW was the leading candidate.

BMW had sponsored the Games in Atlanta. But they just would not commit to Salt Lake City. We went to them again and again. We contacted GM and tried to get them to give us their Saab division to close out the category. They would not do the deal. Mark Lewis spoke with every company imaginable, as did Rob Prazmark.

We never filled the category. By the end of our marketing season, I might have been willing to go as low as $5 million in cash and VIK. I just could not understand it. The Olympics had worked so well for Suburu some years back. They had an ad showing the U.S. ski team in a four wheel drive Suburu station wagon powering by an SUV stuck in the snow. The ad was so memorable, our research showed that a lot of people still associated the company with the Winter Olympics. But despite a great offering, a bargain opportunity, and ample chances to create an auction situation, we struck out.

Another category we had great trouble filling was our financial services category. Merrill Lynch had been a longtime sponsor of the Olympic movement, but they pulled out just before Salt Lake. They had been a sponsor largely because one of their senior executives was on the USOC board. But they hadn't really leveraged their sponsorship in terms of brand association or promotion activities. Again, the financial services category was one where the upscale demographics seemed just right for Olympic marketing.

Mark Lewis arranged meetings with almost every major financial services company. He and I made presentation after presentation, but got little enthusiasm. They were spooked by the fact that Merrill was pulling out. We had high level talks with Morgan Stanley. With the advent of day-trading and Internet brokerages, the financial services market had become a lot tighter. Morgan Stanley was always looking for leverage against the established presence in the industry, Merrill Lynch, and taking over their Olympic sponsorship was the kind of symbolism that played well. We were confident the deal would happen. But in the end talks broke down.

Morgan Stanley had acquired the Discovery card. It was only a small part of their overall portfolio, but it was one part that could not participate in the Olympic program. Visa is, of course, a highly visible sponsor of the Olympic movement. The credit card category was filled. They could have everything but the credit card. Despite their conviction that an Olympic sponsorship could improve the position of their brand in an increasingly competitive marketplace, they could not leave one of their subsidiaries on the sidelines.

Late in the game we had interest from two firms. One was looking at sponsor level figures. But negotiations were dragging on and easily could have led to a dead end. I decided to make a call to David d'Alesandro for two reasons. I knew David would smell a bargain. And I knew that for Hancock, control over the entire financial market, from insurance and annuity products to investment banking and mutual funds, would be a major attraction. After all the travel, preparation and analysis for our many other targets, David simply said yes over the phone. Price and terms we locked in place on the same call. I sure wish we had simply called him first. You just can't predict.

BOMBARDIER

After all the unrequited work on a category like foreign autos, Bombardier was a godsend. Bombardier is the sole maker of something called a "Snow Cat." Snow Cats are enormous pieces of machinery. They resemble the harvesters you see on big farms in the Midwest. But rather than moving across flat corn fields, Snow Cats climb mountainsides, moving and grooming snow and ski slopes, traversing mountain faces with daunting grades. Their track propulsion, like a bulldozer except made of rubber and lightweight materials, powers them in the most hostile terrain. Sometimes they are winched up the steepest grades. A new Snow Cat can cost $200,000.

Snow Cats are an essential part of any alpine ski racing event. In the view of some, Bombardier has no real competitors. If you are running an event like the Olympics, they are effectively the sole provider. So how could you possibly expect a company like that to become a sponsor? Bombardier knew that they had us one way or the other: we would be coming to them with a huge purchase order. And yet they chose to become a sponsor, providing the Snow Cats as VIK under the supplier banner.

Cathy Priestner-Allinger, our director of sport, gets the credit for pulling off that deal. She made the visits, sold the idea, and led the deal with the tutelage of Mark and Don. "We're going to help you out," they said. Bombardier supplied millions of dollars worth of Snow Cats. After the Games, they took equipment back and sold it used. Talk about stepping up to the plate.

Of course there were many more pitches that fell flat than those that worked. We pitched a $20 million deal to Bausch & Lomb, the eye care products company. It was a great presentation with a DVD showing highlights from previous Winter Olympics. Prazmark at IMG had worked up a whole campaign centered on the "official U.S. Olympic sunglasses" that our athletes would wear. It might have worked if it were not for the fact that USOC would not allow us to approach any of the athletes about wearing the glasses. Most of the marquis athletes on the team probably had their own glasses contracts, they explained. Bausch & Lomb took a powder when we couldn't deliver. It was not the only time we fell short.

AT ALL COSTS, PROTECT THE BRAND

The heart of our pitch was all about brand, about associating sponsor products and services with the qualities that the Olympics had come to represent: athleticism, achievement, sacrifice, competition, and ideals like peace and brotherhood. They were the very qualities that typified our higher commitment to the Games, but quantified and packaged for corporate distribution. We would never sell a sponsor on charity alone: the figures were way too big for that.

If brand is what we were selling, and had sold, then we had to make sure the sponsors actually got the positive associations they were paying so much to get. There was a sizeable chunk of money in the budget for something called "ambush marketing prevention." When I first saw it I said, "Get rid of that. Cut that out of the budget." It seemed like a luxury we could ill afford. But Kelly and Mark said, "No, no, no, you can't. You won't be able to sell sponsorships unless you can deliver on your promise to go after people that pirate the Olympic brand." I could not imagine what they were talking about. And then they regaled me with stories from prior Games. During the Atlanta Olympic torch run, the word was that Pepsi had an eighteen-wheel truck that went ahead of the torch to set up in the camera angle of the evening celebration event. Coke was paying millions and Pepsi was looking for a free ride. Nike was the worst offender in the view of many: they advertised during the Games with pictures of athletes, not actually Olympians, but giving the impression that they were a sponsor. Pepsi and Nike were saving money for themselves by shorting the U.S. Olympic team and the Games organizers.

Use of Olympic symbols, or even the words "Olympic" or "Olympiad" without permission were easy ways for companies to get Olympic association free. The federal government had passed a law making it illegal, but many persisted, some in ignorance, some quite purposefully. Some infringements were easy to identify and both SLOC and the USOC would seek remedy—usually by sending a cease and desist letter before filing a formal court order.

In July 2000, SLOC joined the IOC and USOC in filing a groundbreaking lawsuit against cybersquatters who had collectively registered more than 1800 domain names using the protected words Olympic or Olympiad. The suit represented the largest action brought to date under the newly enacted Anti-Cybersquatting Consumer Protection Act of 1999 (ACPA).

Other, more subtle kinds of "parasite" marketing, as it is sometimes called, could involve companies showing Olympic athletes with their brand or even young people in athletic competition during the window of Olympic advertising. All such violations of the spirit of the law were taken very seriously. USOC officials had even threatened to advertise against companies engaging in ambush marketing with PR spots disclosing that the company in question was undermining the efforts of American athletes and the values of the Olympic Games.

Of course, we took a lot of hits in our public relations department for our brand protection efforts. It never goes over well when the guys in the suits come down hard on the little Mom and Pop operations that do not know enough not to use the Olympic rings in their home-grown marketing. The average newspaper reader reacts with distaste and wonders if we "don't have enough to worry about without going after the little people." We read letters to the editor and incredulous editorials about our heavy-handed tactics enforcing Olympic trademarks and symbols. These were the same folks who were apoplectic that we would leave debts and unpaid bills for taxpayers; how did they think we would be able to sign sponsors if we didn't go after the guys who were taking our product for free?

TROUBLING THE CORN

There was a farmer up in Farmington, Utah, who was approached by a man that cuts mazes into cornfields and then sells admission. With the building anticipation toward the Games in the local communities in the fall of 2001, and probably as a gesture of solidarity and support as much as anything else, he cut the maze into a collage of winter sports shapes. It featured the outline of a figure skater and a downhill skier and, unfortunately, the Olympic rings. Someone from our brand enforcement team had to go up there and close them down. They actually had to re-cut the part of the maze that had the rings.

The media got a hold of that particular story. *Sports Illustrated* contacted the guy. E-mails started pouring into SLOC from all over the country about how the Olympics was hurting American farmers. Of course, the farmer who owned the field was not the one profiting from the maze. And the fellow who had to alter his maze design actually ended up thanking us for all the free publicity the story generated for his maze attraction.

The point of the matter is, of course, if you're going to ask companies to fork over millions of dollars for the right to use the Olympic rings on their products, you can't just let it go when someone uses them for free. Mark Lewis had actually had conversations with another national company that cuts mazes into cornfields all over the country about a licensing arrangement with us. I couldn't believe that there is really a national maze cutting company—what a country! Anyway, they passed on the offer. They said they could not afford our licensing fee and they ended up doing mazes with winter sports themes without the Olympic rings in them. He had a right to expect that we would not allow one of his competitors to use the same rings for free.

There is also a rule of law that forces you to take action when you learn about copyright infringement. If someone uses the Olympic rings and we know about it and do nothing, then that can become precedent in the same or similar setting and we forfeit our right to enforce the brand elsewhere. The law prohibits the Olympics or any other corporate brand holder from prosecuting violations capriciously. It's either a zero tolerance policy or it is nothing. We had to act.

We had to get a local tire company to take down a billboard on the freeway that featured five tires arranged like the Olympic rings. And we had repeated run-ins with the Brighton Ski Resort. A clever ad campaign touted the fact that Brighton "was the proud host of zero Olympic events." It would have been clever if it were not for the fact that the word "Olympic" is protected property. Even though they were not looking for positive Olympic association, quite the contrary, and they were being funny, it could create a difficult precedent. The USOC went after them. They relented.

ROVING AGENTS

We had a crew of people driving around to stores looking for pirate products. Our chief of brand enforcement, Ann Wall, was a woman of diminutive stature. She stood slightly over five feet with blond-brown hair and an amiable nature, but she cast a long shadow. She could strike fear in local retailers. Oftentimes, the retailers themselves did not know they were shelving pirated merchandise. Our official licensing program ran the gamut from t-shirts and stuffed animals to snow globes and official 2002 whiskey shot glasses. Much of the legal merchandise came from China just like the pirated stuff. Ann had customs officers in Los Angeles on the lookout for unauthorized shipments, but sometimes things got through. Ann or one of her people would conduct regular tours of the retail establishments in several states and when they found unauthorized merchandise, they would confiscate it. There was no reimbursement for the retailers themselves. They had paid for the material and were just out the cash.

Licensing revenues were an important element in our revenue model. Whereas sponsorship agreements guarantee a certain dollar level of contribution, licensing deals granted us a certain percentage of sales. T-shirts and hats with the 2002 Olympic logos on them were very popular with the local residents in Utah as well as souvenirs for those who traveled to the Games. One of our more popular licensing deals was with Dale of Norway, maker of beautiful Norwegian wool knit sweaters.

As with sponsorships, every licensing deal was a little different. With many it was straight percentage. Mattel Toys gave us a $1 million guarantee with 10 percent of revenues after that. With other merchandisers there were combinations of percentages and fees involved or other contributions. For example, our creative team responsible for the opening and closing ceremonies wanted flashlights for all the spectators. It was a way to involve the audience in the events and the effect of all those flashlights waving together was stunning. Each flashlight would cost about a dollar, right? Even with the batteries included. But when you think that there are 55,000 seats in Rice Eccles Stadium and full houses projected for the ceremonies, it adds up to $110,000 for opening and closing. And if we wanted nice keepsake flashlights with an Olympic logo on it, that would cost a little more. You have to pay someone to pack the flashlights into the Olympic seat packs. Before long you're talking about several hundred thousand dollars for that effect.

So we found a flashlight vendor who was willing to contribute the flashlights for a discounted licensing arrangement. He would produce keepsake flashlights for our ceremonies, and we would allow him to sell flashlights just like ones given out at the ceremonies to the rest of the public.

CULTIVATE THE RELATIONSHIP

Beyond the search for new sponsors, we also made efforts to maximize the value of the relationships we already had. While the basic transaction of sponsorship was often cut-and-dry, there were certain companies that stepped up to bat time and time again when we ran into difficulties. Our best sponsorship companies were true partners in the enterprise. They were the "hall of fame" sponsors.

Think of what Coke did. Coke earned their international sponsor designation with a check for $55 million in cash, not VIK. At that point, Coke would have every right to sit back and assume the attitude of "Okay, what are you going to do for *me* now?" But they just kept giving. They stepped in as a cosponsor of our $25 million torch relay with GM. The torch relay is a logistical nightmare requiring a high level of involvement, not just money. Coke sponsored their own torch runner recruitment, accepted tens of thousands of applications and sponsored a third of our runners. They worked with us every step of the way, providing tables with umbrellas for spectator seating when we described how we wanted to stage little cauldron-lighting ceremonies at mid-day and day's end.

Then they stepped up again to help us with our Olympic Square in downtown Salt Lake City. We were trying to establish Olympic Square as a credible venue where people from the community could come and have an authentic Olympic experience for no money at all.

We thought of running parades through the square with some of the set pieces from the opening ceremonies. We would put the official Olympic products store in the square and try to lure athletes to public appearances and autograph signings. But we felt we needed more for people to do. Coke said, "We can help." They designed and erected a Coca-Cola activity site at a cost of several more millions to them. It was designed and created expressly for people in Salt Lake City. They called their exhibit "On the Ice" and staffed it with Coke employees. They built a 110-foot ice luge track with a 90-degree turn. There was a 40-by-12-foot hockey rink with a regulation goal and a 50-foot sheet of ice for curling. It was all so regular people could experience what some of the athletes experience. All free of charge. Their Coca-Cola On the Ice site had 470,000 visitors!

Coke just kept on giving. Of course, there were two motivations: one, to help their company and two, to be a good partner in the Games. We heard from the more experienced Olympic sponsors like Coke that for every dollar they spent on our sponsorship, they needed to spend one to two dollars more to "activate" their sponsorship. By that, they meant doing things that publicized the fact that they were a sponsor. Remember, for their Olympic sponsorship, we didn't give them ad time on TV. We didn't give them billboards. We didn't even show their names inside the Olympic venues. What they get is the right to use our Olympic logos and trademarks in their advertising and promotions, and for that, they have to spend more money with broadcasters and publishers. And yes, they can spend money around Salt Lake City which helps the Games and at the same time helps associate their brand with the Games. And Coke did that, big time.

Coke wasn't alone. Other "hall of famers" also stepped up to build attractions for our Olympic Square: Samsung, Pfizer, Kodak, Anheuser-Busch, AT&T and others. The team at Bud was always ready to help out when we needed them. Gateway, McDonald's, and Smith's built features for the athlete village. They made the Games better for the athletes even though very few spectators would ever see their efforts.

Visa had a lot more on their mind than to worry about us, but every time we needed to fund a special event or host a group of some kind, they were there to support us. Sead Dizdarevic of Jet Set Sports had circled around the Olympic movement for years, but in Salt Lake, Mark Lewis convinced him to become a full sponsor. More than money, Sead contributed hospitality elements, tens of thousands of tickets for our youth programs, and even a magnificent Christmas party for all SLOC employees.

My friend Kem Gardner was chosen by his fellow board members at Intermountain Health Care to oversee the company's support. In the end, IHC gave us not only the $9 million they had promised, but also recruited hundreds of their doctors and nurses to contribute time as medical volunteers. We never could have paid for the quality and quantity of what they put into the Games. And they did it all as a donation, not even demanding sponsor or supplier rights.

THE RINGS ON THE MOUNTAIN

Another partner, Utah Power, had already signed on as one of our key local sponsors. As the local energy provider in the state, they were an essential partner to provide the billions of kilowatt-hours that would be required to run all of the equipment and systems at our various venues. They came through for us in other ways too. We had seen how in Lillehammer, organizers had lit up some Olympic rings in a farmer's field near the stadium for the opening ceremonies. It was a lovely touch. Then, in Sydney, the rings on the harbor bridge were so dramatic. They really were a focal point for media attention and an ever-present reminder from almost any vantage point in the city that the Games were on.

We decided to put rings on the side of a mountain. We ran the idea past Bill Landels, EVP of Pacificorp which owns Utah Power; he loved the idea. The company made it their own. They offered to build the rings with us and to cover the costs of installment and lighting and disassembly. They were not insignificant costs. It was a big project. We would string the lights on electric cable connected to independent power generators. Together the rings were the size of 10 football fields, with thousands of high output, low energy bulbs, strung on three parallel electric cables that formed the five Olympic rings. Then there came the flack from the environmental activists.

As soon as the good people at "Save Our Mountains" heard about the plan, they began making hay. They charged that the installation would damage the ground cover on the mountain leading up to the site of the rings. I made one of my regular appearances at the Salt Lake City Council Meeting to describe our precautions: the whole program had been environmentally engineered to protect the land. We agreed to re-grade the dirt road when we were done as it had become rutted over prior years. In reality, we would be making it better than its current condition at the time. We also agreed to plant seed when we were through. Finally, we agreed to pay $25,000 to the Nature Conservancy endowment. The environmental groups still said no. If it were not for the courage of Mayor Rocky Anderson standing up to some of his natural constituents, we may not have prevailed. That, and the generosity of Utah Power. They bought thousands of special light bulbs for the project and their own union workers trudged their way up the mountain to install it. In they end, they sought no credit for their generosity. We had agreed to stage a special ceremony at SLOC headquarters for the press heralding Utah Power's support and letting them turn on the switch. But with all of the environmental noise being made, they told us to just go ahead and illuminate it quietly on our own.

It was not exactly the kind of thing you could do quietly. When we tested the installation by illuminating one ring for a few moments a few months before the Games, there were reported UFO sightings in the valley. That solitary ring looked like a giant spacecraft in the pitch black sky: the mountain was invisible at the late hour we chose for our test. A TV helicopter caught the test on tape, however, and spoiled the sightings with the truth. The rings themselves were a signature piece of the overall look during the Games. We even had requests from the community that we illuminate the rings in the early morning as well as in the early evening so the early business commuters could enjoy the Olympic spirit. Few people knew, but it was all made possible by Utah Power and their parent, Scottish Power.

DECRYING OLYMPIC COMMERCIALISM

It would be hard to overstate the contribution that our 63(!) Olympic sponsors made to the 2002 Games. In some countries, where the Games and Olympic committee are financed and backed entirely by the government, sponsors are icing on the cake. In the U.S., unlike every other country in the world, the sponsors pay for the Games. They are the appetizer, main course, and dessert. They gave us money directly and they gave money to the broadcasters for advertising which they in turn gave to us. Ticket sales and donations rounded out our budget. The government provided what it uniquely provides its citizens: transportation and security. The government wrote us no checks; it did not pay one dollar of our direct SLOC budget. No, sponsors did most of that.

I am always mystified by those who say the Games have become too commercial. They also complain that tickets are too expensive for average people. And of course, they would blanch at the thought that the taxpayers should pay for the Games. But just who should pay then? The tooth fairy? Games are expensive because they involve millions of people and are broadcast to billions more. Without the sponsors, we couldn't have Games in America. And I for one think our country needs to show that we can welcome the world to our shores, can serve the citizens of hundreds of countries hospitably, and can root for their heroes alongside our own.

The amazing thing to me is how little commercialization there is in the Games. In every venue, names of sponsors are blocked out. There is not one visible commercial logo or name. See if that is the case at any other sporting event in the world. In the Olympics, it's taken to such an extreme that bottles of water served to athletes, if they will be seen by TV cameras, have the names of the manufacturer blocked out. Cup holders on the seats in the arenas which have beverage names affixed to them are blocked out with tape. The name of the clock manufacturer on scoreboards is not to be above a certain size: IOC representatives measure the letters to make sure. If they are too large, they are covered in tape. Look at the ski bibs of the winter athletes and the jerseys of the skaters: not a single commercial logo. The Olympics even works hard to keep athletes from wearing any item with excessive-sized brand identification on it. There are definitive rules on this that each country must sign. Over-commercialism?

I believe the Olympics are an excellent sponsorship opportunity for many companies. But I have also come to believe that some of the executives and companies that decide to support the Games have other motives as well: they believe in the mission of the Olympics. In making a decision on what sport sponsorship to choose, there are of course numbers to compare. But ultimately, judgment and emotion and feelings enter the decision-making process. And time after time, companies decide to sponsor the Olympics, often to an extent and with a degree of loyalty that I cannot explain solely based upon the numbers. The Olympics play a role in the world that transcends sport. Some people see that, feel that. People like David d'Alessandro—he was outspoken in his criticism because he loves the Games. And when we needed help, he came through. Dick Ebersol and his management team at NBC—they pretend that they broadcast the Games for commercial purposes. Perhaps. But Dick and his team are Olympic converts. They love the Games, the athletes, the Olympic moments. When we sold sponsorships, it was not just because we had a finely tuned pitch. It was also because we broke through. Prazmark's DVD of

Olympic moments reminded them what the Games are about, what they do to people. And so, in a lot more cases than you would predict, people sign up as sponsors. And to the guys who go out on the road, hoping to find Olympic converts like ourselves, those folks are heroes. Every single one is in my hall of fame.

Chapter 11

FUNDS FROM THE FEDS

No matter how well we did cutting costs and raising revenue, we couldn't have Games without the support of the federal government. We counted on them to provide public transportation and public safety, as they had for prior Olympics. Our challenge was twofold: these would cost much more in Salt Lake than they had before, and Congress was in no mood to help a scandal-plagued effort.

For public transportation alone, Salt Lake was budgeted to cost almost five times the Atlanta bill. How was it possible that smaller Winter Games would be so much more expensive than larger Summer Games?

Partly, it's just the nature of Winter Games. The high traffic summer venues tend to be in coliseums and stadiums with pre-built infrastructure. They're next to interstates, with off-ramps and parking lots. The high demand alpine venues are on mountainsides, off narrow, two-lane roads. They have almost no parking. We had to construct access roads, widen highways and overpasses, and build a network of massive park-and-ride lots.

There was another reason Salt Lake would be more expensive than Atlanta. Utah was just starting to upgrade its transportation infrastructure; Atlanta had just completed theirs. When the Games were awarded, Utah was beginning a fifteen-year upgrade of the interstate highway system and a decade-long transit program. With Olympics now scheduled only a few years away, projects that were critical for the Games needed to be accelerated.

When Atlanta won the Games, it was in the final stages of a multi-decade interstate upgrade, subway expansion, airport expansion, and traffic-flow computerization program. These projects had been done through the normal federal/state transportation spending process over a period of many years.

Before we went to Washington with our transportation requests, Utah had already taken advantage of the Olympics halo to get some funding of its own. Shortly after the Games were awarded, the state put together a wish list of transportation projects that could in any way be associated with the Olympics. These were not projects SLOC had requested or, in many cases, needed. Some communities far from our venues asked for federal money to support projects they asserted were needed for the Olympics. The total requests approached $4 billion. Of course, the feds sent them packing.

By the time I arrived, requests had been narrowed down from $4 billion to under $400 million. This revised list, with appropriate documentation and valid Olympic ties, was now under review by Congress and the U.S. Department of Transportation. We were awaiting word.

Separately, the state decided that reconstructing and expanding I-15, which runs the length of the Wasatch Valley, could not be put off until after the Games. Instead of waiting for federal funding, they borrowed $1 billion for a jumpstart. As the first large-scale design-build project in America, they could complete the reconstruction in time for the Games.

Transportation funding was only the start of what we needed from the federal government. The Games would need hundreds of millions of dollars worh of federal support from a long list of departments. In addition, we needed policy actions. We would need an exemption from customs duties for all of the athletic equipment that would be arriving with the athletes. We would need special visa accommodations for athletes and officials. There was the matter of completing a land exchange between Snowbasin and the U.S. Forest Service to allow an access road to be built and financed. All of this and more in a climate that was already skittish about Atlanta's "pork-barrel Olympic spending abuses," and where the scent of our bid scandal was still fresh.

TAKING OUR LICKS

To say the scandal had a polarizing effect on federal appropriators is like saying the Yankees are not very welcome in Boston. When the bid scandal broke in November 1998, SLOC was just gearing up for the 1999 appropriations round. An already backbreaking lift for the Utah Congressional delegation would become even more difficult. SLOC's one employee working on federal funding, Cindy Gillespie, had been pulled from her government work to help look through old bid committee files. One of my first decisions was to get her back into running our federal lobbying effort.

By the time I arrived at SLOC, two of the most powerful members of Congress were sending signals that hearings on the Olympic scandal were in the offing. It was rumored that Senator John McCain of Arizona, a long-time opponent of inappropriate federal spending for international sporting events, and Congressman John Dingell of Michigan, an aggressive investigator of any potential impropriety, were considering reviewing all federal spending on Olympics going back to the Los Angeles Games of 1984.

Senator McCain and Senator Ted Stevens of Alaska were threatening that Congress might revoke the tax deductibility of sponsorships. That would nail the coffin of the Salt Lake Olympics and future Games. Further, Stevens and McCain threatened to revoke Olympic broadcast licensing rights after the NBC contract expired in 2008. And while Senator McCain had a history of fighting waste in Olympic funding, Senator Stevens was the author of the U.S. Amateur Sports Act that created the USOC. He is affectionately called "the father of the U.S. Olympics." When Ted Stevens started to criticize, everyone in the Olympic world sat up and took notice. It was finally time for real reform at all levels of the Olympic movement. And while all that was happening, our Games needed record breaking federal support.

INITIAL STEPS

Our approach in Washington was the same as with the media: tell the truth, be open and transparent, and be clear about what we will need to succeed. My first trip to Washington was to meet with the people who would carry the mantle of the Salt Lake Olympics in Congress—the Utah Congressional delegation. Utah has a small delegation—two senators, like every other state, but only three Congressmen. These five men had borne the brunt of the snide comments and asides from their colleagues in Washington each time a scandal story appeared in the *Washington Post*. Nevertheless they greeted me warmly. We would need the support of the federal government on an unprecedented level and we would need their commitment to be in the lead in Washington. One by one, they gave me that commitment and, to a man, they lived up to it. From that first meeting, Senator Hatch, Senator Bennett, Congressman Hanson, Congressman Cannon, and Congressman Cook made the success of our Games a top priority.

As the "Father of the U.S. Olympics," Senator Stevens was another "must see." In addition to his involvement in the Olympics, he chairs the powerful Senate Appropriations Committee—the Congressional arm that writes the annual funding plan for the entire federal government. It was imperative that Senator Stevens understand both our financial dilemma and our commitment to restore credibility. As the

Utah member on the Appropriations Committee, Senator Bennett graciously arranged and attended the meeting with us.

I had been forewarned that Senator Stevens is not a chatty person. He gets right to business and he is direct and straightforward in his speech. Senator Bennett said to look at his tie to judge how to make my pitch. If he is wearing the Incredible Hulk, get ready to battle. If he is wearing his Tasmanian Devil tie, just pack it up. I was lucky—no Hulk or Devil.

Over the years I would come to know the Senator well; underneath the gruff exterior is a brilliant mind and a heart committed to America. On my first visit, I wanted to convince him to give us a decent shot at trying to pull off the Salt Lake Olympics. I rehearsed our commitment to ethical conduct, openness, and fiscal responsibility. He gave me his opinion of the IOC in blunt terms. He also told me money was tight and that we would have to prove we needed it. But he said that if we upheld our end of the bargain, he would be there to help put the Salt Lake Games back on track.

Next, I went to see Senator John McCain. In the Olympic world, Senator McCain was viewed as the alter ego of Senator Stevens. Where Senator Stevens sought to protect the Olympics, Senator McCain had earned the unfair reputation of being out to destroy the Games. In reality, the Senator did not oppose the Olympics—he simply opposed the federal government paying for the Games, particularly when he saw any waste and abuse. And he had plenty of examples.

In 1993, Congress appropriated millions of dollars for military support for the 1994 World Cup Soccer Games. But the soldiers there were given non-military duties. They drove buses, carried luggage, handled communications—anything that the organizing committee needed a strong back and a reliable body to do. It saved the World Cup millions of dollars.

But the 1994 World Cup, unlike the Olympics, were a for-profit corporation—and they made an enormous profit. Then they made two mistakes that would cause international sports problems in

Washington for years to come. First, they announced that the reason for this profit was the millions in taxpayer money and military support and, second, they decided to pay their CEO a $6 million bonus.

Senator McCain went ballistic. He fired off a letter to Attorney General Janet Reno telling her to recover the money from the World Cup organization. She sent back a sarcastic response pointing out that she could not recover the funding because the organization was only following the law and spending the money that Congress had directly appropriated to them. Since that time, Senator McCain had been a man on a mission. Every time an appropriation came up for an international sporting event—even the Special Olympics—he opposed it. Every time, he lost the vote. But he kept all future organizing committees on their toes justifying their funding and being extremely careful how they spent it.

My meeting was to tell Senator McCain that we needed the federal government to provide more support for our Games than for any other Olympics in history. Fortunately, I knew Senator McCain from Republican political circles. He was cordial and friendly. His anger was focused on the IOC and he reacted positively to SLOC's new ethics rules. He commented on some of the changes he had heard we were making—like no longer having private cars and drivers for every IOC member. But he was also direct about his dislike of taxpayer funding for Olympics. While the meeting did not change his position, it did establish an open line of communications which proved invaluable.

The most unusual meeting of my first trip to D.C. was with Senator Ted Kennedy. Senator Kennedy obviously has a great deal of power in Washington; I knew that as the Senator from my home state and as someone I had once run a campaign against. Many of his colleagues in the Senate would look to him to see whether or not they should support me in my new role as Olympics chief. A quiet word from him could help me succeed or it could make it easy for me to fail. Additionally, as my home state Senator, I knew it was the appropriate courtesy to ask for a meeting with him before I went too far in making contacts on Capitol Hill.

Senator Kennedy and I met for close to an hour that day and he made it clear that he was committed to helping me in Washington with the Olympics. Any concern that he might hold my earlier campaign against me and against the Olympics was gone. Not only did he and his staff help us out when we had military issues, but several times when Democratic members and the Clinton White House checked with Senator Kennedy to check out this Romney fellow at the Olympics, we were given a wholehearted endorsement.

My first visit also included a meeting with the co-chairs of the White House Task Force on the Olympic and Paralympic Games. Originally chaired by Vice President Al Gore, the task force was very ably directed by two co-chairs, Mickey Ibarra of Utah, the White House special assistant for intergovernmental affairs, and Thurgood Marshall, Jr., the secretary of the cabinet. The task force was a tremendous ally for us in cutting through the red tape and time-consuming bureaucracy of federal departments in order to get things done within the abbreviated Olympic timetable.

I had a little fun at Cindy's expense at the White House that day. She was a little nervous that her new Republican boss might not behave appropriately when he met with the White House Democrats. As a life-long Democrat, Cindy had worked closely with the Clinton administration to prepare for the Atlanta Games and now for Salt Lake. Both on a personal and professional level, people in the White House had become her friends. As a lifelong Republican, I had already made it clear to her that I had strong feelings about President Clinton. In my estimation, he had disgraced our nation and himself.

When we got through the Secret Service checkpoint for clearance to go to the West Wing, the agent handed each of us a badge to wear around our necks. Mine had a big, red A. I turned to Cindy and, in front of the agents, said, "Why do I have to wear this?" Thinking I was confused, she tried to explain that all visitors to the White House had to wear a badge. "I know that," I responded, "I'm asking why *I* have to wear the red A around *my* neck. *I'm* not the one that cheated on *my* wife. *He* should be wearing the scarlet A—not me." I grumbled all the way up the drive and into the West Wing visitors lobby. The look on Cindy's face was priceless.

Our meeting with Mickey and Goody, as I came to call them, was all positive. They clearly understood what it's like to do a tough job in the middle of a scandal and they pledged to provide whatever help and support they could. I was impressed by their commitment, both in that meeting and over the next two years. Mickey and Goody always knew that the Games would actually be held under the next president, but they also knew that it would be the Clinton administration that would put in place the federal underpinnings. They believed in the ideals of the Olympics. Much of our success is due to the leadership they showed daily in pulling together federal operations and support for an event that would take place long after they had left.

SUBSTANCE, NOT FLASH

The Olympics had evolved into an "image-conscious" high-spending movement at almost every level. The K Street Corridor, fondly known as Gucci Gulch, had been the site of SLOC's offices. The Atlanta Olympic offices had been even more ostentatious, located inside a prestigious law firm next door to the White House. Atlanta furnished Cindy with an apartment in the same building as Attorney General Janet Reno and Congressman Joe Kennedy. She was given a BMW to drive the ten blocks from her apartment to her office. Her expense account was basically unlimited. No money would be spared; this to give Congress and the White House confidence in the Olympics.

I thought they were nuts.

In the new SLOC, Cindy would need office space in Washington, but nothing lavish. She found a third-floor walk-up office two blocks from the Capitol—right between Burrito Brothers and Bubbles Hair

Salon. The stairs to our office were so narrow and so steep that one SLOC employee couldn't get up them. I had not given Cindy enough money for furniture so she had called the General Services Administration—the government agency that does all the buying for the federal agencies. Surely they must have some furniture that they were getting ready to throw away? Indeed, they did, so we got desks with broken legs, credenzas with doors that fell off, mismatched chairs and a bookcase with no shelves. Cindy hated it—I thought it was perfect. It sent just the message I wanted to send in DC—there would be no extravagance and no opulence at these Olympics.

Another Washington activity that was severely curtailed when I arrived was the giving of small gifts. But considering that we were under investigation for giving improper gifts during the bid, I couldn't imagine how we would give gifts in DC with a straight face now—or who would be brazen enough to take them. That line item was one of the first to come out of the budget.

But even as I refused to spend money on offices and gifts, I asked Cindy to put together a budget for a Washington operation that could deliver the kind of funding we needed. SLOC already had contracts with two individuals that Cindy had worked with for many years. Jody Trapasso was a well-known Democratic operative who had been part of President Clinton's original presidential personnel team. Jody had personally been involved in hiring almost every major and minor appointee in the Clinton administration. He had left the government in 1995 and was a natural to serve as our liaison with the administration.

Mike Huerta was also under contract to us at that time, and Cindy proposed bringing him in-house as a part-time employee. Mike was an incredible resource. He is one of the most capable and competent people I have worked with. Mike has an extensive background in transportation, having served as the port director in San Francisco and New Jersey, as well as chief of staff at the U.S. Department of Transportation. Later, as the assistant secretary of transportation, he oversaw Olympic-related activities for the Atlanta

Games. He had firsthand knowledge of our unique transportation challenges.

Cindy asked for new spending in two areas. First, we didn't have anyone on staff that specialized in the Congressional appropriations. The appropriations process is very specialized and we were having a difficult time making any progress with House budget appropriators: the committee staff had not forgotten Utah's original request for $4 billion. Cindy found a small firm with a new partner named Jean Denton. Jean had just left the House Appropriations Committee staff, so she knew the players and the process. Jean charged about half of what other firms wanted, and she guaranteed that we would have her primary attention and focus. There was just one problem. She was almost eight months pregnant. She would bring the House transportation appropriations staff out to Utah the following week and then fly back in time to meet her doctor's moratorium on air travel.

On that trip, the lead staff person for the subcommittee was a bright and handsome young man named John Blazey. John was extremely skeptical of the need for any expanded transportation system for the Olympics. After a morning of touring venues in the Salt Lake Valley, our team took Jean and John up to Park City on a bus loaded with state and SLOC transportation officials. The interstate from Salt Lake City to Park City has the steepest climb of any interstate in the country. As the bus was making its way up, and our staff was explaining how difficult it would be to transport thousands of people up this mountain in the snow and ice, fate decided to help us prove our point. Smoke started pouring from the engine compartment and the driver ordered all aboard to abandon ship. So, there they stood by the side of the road—the transportation team for the Salt Lake Games, a very pregnant lobbyist, and one of the key people who would determine whether or not we would get the federal support we needed. They were rescued by a passing bus of tourists. The driver of the tourist bus announced over the loudspeaker that the group they had just rescued was planning the transportation system for the Salt Lake Olympics. Priceless.

Apparently, John realized that if we could not even make it up the mountain with a single bus, we were going to need some help to pull this thing off. He spent several more months digging into our requests, even traveling to Sydney that summer to see how other countries put on Games. Eventually, he and others were convinced that our requests were essential for an effective transportation system. But it all started with that one broken bus.

Cindy wanted to hire another transportation lobbyist in order to stop the particular lobbyist from killing our funding requests. As I mentioned, a lot of people in Utah were trying to get funding out of Washington by pretending their projects were Olympic. The Wasatch Front Regional Council was one of those organizations, and they hired Pat McCann, a very well respected transportation lobbyist. Pat called Cindy to tell her that he had been hired for one purpose—to stop her. They wanted more federal money left over for themselves. This was one of the odder hires we did, but I said yes and Pat was retained. Pat turned out to be an extremely valuable member of the team.

One month into President Bush's administration, I called my old friend from Massachusetts, chief of staff Andy Card to ask for support and a contact point. He assigned us to Joe Hagin, deputy chief of staff. By early February 2001, Cindy and I were on our way to Washington to meet with Joe and with several members of the new cabinet. The new administration was no nonsense: instead of having us coax funding from each congressional committee, President Bush put all Olympic matters in his budget. That was a first.

Our meeting with new Health and Human Services (HHS) Secretary Tommy Thompson was also an encouraging change. A former governor, Thompson didn't put up with the Washington bureaucratic processes. I had come to see Secretary Thompson because, in spite of the commitments made by the previous HHS secretary, Donna Shalala, we were not getting any support from the Center for Disease

Control (CDC). This was particularly puzzling because Secretary Sha-lala at the Sydney Olympics had introduced herself to everyone there as "Mitt's banker." Everyone thought it was quite amusing—and I would have too if HHS had been willing to provide any support. But as it was, they were the one department that had done nothing.

I told Secretary Thompson about our problem. He swiveled his chair around to the phone and told his assistant to get the head of the CDC on the phone. "When?" she asked. Now, he said. Should we give him a heads up on the subject and let him call you back? No, he said. Get him now. While we waited, he noted that if the bureaucrats had their way, his staff would talk to the CDC director's staff and maybe in a month we would have an answer.

When he got the director he asked him why they were not in Salt Lake helping prepare for bio-terror and disease control. The director said he would look into it. Thompson told him to go there himself and give him a personal report within a week. The director asked for more time. He was told no.

That resolved, we thanked the secretary and headed to our next meeting with Attorney General John Ashcroft.

Like Thompson, Ashcroft was also making things happen. A num-ber of security-related decisions were stuck in the bureaucracy at Jus-tice and needed to be shaken loose. The attorney general was very direct and to the point. The Olympics, he said, were a terrorist target and Justice would treat the Games as such. He and the DOJ would be fully committed to the safety of our Games; Olympic decisions would be made directly from his office. In fact, prior to the Games, he per-sonally visited Salt Lake and walked or skied the perimeter of each venue.

Over the course of 2001, we would meet with all the members of the cabinet and would find unprecedented support for our Games. A solid groundwork had been put in place by the Clinton administra-tion, and the Bush administration was committed to building on that groundwork. They wanted the Games to succeed. This partnership escalated after September 11. Officials working on the Games became so intertwined with our staff, and our purpose became so united, that it was hard sometimes to remember who worked for SLOC and who worked for the government. We became one team.

BEING SUCCESSFUL IN WASHINGTON:

1. Tell the Truth—the Whole Truth

The perception in Washington was that the folks from Utah didn't tell the truth—partly because of the bid scandal and partly because of the state's earlier request for billions in "Olympic projects," some located hundreds of miles from the Games. Shortly after my arrival, there was one more truth stretching exercise underway. The City of Salt Lake and the Utah Transit Authority (UTA) were lobbying in Washington for a new light rail project, connecting the airport to the university.

The City and UTA believed Washington would never provide the money unless they were told that we couldn't do the Games without the light rail line. Two weeks into my new job, I received an urgent message from Mayor Deedee Corradini requesting my signature on a letter to Washington indicating that the city's light rail project was "essential" to our Olympic Transportation Plan. I asked our transportation and federal relations staff if that were true. No. Light rail would be helpful in moving people during the Games, but it was by no means a "must have." I refused to sign the letter.

I had set off a firestorm. But the more I looked into it, the more convinced I was that by exaggerating the Olympic connection of the project, the City was actually hurting, rather than helping the project. Under all the normal criteria, this project would probably have been funded by Washington. But because they were putting an "Olympic" label on it, the project was receiving special scrutiny from Washington and had become a political hot potato.

Again in May, I was asked to sign a similar letter. At a meeting designed to get me on board, I persisted. One county's commissioners said the only reason they had supported the Olympics in the first place was for the legacy benefits. A similar view was expressed by Will Jeffries, head of the Wasatch Front Regional Council, who threatened that if we did not play ball on light rail we would have a hard time getting the money we needed through his operation to build the intersections, parking lots, and roads that were essential for the Games.

We did not back down. I agreed to support the project but I refused to say it was a critical component of the Olympic transportation plan. We were viewed as the villains who were preventing the city from getting the light rail project they had been promised by the bid committee.

In the end, we were able to get all the parties to join forces and present an unvarnished proposal to the federal government. Congress and FTA then agreed to a full-funding agreement to do a portion of the light rail project that could be built before the Games. Truth had been the most convincing argument. Ironically, while light rail was indeed helpful for our transportation during the Games, it was closed down by the Secret Service on the nights of opening and closing ceremonies.

2. Find the Right Fit

The federal government is not like a large corporation with centralized decision-making. It is more like hundreds of independent entities, each pursuing their own agendas. Getting help from Washington depended on matching our need with a specific agency's mission. When we needed support for the Paralympics, for example, we looked to see which federal agencies had programs that supported the disabled. Almost all of them, it turned out.

We would also adapt our plans to meet the federal goals. Bus drivers were an example. We needed about 1,200 buses for the Games, far more than were available in Utah. Like Atlanta, we hoped to convince cities across America to loan us their transit buses, during their busiest season, for free. The biggest obstacle was the cities' concern about who would drive them.

The buses that had been loaned to Atlanta were treated terribly. Atlanta used soldiers to drive the buses—soldiers who were only given a few days training before being put behind the wheel. Buses were returned with missing fenders, ripped sides, ruined engines, and broken headlights. We would have to guarantee experienced drivers. Tom Halleran, our head of transportation and a longtime bus guy, decided that the best way to get the transit authorities on board was to ask them to send drivers with their buses—and we would pay the drivers union wages. We got more driver applicants than we had positions—drivers who were willing to take vacation during the Olympics and drive buses for us. We covered their travel. We housed them. We provided uniforms. And because the Department of Transportation worked in partnership with us to talk to the transit authorities and talk to the unions, we were able to design the program so that the federal government could reimburse the hourly cost of the drivers.

Most important, the Olympic transportation plan in Salt Lake worked. I believe it was the first time any Olympics in history had a transportation system that worked from day one. We were proud and the U.S. Department of Transportation was proud. The bus drivers who displayed their home city on their panels were proud. They reminded us that we really were hosting America's Games.

3. Never, Never, Never Give Up

If you work at it long enough, there is always another way to get the help you need in Washington. We planned to build our athlete's Olympic Village at the University of Utah. After the Games, it would become married student housing. The available space was actually part of an historic military fort. It still belonged to the National Guard. For more than two years, Congress had worked to relocate the Guard unit to another site so that construction could begin. The schedule was tight.

In September, Congress passed a Military Construction Appropriations bill that included $20 million for the relocation of the Guard unit. The unit could move and the land would be ready for construction.

But Congress had just given the president the line item veto, and this bill was the first time President Clinton would use it. The headline in the *Washington Post* read, "Clinton Vetoes Olympic Village." This came as a shock to the White House. No one had known that the money was to make way for the Olympic Village. Then, the Supreme Court decided to review the president's line item veto authority: Congress could not fix this until the following year—too late for us to finish the Olympic Village on time.

Cindy didn't give up. After being told by lawyer after lawyer that there was no way to fix the problem, Undersecretary of the Army Mike Walker found a solution. Secretary of the Army Togo West ordered the Guard unit to vacate the land. He didn't relocate them— he just directed them to leave, pronto. The document ordering the Guard to vacate the land gave the lawyers what they needed to transfer the property in time to start the Village.

PUBLIC HEROES

At one time, people in public service had the choice to go into the private sector and make money. While politics and bureaucracy may have taken away some enthusiasm over time, when given the chance, the idealist comes back out. In spite of the scandal, people wanted the Games to succeed and they thoroughly enjoyed helping us.

A few months before the Games were held, I asked Scott Givens to create the "Olympic Order of Excellence" for honorees from government. SLOC senior management must agree on each recipient. We presented these awards in April 2002. I left my campaign in Massachusetts to say thank you to these individuals.

Ron Acker, a senior member of the visa services office at the State Department, began working with Olympic issues for the Atlanta

Games. The image of government employees who come in at 8:00 a.m. and leave at 4:30 p.m. does not apply to Ron. For the month that athletes were coming into America for the Games, Ron took a sleeping bag to work and slept under his desk. Twenty-four hours a day, he monitored flights, passports, visas, and made sure that everyone got into the country in time to compete. He developed the new electronic visa procedures and personally convinced the FBI, Secret Service and CIA that they could work. And, after nine years of working to make the Olympics a success, we invited him to join us in Salt Lake for the Games. But Ron's priority was making the system work and he knew he needed to be in Washington. Ron made America look good to the world community. Together with Secretary Armitage in the ceremonial 8th floor diplomatic reception room, we presented the award to a surprised public servant.

John Blazey was the staffer in the bus that broke down on its way to Park City. Since that time, he had immersed himself in the intricacies of the Olympics and, in no small measure, our success in Washington was due to his involvement. John was always our toughest questioner, but he had also come to believe in the power of the Games. He was determined that the image we would present to the world would reflect all that was good in our country.

In typical fashion for John, he did not come to the Games as a dignitary or honored guest. Instead, he asked Cindy if he could work as a volunteer. He put in long hours and long days as a member of our team.

I flew to Salt Lake to give the third Order of Excellence to John Hoagland. Years earlier, the U.S. Forest Service had tapped John to head their Olympic team. Under John's direction, the Forest Service handled a politically explosive land transfer in order to create Snowbasin, site of Olympic Downhill Skiing. They helped develop the Paralympic events at Snowbasin under our Americans with Disability Act program. After September 11, the Forest Service stepped up with even more personnel capable of handling difficult and dangerous security assignments on tough mountain slopes. Now that the Games were done, John was taking the retirement he had waited for. But first, we needed to say thank you.

Everything we did at the Olympics was because of the people who shared our vision and stretched to achieve it. Thousands of public employees took part in making our Games a success. The Games really were a national event.

Chapter 12

REACHING INTO
THE COMMUNITY

In most Olympic cities, there is a normal progression of attitudes about the Games. When the IOC president announces that the city has been selected to host the Olympics, there is spontaneous celebration. That was surely the case in Utah. President Samaranch's announcement was broadcast on a super screen in front of City Hall. When he designated Salt Lake City as the winner of the IOC vote, the air was instantly filled with a hail of hats, hands, confetti, streamers, and cheers. The visual was broadcast hundreds of times in the years that followed. For most host cities, there begins from that moment a steady slide of public support and confidence. The media gleefully leads an agonizing reappraisal. Every imaginable interest group will claim that the Games will hurt their constituency and as a result, they will look for financial or other consideration from the organizers. And the inevitable mistakes and failings of the people who run the Games will be exposed time and again. The net result is that the sentiment in the community for the Games drops to its nadir just before the Olympians arrive. The CEO of the

Lillehammer Games reported that less than 20 percent of the populace viewed the Games positively prior to the arrival of the Olympic torch.

Salt Lake City community support didn't follow the slow descent pattern: community support dropped like a stone. There were polls taken, of course. Three out of four Utahns thought the reputation of the state had been hurt by the scandal. Three out of four thought Salt Lake City was to blame for its own woes. More than half of respondents expected that some sort of taxpayer bailout was likely; only 44 percent thought the Games could secure adequate financing.

Almost a year later, we had made a start on turning around attitudes. As of December 1999, 64 percent favored hosting the Games and almost 80 percent thought SLOC would be successful. Belief that we could secure adequate financing rose from 44 percent at the beginning of 1999 to 66 percent by mid-2000 and continued to track upward. Two-thirds of respondents thought the Olympic movement had been improved through the whole experience of the scandal. The sense of reappraisal was an upward trend, not a downward one.

The extent of our effort to rebuild confidence and positive sentiments had known few bounds. From media to government, from homeless advocates to gay and lesbian activists, and from churches to corporations, we walked every imaginable road to recover what had been lost. The most visible of our efforts were played out in the media. The most hands-on campaign had been face-to-face selling in communities up and down the Wasatch mountain front.

TOWN COUNCILS AND COUNTY COMMISSIONS

I think I know which comes first between the chicken and the egg, but I can't tell whether public opinion or politician rhetoric precedes the other. I do know that after the scandal broke, politicians were vocal in their criticism of everything SLOC. Maybe they just wanted to catch up with public sentiment. Or perhaps they were hoping that by expressing vehement critique now, people would forget that they didn't have much to say when it would have made a difference. Whatever the reason, a number of politicians and their like were highly critical, even cynical.

The City of Salt Lake had a top administrator who was particularly unforgiving. Roger Black was not a politician, but he followed the lead of his boss Mayor Corridini in strenuously resisting our plans. At one point, I quite vehemently expressed my dissatisfaction with his take on Games preparations. Of course, he was expressing the viewpoint of the mayor, but I couldn't very well vent my frustration at her—she was one of my bosses. When the mayor left office, Roger was out of a job.

I knew I had a big task ahead of me to rebuild trust with municipalities. Fraser added that we also needed hundreds of permits and approvals from them. We needed a full time person to run point for us with local governments. Roger came to mind. I asked him to lunch and made an offer. First, though, I had to eat humble pie. I acknowledged that he had been loyal to the mayor, and direct and perceptive with us. He knew the municipal obstacles and personalities better than we ever would. In short, SLOC, and I, needed his help. He had already begun to respond to much better offers than ours. But like so many others, he put things aside for a couple of years for the Olympics.

Shelley Thomas and Roger convinced me that I needed to personally visit communities across the valley. "Answer questions, clear up misperceptions, and gin up the Olympic Spirit with videos and a rah rah speech." I would appear in town meeting-like events in each of Salt Lake's seven council districts as well as many other towns and cities.

There were a lot of concerns. First and foremost for local officials, the $59 million in deferred sales tax revenues. The success or failure of the Games would have a direct financial effect on them. They had also heard horror stories from Atlanta about having basic services overrun by the influx of visitors. They worried about basic security provisions, about traffic, about a migration of homeless people from around the country, and about the environmental impact of the Games.

The meetings were invariably well attended. The high school gymnasium would be packed. On one occasion, Roger called me, having gone ahead to the site of one of these meetings. He warned me that it would be a full session and that most of those in attendance fell into one of two camps: "They've either got blue hair or hiking boots." The senior population tended to worry about taxation and the environmental lobby wanted to make sure we dealt responsibly with natural resources.

When issues were raised, some folks were just itching for a fight, but I saw no profit in obliging them. Even though it often seemed that their concerns may have been exaggerated, on most occasions I would nevertheless concede the point. My retort had nothing to do with their challenge; instead, I reminded them of the greater purpose of the Games. "Yes, the traffic *will* be bad, there *will* be environmental impacts, but we have a once in a lifetime opportunity to be of service to the world. It will be worth the sacrifice, won't it?" "Yes, security forces *will* make our city look like an armed camp, but we and our visitors from all over the world will be safe, right?"

As it turned out, traffic during the Games was relatively light, we had zero net environmental emissions and security was tight but not intrusive. Prior to the fact, however, there was no way to allay fears. Whether in Washington, D.C., or in Provo, Utah, I found that disputing people's concerns usually led to defensiveness and entrenched positions. I'd look instead for a transcendent value upon which we both could agree.

I remember in particular an audience in Heber City, Utah. This is a small farm community in a lovely valley near one of our venues. Athletes competing in biathalon and cross country events would be staying in the small motels in the town where travel to the competitions would be fast and easy. Well, one questioner was concerned that because we had rented all the motels for the athletes, there wouldn't be any "international jet setters able to stay in Heber—people who will shop in our stores." Now, Heber is a farm town, a cowboy town. Somehow I couldn't see those jet setters setting in Heber, buying Big Gulps at the 7-Eleven. But you know, he was right, and I said so. They would be sacrificing what they could sell to spectators by having athletes. No one objected. In fact, the remarkably good people of Heber City, Utah, applauded, generously.

The message of serving the world was made for the people of Utah. People don't mind giving of themselves for a worthy cause, they rise to the challenge. What they mind is being patronized and being told that their concerns are not valid. Despite the host of difficulties some people felt the Games were likely to bring, the unavoidable fact of the matter was that they were coming. We could alter our preparations in anticipation of greater trouble, but the Games would come.

The problem with the cities and towns was not their worries or their wearying doomsday scenarios, it was that some saw the Olympics only as a way to make a few bucks. The hope that the Games would bring financial dividends had been a part of the early appeal of the bid: increased visibility could bring greater economic development. But it was not long-term growth that many of these municipalities sought, it was windfall. And they wanted SLOC or the federal government to pay. Of course, to the team that was working to cut unnecessary costs and to bring in new revenues to enhance the Games, the thought of paying tribute to localities was anathema.

Midway is a delightful mountain community that played host to our cross-country skiing. They did a spectacular job. Soldier Hollow was situated on the side of a stunning mountain. Olympic audiences could literally watch almost the entire cross-country race from their seat in the stands. Whereas most international competitions in these sports have courses that weave in and out of alpine forests, almost invisible to the spectators, our Soldier Hollow designers had constructed a course with all the dips and curves and stretches in an elaborate pattern that was almost entirely visible from any vantage point.

While cross-country skiing is low on the list of compelling winter sports for American spectators, it is as popular as football or baseball to the Scandinavians. We expected crowds. We had constructed a temporary parking structure in a farmer's field not far from the course and the road that accessed the field was perfectly adequate for heavier traffic. But we decided to use a secondary access road for the athletes themselves so that they would not be delayed by spectators. The world's cross-country and biathlon competitors were staying at a mountain resort called the Homestead and there was an old, weatherbeaten back road that led from the Homestead to the venue. This road was nothing fancy. It had potholes and cracks, but we would only be sending a few athlete vans down it over the course of the Games, nothing like the crush of Olympic spectators.

Midway decided that if we were going to use the old access road from the Homestead, the city had a right to demand that it be repaired and repaved. It was a $100,000 expense. We did not need that road repaved. But Midway would not grant us the permits we needed to operate the venue unless we agreed to pay for the repairs. They had us over a barrel. Here we were, struggling financially, striving against the scandal to scramble together enough resources to stage the Games and bring honor to the state, and Midway was looking for a freebie, a handout from us. It absolutely steamed me, and I wouldn't do it. I could not agree.

It was ultimately settled. We paved the road. But the staff had to get me out of the way first. I was not about to compromise on this one. I would not let SLOC be held hostage. Nevertheless, we needed to move forward with the business of the Games. I agreed to step aside so my team could carry on negotiations.

Fortunately, the sentiment of the Midway citizens was a far cry from their politicians. Perhaps more than any town in the Olympic region, the people of Midway hosted the world with warmth, hospitality, and panache. Under the leadership of one of the town's premier citizens, Tom Whitaker, and with the help of scores of volunteer leaders like Valerie Kelson, the people of Midway built a western pioneer village surrounding the ski venue. They literally moved historic cabins to the site, built an Indian village, filled corals with bison, staged live entertainment, and even operated a series of

horse drawn hay rides for spectators. In the center of the competition area, a cowboy campsite bustled day and night, stocked with
veritable cowboys and mountain men caring for horses and preparing meals at the chuck wagon. Foreign visitors were delighted to get
their first real taste of the cultures of the Old West. Locals brought
their families to see roots of their heritage. And adding enormously
to the experience was the regular arrival of the historic Heber
Creeper: a vintage steam locomotive and train that was given a special landing at the venue, allowing spectators to arrive by rail. The
entire operation was built and staffed by the people of Midway, plus
some friends from the surrounding communities. Each time I would
get heartburn about some government type trying to hit us up for
money, all I had to do was think about the service and dedication of
the citizens.

Midway's politicians were nothing compared to some. Salt Lake
County and other municipalities very nearly got away with imposing
property taxes on our venues, including even the office fixtures and
computers in our headquarters. That would have been a seven-figure
problem for the Olympics and manna from heaven for the county, city
and towns. The state tax code makes it clear that certain organizations are exempt from property taxes. Exempt organizations are those
that perform a charitable purpose or that carry out some function on
behalf of the government. Since Salt Lake City itself had actually
contracted with the IOC to stage the Olympic Games, it seemed
pretty clear to us that we were fulfilling a government responsibility.
But the county tax assessor and some county commissioners saw an
opportunity to bring in some extra money. Again, with all that was
being done by so many people to make Salt Lake and the surrounding communities look good to the world by hosting successful Games,
I couldn't believe the selfishness of a few. I went to the county's tax
hearings and personally testified. The mayor testified on our behalf as
well. Even the state argued for us. The first decision of the county was
against us. Ultimately, the courts saved our bacon.

There were communities where political maneuvers gave us heartburn, but they were the small minority. The municipalities that gave more than was expected vastly overwhelmed the few examples of overreaching. Venue cities like Provo and Ogden decorated their streets to the nines, all at their own expense. Even more impressive was the effort, decoration, and celebration in communities that did not even host an event. Municipalities all over the state purchased Olympic banners and flags for street decoration, held festivals and galas, linked school programs to visiting Olympic athlete nationalities, arranged bus trips for their citizens to Olympic events, and cheerfully backed their citizens and employees who served as Olympic volunteers.

SHARING THE OLYMPICS WITH THE COMMUNITY

I was once invited to the Super Bowl by a business colleague. From my stadium seat, I looked around to an audience that had come from many places, but for the most part, not from the state. It struck me that the local papers were full of Super Bowl stories but that the stadium was not filled with many of the locals who were hosting us.

When the Olympics became my job, one of the first things I decided to do was make sure that the citizens of Utah would be able to experience the Games. That became one of the primary objectives of the Games.

Event tickets are massively expensive, at least for the high demand events. But I had learned from Sydney that the experience doesn't require great front row views to touch the heart. It just means being there, feeling the spirit of the competitors and the spectators. With this in mind, we embarked on a ticket strategy that would get as many Utahns to the Games as possible but also allow us to make the money on ticket sales that our budget required. I called our plan, barbell pricing. At one end, we had a big block of very expensive tickets, priced as high as the market and the IOC would allow. At the other end, we had a large block of very inexpensive tickets, largely for the locals. We did not have a lot of pricing in the middle. At figure skating, our better seats went for over $400, but our seats in the balcony went for $35 to $50, even for the gold medal rounds.

Some events, like cross country and biathalon were not in high demand from our visitors. We priced them at very low levels and heavily marketed them locally to get as many Utah parents and kids into an Olympic event as possible. Our estimate was that over 40 percent of all the tickets sold for the entire Olympics went to Utah residents. That was like no Super Bowl. The Games were shared with the people who produced them.

I don't know who came up with the idea for selling Olympic license plates at a markup over regular plates and using the proceeds to buy tickets for Utah kids, but it was a good one. Cindy Gillespie took the idea even further: she would ask the U.S. Department of Education for funding to pay for tickets to the Paralympics for local children. Mark Lewis worked out a contribution from Jet Set Sports, one of our sponsors, to provide even more tickets to our kids. When we added it all up, we were able to buy or give away 60,000 tickets to kids for the Olympics and 72,000 for the Paralympics. The challenge of actually getting kids to the venues, clothing them for cold weather, and making sure they had adult supervision was an enormous task, skillfully managed by Judy Stanfield, our education director and formerly a school principal herself. She knew the ropes of Utah schools like none of us ever could.

As an experienced educator, Judy knew all the tricks to get kids really involved. We announced the "One Town, One Country" initiative. Each city or town and all its schools adopted a foreign country. We coordinated the country selections so that we covered every country with at least two communities. The school kids learned that country's national anthem, studied its culture, learned about the athletes it would be sending to the Games, and made individual copies of its flag. Then, when the Games began, we encouraged the kids, and the town citizens, to cheer that country's athletes, in addition to our own. We even had kids from the schools welcome the team at the airport and sing their national anthem at our official greeting ceremony at the Olympic Village. Utah kids made paintings that we used to decorate the thousands of athletes' rooms and the shared spaces in the Olympic Village. And when the competitions were underway, I am sure some athletes from the smallest and least well-known countries were surprised to hear cheers and see flags waving in their honor.

As a side note, one of the regular digs from the media is that American audiences aren't welcoming to other nation's athletes. Supposedly, Americans are homers. Well, this "One Town, One Country" program sure changed that. And I observed as well that American audiences at the Games were enthusiastic supporters of excellent performances, regardless of the nationality. But the newspaper articles printed the old canard anyway. I figure some reporters just can't get enough of an old story, even when it is no longer valid.

I thought one of the most innovative ideas to bring the Olympics to the people was the Youth Sport Program, led initially by Shelley Thomas and directed by Bob Bills. SLOC built sport equipment that could provide some of the features of a true Winter Olympic sport. There were luge sleds that worked off a ramp and, my favorite, a trampoline system complete with bungee attachments that enabled a person to get the feel of freestyle aerials. I actually took this to New York for the *Today* show: Ann Curry and I got harnessed up and did a demonstration. She did great; I could not get myself high enough to do the flips. No matter, I was only on national TV with all my friends and family laughing at me.

The equipment was a hit with kids in schools across Utah. We had teams of SLOC people, many of whom were themselves accomplished athletes, drive our equipment to literally hundreds of schools, giving kids a taste of Olympic Winter sport. The kids didn't just watch, they got to try the sport. And even though Utah is a winter sport Mecca, very few Utah kids have ever been on the slopes. Almost none had tried luge, bobsleigh, or freestyle, at least until our youth sport team arrived at their school. Sometimes, our folks found kids who had such a level of interest and proficiency that we enrolled them on pre-Olympic training programs. We found, for example, that several children at a special school for the hearing impaired possessed unusual skill in perceiving the motions and positioning of their body, a talent which proved critical to success in luge. Several followed through to enter junior, pre-Olympic programs.

Street-to-Sport and Sport-to-Sport programs went a step further. Street-to-Sport took troubled or at-risk kids to the ski resorts, taught them to ski, and got them into a sport and off the street. It was funded by the ski resorts, like Park City Mountain Resort and sponsors like Delta Airlines, another of our hall of fame sponsors. Sport-to-Sport looked for kids that were good in one sport that was not in the Winter Games and helped them transition their skills to an Olympic event. Our most noted success was a boy from Heber City who was a terrific gymnast and tumbler: he became an accomplished freestyle aerial competitor on the U.S. Junior Olympic team.

In all, more than 600,000 Utah school children were given Olympic-related experiences. Olympic venues were made accessible to the local public through "wanna-be" camps we organized in the years leading up to the Games. People of all ages signed up for weekend camps in which they received instruction in a new sport and actually tried the Olympic field of play.

My pride and joy when it came to sharing the Olympics with the people of Utah was Olympic Square and the Olympic Medals Plaza. With eight blocks of displays, parades, music, entertainers, and food, the Square was a gathering place. Lines to get in could take well over an hour. Once you got inside, there were no more checkpoints. In addition to our own Olympic store, Coke, Samsung, Kodak, Pfizer, and other sponsors created interactive pavilions for the visitors inside the Square. It was filled from about noon until midnight for seventeen straight days.

The top billing in the square was for the free nightly concerts and the awarding of medals to that day's champions. Twenty-thousand people, half standing and half sitting, filled an outdoor arena for more than two hours of awards, entertainment and music, followed by a fireworks show. And all the tickets were free. We paid to bring in top talent: The Dave Matthews Band, Barenaked Ladies, Sheryl Crow, Brooks and Dunn, Marc Anthony, NSYNC, Foo Fighters and other greats. Olympic Square and Olympic Plaza were financed by the business holding company of the Mormon Church, Hallmark and other sponsors.

MINDING THE CRITICS

Despite our best efforts with the media and our work to include Utahns in the Olympic experience, there was no respite from outspoken critics of the Games. On the one hand, we very badly wanted the public sentiment and support for the Games to grow. If government officials and insiders were throwing stones, I worried that might shake public confidence. But on the other hand, most of the public gadflies and detractors actually helped. They kept us in the news and they kept public expectations in line. The more they heard about impending traffic nightmares, the more they were likely to respond to our share-a-ride program. We didn't have to warn people, the critics did it for us.

There's another aspect of expectations that is just as important. How does the world at large, and the media, expect your Games to match up with Olympics of the past? If expectations are unrealistically high, everyone will go away disappointed when they do not live up to those expectations, even if they are very good. There is a balance to be struck between building support for your enterprise and over-promising. Atlanta had made the mistake of guaranteeing the "best Olympics ever." Then when things went wrong, that was the self-declared standard against which they were measured. Technology systems were to be the most sophisticated in the world; they weren't, and the media howled. Transportation systems were to perform almost flawlessly. When they didn't, the media couldn't wait to get to their computers to tell all. In reality, Atlanta put on really good Olympics, but that was overshadowed with stories about unfulfilled promises.

I didn't want to suffer a similar fate. Our critics made sure that neither the people of Utah nor the media fell prey to unrealistic expectations. We were careful not to become so defensive in our response to the critics that we over-promised. We guaranteed that the Games would showcase remarkable athletes and unveil stories of courage, but we didn't promise flawless computer systems or smooth transportation. With IBM withdrawing and our SLOC team cobbling together, for the first time in Olympic history, a broad group of technology providers, the probability of some kind of technical glitch seemed quite high. I explained to the media, "There is no way this can work, but we will respond to problems quickly."

Interestingly, my efforts to keep expectations in check was misunderstood by our sponsor, SchlumbergerSema, and the IOC. After my comments about the inevitability of problems, they called to demand a retraction. I was casting aspersions on the quality of their work and capability of their people. Of course, that was not at all what we intended; we were able to talk them down from their emotion. But in the future, I used more diplomatic phrasing. But the message still got through.

We responded in similar manner when concerns arose about the effect the Games would have on the homeless. Here the critics were experienced advocates: they knew how to get their alarm into the media. In fact, one advocate group even published an annual report card on SLOC, showing how well—or rather not well—we were doing in addressing problems of homelessness and the like. The papers ate this stuff up. Ed Eynon, Bill Shaw and I met with these groups on a regular basis. It was impossible for an Olympic organizing committee to solve all the social problems of Utah, but we could do everything in our power to help. We could also seek to minimize any negative impact the Olympics might have on the homeless. Here, the detractors provided another vital benefit: they acquainted us with issues we might have missed, and opportunities to help we might have overlooked. As a result of their work, we found truckloads of excess VIK, food for example from Kellogg's, that neither the USOC nor we were going to use. These we donated to the Utah Food Bank.

We didn't always agree with the critics. Sometimes, we felt they were overstating a problem to gain advantage. There was a barrage of media accusations that the Games would hurt the homeless and overburden our social service providers. The advocates reported that in Atlanta, the homeless were bussed out of town to make the city look better for visitors. I simply stated that we would do no such thing: "the people should see our community as it is, not as some would like it to appear." The bigger concern was that there would be a massive influx of homeless who would come to "work the Games," there would not be enough capacity to care for them. We were skeptical: would homeless from other states journey to Utah in the cold of winter? The critics said that Atlanta had seen a huge inflow, but our Atlanta alums couldn't remember seeing it. The advocates brought in social service providers from Atlanta to tell the media about the huge flood of homeless we would see.

When we went to the Sydney Games, I decided to visit the social service providers there to find out what they were experiencing. In my meeting with the manager of the largest shelter network in Sydney, he said that he too had been told to expect hundreds of new homeless. They had built extensive new capacity and recruited additional volunteers to staff shelters and serve meals. But there was no increase at all. The other shelters I visited had similar stories. The problem was overblown there as it was in Utah. I learned something else as a result of my inquiries. I had hoped to have some homeless mothers and children attend the Games as our guests in Utah. Sydney had tried the same thing but found that the homeless did not feel comfortable with the "high roller" crowd. They didn't want tickets. But they did like watching the Games on TV. So instead of pushing free tickets, we arranged TVs for shelters.

Despite the experience of Sydney, we wanted to be prepared for any increase in homelessness we might see. We worked closely with shelter administrators to build their capacity toward Games time. We added beds and, in response to concerns about access to medical care, we set up an accredited cross-town shuttle to get people from the shelters on the west side of Salt Lake City to the hospitals on the east side during the Games. We brought Olympic athletes into the shelters to meet with homeless children. Much of the success of these programs was due to the efforts of our partners in city and county government. They stood up for the homeless communities. Later, the director of the downtown Salvation Army shelter, Major Wayne Froderberg, remarked, "There's been an outpouring of resources. Everybody has said, 'We want to include those who are disadvantaged' in the midst of the celebration. And I believe the community has accomplished just that. I'm proud to be a part of that contribution." He added that one of the lasting benefits of the Games to the community would be the legacy of heightened collaboration between the various agencies providing charitable services.

One reason I got along well with the advocates and critics was that I respected their concerns. It was easy for me to see the negatives associated with the Olympic effort—how economic growth and development was a two-edged sword, how the public would have to assume any debt should the Games prove unprofitable. I had had similar views from my earlier vantage point in Massachusetts. The difference was that I subsequently saw an imperative to fulfill the obligations Salt Lake City had entered into with the international community. And I came to appreciate the greater social benefit the Games could play for the youth of the world.

I sought out our most vocal critics like Steve Pace of Citizens Against Olympic Waste. I asked him for a t-shirt like the one I saw him wearing on TV, printed with the words "Slalom and Gomorrah." And he sent me one. I respected his views even though we usually disagreed; his criticism was a foil against which we would be given the opportunity to clarify our policies with the public.

GETTING SCARY

As much as we got used to constructive critics, we never got over the truly wacky ones. At least once a week Donna Tillery, my incredible assistant, would arrive at my desk with a bizarre letter of some kind. I asked her to give them to me rather than to throw them away. I wanted to see what the lunatic fringe was saying. Maybe I wanted to know whether I needed to take cover.

One highly credentialed soul was convinced that we were going to suffer a massive terrorist event. This conclusion he reached well before the September 11 disaster. That event only heightened his fears and concerns. His knowledge of possible sources of terror led me to believe he was informed. He wrote me as many as twenty or thirty times. He also wrote each Olympic sponsor CEO when they were announced in the paper, encouraging them to withdraw. His credentials and arguments led to a few calls or letters. At the request of his local legislator, I met with him. Not a good idea. My attempt to reassure only inflamed his passion for stopping the Games. I'm sure he was as relieved as I that no terror event materialized.

Another brought forward a plan to finance the Games. His approach was highly professional and filled with reputable references. But I was cautious. I invited the FBI, whose headquarters was in our very same building, to sit outside my office as I listened to his pitch. It turned out that he was a con artist. He had a scheme where SLOC would buy hundreds of millions of "government bonds" which "his organization" would loan to foreign countries resulting in 100 percent profits with no risk. If you don't follow that, neither did I. Our FBI friend had a word with him after he left.

One unsigned letter decried the fact that we had hired Canadians to do what Americans could do as well. I presume the author was referring to Cathy Priestner-Allinger, our head of sport. Yes, she was Canadian but her skills were quite unique.

I kept a file of what I labeled "hate mail." By far the most correspondence I received involved the Mormon church and my membership in it. Even though many included ample repetition of the "f-word," I saved the letters just in case the FBI needed leads if I were to disappear. The fact that Fraser and I were both of the same faith drew a great deal of venom, as well. "Just how white, rich and Mormon will these Games be? That sums up our senators and representatives in Washington: the ineffectual five." I'd never really lived in a place where anyone cared what religion I was. I found this anger more than a little troubling. I understood a little better what my Jewish friends encounter, albeit more violent and dangerous in their case.

The Utah State Government Watch Dog Group of Provo Utah was vehemently anti-Olympics and anti-Mitt Romney: "Mitt Romney took this job because he has higher political aspirations in the state of Utah.... After all, he could not win a Senate seat in Massachusetts—so why not come West to 'Mormonland' to try again." I ignored the group's final recommendation and returned to Massachusetts.

Despite the angry rhetoric, I must admit that I generally found the invective to be humorous. It provided a light respite from the real problems. And it surely did not deter our effort to share the Games with the entire community or dim our Olympic vision.

REACHING INTO THE COMMUNITY

If the place where you work and the place where you live are not diverse, it is easy to forget the people of diverse backgrounds. It is also easy to forget to consider whether and how you are reaching them. Because the African American community is so small in Utah—about one percent of the population—many assume there is little ethnic

diversity. But Utah has large Latino and Native American populations. The last thing we wanted in the legacy of the Games was that
we had failed to involve ethnic minorities in the Olympic experience.

After I had been with SLOC for about a year, our volunteer project
team produced TV spots to help launch our volunteer recruiting campaign. They put together some clever ads with tag lines like "Make
the Olympics without breaking a sweat" and "17 days of work, a lifetime of pay." Most of our airtime was contributed by our television
and radio broadcasting sponsor, KSL. A local Telemundo affiliate
approached SLOC about selling some space on the Spanish broadcaster
for the ads and they were rebuffed. Our people responded somewhat
defensively, in part due to the fact that we had not budgeted money to
purchase airtime from independent broadcasters. But the ethnic association of Telemundo brought criticism about racial insensitivity.

At that point, we about-faced. I apologized for our blunder. We purchased $5,000 worth of Spanish-language advertising and I went to
work with Ed Eynon to formalize an enhanced minority outreach program for our volunteer recruiting effort. I hoped to substantially
increase the participation of our Utah minority communities in the
Games. Specifically I wanted a program to recruit people from different ethnic backgrounds as employees of SLOC and as Games-time volunteers. I also wanted to find a way to identify minority-owned
businesses that could compete for SLOC business. I was proud that our
largest single SLOC contract, for $70 million, had been awarded to an
Hispanic owned and managed company, but we felt we could do more.

Ed and his staffing director Steve Clark recruited members of the
African-American, Asian-American, Native-American, Hispanic-Amer-
ican, Pacific Islander, and other minority communities in Salt Lake City
and the surrounding areas to act as liaisons between their communities
and the Olympics. He hired Jorge Arcelareta as a full-time coordinator.
We formed a Minority Outreach Council to share insights and recommendations. Procurement needs were brought to the council so the representatives could help us find locally owned minority-run suppliers

when possible. I regularly attended meetings of the Hispanic Chamber of Commerce to show our interest in procuring from their businesses. Our Minority Outreach Council members helped us identify the media outlets, newspapers, Internet sites, and radio programs that best served their ethnic populations so that we could maximize the exposure of our recruitment messages in minority communities. The second time around we got high marks from opinion leaders in minority media and from the state director of minority affairs. Within six months we had more than doubled the number of ethnic minorities employed at SLOC. It was a record in which we took pride.

Our efforts to reach into the entire community did not stop with ethnic minorities. We formed an Interfaith Council that represented the Olympics in staffing and volunteer needs to the various religious denominations in the state. We had representatives from the American Association of Retired Persons linking us with the retirement and geriatric communities in the area. We also formed a Council on Disability. While the council focused on matters of Games-time access, it also identified opportunities for volunteering for disabled persons. On one occasion, our SLOC board of directors was meeting in a building that I had learned was next door to the headquarters for the Salt Lake City chapter of the Gay and Lesbian Alliance. After the meeting, I walked into the GLA office and asked if they would consider helping recruit volunteers for the Games. They jumped at the opportunity.

We also wanted to make sure that SLOC employees from minority backgrounds felt comfortable at SLOC and had ample opportunities to express concerns or criticisms about their work experience. I had read about previous Olympic organizations where minority employees had stepped forward at the time of the Games to complain that they had been discriminated against in hiring and promotion practices. We wanted to make it clear that we would not tolerate any type of discrimination at SLOC. We had two members of our board of directors, Lillian Taylor and Richard Valez who came from minority backgrounds themselves, interview all of the minority employees in our organization annually. They could ask if there were any problems, if they thought they'd been treated unfairly, or if they'd been harassed in any way. They asked questions about compensation levels and whether they thought they had equal access to promotion and advancement. They also interviewed a cross section of the staff to ask if they had seen inappropriate treatment of minority colleagues. Every year the human resources subcommittee of the board of trustees prepared a report that was made available to the public.

We may have had the best outreach effort in Olympic history. There's really no way to make a comparison. Organizers from other countries that had hosted Winter Games did not have similar demographics: Japan, Norway, France. Atlanta was aggressive in its hiring outreach. Whatever the record of others, we were determined to take the Olympics as deep into the various strands of our social fabric.

TOUCHING UTAH'S BILLIONAIRES

My interest in the billionaires was serious: I wanted to touch them for a generous contribution to our donor program. Kem Gardner headed our donor program and he knew where to focus: billionaires.

Jim Sorensen:

Through one of the Sorensen's nephews, Mrs. Sorensen had been introduced to providing sponsorship for the Soldier Hollow biathlon and cross-country venue. She had agreed to meet with Lyle Nelson, one of the directors of the venue, to discuss the prospects for a gift of some kind. I was pleased to join in the meeting.

Mrs. Sorensen graciously invited us to attend lunch at her home. The home had a beautiful entryway and a spectacular view of the mountains. Mrs. Sorensen tended to give to educational causes. Mr. Sorensen was reported to have offered $20 million to the University of Utah for its medical school on condition that the school be renamed in his honor. A semi-revolt of faculty and board members occurred, reportedly because they did not want the school named after a person who had "only" given money and created a major medical company. Mr. Sorensen graciously withdrew his $20 million offer.

Despite our delightful luncheon, Mrs. Sorenson chose not to donate. My efforts to meet with Mr. Sorenson were just as fruitless. Though numerous introductions were offered by mutual friends, he never submitted to a meeting.

Ray Noorda

For our first meeting with Ray Norda, we took a whole team. Chairman Bob Garff, who knew Ray best, kindly set up and attended the event. Because Ray had made his fortune in the high-tech world and because he reportedly had interest in some kind of Olympic involvement with one of his new IT ventures, we brought Alice Mahmood, our head of IT, along with the usual pitch team of Mark Lewis, Don Stirling and me. Mr. Noorda worked out of an office in Orem, Utah. The offices were extremely modest, with small spaces and institutional furnishings. This was a man who did not want to waste his money on ostentation.

Ray Noorda was dressed in Levis and a golf shirt and sported well-worn jogging shoes. He listened quietly to our pitch, and let Ralph Yarrow, his chief executive officer for The Canopy Group, a venture capital firm employing Ray Noorda's resources, do most of the talking. In our first meeting, the focus of our discussion was to explore possible ways Mr. Noorda's new venture companies might contribute and benefit from the Olympics. But given the small scale of most of The Canopy Group's early stage companies, this seemed to be a difficult match.

In April 2000, Bob Garff and I traveled again to meet with Ray Noorda and encouraged him to make a personal contribution of $1 million. At the end of the meeting, he said that he would do something for the Games and that he would get back to us with specifics. In most sales settings, ending a meeting without a fixed commitment means you're getting bupkis. But he called back several days later and pledged a full $1 million.

Prior to the meeting, we had heard widespread rumors about Ray Noorda's ill health. But in my interaction, I saw a clear head, a clear purpose, and a clear decision. Ray took nothing personal from his gift; he made it to support the state in a critical time.

Alan Ashton

Our first meeting with Alan Ashton occurred in the summer of 1999. Jeff Robbins, a friend of Don Stirling's and director of a Utah sport marketing effort, generously arranged for a luncheon for the four of us at Thanksgiving Point, a massive, multimillion dollar cultural center that Mr. Ashton had developed in Utah Valley.

We pitched Ashton very gently, having heard that he did not want to be asked to give money to the Olympics. Ashton made it clear that in addition to his church, his charitable priority was building a family-centered oasis, if you will, that could be shared by the people of Utah for generations to come. The setting would include gardens, a waterfall, and extensive recreational facilities. The site already boasted unique shops and dining, a museum and an 18-hole golf course. He indicated that he had considered a hotel for the premises, but decided against it because of the requirement for Sunday employment, the Sabbath day.

More distinctive even than his plans for Thanksgiving Point was his entirely normal lifestyle. A man very near retirement age, he was coaching tennis for the Orem High School. He enthused that they were making great progress towards becoming one of the best teams in the state. In addition, he was teaching a daily scripture study class to high school students. This was one of the most gentle, dedicated and kind people I had met.

Chairman Bob Garff and I met with him again in April 2000. As before, we spent a good deal of time talking about his tennis game and his commitment to teaching young people. While Ashton indicated that he had developed a superb 18-hole course at Thanksgiving Point, he himself was only a beginner and never counted his strokes when he played the game. His tennis, however, was at an entirely different level. He regularly played with college tennis athletes and often beat them.

Once again we made the pitch, explaining in our view that this was a defining moment for Utah. Ashton indicated that he had spoken to his wife prior to our lunch and that they had decided that they would make a contribution to the Games.

Jon Huntsman

Jon and Karen Huntsman are probably Utah's most well-known billionaires and its most noted philanthropists. In fact, they are among the most generous billionaires in the nation. They have devoted $200 million to a local cancer research center and hospital. Following the earthquake in Armenia, they sent their own personnel and sizeable funding there to build a factory to produce cement, the critical component for rebuilding the country. There is virtually no major charitable project in the state that does not benefit from a Huntsman gift, usually very large.

Jon earned his money. He acquired unprofitable divisions of oil and chemical companies, turned them around, and built one of the largest chemical companies in the world. Though a private concern, it reportedly has experienced ups and downs over the years, but the Huntsman giving has never slowed.

As you'll read, Jon was very critical of the Olympic bid and its management. Apparently his good sense carries into community life as well as business. So asking him for a gift for the Olympics was not going to be easy. The key to unlocking the Huntsman generosity is the heart: Jon and Karen met an inspiring Paralympian and immediately offered to give $1 million to the Paralympics.

Earl Holding

Now here is a character. Like all the other Utah billionaires, Earl made his money himself. His fortune came from selling and distributing gasoline, lodging, and real estate in California. Earl was an odd mixture of lavish spender and skinflint. He was building a new 700 plus room five-star hotel in Salt Lake City. His goal was to create what he said would be "the most beautiful hotel in the world." He may have succeeded. The imported marble, woven rugs, and chandeliers are extraordinary. He also owns Sun Valley Resort in Idaho which he transformed into one of the most luxurious resorts in the country. Finally, he was developing his ski resort in Utah, Snowbasin, into which he was investing a reported $100 million. All of these projects he did without any bank borrowing: Earl pays cash.

Now the other side of Earl. Guests at Sun Valley tell of frequent nights when they see Earl and his wife preparing and serving food in the restaurant. It's not just a photo-op, it's a workshift. A waitress at the Grand America Hotel said that Earl came in after she had set several hundred place-settings for a banquet. He saw that the settings had spoons. He asked what was being served. She told him. He noted that there was nothing that required a spoon so she should go back and remove them all: "spoons are the easiest thing for people to steal; only put them out if you have to."

Earl's developments of the Grand America hotel and Snowbasin were enormous assets for the Olympics. They must have cost him hundreds of millions. But he spent months, years, trying to negotiate a better price with us over the room rate at one of his other hotel properties. And he would not budge. We in turn spent months trying to get Earl to contribute something to our donor program. Zippo.

No, we did not get a contribution to the donor program from the Holdings, but we got millions of dollars of other contributions. We would have been in a very tight spot without their generosity.

THE BIG CONTRIBUTIONS

Without question, the people who gave the most were the 23,000 volunteers for the Games and the 3,000 for the ceremonies. For those who would serve during the Olympics, we needed 17 days; for those in the Paralympics, it was 10 days. Typically, that meant people had to take vacation days. In some cases, employers allowed their employees to take unpaid leaves. Whatever the circumstances, it was an enormous sacrifice.

We just couldn't understand why we needed so many people, more than 23,000 in all for both Games. Jean-Claude Killy of France had told us to cut to the smallest number possible given the expense of training and providing. In fact, Fraser and I spent numerous sessions with each venue manager getting detailed justifications for every position. The number just didn't go down. It had a lot to do with the enormous scale of an Olympics. Think about it: we had 2,223 port-a-potties, 698 full-size trailers, 2,100 bedrooms in the Olympic Village to set up and clean, 76,125 bed nights, 44,000 towels to launder, 4,000 cars to drive, and hundreds of thousands of spectators to screen at security, usher, feed, and entertain every day. Recruiting and training volunteers was ably organized by Ed Eynon and his HR team, and was itself headed by a volunteer, Steve Young, Super Bowl Most Valuable Player of the San Francisco 49ers. Steve pumped up the volunteer candidates at our many training sessions. His contribution of time and energy was another reason why our program was so successful.

The management task was shared by professionals and by volunteer leaders. Fraser and I were committed to having mature, experienced leaders from the community take the lead management role at each venue. We asked some twenty community big shots and their spouses to give a year of part-time service and thirty days of full-time service as venue chairpersons. Business CEOs, the head of the state AFL-CIO, and public leaders rose to the challenge. They each recruited ten captains who in turn recruited ten more volunteers, forming a management backbone for each venue. Their job was to recruit, retain, motivate, and lead. They also were on the ready if there was a major problem that required a mature head. The owner of the Utah Jazz, Larry Miller, wore our volunteer uniform at his own Delta Center. Every time I saw these folks, I just shook my head: these people were so remarkably willing to serve the Olympics and their community. It takes a lot of heroes to bring off something like the Olympic Winter Games.

Chapter 13

SLOC AND
THE MORMON CHURCH

I would never have guessed that a religion would be such a big matter for the Olympics. I grew up in Michigan; I was the only Mormon in my school. Ann and I had lived in Massachusetts for thirty years where members of my faith made up less than a half a percent of the population. Where I had lived, church affiliation wasn't an issue. But this was in Utah, and for a lot of reasons religion was a big deal to the Olympic Winter Games.

Utah's history sets the stage. The state was settled by Mormon pioneers in the 1840s. Subject to intense persecution in Illinois, the Mormons went west looking for a place "of their own." Brigham Young said at the time that they would "go to a land where there are at least no old settlers to quarrel with us. . . . where we can say that we have killed the snakes and made the roads."

For many years, Utah's physical remoteness and arid undesirability were bulwarks against federal government intrusion into what amounted to a theocracy with Church President Brigham Young also serving as the first territorial governor. This same cultural dominance of the Church continues to the present day.

Salt Lake City is a much more culturally diverse urban center today than ever before. But the history and shadow of the Church's active involvement in civic affairs is still a major subject of discourse in the state. And the fact remains that the Church, as it is called by Mormons and non-Mormons alike, is still an influential institution in Salt Lake City and in the state at large. The governor, the Supreme Court Justices, and many of the key legislators are members of the faith. Neither of the mayors I worked with, however, were Mormon. And there certainly was no litmus test for the organizing committee. In fact, my predecessor Frank Joklik was active in another religious tradition.

The impact of the Church on the Games derived from its impact in the community. First, by virtue of its sheer size—in population, finance, and geography—we needed the Church's support and generosity. But at the same time, we needed the support of the entire community. The perception that the Games were in any way an extension of the Church could make that kind of inclusiveness almost impossible.

Given its long history and deep roots in Utah, the Church owns considerable land, buildings, and enterprises across the state. Of course, there are literally hundreds of Church buildings. But there are also extensive land holdings—some held for future building sites, others held as investments. In particular, the Church owns a great deal of land in locations that would be key to our Games. It owned the land adjacent to our Utah Olympic Park, site of ski jumping, bobsleigh, luge, and skeleton. The only direct path to those venues would be on a road we would construct right across Church land. They owned land adjacent to freeways and highways that we would need for park-and-ride lots to make our transportation system work. They owned the only unencumbered block of land in the heart of downtown Salt Lake City, so-called Block 85. This was the spot we were convinced would be the prime location for our Olympic Square and our plaza for the awarding of the Olympic medals. In short, we needed a lot of property rights.

We also wanted some of their softer assets: translation studios and equipment, translators, printing capacity, auditoriums, and participation by their world renowned Mormon Tabernacle Choir. Just as critical would be the enthusiastic participation of Church members in our volunteer program. We knew we would need particular support from Brigham Young University as well as from Church employees to reach our recruiting targets.

Even more visible in the community are Church investments in local and regional businesses. The Church owns the majority share of the NBC TV and radio affiliate in Salt Lake, one of the city's daily newspapers, a national broadcasting conglomerate, and a book publishing and retailing company, among others. As one of the largest enterprises in Utah, we felt that it was appropriate to ask the Church to donate funds to our donor program, just as we were asking other enterprises to donate or become sponsors.

The importance of the Church to our Games had not been lost on my predecessors. They had worked closely with Church leaders, discussing our requirements and ways the Church might help. A senior Church official had accompanied SLOC management to Nagano to see first hand the type of event that was headed for Salt Lake City. While no commitments had been made by the Church, one important request had been accepted: the Church issued a letter to its members in the Salt Lake City region indicating that it would not be inappropriate to serve as a Games volunteer, even thought the Games schedule would include the Sunday Sabbath. To most, this seemed like an invitation to volunteer for the Games.

At least two things stood between that letter and SLOC receiving contributions and direct support from the Church. One, the bid scandal. Without question, the Church had to have serious reservations about any further association with our organization. The other, the President of the Church of Jesus Christ of Latter-day Saints himself. President Gordon B. Hinckley is the person who makes all decisions for the Church on matters of this magnitude. The support and trip to Nagano by a senior Church official was in no way a decision to go ahead. It was fact finding. SLOC had not yet met the decision maker.

Somehow we had to thread a very fine needle: get the full and extensive support of the Church while at the same time not alienating the broader diverse community. In the end, we could have never succeeded in this broader mission had we not benefited from an unanticipated source.

ROUND ONE: SECURING THE FINANCIAL COMMITMENT

I sat down with Kem Gardner to get his advice on how to approach the Church. Kem had been a long time resident of Utah and had close relationships with several Church leaders. He had been the one to get me into my job, he knew how important the Church was to our success, and he knew the ins and outs of how the Church worked better than I ever would. "President Hinckley will make the decision, you can be sure of that. But it will be critical to have Elder Hales and Elder Eyring on your side. They will probably be the ones to decide if you make your pitch to the President directly or whether they take it for-

"MORMON OLYMPICS"

The term "Mormon Olympics" was not coined by the Church's critics, but by one of its own. Jon Huntsman, Sr., founder and owner of Huntsman Chemical Corp., one of the wealthiest men in Utah and a Church leader, had been a consistent Olympics critic. He questioned the economic benefits, distrusted the IOC process, and feared that the Games could divide the community along religious lines. The fact that Fraser and I were both LDS contributed to that concern. This was the worry that led to the "Mormon Olympics" label.

His criticism began with the bid committee leadership. Knowing Tom Welch as his next-door neighbor, he was convinced that excess and taint could characterize Salt Lake City's bid. The unfolding scandal justified his fears. As I was arriving to take the job with SLOC, Jon was publicly calling for Salt Lake City to return the Games to the IOC. In his view, the best way to make restitution for the bid committee's ethical lapse was to give the Games back, allowing another city to receive the honor of hosting the Games.

ward for you." Elder Robert D. Hales and Elder Henry B. Eyring are members of what the Church calls the Quorum of the Twelve Apostles. You might think that is as high as you could go in the Church, but you would be wrong. The highest authority is with the First Presidency, specifically President Gordon B. Hinckley and his two Counselors, Thomas S. Monson and James E. Faust. By the way, it's Mormon tradition to use these people's middle initials; I have no idea why.

I began with a meeting with Elder Hales and Elder Eyring, as Kem had recommended. They had been asked by the President to coordinate any involvement the Church might have in the Olympics. They were my official contact points. Both congratulated me on my assignment and wished me the very best. They made the first request: would I *please* consolidate all our requests of the Church in one person. They were receiving inquiries from numerous SLOC departments across the entire Church. It turns out that as the months had progressed, SLOC requests for support had continued to mount. SLOC people had

---

Continued from 272

After a fair measure of blunt talk in the media, Chairman Garff arranged a meeting with me, Jon, the governor, and himself. We agreed that the Games may not have been a good idea in the first place and that the bid committee's acts had been disgraceful and unethical. I pressed my view that our highest duty now was to stage them with excellence. We owed it to the athletes and to our country. It became clear that we really weren't that far apart. In fact, before it was over, Jon agreed to host a fundraising function for us in the Huntsman Center. He noted that

he was not inclined to contribute himself, however.

The event was a huge success. We heard from Carrie Strug, the Olympic gymnast from the Atlanta Games who had bravely competed despite a sprained ankle; Dan Jansen, the Olympic speed skating hero who won his gold after four Olympic tries; and Paralympic gold medalist Chris Waddell, who spoke from his wheelchair next to Jon and Karen Huntsman about winning his gold medal in downhill skiing. Jon surprised us all when he announced that he would be contributing a million dollars.

inquired about parking for our downtown accreditation center, permission to use Church parking lots during weekdays, accommodation at apartment buildings, security consulting, orchestra recording support, and on and on.

Their request was easy to accommodate. I sent a memo to all SLOC personnel: "Given the many resources of the LDS Church, it is natural that any number of us might want to discuss possible use of their facilities or capabilities. At their request, all inquiries, even the most preliminary in nature... are to be directed to me first."

My request for the Church was a lot more involved. I had prepared a complete list of the things we wanted. I went through them one by one, ending with a proposal for a $5 million donation to the Games. I could tell as I went along that I had reached saturation: they were still smiling, but they were a little surprised by how much we were after. Finally, they gave me that Ronald Reagan sort of cock of the head and said, in effect, "If you don't ask, you won't get." They told me to go back and reorganize my requests, including the rationale for the Church's participation in each, and bring it to them to review again. After that, they would see if President Hinckley wanted to meet with me. I took that as a good sign.

My follow-up meeting went well and led to their request in my behalf to meet with the First Presidency. Weeks passed; then I got the green light.

By the time of my meeting with the First Presidency, SLOC had gone an entire year without signing a new sponsor. Our budget deficit was not going away. A financial commitment from the Church would not only help us begin filling our financial gap; it could potentially open the door to the hearts of other sponsors and contributors as well.

Elder Hales and Elder Eyring accompanied me to the First Presidency office. Bishop H. David Burton, the Church's manager of its secular assets, was also there. The Presidency was seated at the top end of a "T" shaped conference table. I was invited to sit along the stem side of the T. I had prepared a paper copy of our proposal, laid out in bold Power Point. I wanted to make sure that elderly eyesight had no problem seeing my pitch. After words of congratulations and confidence from President Hinckley, I was invited to proceed. He peppered me with questions as I went along. Most of the inquiries were focused on the Medals Plaza. It was our hope to present the athletes with their medals each evening at the plaza. With the NBC affiliate who would be broadcasting the Games located next to Block 85 and with the Temple only two blocks away, TV camera views of the Medals Plaza would surely encompass the Church headquarters, buildings, and temple, the city skyline, and the mountains beyond. The site was perfect for showcasing the entire city and Wasatch panorama. And, of course, it was the only site large enough for our planned free concerts.

President Hinckley asked several questions about the grade levels in Block 85. Would the site require re-grading? Would that necessitate a retaining wall be built? How deep would the new grade go? Could it encounter archeological artifacts that would impede the process? Block 85's current use was for three separate parking lots, all of which were at somewhat different levels. Despite being the spiritual leader of an international church, President Hinckley was quite clearly an intensely practical man. A former builder and railroad man, he knew the kinds of practical considerations involved in my request. His grade questions caught me a bit off guard but I promised a full report would be forthcoming, as did Bishop Burton.

The boldest request was for $5 million in resources for equipment to transform Block 85 into the concert arena we needed. The most puzzling expressions came with my proposal to use the roof of one of the Church's new buildings as the place to launch our nightly fireworks display.

The meeting ended with thanks but not a decision. The First Presidency would get back in touch with us with the final word in due time. Several weeks passed; that seemed like more than due time to me. I called Elder Hales. "Be patient," he said. The President was carefully considering each of our proposals and would let us know what had been decided.

Not long thereafter, Elder Hales called with the good news. Almost all of our requests were approved, even the $5 million. The funds would not come from the Church itself but rather from secular businesses owned by its holding company. He gave no conditions or requirements whatsoever. Matters were left to my "good judgment." The rejections: the fireworks and the use of Church printing presses: the President did not want to have the Church take printing business away from local printers. When we got the news, the SLOC senior team celebrated, without alcohol, of course.

But it was alcohol that would ignite a media storm not long thereafter.

ROUND TWO: THE ALCOHOL DEBATE

During the Sydney Games, the matter of alcohol became an issue for the city council of Provo, Utah, the site of our women's hockey events. Council members expressed their view that a special permit to sell beer in our Provo venue should not be granted. Articles and letters pro and con received a fair measure of media attention. Very early on, a great deal of press in Utah was generated by an anti-alcohol activist group led by a local physician. He was highly critical of SLOC's decision to secure a sponsorship from Anheuser Busch, a longtime sponsor of the Olympics. Many people in Utah apparently felt that any association with a company that sells alcoholic beverages was inappropriate. And many others were equally incensed that a longtime sponsor's generosity would be maligned or possibly even denied because of religious sentiment.

Given the media attention to the issue at home, I was asked by a Salt Lake reporter in Sydney to outline our alcohol policy. Coincidentally, I had spoken that same day with Gerhard Heiberg, CEO of the Lillehammer Games. He explained that in Norway, it was against national law to serve alcohol in sport venues. The logic was that they did not wish youth to associate alcohol with sport. Fraser and I had discussed among ourselves and with other SLOC managers whether such a policy might be wise for us. Don Pritchard, our director of food services, expressed his view that Budweiser would probably prefer to serve beer exclusively at stadium clubs and hospitality suites rather than at venue concession stands.

The issue came to a head on my monthly radio show when I returned. A caller asked about our position on alcohol. I said that three rules would govern. First, we should be hospitable to our guests from around the world, and that would include offering alcoholic beverages. Second, we should not in any way promote the use of alcohol by young people. And third, we should ensure that any drinking would be done responsibly. Further, I anticipated that our sport venues would sell alcoholic beverages but that the Medals Plaza, where we expected families and young children to attend free, would not. What I had said made perfect sense to me, but I had no idea what a firestorm I had lit.

Budweiser was not happy that I had decided to philosophize on the merits of alcohol at events: "Just make your decision and be done with it." They expressed their concern by letter and ultimately by a visit from the vice president of marketing, Tony Ponturo. He was gracious, understanding, and quite convincing. They were not paying millions of dollars to the Olympics to become my victim. Clearly, they had a good point.

Following the radio show, I sent an e-mail to the board describing my views on alcohol, as I had discussed over the air, and promising a full discussion at our upcoming management committee meeting. Salt Lake's Mayor Anderson took exception with my policy in an e-mail forwarded to the other members of the board. Other board members jumped into the fray as well, mostly in a highly negative reaction to my positions. Remarkably, the comments of my board members and the media focused on the Church and its prohibition to its members from drinking alcoholic beverages. One board member's memo to me began

"Now that you have taken it upon yourself to become a spokesman for the Mormon Church..." The *Salt Lake Tribune* editorialized that I was attempting to impose my religion on other people. Predictably, the many letters published on the topic in the *Salt Lake Tribune* were highly critical and those published in the *Deseret Morning News* were laudatory.

One morning riding to work I heard a radio talk show tearing me apart for my view that alcohol should not be served at the Medals Plaza. Overwhelmingly, the host and the callers saw it as a Mormon issue. I was so disturbed by the religious polarization and by the emotion and anger of the callers that I drove to the studio and went on the show, hoping to diffuse the emotion. Tempers calmed as I expressed openness to input.

Several weeks later, Jay Shelledy, editor of the *Salt Lake Tribune*, opened my eyes. He said that while it is considered impolite to attack another person's religion, in Utah that is done in an indirect manner by talking about alcohol. Attacking Utah's alcohol restrictions is a way of venting frustration at everything one might feel about the Mormon Church and its influence in Utah political, social, and economic life. The media were delighted to tap into the resentments of both poles of Utah society. Talk shows, letters to the editor, and editorials were teeming with newfound passion. To me, having lived my entire life in Detroit or Boston, decisions on serving alcohol were about preventing drunk driving, ensuring crowd safety at large events and the like, not religion. I had touched the third rail in Utah without even knowing it.

Salt Lake Mayor Rocky Anderson went to the media to insist that the Medals Plaza be able to serve beer. He said that a celebration site with concerts which would last late into the night absolutely had to offer alcoholic beverages. Otherwise, some people who might have wanted to attend would stay away. I met with the Mayor that afternoon. My view was that the Medals Plaza was designed to be a family affair: athletes would be given their medals there and concerts would last only one hour. I also felt that it would not be fair to the

Church that had been so generous to us, to sell alcohol on their property. My bottom line: you don't borrow the Rabbi's barbeque grill to cook pork chops and you don't use the Mormon Church's property to sell liquor. Further, there would be some people who would not bring their family to an event where alcohol was being served. If not serving alcohol might keep some people away, serving it might keep others away. There was also the matter of safety: Jim McNeil, Utah's leading producer of rock concerts, explained that an outdoor concert with standing crowds where alcohol was being served could present real crowd safety issues. In fact, a crowd control problem at one Utah concert had resulted in teenage fatalities. Finally, we were pitching Coca-Cola to pay for the concerts: if their sponsorship came through, they would surely insist on venue exclusivity for their products.

Mayor Anderson relented. Maybe it was my compelling arguments. More likely, it was because we found an acceptable compromise. We agreed that alcohol would be served at a site near the Medals Plaza where the events could be seen on a super-screen. We would not confiscate alcohol on the Medals Plaza, but we would not serve it there either.

As all this was playing out in the media, I wondered if I would get a call from Elder Hales. I didn't. In fact, the Church never got into the alcohol debate. I imagine that they cared but that they hoped we would just do the right thing by them. Rocky and I agreed to do just that.

In preparation for our management committee meeting of November 9, I called Rocky and explained that in my view the last thing our community needed was to be further polarized by an extensive public debate on alcohol. We had both done enough of that already. He agreed that as we had reached a compromise solution. It would be best to secure the management committee's support quickly and quietly. He would make a motion to adopt management's proposal relating to alcohol policies on the Medals Plaza. As a result, our alcohol policy was unanimously adopted.

I had learned something about alcohol in Utah that I didn't know before. In Belmont, Massachusetts where Ann and I had lived for the past thirty years, alcohol was not sold. It wasn't a religious issue, of course. Ours was a dry town because of concerns about drunk drivers, youth drinking, and other social issues. My Church expected its own members not to drink as an indication of obedience to their religion. Its opposition to liberal alcohol laws, however, had nothing to do with a desire to impose the religion on others. In fact, the Church's members abstain from coffee and tobacco, as well as alcohol and the Church actually serves coffee in the hotel it owns. If it wished to impose its religion on others, it wouldn't be serving coffee either. No, their issue with liberalizing alcohol regulations derives from the same social consequences recognized in other nations and communities: concern about drunk driving and alcoholism. But that's surely not how it's perceived in Utah where many feel the Church's hand in government is misplaced and too heavy. In Utah, alcohol is about a Church.

Just prior to Thanksgiving 2000, Caroline Shaw and I met again with the publisher of the *Salt Lake Tribune*, Dominick Welch, and its editor, Jay Shelledy. I explained my neophyte status when it came to public sentiment about the Mormon Church. I noted that Boston was more Catholic than Salt Lake was Mormon. And in Boston, I saw no evidence of the religious-based polarization I had witnessed in Salt Lake. Our objective was that the Olympics would bring the community together, much as they bring the world together. I solicited his advice.

ROUND THREE: THE "MORMON GAMES"

In the spring of 2001, SLOC's communications department learned that the *Salt Lake Tribune* was about to go to print with an in-depth story purporting to trace the involvement of LDS Church officials with Salt Lake City's various bids to host the Olympics. The *Tribune* also made a request for copies of all SLOC files with documents pertaining to the LDS Church. It was clearly their intention to stir the coals again. And this time they were not alone.

Similar editorial pieces were appearing in the national press. *USA Today* published a lengthy article one year out from the Games anniversary that began by noting "One year to go . . . Olympic kingdom Games provide opportunity for Mormons . . . to drive home the point . . . 'We're not weird.' " It went on to describe the Medals Plaza as "the church's most conspicuous effort." Other pieces exposing the "Mormon Olympics" angle were in the works at *Newsweek* and *The New Yorker* magazine. And coverage of the issue was resurfacing in AP stories and every paper from the *New York Times* to the *Christian Science Monitor*. I suppose it was inevitable, but by this time I was very, very concerned about another polarizing round of debate. We were set to launch our volunteer recruitment program in little more than a month and the persistent suggestion that the Church was either controlling the Games or using SLOC to promote its own interests was incredibly damaging to building support among people of all faiths and backgrounds.

With the *Tribune* article in the works, we tried something of a preemptive maneuver. We held a press conference at our offices to toast the Games and "the unity they represent and the contributions of all people of all faiths and backgrounds that will make them successful." The attendees included board members and local sponsor executives. People of various faiths were there, including the Episcopal Bishop. Some of us used orange juice for the toast and others used champagne. The idea was to underscore the diversity amongst our trustees and senior executives and to emphasize our sensitivity to inclusiveness. Was it hokey? Yes. Did we know we would get dinged for being hokey? Yes. But we needed to do something that would get some traction in the press on the issue.

I made a candid statement at the press conference: "the characterization of Olympic matters as Mormon or non-Mormon is in my view both divisive and demeaning . . . These are Games for America. . . .

They're Episcopal. They're Catholic. They're Muslim. They're Jewish. They're Mormon. They're Baptist."

Talk show hosts and callers had persisted in criticizing the Church, pointing to its many contributions to the Games. I also addressed the issue of Church contributions in my address: "I was brought up to thank people who made gifts, not criticize them. I have to say thank you for the contribution of the Medals Plaza land and funds to build it out for free concerts." Of course, I was particularly sensitive to the Church's contributions: it was I who had worked to secure them.

Shortly thereafter, I asked Elder Hales to review my requests of the Church in light of the ongoing criticism. I took the blame for having not been sensitive enough to the issue and apologized for subjecting the Church to criticism for being generous. I had simply asked for too much. Elder Hales wrote me a letter asking SLOC to review all my previous requests and pare off any that were not absolutely essential. I turned to SLOC's Interfaith Council to advise us. Most of the members were not troubled by the Church's contributions and support for the Games; they felt they were commensurate with the Church's substantial presence in the community. Nevertheless, we eliminated two of our requested items.

The Interfaith Council was concerned, however, about potential proselytizing efforts by Church representatives during the Games. For most, the concern was put to rest by a public statement by President Hinckley: the Church would not have missionaries proselytizing visitors during the Games. As it turned out, it was other faiths that were busy on Salt Lake City streets during the Olympics. The Mormon Church's restraint and generosity were widely praised.

Knowing that everything would work out in the end, however, didn't help us as we approached our volunteer recruiting campaign. Would Mormons and non-Mormons alike sign up in order to generate the numbers we needed? When Monster.com and our SLOC website began taking applications, we got our answer. We received 68,000 applicants for just over 24,000 volunteer positions. Over a quarter of the applications were from out-of-state. Of course, we did not ask for a candidate's religious affiliation, but orientation and training meetings confirmed what we suspected: this was a diverse volunteer corps. My niece was a volunteer driver at the curling venue in Ogden. Of the twelve drivers in her pool, she and one other were Mormon. All were locals and represented a cross section of faiths and ethnicities. They became good friends and continued their association after the Games. Perhaps that was the most successful aspect

BNL

Given the dignity befitting an Olympic setting, we tried to be somewhat careful about the acts that performed. NBC had committed to broadcast the Medals Plaza performances on national television and while some popular acts can be pretty crusty, we wanted to avoid lewd actions or vulgar lyrics. I asked Scott Givens, our director of ceremonies, to do a thorough search of band lyrics and videos before booking acts. One of the performers we were planning on having had an arrest for drug possession leading up to the Games. We made other arrangements.

One group that kept appearing on planning sheets for the Medals Plaza was listed as "BNL." Scott eventually let slip that the acronym stood for "Barenaked Ladies" but insisted that they would be one of the most appropriate and purely entertaining acts of the Games. I said that was all well and good but that someone had to tell Elder Hales and the LDS Church

about it. Of course, that someone was me.

I first called the CEO of Bonneville International, a Church-owned media company, to gauge his reaction. He knew the group and said they would be fine. His daughter was a huge fan. I plucked up my courage and called Elder Hales.

There was a long pause on the line when I told him. I insisted that they were a great group, that they would comport themselves well and would do nothing to bring embarrassment to the Church or to the Games. "Then why do they call themselves that?" came the reply.

I explained that early in their history they had been asked about their favorite things and bare naked ladies had been one of their answers.

The evening of the event, another one of the Church's Apostles was present. When the band of young men came out wearing Canadian speed skater uniforms, he deadpanned, "I'm already disappointed."

of community involvement in the Games: people overcame polarization and came to know each other on a personal basis. This, of course, was the factor that led the Games to bring the community together: people working side by side with others for a noble purpose, broke down barriers and built bridges.

After three years of criticism and cynicism surrounding the Mormon Church's involvement with the Olympics, it worked out quite well after all. Almost all reports praised SLOC for Games that included diverse members of the community; a few were perceptive enough to recognize that our success had also been helped importantly by the Church's generosity. The free concerts and medals ceremonies were dependent upon their land and development funding. LDS volunteers had shown up in large numbers. The massive building wrap decorations included their structures, even the Church headquarters building. And oh yes, we had massive fireworks displays every night, lit from the roof of their building, after all.

I have often wondered what the Church made of the Olympics. From our standpoint, the Church's contributions were not just helpful, they were critical. I have a reason for feeling that the Church was also pleased. The night of closing ceremonies was a Sunday; the Presidency and the members of the Quorum of Twelve Apostles were not in the stadium for our final celebration. President Hinckley and members of his family instead were on the top floor of the twenty-four story Church Office Building, viewing the proceedings by television. As the fireworks began to ignite across the valley, President Hinckley went to the window and stood, silently. Tears ran down his cheeks. Over one and a half centuries before, his predecessor Brigham Young and thousands of weary, impoverished travelers entered this same valley. Now, their descendants and neighbors had welcomed the world to their mountain home. President Young had said that one day the flags of the world would come to Salt Lake; indeed they had.

Chapter 14

SECURING THE OLYMPIC GAMES

With all the financial, legal, and operational problems we faced, security and public safety issues were not at the forefront of my worries in my first few months at SLOC. I assumed that our role in planning for security was probably not a very big one. After all, public safety is the government's responsibility and surely, for an international event like the Olympics, the federal government just took over security and told us what to do. That's what I thought. The truth turned out to be very different.

Not long after coming on board with SLOC, on one of my trips to Washington, D.C., I met with Louis Freeh, then director of the FBI. At the end of our meeting, he remarked that the FBI expected to see a substantial increase in terrorist activity. This was not an offhand comment. He waited until my colleagues had left the room, looked me in the eye, and leveled this warning with deadly seriousness.

That got my attention. I knew that there had been terrorist attacks in Munich at the 1972 Games and in Atlanta in 1996. So I did a little research. And what I learned troubled me greatly. There have been some excellent reports written on the Munich attack. Several things are striking: it was easy for the terrorists to get into the Olympic Village and easy for them to take hostages because security was lax. In Munich, security was primarily the responsibility of the organizing committee. The procedures for working with the police in case of an incident had not been well thought through or well-rehearsed. So when the hostages were taken, the left hand did not know what the right hand was doing. It took way too long for the police to respond. Further, the person who negotiated with the terrorists was a member of the organizing committee. For the first critical communications with the terrorists, an untrained executive negotiated for the lives of athletes. Today, it seems incomprehensible that this ever happened.

Every Olympics learns from prior Games. Munich taught new lessons for securing athletes that are now standard practice. One of the most secure locations is the Village. Among the steps we took were double-fencing, cameras, motion detectors, bio-hazard detectors, food testing, mail testing, and screening people and goods twice before letting them in, and an inner, even more secure location that only the athletes could access. High-threat delegations, such as the Israelis, are given the most secure locations within the Village and are allowed to bring their own security. Everyone given access to the Village goes through background checks—even volunteers. Drills are run repeatedly on how to deal with an attack—any scenario that can be dreamed up is planned for and rehearsed.

Lessons had also been learned from the Los Angeles Games—particularly the need to do background checks on all employees and volunteers. It turned out that in Los Angeles, because many background checks were not completed before the Games began, convicted felons held critical posts—even security posts. I heard from the public safety leadership in Los Angeles that they had more problems during their Games with crimes committed by volunteers and employees who turned out to have records than they did from any other source. So, we started early and anyone who didn't pass a background check couldn't work or volunteer for our Games.

But it was the lessons learned from Atlanta that had the most impact on security and public safety preparations for Salt Lake.

Reports from the public safety community were highly critical of Atlanta's planning and implementation. And, unfortunately, it reflects how slow we were as a nation to begin to recognize that terrorism was becoming an issue in our country. When Atlanta began preparing for the Games, there had not been a terrorist attack on U.S. soil. Then, in 1993, the first World Trade Center bombing happened, and most of us heard of Osama Bin Laden for the first time. Not long thereafter, Timothy McVeigh stunned us all by his brutal attack on innocent people in Oklahoma City.

For the security and public safety planners in Atlanta, each new incident, and the increasing intelligence, sent them reeling to develop ways to prevent and respond to these types of attacks. In Atlanta, where there were literally over thirty different public safety agencies—federal, state, and local all "in charge" of securing a piece of the Games, turf wars and jurisdictional disputes were the rule, not the exception. An attempt had been made to pull everyone together to develop a coordinated plan, but it had fallen apart as the potential for a terrorist attack increased and every agency focused on making sure that their piece of the security puzzle worked—even if all else failed. About a year out from the Games, Vice President Gore came to Atlanta for a security briefing and asked a straight-forward question—"Who's in charge?" The answer back was "it depends." Accurate, but not a good answer. When you are holding the largest peacetime event in history and terrorism has been launched in your country, you want someone who can tell you that they are responsible for the overall effort. In Atlanta, no one was.

THE SECRET SERVICE

With one year to go, and perhaps to try to compensate for the lack of a comprehensive plan, the federal government began to infuse massive resources—over 14,000 troops were sent in. Federal law enforcement agents also came in by the hundreds. They plugged all the holes they could—and then prayed that no one would break through the ones that remained. Unfortunately, someone did. Not many believe that much could have been done to stop the attack in Atlanta—there will always be a place you don't secure and the bomber would simply have gone to another site. But that knowledge didn't do much to give the public safety community in Atlanta comfort when it was all over.

Although I never met the men and women who worked in public safety in Atlanta, I did hear repeatedly about the actions they took when the Games were over. They held a three day summit with the law enforcement community in Salt Lake. One by one, they implored Salt Lake not to repeat their mistakes. Although they had done everything they could in that last year, they carried regrets for what had gone before and they felt a personal responsibility to share the hard lessons they had learned. Their truthfulness hit home with the leadership in Utah. And it hit home with the federal government—which hadn't been much better organized than the locals.

So, following Atlanta, the White House decided to create a structure that would put somebody in charge. President Clinton issued Presidential Decision Directive 62 that set out a hierarchy for all so-called "National Special Security Events." It put the U.S. Secret Service in charge of planning and operational security, the FBI in charge of intelligence and the immediate response to a terrorist incident, and FEMA in charge of handling the consequences of an event with mass casualties. This meant there were three human beings who were in charge of making sure that everything came together in their area of responsibility. There was one human being on the federal level, Mark Camillo from the U.S. Secret Service, who was responsible for making sure that all the federal agencies worked in coordination to plan for their Olympic roles and then operated as an integrated force to prevent something from happening at Games time. Mark was one of a number of truly high caliber federal law enforcement agents that were assigned to Olympic duty. There was someone we could turn to for decisions and there was someone who would be held accountable if things went wrong. Mark summed up his job pretty succinctly: "My job is to make sure that the FBI and FEMA never have to work during the Games. We prevent—they respond. If they are ever called in, we've failed in our job." He was straightforward and knew exactly what he had to do—I liked working with him.

At the FBI, Ray Mey was appointed by Director Freeh in 1997 and oversaw Olympic planning through 2002. It is very unusual for an agent to stay in one job like this for so many years, but Freeh knew that the Olympic planning effort needed continuity, so he committed to leave Ray in place until the Games were over. Dave Tubbs and then Don Johnson served as the Special Agent in Charge for the FBI, and they were both no-nonsense, get-the-job done leaders. Over the years, the Secret Service and the FBI brought in a number of agents and planners too numerous to mention here, but to a person, they were dedicated to keeping our Games safe.

THE LYNCHPIN UOPSC

On the state level, Utah had also tried to put in place a structure that would produce a coordinated and integrated public safety plan and, just as important, put someone in charge. SLOC actually had a seat on the Command, as it was called. It was unprecedented to put a private sector enterprise in a law enforcement entity, but it reflected the reality of the job to be done. The model developed in Salt Lake was good. And, like any model, it was only as good as the people in the positions.

The Utah Olympic Public Safety Command (UOPSC) was created by the state legislature in 1998 with the authority to plan and direct the Olympic security and public safety efforts of various state and local police agencies in a unified way. We had state and local law enforcement agencies, along with fire, Emergency Medical Service, and public health, each playing a public safety role in Salt Lake.

It's no surprise that this new model for law enforcement wasn't exactly popular right up front with all the sheriffs and police chiefs.

So Governor Mike Leavitt did a very smart thing. He named the commissioner of public safety as the first commander of UOPSC; Craig Dearden had been the sheriff from Weber County. Leavitt knew that in these early days, it was important to have someone in charge who could gently bring all the various sheriffs and police chiefs to the table and get them comfortable with the new way of operating. As one of the them, Craig was perfect for this task.

If the task of organizing the public safety community was daunting, it was nothing compared to the real work they had to do—keeping this Olympics safe. The sheer enormity of the job was amazing. We had venues, like Snowbasin, that were literally vertical mountain cliffs. How do you secure the perimeter of a mountain? We could set up mags at the base of the venue, make people go through those (although since many came with skis, this would be challenging), and we could use snow fencing to create walkways to keep the public where we wanted them. But what would stop someone from coming into the venue illegally by skiing over from the other side of the mountain? A single terrorist, with a mortar on his back, could wreak havoc. Fences? When you have a snow base of 20 feet and a storm can drop several feet in hours, fences won't work. Cameras? Again, the weather makes it difficult to use them and the response plan, once you see the skier, can be quite dangerous—it's probably a helicopter flying up the mountain and dropping off a SWAT team—not quick and certainly not easy if the mountain winds are gusting. So the answer, by and large, had to be large numbers of patrols. I probably have the most admiration for the men and women who pulled alpine patrol duty. The feds decided to take responsibility for these patrols and they used a lot of Forest Service and Secret Service agents. Think about it. Miles of perimeter to be patrolled on skis, 24-hours a day, in temperatures well below freezing, strong winds, and high altitude. We had patrols at all our mountain venues. Anywhere where a rocket could be launched and hit a venue, there was a force that could stop them.

LOOSE LIPS

When I came aboard in 1999, the UOPSC planning structure was in place and a lot of preliminary work had been done. But we were a long way from having a detailed, unified plan and the tough work of saying "no" was about to start. Since planning was done from the venue level up, each local sheriff or police chief had been involved in developing an initial outline of the public safety plan for their area—and in this process each had developed their wish list of what they needed for the Olympics. Needless to say, most of them were grabbing for the brass ring with gusto. They all needed new equipment—police cars, radios, riot gear—you name it, they needed it. And for some reason, they needed it permanently. When the feds offered to loan the equipment, or when we had sponsors who were willing to bring it in temporarily, that was always a problem. Only permanent, leave-behind stuff would keep these Games safe.

And some of the requests were amazing. One sheriff felt an armored personnel carrier was needed for his county. Another local agency came to my office to explain why it was important that we acquire a helicopter for their proprietary use. Another needed two boats—a special type of expensive hydrofoil—to have "just in case" a plane crashed into the Salt Lake and they had to rescue people. And the universal expectation was that SLOC or some state or federal budget would pay for it all. A real boondoggle was in the works.

The Utah Congressional delegation was a tremendous help through all of this. They recognized that the only way we would be able to avoid the turf problems of Atlanta was if UOPSC was actually empowered to set the public safety plan and then enforce it. They also recognized that no matter how many laws you pass, real power comes from money. So the delegation took the politically difficult step of refusing to consider any requests for public safety funding for the Olympics unless those came through UOPSC. And, to ensure that SLOC and UOPSC worked together, they refused to take those requests through any channel except Cindy Gillespie. This single action did more to empower UOPSC and force everyone to work together than any other step we took.

As could be expected, some of the sheriffs began to fight back. And they went for the jugular. County commissioners began passing regulations giving the sheriff the authority to deny our event permit. Without the permit, we couldn't hold the event. And to get the permit, we would have to meet their demands for equipment and personnel. It was blackmail plain and simple—but it got our attention. And Washington's. Mark Camillo, the Secret Service agent in charge of Olympic security, came to see me and others worried that the local jurisdictions were digging in and becoming silos. Our well-coordinated, centralized planning effort seemed to be slipping away.

With the Games two years away, the attention of the media was also shifting to Olympic public safety planning. And, as the sheriffs flexed their muscles, one or two found that they liked being in the limelight. I would wince when local law enforcement came on TV to talk about our public safety planning. Inevitably, the reporter would ask that age-old trick question, "What do you worry about the most?" And then, astoundingly, the official would lay out for the world the type of attacks we feared most—what would be the hardest for us to stop. It makes for great drama. But there's nothing like exposing your weaknesses to the enemy. While I certainly could not claim to be an expert on anti-terrorism, there was one thing that was clear: security preparations for the Olympics did not need to be spelled out in the world media.

And it wasn't just local officials that were talking. Commissioner Dearden, Commander of UOPSC, decided the best way to keep the press from talking to the sheriffs was to get out there first himself. To be honest, we had a genuine disagreement among all of us as to the proper amount of information to give out on security issues prior to the event. I supported the Secret Service communications plan; their standard line is to just say that they don't talk about security preparations. Frankly, when you are dealing with terrorists, I think people understand that. The governor and mayor agreed with me. I thought Commissioner Dearden did too.

So I was a bit surprised to see Commissioner Dearden on the evening news one night describing various drills that our law enforcement personnel were running to prepare for bomb attacks at Olympic venues. The footage showed a federal bomb squad, dressed up in their moon suits, detonating an incendiary device that sent a car tire 100 feet into the air. Commissioner Dearden talked with the reporter for a few minutes and actually outlined which public places he thought would be safest during the Games and which felt were more vulnerable. I was infuriated. I asked our communications director to order a copy of the tape from the TV station. I watched it again and again, dumbfounded.

There was even a story in the *Wall Street Journal* about the counterterrorism precautions being taken for the Games. There was Commissioner Dearden describing how officers were training for the possibility of chemical and biological attacks. There was a picture of people in anti-contamination suits carrying a dummy in a body bag—some sort of "dirty corpse" drill. Someone had invited a photographer. It made for great theatre, but it was inconceivable to me how this kind of article—and there were others like it—could actually reduce the risk of terrorist incidents. If anything, I thought, such grandstanding could only increase the likelihood of attacks. It certainly increased the number of frightened callers to my office. The commissioner felt he was making the citizens feel safer. I felt that instead, he was inviting trouble.

My concerns were intensified because we still were not making progress on finalizing a public safety plan. The U.S. Secret Service had stepped up their involvement in the planning process and were now assigning senior people full-time to Olympic planning.

At this point, probably the single biggest factor holding up finalizing a plan was the question of who was paying. UOPSC had pushed the planning process as far as they could without some clarity. No one was willing to sign off on a plan when they did not know what their organization's financial obligation would be. While it was clear that there would be massive federal support, it was not clear whether that support would cover the entire plan. We couldn't find out how much the feds would cover until there was a plan—and we couldn't get a plan because we didn't know how much they would cover. It was a chicken and egg dilemma.

SHOW ME THE MONEY

In the spring of 2000, we had our first break-through. Ironically, it was by turning a liability to our advantage. In February 1998, while all the SLOC leadership was in Nagano for the Olympic Games, the legislature snuck through a special sales tax on Olympic tickets. It was a bitter blow for the cash-strapped committee. We couldn't increase the price of tickets to cover the new tax; we would just have to pay it out of our revenues. So, it was $13 million lost to us—and we got nothing for it.

Everyone was looking for a way to get the cities and towns on board with UOPSC, but the problem was finding a source of money. The ticket tax was a sore point with us at SLOC, and we had always hoped to be relieved of it. I suggested to the governor that SLOC would give up trying to invalidate the tax in the courts if he would be willing to allocate the entire amount to UOPSC, so that the cities and towns would know that there was a dedicated fund to cover their costs. It would give UOPSC leverage to enforce a plan. SLOC would also agree to become the payor of last resort for any costs outstanding when the Games were over. We had a plan.

After weeks of intensive lobbying with county commissioners, sheriffs, and state legislators and with the heroic assistance of Lane Beattie, Senate majority leader and future State Olympic Officer, and Mayor Anderson of Salt Lake, a deal was struck. The model for Olympic security planning that had been a paper tiger now had teeth.

Even with the core money available, and with the federal coordination going well, it would be several months before a comprehensive, detailed plan was in place. Part of the problem was that local law enforcement just isn't used to doing long-range planning, and we were asking UOPSC to put together a level of detail that was unfamiliar. And, the staffing at UOPSC was inadequate for the task to be done. The leadership knew what needed to happen, but the second tier of planners and computer programmers necessary to put together something this complex just weren't there. Considering that this is what we did at SLOC, I thought we could probably provide some support.

At SLOC, security fell under Doug Arnot, our managing director of event operations and, ultimately, under COO Fraser Bullock. Doug has a wealth of experience doing detailed event logistics. Everyone agreed that it was time to lock SLOC, UOPSC, the Secret Service, DoD, and the FBI in a room until decisions were made. We brought over the team that had prepared the detailed security and public safety operations plan for law enforcement for the Sydney Olympics and they organized the data as the group progressed. Together, the group mapped out the missing particulars: where barrier fencing would go, where the guards would stand, how many magnetometers would be needed to process the crush of spectators, how many volunteers would be required to work each one, what the level of law enforcement representation would be inside each venue, and what the cost and scheduling would be for each item. When they were done, we had something no U.S. Olympics had ever achieved—a comprehensive, coordinated public safety plan that everyone had agreed to follow.

It was a critical step to have the specifics in place. With a comprehensive plan in hand, sanctioned by state and federal authorities, preparations and training could move to a new level. As we moved into this next phase, there were some leadership shifts that brought new capabilities to the effort. In November, Commissioner Dearden resigned to take a position back in his home county. Fortunately, a few months earlier, the governor had created an executive director position at UOPSC—someone who would run the day-to-day Olympic public safety effort. Dave Tubbs, the senior FBI agent in Salt Lake, retired and took this position. Bob Flowers, a sheriff from southern Utah, moved north to become the new commissioner of public safety and commander of UOPSC. Bob and Dave made a great team heading UOPSC. Dave was replaced as special agent in charge at the FBI by Don Johnson, who came from Oklahoma and brought first-hand experience in dealing with the response to a terrorist attack.

There was one other member of the senior security leadership team that had come aboard in 2000. General J.D. Johnson who would have command over the National Guard and Reserve troops that DoD would send into Salt Lake. General Johnson had, arguably, one of the most difficult tasks of the group. Because of continuing Congressional investigations and pressure over limiting the use of the military at special events, the Pentagon was slow to begin establishing their Olympic force on the ground. After considerable pressure from us and the state of Utah, the Defense Department finally assigned General Johnson and sent him in with a very small, core team to start planning. But they didn't release the money that Congress had set aside for the effort. Red tape and lawyers had it all tied up so the General was sent to Utah to do the job but given no resources to work with.

I didn't learn all of this until much later, because J.D. was never one to complain. But for the first few months that the military's Olympic command operated, it was financed by General Johnson. He paid for everything, from making keys for the locks on the offices to buying computers and paper so they could work. I told him later he should never have done that. His answer was typical of the kind of people we have in our armed services—he had a job to do, and he knew it could not wait for the bureaucrats to figure it out. The military was late coming in and he didn't have a day to lose. General Johnson knew his mission was critical; a few months later, after September 11, we would all be glad that J.D. Johnson didn't wait for the Pentagon to come through to start working. He was ready to take on an expanded mission because of the groundwork he had laid.

THE LAST PIECE

Our plan called for some 77 kilometers of fencing, hundreds of magnetometers, and 4,000 law enforcement officers. Prior to the Games, there were only 3,500 officers in the entire state of Utah. UOPSC projected that about 1,300 officers could be borrowed from local Utah law enforcement and from the state police. Another 700 officers could be counted on from neighboring states and other communities but they would need housing and transportation—not to mention everyone would need special uniforms for standing patrol in the cold. All totaled, the personnel costs for state and local government were projected to be $30.7 million. The state's redirection of sales tax to public safety would cover $13 million. SLOC contributions through Olympic sponsorships and Department of Justice grants over the past several years provided an additional $5 million. But $12.7 million remained and SLOC just didn't have the money. We knew we would have to ask Congress to provide the funds. And even with the additional funding, we were still 2,000 law enforcement officers short. The Secret Service had agreed that these positions should be federal officers that would be pulled from the federal agencies. But, since they would all have to be brought into Utah, the cost would be high. They would need transport, housing, food, training, uniforms and equipment. This would be the largest movement of federal law enforcement personnel in our country's history.

On top of this, the military would play a significant role. Thousands of troops were required to perform military support missions for the plan. They would bring in bomb dogs and inspect venues and vehicles, they would fly air patrols, and they would run specialized law enforcement communications. But, like the other aspects of the plan, no money had been appropriated to carry out the mission.

The number of federal law enforcement officers needed for Salt Lake was much higher than for the larger Atlanta Games and we knew we would have to explain this to Congress. The bottom line was that we needed more officers because we couldn't use the military to the degree they were used in Atlanta. During Atlanta's Games, federal troops played critical public safety roles. But there were reports that they were also used in other ways. When the organizing committee couldn't find enough bus drivers for the Olympic system, military troops were trained to drive the athlete buses. When volunteer security personnel abandoned their assignments after the bomb exploded in Atlanta's Centennial Park, state officials turned to federal troops. And in the days before the Games began, after hurricane force winds devastated certain Olympic facilities on the coast, the Navy had been called in to rebuild them. In all, Atlanta employed 14,000 federal troops to fill a variety of last minute needs, including public safety.

Senator McCain in particular was irked to learn that in Atlanta federal troops were driving buses, standing at security posts, and docks. As Washington's number one watchdog against waste, he saw the Atlanta Olympics as a prime offender, and nothing in SLOC's history suggested we would be any different. After Atlanta, McCain championed legislation that specifically limited the involvement of federal troops at Olympics to public safety details. It further required the Justice Department to certify that requested services would be of a nature that only the military could provide.

In late November 2000, Thurgood Marshall, Jr., and Mickey Ibarra summoned representatives from the various public security agencies to the White House to assess their commitment to the Olympic public safety effort and to determine whether there was agreement that the federal departments and agencies should provide 2,000 officers and other equipment, in addition to the military personnel. Essentially, this meeting was to obtain the buy-in of the top levels of all the departments for the comprehensive security and public safety plan that had been developed by SLOC and UOPSC under the guidelines of the Secret Service.

It was pretty obvious which way the meeting would go. What wasn't obvious is that this sort of "assuming responsibility" meeting rarely happens in Washington. The transition of the presidency meant that there was a need to have real certainty before the change in command occurred, and Mickey and Goody had set the stage to give us that certainty. When we left the White House that day, we had a commitment from the federal government to provide the people and equipment we needed to secure Salt Lake. Now, all we needed was for Congress to fund that commitment.

THE BUSH ADMINISTRATION

With the inauguration of the Bush administration, our continual push for federal funding got a little easier—at least on the security front. For the last ten years, Atlanta and Salt Lake had performed a complicated dance in order to get federal support. We would work with a federal agency, figure out what the agency's role was in the Olympics, figure out how much it would cost the agency to do its job, and then SLOC would have to go to Congress and ask them to fund the role. I always thought it was ridiculous that I had to ask Congress to give an agency money to do their job; why couldn't they just budget for it? Well, when the Bush administration came in and heard what was going on, they thought it was nuts, too. Particularly when it came to security and public safety. The new Olympic liaison, Deputy Chief of Staff Joe Hagin, was clear when he talked with us. If the federal government had a role in the security and public safety plan, and if there was concurrence in the agencies that they needed to carry out these missions, then the money would be in the first Bush budget submission to Congress.

And it was. The Bush budget included $130 million for Olympic needs, largely to provide the 2,000 federal law enforcement officials that were in the plan. Suddenly, instead of going over to Congress and begging for money, we were walking the halls with the Secret Service and the FBI, supporting a budget request made by the President so that the Olympic public safety plan could be implemented.

Many of the problems we faced at that time dealing with the hodgepodge of agencies and appropriations subcommittees that divvied up public safety are no longer an issue. The creation of the Department of Homeland Security essentially provides one-stop shopping now for most of the agencies that play a role in securing an Olympics. By the same token, Congress reorganized the appropriations committees as well, so that there aren't five or six different subcommittees overseeing security.

Fortunately, Congress got it, and the security plan got the funding it needed. Not only that, but the effort that we made over the months to discuss the plan in detail with Congress—usually with SLOC, UOPSC, the Secret Service, FBI and Defense doing the briefings together—solidified in the minds of those in Washington that this was an integrated plan and that we would implement it in a unique way. Federal, state, and local government would be working hand-in-glove with the organizing committee during the Games.

Chapter 15

SEPTEMBER 11

The morning of September 11, 2001, I was in Washington, D.C., working on security preparations for the Games. The last $13 million in federal appropriations required by our plan had been included in the Senate budget but missed by the House of Representatives. There had been confusion in the House committee about a similar figure requested by the FBI. They had mistakenly deleted what they thought was a redundancy. We were anxious to meet with key legislators to clear up the confusion and reconfirm their support.

We had planned to be in New York City on the 11th. That was the date originally set by our public relations people for announcing the names of our Olympic torchbearers. Our team had planned an elaborate press conference adjacent to the World Trade Center at Battery Park. But we delayed the announcement in New York to accommodate our meeting on Capitol Hill.

Cindy Gillespie had scheduled a meeting with House and Senate appropriators in the U.S. Capitol building for 10:00 a.m. on the 11th. I met Cindy at 8:00 a.m. to put the finishing touches on our presentation. She had an office in the Ronald Regan building on Pennsylvania Avenue, just blocks from the White House. I was on the phone to Salt Lake City, doing a radio interview. The interviewer interrupted to say there were reports that a plane had hit the World Trade Center. I hung up and turned on the small TV in the office.

Like so many other Americans, I watched in horror as flames poured from the North Tower of the World Trade Center. I called my wife Ann; she was watching coverage on the *Today* show. It seemed like a dreadful accident, Ann wondered out loud how a plane could fly into a building in clear daylight. Could it have been done on purpose? Then a plane hit the other tower. We watched it happen on TV. We were stupefied. These were deliberate acts. This was terrorism.

Soon, damage to the Pentagon was reported, absent any video footage. The worst place to be right then was a government building like the one we were in. It was also pretty obvious that Washington, D.C., would soon be grid locked by a massive evacuation. We left the building and found Cindy's car.

We drove north toward Alexandria, Virginia, where Cindy shared a house with her sister. Interstate 395 comes within a few hundred yards of the Pentagon, and as we reached the Pentagon exit, we found abandoned cars blocking the two right lanes. Stunned drivers and passengers were leaning on the guardrail to watch the flames coming from the Pentagon. Acrid black smoke poured into our car. It didn't smell like burning jet fuel or a house fire. It smelled like nothing I had ever smelled before. Like war. Things that do not normally burn ignite and smolder under the extraordinary heat of military ordinance—or in this instance, the heat of a plane filled with fuel penetrating a building at 500 miles per hour. It was combusting concrete and metal that I smelled.

It immediately struck me that the world would never be the same. My mind raced to think of all the implications. I made no effort to order or weight them. I did not think about the Olympics. I thought about thousands of children who must have lost a parent. I thought of wives and husbands. I thought about a worldview that had grown accustomed to thinking in terms of lifestyles, not life and death. I did not tear or sob. I sat emotionally stunned. I called Ann again. Together we called our sons. Despite the very public nature of that national tragedy, it was felt in individual families in very intimate ways.

Eventually, my mind did return to the Olympics—the effort that had consumed our lives for close to three years. I knew instinctively that the events of that day would have a profound effect on our work. There would undoubtedly be calls for the cancellation of the Games. It was even possible that individual athletes, teams, or entire national delegations would make the decision to stay home. Security and transportation, particularly air travel, would be more complicated than before.

But there was no question in my mind about the ultimate outcome. We would forge forward. We would review our security plans from top to bottom and make appropriate adjustments. Inasmuch as we were able, we would provide public reassurance about our extensive security provisions. In many ways, our staging the 2002 Winter Olympic Games in Salt Lake City would be more important than ever before. Whereas nationalism and pride were the hallmarks of international competition, our Games would have to be about something more. In the face of such hatred and violent prejudice, the Olympics needed to stand as a visible demonstration of solidarity and the enduring principles of civilization: mutual respect, fair play, brotherly competition.

A MESSAGE OF UNITY

With deaths being counted and mourning only beginning as the survivors were notified, I did not feel I should make a statement about the implications of the tragedy on the Olympics. Those considerations paled in comparison with the impact on families. A call came from Caroline Shaw, our communications chief, asking me for a statement. I said to wait at least a day. My position was that we had no comment with regards to the Olympics while the appalling tragedy was so fresh.

The time would come when we would need to reassure the public of our security preparations and to beef up our current plans. But while the smoke was still pouring into the streets, it wasn't the time.

Within a few hours Alan Abrahamson from the *Los Angeles Times* called me on my cell phone. Alan asked me how the outlook for the Games had changed. I repeated to him my surprise that anybody wanted to hear from the Olympic organizing committee on that day, but he begged to differ. He remarked that in a time of national duress, the Olympics and its message of international cooperation and peaceful humanitarianism would be a part of the story, part of the healing. He predicted that before the day was over, I would end up changing my mind. I told him I would contact him if I did.

He was right. By the end of the day, I kept to a basic message, limiting elaborations:

> Tears and prayers flood our hearts. But not fear. As a testament to the courage of the human spirit, and as a world symbol of peace, the Olympics is needed even more today than yesterday.
>
> Of course, the conduct of public safety can never be the same. I look to the federal government to revisit public safety plans for these Games. We will remain fully engaged in that effort and will make it our highest priority.

I spent the night at the Marriott Courtyard in Alexandria. I watched the news coverage through the early hours of the morning and, like most Americans, tossed about with dreams of disaster.

The next morning, with TV reports of Germans singing our national anthem at the Brandenburg Gate and French papers exclaiming *"Nous sommes tous Americains* (We are all Americans)," my emotions broke. It is always the best in humanity that strikes me most deeply. Later, the stack of faxes and e-mails from Olympic committees around the world that appeared on my desk included Iran, Russia, China, and others. As countries that have been our competitors, even enemies, rallied to support us, I again choked with appreciation.

That morning I crafted an e-mail to all of our employees. Here's part of what I wrote:

> Like you, I have been overwhelmed with emotion. The horrific reality of the attack on civilization and the incomprehensible scale of human suffering have led each of us to our own form of prayer and mourning. Everything which is part of our everyday we rethink in terms of new priorities. Where does the Olympics fit?
>
> In my view, the work we are doing is more important today than ever. The Olympics is a sporting event and much more: it is a world symbol of peace, of the bond of humanity, and of the triumph of civilization over barbarism. The celebration we are planning is less of a party and more of an affirmation...
>
> Today would be even harder for me if I were out trying to make a few bucks. I am honored that I can join you in work that means so much to our nation and to the world. In the annals of Olympism and the history of Utah, this may stand as one of the defining hours. I am confident that we will perform with honor.

Days later, when I finally managed to arrive back in Salt Lake, we assembled the entire team outside our headquarters building on the Gallivan Plaza. We said a prayer. We sung the national anthem and God Bless America.

A POST-9/11 WORLD

It is an understatement to say that September 11, 2001 changed our perception of security. While we had always contemplated the possibility of a large-scale terrorist incident in our planning, it was completely different to suddenly find the threat so real. While we planned for international terrorism, our discussions centered around the threats closer to home.

For me, two things were clear. First, I knew I could not let people come to Salt Lake unless I believed everything that could be done, had been done to keep them safe. And, second, unless the federal government stepped up and assumed responsibility for meeting this new terrorist threat to the Salt Lake Games, there would be no Games.

On the morning following the attacks, Cindy and I called Senator Hatch, who was in his Senate office, and asked if we could get together to talk about how to go forward. He told us to come right over.

I was the only person going into the Hart Building when I arrived that morning. Behind his desk, Senator Hatch was reading newspaper articles that had been highlighted for his review. We spent much of the morning talking about what had happened and how it was likely to change the country. He assured us that Congress would recognize the need for additional security. But with only four months left and the official federal budget close to completion for the year, I was wary of bureaucratic inefficiencies. Cindy had previously suggested to me that I ask for Senator Hatch to arrange a summit with the attorney general, secretary of the army, each of the public safety agency heads, and key Congressional leaders. Literally, we were asking for a summit to decide if the federal government wanted our Games to go on. It would take an enormous commitment of resources and people; we did not have the time to spend going through the normal Washington decision-making process. Senator Hatch liked the idea and committed to make it happen. We would shoot for three weeks away. In the meantime, the UOPSC and its federal partners would redo the public safety plan so we would know what was needed.

Within days, SLOC, UOPSC and the key federal agencies sat down to revisit every detail of our plan. When they had scrubbed it thoroughly, they presented to the governor, the mayor and me their recommendations for needed enhancements. There were training facilities and temporary housing for the athletes near the venues that had not been slated for enforced perimeters. They would all have to be secured. We would need a far more comprehensive and aggressive plan to patrol the airspace above the venues. An air CAP (Combat Aircraft Patrol) and a possible shut-down of the airport were on the table. The Secret Service felt strongly that we should assign military or law enforcement personnel to our magnetometer stations, which in our original plan were slated for trained security volunteers. The governor decided to cancel an event he was planning for the public and SLOC eliminated or scaled back others we had planned. The only question was whether or not to merge the city's plans for nightly celebrations at city hall into other Olympic events that were already in secured venues. While I strongly felt that in this time of limited resources it was inappropriate to divert law enforcement personnel, equipment and fencing to cover this event, the mayor felt equally strongly that the city should continue with its plans. We agreed to disagree for the moment.

The estimated cost of these enhancements would be $40 million, $30 million for additional personnel and for improvements in the air defense system. About $10 million would be directed toward UOPSC for purchases of equipment and fencing as well as additional personnel costs for venues under UOPSC's command. Cindy and I met with Senator Bennett over the weekend to discuss the figures. He felt confident that his colleagues in the Senate would do what was necessary to protect the Games. He also expressed his view that the Games would not be a target of international terrorism. Bin Laden, he explained, was far too effective a politician to wish to alienate the entire world by attacking the Olympics. And, his modus operandi was to lay low following an attack. The World Trade Center and Pentagon attacks had probably taken five years to prepare, and were Bin Laden's greatest moment. Bennett believed that he would lay low for a few years before bringing out another team of terrorists. We all hoped he was right.

As the Secret Service, FBI, DoD and FEMA passed the revised plans up the chain for review back in Washington, I had a conversation with our White House liaison, Joe Hagin. Congress and the White House were working on an emergency supplemental to help New York, rebuild the Pentagon, and begin to prepare for war. Our money needed to be in that supplemental so we were racing the clock to get the new security plan approved. Joe told me that it was definitely on everyone's radar screen that more money and more troops would be needed for Salt Lake. He expressed confidence that by the time we held the meeting that Senator Hatch was organizing with Attorney General Ashcroft, Army Secretary Thomas White and other key decision-makers, there would be federal agreement on a revised plan for Salt Lake.

THE SUMMIT

Wednesday, October 3rd, was the date set for the Olympics security summit. Senator Hatch had obtained commitments from the attorney general, the directors of the FBI, Secret Service, FEMA, the secretary of the army, Speaker Dennis Hastert, Senator Stevens, as well as several other Washington power notables. Governor Leavitt would represent the state, Mayor Anderson would represent the city, Dave Tubbs would represent UOPSC and I would represent SLOC. Cindy spent the week before the meeting back in Washington making the rounds with Mark Camillo, Dave Tubbs, Bob Flowers, and Don Johnson to explain the revised security plan to Congressional staff and answer questions at the various federal departments. She called me one afternoon to tell me how much Washington had changed. The front lines were no longer on foreign shores; they were now in America. There would be no more lobbying for military support for Salt Lake: the military would stand with us to secure the public.

Tuesday afternoon was capped by a call from Senator Hatch informing me that he had succeeded in arranging a meeting with Senator John McCain. I drove directly to the Senate office building and met Hatch on the way. Senator McCain was waiting and ushered us into his office. Like everyone else, the events of September 11 had sobered him. He got right to the point. He told me that he believed it was important to America that the Games go on and important to the world that the nations come together in a show of peace. He made it clear there would be no problems from him when we came to Congress for the funding necessary to keep the Games secure. We would have his support, and we did. Over the years I have worked with him, I have come to understand that Senator McCain is a true fiscal watchdog but first and foremost, he is a true patriot.

The security summit on Wednesday provided the official affirmation that the federal government would do everything necessary to secure the Games. By the time the meeting was over, Secret Service Director Brian Stafford had briefed everyone on the revised security plan, the attorney general had committed the federal law enforcement agencies, the secretary of the army had committed the troops, and the Speaker of the House and Senate Appropriations Chairman Ted Stevens had committed the funding. In three short weeks, we had revised our plans, reached concurrence at the top levels of the federal government, and received Congressional commitments. Apparently government can move quickly when it needs to. And, on the flight home with the governor and mayor, we were aware that now, it was our turn. We had a lot to do in three short months.

PUTTING IT ALL TOGETHER

The next three months were a whirlwind of activity in the security area. Frantic efforts to get more fencing, more barricades, more mags, consumed our procurement staff. General J.D. Johnson was training troops around the nation to prepare them for Salt Lake. This wasn't a normal military mission; they were coming to be a presence and to perform critical roles, but no one wanted Salt Lake to feel like an armed camp. The military would be interacting with the public at the mag-and-bag operations. General Johnson put together a special tape on how to talk to and treat civilians when they're inspecting them. It was incredibly effective. At Games-time, one of the biggest surprises to the world community was that they showed up at Salt Lake and found the military to be friendly and courteous, not at all the image they expected. In my mind I said, "thank you, J.D.," every time someone stopped me to compliment our armed forces. It was a great effort.

Mark Camillo was working with DoD, FAA and others on the new air CAP. While in the end the feds could simply order the air CAP, they worked with everyone to prevent unintended problems. For example, it was clear early on that the airspace would be shut down during opening and closing ceremonies, but if that happened, how would NBC get their camera shots? For years, we had designed the ceremonies so that some of the effects could only be seen by a camera shot directly down into the stadium. It was too late to change the ceremony. A compromise was finally struck by limiting the helicopters to just the one TV feed, locating the helicopter one half mile from the stadium, and putting armed law enforcement in the chopper with the cameraman. I've always wondered what it was like for that guy to be up there shooting the ceremonies knowing the other people on the chopper were there to shoot him if he tried anything unexpected.

One of our biggest challenges during this time was making sure that the athletes felt safe. While I had no doubt that any athlete that made the Olympic team would probably risk life and limb to be in Salt Lake, I also knew that the decision would probably not be theirs. Their National Olympic Committee and their National Sports Federation would decide whether or not their athletes would be safe in Salt Lake.

In late September, I got a call from Gary Bettman, commissioner of the NHL, expressing his concern that owners or players might be fearful about coming to the Games in Salt Lake City. Clearly, without the NHL players, the Games would suffer a severe blow. And, if his NHL athletes were nervous, then we could certainly expect that other federations and other nations would be too. So, we tackled this on three fronts. First, I met in New York with Bettman and NHL representatives and gave them a thorough review of our plans. Once they had this briefing, they were okay; it was clear everything that could be done, was being done. Then, we invited all the national Olympic committees to send their security directors to a two-day meeting in Salt Lake where UOPSC, SLOC and the Secret Service walked them through the security precautions we were taking. They left convinced that the United States was pulling out all the stops. And, third, Undersecretary Dick Armitage at the State Department got our U.S. ambassadors to help around the world, making sure that countries that were uncertain about security knew how much the U.S. was doing to keep the athletes safe. In the end, it worked: when the Games opened on February 8, no athlete stayed away because of security concerns.

Even though we had a revised plan, we never stopped looking for holes or problems. And, occasionally, we would find them. About two months before the Games, we decided that the athlete transportation plan really needed to be stepped up. When you looked at it, this was the point where the athletes were the most vulnerable. They were leaving a highly secured village and going to a heavily secured competition venue. But in between, they were in a bus or a van and susceptible to attack or kidnapping. The Secret Service decided to take responsibility for increasing what we called "in-transit security" and they provided officers to travel with some delegations, escorts for others and a mix of precautions. One of the precautions was putting GPS locators in each vehicle, and requiring the driver to report to the transportation center as he left a venue and at designated points along the pre-set route. That way, we would know instantly if a vehicle steered off course.

This worked beautifully—so beautifully, in fact, that one of our "incidents" at Games-time came from the GPS monitoring. In the transportation command center, one of our staff noticed a bus moving off-course. He tried to reach the driver by radio, but he didn't respond. He alerted the law enforcement officer sitting in the command center and he tried to reach the driver. Still no response. They called the security command center and the police went into action. Monitoring the bus's movements, they directed the police to interdict the wayward bus. SWAT teams were called up because we either had a lost driver or someone had taken over the bus. Then it halted and in minutes, the police had the vehicle surrounded, as well as the McDonald's where the driver had taken the athletes to get something to eat.

Ultimately, no amount of preparation can ever allay all your fears—nor should it. In the end, no security plan is foolproof. So, in spite of all the experts and all the specialized equipment and all the people we had assigned to security, I went in the Games with my breath held just a little. We had done all we could—but would it be enough? I'll be truthful. With each day that passed, I gave a sigh of relief and then held my breath through the next. One night, just as a concert was starting, my wife's cell phone rang. Mine was turned off. It was UOPSC Commander Bob Flowers. They thought they had found anthrax at the airport, they were clearing the facility and would be holding a joint press conference with the Homeland Security spokesperson shortly. I got up and went to the command center to work with everyone on contingency and evacuation plans. Later that night, word came through that the first test had been false: the powder was harmless. We had made it through another day.

Those may have been the longest seventeen days of my life, but they were also some of the absolute best. In writing my speech for closing ceremonies, I tried to say thank you to the thousands and thousands of people—volunteers, cops, federal agents, military troops, firemen, public health workers—who had toiled behind the scenes to keep these Games safe. It was an unprecedented security effort and it was effective because at every level, from the forest service ranger on patrol at 2 a.m. in the mountain cold to the military soldier screening vehicles to the volunteers keeping people out of secured areas with a smile, everyone did their jobs as if the lives of those around them depended on them performing perfectly. Which they did.

There are inflection points in history that mark the departure from one course and the beginning of another. September 11, I believe, will mark a shift in numerous dimensions of human endeavor. Most poignantly, the growing human expectation of predictability and safety had been shocked by an undeniable reality of vulnerability and uncertainty. Politically, the Cold War competition between two super-powers was replaced by a "clash of civilizations." A large and mighty military power had been frustrated by a tiny band of treacherous, agile terrorists. September 11, 2001 is a defining moment for our country and for the world. It was a dramatic manifestation of many streams of change that continue to play out around us.

Against this new historic course, the Salt Lake 2002 Winter Olympics in their own way were also defining. This was the first international event since the attack, and it was in the United States. Seventy-seven countries were there, holding aloft their colors and parading the excellence of their youth. Even in an uncertain world, civilization would proceed, nations would gather, freedom would ring, and young heroes would be celebrated. We would not sacrifice those things that made humanity God's greatest creation.

Chapter 16

Heart and Meaning

Of course, the athletes are the center of the Games. Olympians would showcase the qualities of the human spirit to the world. So sport and athletes came first; field of play, accommodations, doping control, everything to verify the integrity of the athletic competition. The broadcasters and media were our willing cooperators. They dispersed the sporting images and told their stories. But there was more. We needed music and color and cheering spectators. The power of the athletic achievements to touch hearts derived in part from features that surrounded the performance itself.

Creative features would heighten emotional impact. If we were to succeed in our vision, every creative element had to support the Olympic performance: the ceremonies, the decorations, the music, the medals, the entertainment, the artistry, and even the volunteers. For that to happen, each element had to reinforce the others. We needed a single message, one theme that connected every creative element.

The theme of our Games was "Light the Fire Within." Gordon Bowen, my friend from McGarry Bowen, had produced marketing campaigns for the likes of Coca-Cola, American Express, Verizon, and AT&T. He committed to help with ours but just couldn't find the time to devote to the effort. I pushed hard one day after struggling for the umpteenth time to put words to our vision of the Games. He sat down and began writing. He called me a couple of hours later with ten lines, seven of which were a good deal better than anything any one of us at SLOC had come up with in several months of trying. We are not all created equal. Gordon's talent left us speechless, and appreciative. One of the lines was "Ignite the Fire Within." I really liked it. I ran it by Scott Givens and the senior management. Sold. Great. I called Gordon and told him which line we had chosen. He was pleased to have helped.

Several days later, Gordon called. He had just had lunch at a small restaurant in Salt Lake City called Guru's. On their menu was the same line: ignite the fire within. Our legal team did a copyright search and found the phrase "the fire within" had in fact been secured by yet another Utah company, Franklin Covey. One of the founders of the restaurant had once worked there. We called Franklin Covey and got their permission to use the phrase for the Games. Not wanting any legal problems, we also worked out an arrangement with the restaurant people.

We changed from "ignite" to "light" after speaking with our composer, David Foster; "light" was a lot easier to work into music lyrics. Every time I saw the phrase, I thought of the time, legal work, and effort to come up with it.

Visually, we would connect our creative elements to the theme. When we were dealing with fire, as with the torch and the cauldron, we wanted to somehow have the flame visible on the inside, then emerge into the air. We wondered if that would be possible. In other media, Scott felt that the contrast of "fire and ice" or "reds and blues" was best to carry our message. The red and fire represented the inspiration of the athlete; the blue represented the challenges they had overcome. They had lit the fire within. Given how little money was left in our creative budget, it was all the more important that all our elements reinforce the same theme.

SYDNEY SUCCESSES

A year and half into the job, the opportunity finally arrived for Fraser and me to have our own Olympic experience. It was surely a source of amusement that neither Fraser nor I had ever actually been to an Olympics. That isn't quite true: Fraser had done some work for Visa back in the '80s and was their guest for one day at the Atlanta Games. When asked by the media about my Olympic experience, I used to say that I had been to every Olympics since 1960. I had seen Ali box. I had seen Fleming skate. I was as familiar with the stories of Jenner, Korbit, Hamill, Mahre, Moses, and Eruzione as anyone. But I had attended the Games the same way everyone else in America did, on television. I had never actually been to an Olympic event, never once. It was time to see the Games in action and check our preconceptions at the door.

We wanted to suck as much experience from the Sydney Olympics as possible. In addition to our first hand anecdotal observation, Fraser and I organized a systematic approach to learning. First, we embedded SLOC staff as paid Sydney organizing committee employees for several months leading up to the Games. Second, we assigned our entire management team to assess all practices that fell within their SLOC functions. The results from these efforts were to be gathered, communicated, and promulgated in a defined protocol. To make sure that everyone was on track and keeping up, we gathered every morning as a management team to report on the prior day's work and observations. We rented a hotel room in Sydney with a balcony overlooking the city; every morning we assembled for breakfast together and detailed our findings.

The Sydney Games were flat out impressive, there's no denying it. In so many ways, what we saw there were case studies of what to do and how to do it. In particular, I was overwhelmed by the sheer spectacle of it all. I remember sitting in the stands during the opening ceremonies with a stew of emotions brewing inside of me. Part of me was drawn in and exhilarated by the opulence and imaginative wonder of the show. The stadium itself was capable of inspiring awe. Built expressly for the Olympics, it featured huge cantilevered pulleys that flung multiple props and performers simultaneously into the air at the touch of a button. The cast of 12,500 included tattooed fire breathers, flaming stilt walkers, tap-dancers on tin roofs, and 120 galloping horses. The wonder was accompanied by a sinking sense of dread. Sydney was drawing the lines of comparison by which our efforts would be measured. They seemed to be setting the bar impossibly high.

The University of Utah's football stadium where our ceremonies would be held could hardly compete with Sydney's state of the art Olympic arena on technical merit alone. At one point, we inquired what it would cost to stretch a cable above our stadium from which we could hoist by pulley an actor; the figure was $1 million. Sydney had multiple hoists and for massive props as well as actors.

I admit to having terribly inappropriate, mixed emotions when their mechanical cauldron stalled halfway up its track. It had been ignited in a pool of water, raised around torchbearer Cathy Freeman, and was on its way up a cascading waterfall to its final resting place on a pedestal at the top of the stadium. It was a remarkable spectacle, but about halfway up, the burning cauldron stopped in its track. For several minutes it didn't move. Perhaps it would just be stuck there. If so, the small portable tank of fuel that was feeding the flame would soon be empty, extinguishing the flame. Remember the words of Henry Higgins in *My Fair Lady*: "How simply frightful! How humiliating! How *delightful*!" Both to my relief and to my disappointment, it suddenly jerked upward on its path again. The crowd cheered more loudly than had it worked without challenge.

It turned out that the stall was the result of a malfunction by a tiny $1.50 electrical contact: its job was to confirm that the safety locking device was firmly in place. When it failed to do so, a person was sent running to personally inspect the locking mechanism. When all was in order, it again began its ascent, arriving at the top and connecting to the fuel lines just minutes before the flame would have expired. But the near-miss cauldron lighting was followed by what seemed to be ten solid minutes of dazzling fireworks bursts. The ceremonies had been an unqualified success. In truth, I was happy for Sydney and for the Games but I was also more than a little intimidated at the prospect of producing our opening.

A JEWEL OF A CITY

Another area where it seemed we would never be able to measure up with Sydney was in the scale and majesty of their decorations. Sydney's Olympic budget was estimated at $5 billion, including a much-publicized last-minute $84 million bailout by the government of New South Wales. That's more than two times what Atlanta spent and almost three times our budget. Much of that money came from government support. A lot of it was earmarked for infrastructure improvements and decoration.

Streets were resurfaced. Grass acreage and seating were expanded in city parks. Footpaths were widened and paved with granite. Theaters and visitor centers were constructed. New light poles were installed on every major thoroughfare and pedestrian plazas were installed with granite chairs. Subway stations were rebuilt and subway tunnels widened. The city looked brand new. There were Olympic flags and banners everywhere you looked. The harbor seemed jammed with food, entertainment, and wall-to-wall party people every hour of the day and night. The harbor itself was resplendent and formed a natural focal point for all the energy of the Games. The Harbor Bridge with its oversized Olympic rings reflecting off the water at night, the Opera House lit up like a temple: you couldn't help but be impressed. And I knew how much it cost.

I made comments to the media about not expecting Salt Lake City's Games to be nearly so flashy. I said I hoped they would be "an example of American ingenuity" not a "testament to excess." I pointed out that all of the improvements and decorations would have an impact on those attending the Games but would not really be conveyed to the television audience. But I knew I was overstating my case. What Sydney had invested in décor and entertainment enthused the crowds of spectators and thrilled the local citizens, most of whom could never make it to an Olympic event. It was an integral part of sharing the Olympic spirit. I knew we would have to do more in Salt Lake City to enhance the feeling of celebration, hospitality, and significance of the Games. I also knew we had slashed the "look of the Games" budget by more than half to barely $9 million. Sydney spent more than three times that amount on decorative banners alone. Likewise, I had cut opening and closing ceremonies budgets to $20 million, less than a quarter what we estimated that Sydney had spent. We had some serious work to do.

MORE FROM LESS

Which brings me back to stretching to achieve impossibly high objectives. Time and time again, we had turned to one or another of our directors and asked for near miracles.

For all things relating to the creative functions, I turned to Scott Givens. We needed him to bring heart and meaning to the Games, achieve the scope and sweep of Sydney, but with less than a tenth of the bankroll. We needed big ideas—big enough to fill the city with the magic of an Olympic celebration. We could not afford to fund a battery of infrastructure improvements, let alone a banner for every streetlamp, so the projects we chose to fund needed to be high impact. We needed more from less. We needed water from stones. Scott went to work thinking big, bold, audacious thoughts.

CREATING A CENTER FOR OUR GAMES

If you only have enough money for a dozen roses, you don't put one in each of twelve rooms, you put them all in one vase in the one room where people gather. That's what Scott wanted for Salt Lake City. The creative team's first challenge was to create a focal point. We wanted to find a single place to concentrate our crowds, our entertainment, our decorations, and our energy. It was our only hope for anything like the energy we felt while we were in Sydney.

That's why all my predecessors and I focused on Block 85. I've already detailed how the Mormon Church stepped up with the donation of Block 85. It would accommodate over 20,000 people at once. We saw it becoming the living, pulsing center of the city during the Games—a place where people would congregate night and day just to be a part of things. That is what Sydney had and that is what we desperately needed—all the more so given the fact that our Games would be during the winter. It would be cold outside and people would need a reason not to stay indoors. Block 85 gave us the space; Scott would have to use it to create a compelling celebration center. One feature would be decoration.

Musing on the fact that the Salt Lake City was the largest city ever to host a Winter Olympics, Scott and his gang hit upon an idea of pure genius—building wraps. Huge building-sized images of Olympic athletes would be draped on the biggest buildings of Salt Lake City's skyline.

The size of the images themselves would, of course, lend a heightened sense of drama to the city. The subjects of the pictures—a biathlete, speed skaters, a hockey goalie, a slalom racer—would reflect our focus on the athletes. All through the streets of Salt Lake, people would encounter towering images of athletes in action. One by one, they would pass by until you found your way to the Medals Plaza at Block 85. There, all of the images on the skyline would suddenly line up side-by-side all around you. Talk about a big idea.

On our budget, we could only afford one "view" of the city, so Scott aimed to make it an absolutely unforgettable one. The building across from Block 85 housed the local NBC affiliate and would serve as the camera platform for broadcasters worldwide. With massive 20-story building wraps as his canvas, Scott and his team imposed athletes on the city and beneath the towering mountains surrounding it.

Each building wrap cost approximately $100,000. There were twelve of them. We spent a little more securing display rights to every other large building in town so that no guerilla marketing campaign could use our innovation to sell merchandise. We also paid to light each building. Our entire building-wrap project cost little more than $1.5 million dollars. In comparison with other Olympics, it was hardly any money at all. And it rivaled the best that had been seen anywhere before.

THE RINGS

Nothing says Olympics like the Olympic rings, of course. Lillehammer had lighted rings on a field next to a farm, next to the mountain village. Salt Lake City mountains were far too big for that scale of display.

Scott came up with a low-tech, low-cost solution that was big enough to fill the imagination. All it would take would be 2,500 industrial-size lights strung on electric cables, formed as rings on the side of a mountain. We countered that the snow would bury the lights and that there was no electricity up on the mountain. Scott answered that we could string the cable and lights on seven-foot poles, above the depth of the snow, and we could bring in massive portable generators.

I remember the day Scott Givens bounded into my office and drew open the shades at my window. He pointed to one of the prominent peaks that looks over the city. "There, Mitt," he said, "that's where we'll put our rings." Scott could see me trying to visualize metal rings propped up far away on a mountainside. "No, Mitt, the whole mountain. We'll cover the mountain with our rings." It was a big idea. We went in search of a sponsor to fund it and lucked out with our friends at Utah Power and their parent, Scottish Power. The electrical union members worked several weekends to install it. When they were lighted, they drew gasps from all over the valley: they could be seen by hundreds of thousands of people. They were magnificent.

THE CAULDRON

The Olympic cauldron is another focal point and, like our building wraps of athletes and the Olympic rings on the mountain, ours could be seen from the Medals Plaza. Sydney's cauldron reportedly cost $8 million. Our skinnied-down cauldron budget was $450,000, a figure we boosted just prior to the Sydney Games with an additional $1 million—still chicken feed compared to Sydney. I had remarked to Scott that with our budget, we would be welding two Weber grills together, igniting a small pool of charcoal lighter, and hauling it up a flagpole.

Scott conceived of a glass cauldron; the flame would be able to be seen both inside and outside the bowl of the cauldron. It would not have to be as large as Sydney's because the flame could be seen inside the bowl and hence, it would not burn half as much fuel. And gas was a major expense of the cauldron. It would be spectacular and memorable in its own way. A glass cauldron had never been done before. It would allow you to see the Olympic flame actually tumbling and rolling in the bowl. Now we just needed someone who could design and build it.

We had heard about a company that had done amazing things with water and fire. Their work was front and center at the opulent Bellagio Hotel in Las Vegas. The company was called Wet Design. They were essentially a group of mechanical engineers, coincidentally out of the University of Utah. They had patented a new, more spectacular way to drive streams of water into the air, for fountains and other applications. Scott and I went down to Las Vegas to see their fountains and to watch the "O Show" spectacular, featuring the latest in fire and water technology. It was impressive.

It may not seem like an obvious choice to turn to a group of fountain specialists to design a cauldron, but we needed innovators and these guys were known for it. It would turn out that running water would be an essential component of the cauldron design. The only way to keep soot from the flames from building up on the glass was to have water running down the surface. In the end, the running water gave the impression of melting ice, but the water was primarily a technical element. If one of the water nozzles broke and an area on the cauldron got dry, the soot would adhere to it and turn it black. It was merely one of a host of technical problems we would end up having to solve on our way toward realizing our vision—a vision we may not have had the courage to pursue had we known up front how technically demanding it would be.

Several months later, Scott Givens and I made a trip to Los Angeles to check on Wet Design's progress. They had constructed a scale model of the cauldron. Given the complexity of our design, we were more than a little anxious to see how well it was working. Visions of Sydney's $8 million cauldron, malfunctioning because of a simple switch, were always in our minds.

We arrived in the early evening with the sun well above the horizon. We fired it up as soon as we got there. On hand was the entire team from Wet Design as well as representatives from the local fire department, the Salt Lake Fire Department, the Los Angeles gas company, and our gas company, Questar. It lit easily and produced a flame with the precise characteristics we had been looking for. The folks at Wet Design had made two practice runs earlier in the afternoon. Both times, the fire department was called in by the neighbors. It seems that the fire department representative on the spot was unable to call off his colleagues despite his repeated entreaties from his hand held radio. Something about flames leaping 25 feet in the air will do that.

After dinner, we lit up the cauldron once more. This time we drew quite a crowd in Wet Design's largely Hispanic neighborhood. We had tapped into the main gas line supplying the neighborhood; presumably, our cauldron was drawing so much fuel that gas ranges and appliances could hardly produce a flame. Jim Doyle, the project manager, was barraged with questions from onlookers. "It's for an amusement park in Malaysia," he explained. The cauldron was one of our surprises: he didn't want to blow our cover.

Earlier tests had in fact produced an unimpressive flame. Flames, it seems, have a tendency to stick close to one surface. Our cauldron flame stuck to one glass panel—it didn't tumble and roll, it just hugged one of the sides. So Jim Doyle designed three long stainless steel fingers that reached up into the bowl and shot air in a circular pattern near the flame's base. By the time the design was complete, we had gas entering from the bottom, jets of water running down the glass sides from the top and fingers of oxygen blowing in a swirling pattern. We had heat resistant panes on the inside and shatter resistant panes on the outside. The water presented further complications. It had to be heated prior to lighting the flame to keep the panes of glass from freezing, but as soon as the cauldron flame was ignited, we had to be able to switch off the water heaters and engage several large air conditioning units to pull the heat out of the water before going back up to cycle past the 900 degree blaze. The cauldron was 117 feet tall, presenting serious wind factors that had to be engineered. It weighed over 29,000 lbs., making transportation and installation at the site even more complicated. And it drew sizeable quantities of water, natural gas, and other gasses from tanks nearby.

Despite the complexity of the mechanisms, the effect had the grace of simplicity—a translucent bowl with a flame that rolled, tumbled, and bounced from wall to wall, occasionally taking giant 25 foot leaps into the sky. It was beautiful. All of it done at a fraction of the cost and using a fraction of the gas as the big boys in Sydney and

Atlanta. The cauldron had distinctive grace and artistry. It was unforgettable. Just what we had hoped for.

COLORS

We got ideas about our colors in Sydney. We noted that over very large spaces, like the Olympic stadium, if the decorations featured multiple colors, they became indistinct and blended together. Sydney had purples and greens and gold. The colors were fine up close, but at a distance, they competed with faces and clothing colors in the crowd; you couldn't pick out the banners or decorations. Repeating colors across broad panoramas had much more impact. Fresh from our experiences in Sydney, I asked Bob Finley, our director, to review our color scheme plans, street by street, venue by venue, building by building, and simplify. In fact, I wanted only one color—blue.

There is something about the color blue that really comes to life on TV. Sydney used a great deal of blue in their decoration, and we would too. I would look at the blue bunting in the Olympic stadium and it was nothing special, but on television it burst to life. I wanted lots and lots of blue.

Our creative team didn't entirely agree. They insisted that one color alone was too boring. Surely there was some room for contrast and variety. We came to a compromise and arranged our colors geographically. As you approached a SLOC venue all you saw initially was blue—blue banners, blue placards, blue fencing, etc. As you got closer to the venues, however, the color schemes warmed. Yellows and oranges gave way to red at the venue entrance—the "hot spot." We didn't mix colors per se, the yellows went with yellows and the reds went with reds. And the field of play was all blue again, so it would pop on TV.

The blues and reds were another way of telling the "Fire Within" story. Ice is blue and fire is red. The mountains of Utah are blue. The hoodoos and rocks of the desert are red. Fire and ice were everywhere in our décor. All SLOC publications featured the blues and purples of the mountains on the cover, but the inside title page, or the endpapers, were red. Tying elements around our theme underscored our message. Given our budget limitations, we felt it was even more essential to use all our creative elements to drive a single theme. I think Scott and his team succeeded.

OPENING CEREMONIES

Opening ceremonies set the stage for the entire Olympics. They tell the spectators and the audience what to expect, what to look for. Sydney's ceremonies said: "Let's get together and party." Atlanta's said: "We are the greatest." We wanted The Winter Games of 2002 to touch the heart: "watch these athletes: they will light a fire within you." Or, in one word, "inspire."

I had imagined that Olympic TV ratings peaked for figure skating or hockey. In fact, in terms of world audience, the opening ceremonies is the biggest moment by far. Viewership cuts across both genders, all ages, all cultures, all demographic groups. Our opening ceremonies broadcast would be seen in 160 countries by over 2.1 billion people, the largest televised audience in Olympic Winter Games history. There would be dignitaries in attendance, including the president of the United States.

I thought of Mike Eruzione's comment that his most meaningful Olympic moment was walking into the stadium during the opening ceremonies, representing his country. Dick Ebersol, president of NBC Sports, noted that for 95 percent of the world's athletes, the opening ceremonies is *the* moment—*their* moment at the Games. Very few athletes would stand on the medals platform. We couldn't control what the athletic performances of the Games would be, but we could make a great opening ceremonies performance. Once again, money was an issue. And again, we needed to find a way to do more with less and at the same time try to find additional funds.

Those of us who had come together to produce the Games had been drawn by a sense of purpose. It followed that the opening ceremonies would convey meaning and purpose as well. So often, Olympic ceremonies were variety shows with songs and dancing and plenty of flash but little meaning. We wanted to say something, something about the athletes, about the world family, about the power of one person to inspire another. Our Games had a message; so should our opening.

In my first address to the board, I said that I didn't want our ceremonies to be "just another Hollywood minute." I drew a line of comparison with Super Bowl halftime shows—those are classic examples of variety show programs that can be entertaining but that don't have any particular theme or message or meaning. "Have you been inspired by a halftime show lately?" I asked. "Have you had it bring a tear to your eye?" It's just another Hollywood variety show, and I wanted more than that.

My comment actually had repercussions. It was at the time that we were first accepting bids to produce the ceremonies. The Disney Company took umbrage with my use of the phrase "Hollywood minute." They were a leading contender for our business given their experience with large-scale productions. We had high hopes for a quality proposal, but they dropped out of consideration, citing my statement and saying they did not want to have anything to do with ceremonies as I had described them. I figured "good riddance." If they didn't like the idea of ceremonies with meaning, not glitzy variety shows, we were better off without them.

The person who would guide our ceremonies effort was Scott Givens, and at his side was our director of ceremonies, Sayre Wiseman. A normal human would have been overwhelmed with what Scott had on his plate: all design and creative, decorations, publications, entertainment, and ceremonies. Any one of those areas could consume him; more likely, he would divide his time ratably among all his responsibilities. That's not what I wanted. I told Scott to spend 90 percent of his time on opening ceremonies and 10 percent on the rest; he laughed.

I persisted: opening ceremonies were just that critical. I also had Scott report directly to me. Most Olympic CEOs do not concern themselves with the details of ceremonies. I wanted to be very much involved.

BOOKING THE SHOWMAN

We put out a request for proposal to produce our ceremonies and received over sixty responses. A number of them were quite impressive. In the end, we went with Don Mischer Productions. Don had produced the ceremonies in Atlanta. As we pulled up to Don's office building, it was easy to see that his production company wasn't of the scale of the others. Then we entered the office. It was tiny. It looked like he and his secretary were the only people who worked there. This was Don Mischer Productions. Here was the one man in the country who had staged an opening ceremonies in the past two decades. But there was one thing that impressed me about the office: the Emmys.

Don sketched out his idea in a relatively prosaic way. Don is not the promoter type. He under-states. He under-promises. He points out the complexity of things. So, naturally, I was immediately inclined to like him. He talked about his experience in Atlanta and how many difficulties they had. Yet, he said, it was the highlight of his career and for those in the team he had pulled together. They never imagined having the opportunity to do it again, but they would jump at the chance.

His show began with a central character, someone he called the "child of light." The child was alone in the woods being buffeted by a storm. At some point, a shaman or angelic personage visits him and gives him light. The child in turn gives light to other children who fill the stadium floor. They were broad strokes, but there were characters and conflict and purpose to what he was proposing.

I also knew from examples I had seen of Don's work that he was capable of connecting emotionally with an audience. Atlanta's ceremonies had been criticized by some in the IOC. Much of what the

IOC objected to what was what Americans liked. And Don had been required to insert segments by the organizers. Of course, there was also a lot of pressure on Atlanta as the 100th anniversary of the modern Olympics. I had watched the tapes of the last ten Games, and I thought Atlanta's ceremonies actually stacked up pretty well. There were several moments of pure magic.

One was the tribute to the ancient Olympic Games. Don had fashioned an image of an enormous vase from cloth. On it, he projected silhouette figures of athletes. Each struck various traditional Greek poses that were transferred to the "vase" surface in massive fifty-foot dimensions. It was spectacular. It was a powerful, visual way to connect the historical with the modern. Having Mohammed Ali light the cauldron was likewise a lasting and emotionally resonant moment. Celine Dion did a remarkable job; Don had found ways to accent key passages in her performance with tens of thousands of flashlights in the audience.

I also liked his approach to building his production team. Don assembled a team of independent professionals: the "best of breed." With the kind of clout he has in the industry, he is able to attract the best names in the entertainment business. If fireworks were a part of the show, he would hire the best fireworks person in the country. I didn't have much experience with putting on shows, but I was very much inclined to Don's approach. It would mean additional time up front pulling the team together instead of the "plug and play" solution that the other candidates offered, but it seemed to offer the very best talent. Scott felt the same way. He said that you could not hope to have on staff from year to year the kind of talent that you could plausibly assemble around the Olympics.

At this first meeting, Don had assembled some of those he would have on his team. Kenny Ortega was a producer and veteran choreographer for stars like Michael Jackson and Madonna. He had worked with Don in Atlanta, as had musical director Mark Watters. Producer David Goldberg committed to run the production's budget, operations, and logistics—a thankless but critical task. And producer Geoff

Bennett would direct all matters relating to the thousands in the volunteer cast, a job he had performed brilliantly in Atlanta as well. We awarded the contract to Mischer.

One of the first decisions was what kind of surface we would have for the stage: wood planking, solid ground, or ice. We couldn't resist the notion of an ice stage. It fit with Winter Games. It was a nod in the direction of the athletic competition. But more than that, it brought speed and movement. One hundred fifty yards or so is quite an expanse. If you think of a halftime show at college football game, it conjures up tuba and trombone players looking like ants, and moving about as fast. Even when the cheerleaders ran across the field, it seemed to take them forever. Ice would allow people and props to move with grace and speed, to cover the full expanse of the spectators' field of vision.

But ice was challenging technically. Massive compressors would be required, larger than anything that had ever been pulled together before. Pipes for the chilled chemicals would have to be laid beneath the surface. And then there was the problem with the shape of the football field. Football fields are convex for drainage; ice surfaces need to be entirely flat. We ended up having to cover the entire floor of the stadium with dirt, level it, and pave it with asphalt before we could lay down the pipes.

Ice also complicated our casting. Many cast members would need to be expert skaters, probably including professionals. We would need to pay, house, and transport them to Utah. Volunteers would also need skating skills. Ice was a big decision. Save on the little stuff and the things that don't really matter, go for the big things people will never forget. Yes on ice.

FIGHTING FOR A STORY

Don's early incarnations kept the child of light and embellished the theme. He added a closing "carousel of light." It was an enormous contraption like a Christmas tree with movable branches that we would build up in the center of the field. It would lift the child of light and other children up on its "branches" and rotate them in front of the audience, to our grand finale music.

The idea of a western celebration of some kind also figured in the early drafts. Cowboys and pioneer women were going to construct a frontier town in the middle of the field. Cast members would hammer, frame, and saw away. Pulleys and clasps would raise and place prefabricated set pieces, assembling a town in minutes.

I liked the visual effects, but I was concerned that we would fail to touch hearts. I wondered whether we shouldn't have characters and conflict resolution. As an old English major, I thought we needed to tell a story to draw in the audience. Apart from the child of light who was really more of a thematic element, there were no "characters" per se, no basic conflict, and no dramatic arc.

Don insisted that it is impossible to tell any kind of intelligible story on a football field. We could make reference to dramatic events. We could re-create moments from history that people would recognize. But without recourse to spoken dialogue, even to facial expressions, he thought it very ill advised to stage a play in a stadium. The visual distance to the field and the multilingual character of a worldwide viewership precluded the very elements that captured audiences watching a musical or play. I countered that ballets and large-scale pageants succeeded in conveying complex storylines without words or intimate audiences.

Don and his team worked to see if there was a way to tell more of a story. But they remained skeptical that anything like a play could be effectively produced on a football field in February. Their focus was on visual effects that would connect with the audience. Iterations of the script kept coming back with more music and choreography. At one point, even the role of the child of light was diminished. At the very least, I wanted that child of light as a consistent presence. He represented the power of the Olympics to inspire the youth of the world. He captured the spirit of our motto, "Light the Fire Within."

We agreed that the child of light would introduce each of the artistic segments. He would usher in the pioneers, lead in the Native American nations, and introduce the parade of athletes. The child of light opened our Medals Plaza to festivities every night. The child of light was at the head of every parade in Olympic Square. But I also came to recognize that Don and his team were right and I was wrong. A true story line was not the way to connect with the audience; rather, symbols, references to familiar stories, and powerful music and images would touch the hearts of our audience.

The day after the performance, Dorothy Hamill was interviewed on TV. She had been overwhelmed by the ceremonies; "I cried during the whole thing," she said. And I thought to myself, "Yes!" That is precisely what we were shooting for.

WOW MOMENTS

The entire ceremonies team concurred that memorable ceremonies had moments that stood out, that awed the audience. We looked to include what we called "wow moments." They were the big ideas that held up the show, like poles in a tent. After watching tapes of previous opening ceremonies and reviewing the press coverage to see how each was received, it was evident that different Games were remembered for defining moments. In Atlanta, they were the Ali cauldron lighting and the Greek athletes silhouetted on the massive vase. In Lillehammer, it was the torchbearer who launched from the Olympic ski jump. In Albertville, an enormous Maypole-like device presided over the entire ceremonies and formed the center of each artistic segment. We started by asking ourselves what the postcards of our ceremony would show: what would be the moment to remember? How would we build such moments into the show?

Like the Maypole in Albertville, we expected our ice stage, magnificently sculptured and lit, to be a memorable feature. The lighting of the cauldron by Mike Eruzione and the Miracle on Ice team would stand out as well. But because he and they were in some ways a logical choice, it would not be as big a surprise to the audience, and wow moments are fueled by surprise. Scott Givens and Jamie Rupert had an idea for turning the normally staid presentation of the Olympic flag into a wow moment.

There would be eight individuals who would present the Olympic flag. We would choose one person to represent each of the five continents symbolized by the five Olympic rings. The three remaining slots would draw from the three pillars in the Olympic movement: Sport, Culture, and Environment; one person would be chosen to represent each. It was a compelling idea, just the sort of symbolism that Olympic audiences appreciate. More important, it reinforced our theme and focus on inspiration. All of our torchbearers had been chosen because they had inspired those around them through their sacrifice, commitment, or courage. Now we would also choose eight inspirational figures from around the world to stand together at a crowning moment of our ceremonies.

The list of potential candidates was very long, but the shortlist came easily. Despite the distance to be traveled and the short notice, our nominees were anxious to serve: Nobel Peace Prize laureate Bishop Desmond Tutu representing Africa; Australian Olympian Cathy Freeman representing Oceania; astronaut and former Senator John Glenn representing the Americas; steelworker turned president of Poland Lech Walesa representing Europe; Japanese Olympic ski-jumping hero Kazuyoshi Funaki representing Asia; Academy Award-winning director and producer Steven Spielberg representing culture; marine life environmentalist Jean-Michel Cousteau (son of Jacques Cousteau) representing the environment; and, lastly, IOC executive director and legendary winter Olympian Jean-Claude Killy representing sport.

For three months, Scott and I kept our secret as we sent out letters tracking down our guests. All the media speculation was on the choices of torchbearers. And here we were flying in the likes of Steven Spielberg, Desmond Tutu, and Lech Walesa. That night, when their names were read, and when they marched out together representing the peoples and ideals of the world family, I for one was deeply moved. I was standing next to IOC President Jacques Rogge: "that was something we will not ever forget."

Other crafted "wow moments" included our personage of light skating across the ice with fireworks on his skates igniting the Olympic rings in flames on the surface of the ice; the gathering of Native American nations in their tribal dress, each chief riding in horseback to extend good wishes and blessings to the athletes of the world in their native tribal languages; our remarkable fireworks display choreographed first to John William's newly composed Olympic anthem and then to Beethoven's *Ode to Joy*; and, of course, the presentation of the World Trade Center flag—perhaps the supernal moment of the entire event. Those moments were deliberately crafted for drama and emotion, to become the pillars that would support the competitions.

MUSIC

Music was the key to the heart of any audience. Our selections and our musicians were critical to our success in touching hearts and communicating meaning. Given the size of the TV audience for the opening ceremonies, top artists are usually willing to perform without charge (although their travel, personnel and technical costs can be quite large). Because our Games were in Salt Lake City, I wanted both celebrity artists and new performers, celebrities to show that we had world-class Games, and new artists to show emerging talent.

By and large, we wanted newly composed music, fit precisely to the story being told in each segment. We also hoped to find other preexisting scores that would draw the audience to familiar memories.

We also wanted an anthem and a pop song that could each become something of a signature piece. We knew from the outset who we wanted for the anthem: the master of Olympic anthems, John Williams. I called him with Don and asked if he would compose for our Games. He agreed. His composition blended a symphony with the voices of a choir. It could not have been better suited for Salt Lakes's Mormon Tabernacle Choir and the Utah Symphony. Such an anthem is performed live at the ceremonies but it is also recorded and then played on track, to supplement the obvious problems associated with trying to microphone a symphony and choir outdoors, possibly in inclement weather.

Returning from a sales call on a prospective sponsor, I rushed to Utah Symphony Hall to hear John Williams conducting the symphony and the choir. The symphony was on the stage, the choir was in the first 25 rows of the audience seats. I stood with him at the center between them for the most powerful musical performance of any kind I have ever heard. His piece would be a wow moment.

For the pop theme song, I had to become educated. Don Mischer and Scott Givens loaded me down with stacks of CDs to listen to, looking or rather listening for a composer. I worked my way through them during drive time to and from our home in Park City. I suppose it's not surprising, but I was very impressed with the work of David Foster. Don and Scott arranged a meeting with Mr. Foster at Don's office in California.

He generously offered to write something for us free of charge. Apparently, he offered more than one choice. Scott and Don wouldn't let me listen to the first one for fear that I might select it. In Scott's words, he doubted my ability to separate the mechanics of a song itself from the strength of the performer. The number was performed by a dynamite studio singer and the song sounded fantastic, but Scott was convinced it wasn't right.

Foster sent a second composition, called *Light the Fire Within*. This one they let me hear! I thought it was brilliant—just the right message, just the right tone, soaring melodies, and power to rock the soul.

The next task was finding someone to sing it. LeAnn Rimes was a perfect fit. Her style was spot on—wholesome but adventurous, pretty, young, and rising. I spent hours listening to her tracks trying to determine whether she had the voice to carry both the soaring high notes and the subtler elements of the song. It sure seemed so to me. Of course, what did I know? Don, Scott and David were probably just trying to get me involved, but it was great fun. She did a tremendous job.

Our decision to include Sting's *Fragile* number was made after the September 11 attacks. Sting's ten-year-old hit had been enjoying something of a revival. Its lyrics captured the deep feeling of loss and bewilderment that typified much of the world's response to terrorism—in Jerusalem and Nigeria as well as in New York. And it did it in such a graceful way. We had a stunning arrangement that brought in Yo-Yo Ma playing a cello descant and the swelling back-up vocals of the whole Mormon Tabernacle Choir.

The Dixie Chicks did come, though they were skipped by NBC in favor of a commercial break. They sang their hit *Ready to Run* as the culmination of the settler sequence. The song begins, "When the train rolls by... " and the number featured two cloth and wire trains working their way down the stands from either end of the stadium. They met in the middle and a golden spike of fireworks shot up in commemoration of the historical meeting of the eastern and western lines at Promontory Point in Utah. We had a cast of hundreds dancing and clogging. The Dixie Chicks number led into "She'll be coming round the mountain" and the whole audience sang. It was fantastic. I had pushed hard to involve the audience wherever we could, particularly with singing. The community in Utah is atypically devout—Mormon and other denominations, too. There is a lot of singing in Church on Sunday. It's not an exaggeration to say that you wouldn't do too badly taking a random group of people off the street and handing out four-part harmonies. I wanted to get people clapping and singing and harmonizing and that number just came alive for me. The critics pretty much panned the train segment and singing, which proves it was emotional and moving. In the stadium that night, the culmination of all that energy was just electric.

FIREWORKS

Our fireworks display at the opening ceremonies lasted roughly ten minutes, instantaneous compared to Sydney's lengthy forty-minute barrage. But we kept all the fireworks the same color, white, and we affixed launchers to the stadium itself and rocketed them in choreographed sequence to John William's anthem, the symphony and choir. For the closing ceremonies, we put our money on eight massive shells from Japan, and combined them with hundreds more.

The final fireworks show for the closing ceremony ended up being a million dollar show. But that money wasn't in place until very close to the Games. Nevertheless, the big 24-inch shells had to be ordered from Japan nine months out to allow time for shipping (they're basically bombs so you can't send them on a plane). The largest incendiaries allowed by U.S. law, they go up about a half-mile and burst to a 3000-foot diameter. They were spectacular. At $25,000 each, no one had ever launched eight of them in this country. We pulled the trigger on those nine months out. I didn't know where the money would come from. I told Scott I'd pay for them myself if I had to. I said, I don't know if we can afford the rest of the show but we're going to buy those shells. Later we filled in with domestically made smaller fireworks that we could order at the last minute, but we put the big guns in place.

HEDGING OUR BETS AGAINST THE POSSIBILITY OF SUCCESS

Given the remarkable financial success that the 2002 Winter Olympics ultimately enjoyed, it is difficult to fully capture how tenuous and uncertain our financial prospects seemed up to the very end. We knew that our financial health was always precarious: if all went as planned, we would be fine, but if we hit major bumps in the road, there was little forgiveness.

Chronic uncertainty led us to protect our contingency fund and plan for disaster, and it forced us to do more with less. But success was also a distinct possibility. So early on, as I was slashing budgets in ceremonies and "look of the Games," I gave a contradictory instruction to Scott. Spend as if you were about to go broke, I told him, but work up your plans as if money were no object. Our calculation was that it would cost roughly ten cents on every dollar to have plans in place in case more resources became available. That was money I wanted to spend.

Our initial commitment to Olympic decorations was the Cityscape program of building wraps, similar banners of athletes on the back of the bleachers at Olympic venues, and then, of course, the field of play itself. Decorations for the field of play were the only ones mandated by the IOC—they wanted things to look good on TV during the competitions. But while we limited ourselves to broad strokes, our "look" designers were drawing up plans for Olympic kiosks, Olympic concession stands, and bleacher trimmings. And it was a good thing too.

We got the first pretty clear reading that we were in good financial shape only a few months before the Games began. When we did finally see our way clear to spending more on the spectacle of the Games, it was too late to develop new plans. It was only because of our preemptive design work—a sort of contingency planning in reverse—that we were ready to fill in the gaps in our design. We put flags and banners around our venues and built huge towers featuring placards with images of Olympic athletes to beckon spectators from the parking lot to the general entrance. We were flush when it was time because we planned for unpredictable success.

It is hard for me to characterize the success of our creative team; I'm too biased I suppose. Biased or not, I cannot imagine a more

powerful and captivating creative program. From ceremonies to decorations to design, every feature tied together, or as Scott Givens liked
to say, "they got along." The result was that the Games of 2002 said
something. They were more than a party, more than a sports event.
The Games had heart and meaning thanks to the vision and dedication of people like Scott and Don and those who worked with them.

HAVING HEART

There was one family, one person really, that made it possible for us
to have a spectacular cauldron, to have an ice surface in the opening
ceremonies, and to have such an extraordinary fireworks display.
Spence Eccles had long ago been a member of the U.S. ski team. When
I arrived at SLOC, he was a member of our board. Ann used to say
he was a very handsome man, and I guess she was right. I liked him
more for other reasons.

Spence was the first citizen of the Olympics of 2002. His voice of
experience was the safe harbor in turbulent board meetings. When the
swirl of scandal threatened to derail the Games, he was steady as an
oak. Even at the final trial of Tom Welch and Dave Johnson, he put
the nail in the government's case: "they didn't do anything illegal."
Spence wanted nothing to take away from the athletes and the
Games.

Spence had agreed to donate at the gold level, $1 million. He also
signed up family members, further boosting our balance sheet. But
with several months to go before the Games were to begin, I realized
that we couldn't wait until the last moment to make a go or no-go
decision on some expensive enhancements to our opening ceremonies. Ray Grant, Don Stirling and I had pitched Spence time and
again on various Olympic projects. As the lead trustee for the charitable trust established by his deceased aunt and uncle, The George S.
and Dolores Dore Eccles Foundation, his support for a grant could
be dispositive. Spence's gorgeous daughter Lisa was the executive

director of the foundation: she explained that the foundation gave primarily to the needy and to cultural charities in Utah. But we argued that the opening ceremonies would be the biggest cultural event in the state's history.

The day that the Wet Design folks brought us the three-and-a-half foot scale models of cauldron designs, I knew Spence had to see them. Together with Don Mischer's model of the ice "stage" for the ceremonies, Don Stirling and I took the models to Spence's foundation office. "Spence, we are either going to have two Weber grills on a flagpole or we're going to have this art." By the end of the day, the foundation had committed to provide the millions it would take to build the ice and to sculpt the cauldron.

Spence's generosity didn't start or end there. The family and foundation built an ice arena we would use for Olympic practices. And they built a legacy footbridge connecting the athlete's village to the ceremonies stadium at the University of Utah. We named Spence the Mayor of the Olympic Village: he was there every day, greeting athletes from around the world in welcoming ceremonies. Had he not been running and then merging a major bank at the time, Spence would have been a perfect choice for the CEO of the Games.

Time and again, we were reminded that the success of the Games would be due to commitment to a shared vision. Spence was one more example.

Chapter 17

The Games Have Arrived

The dividing line was the Utah border. Once the torch crossed it, the Games preparations were over and the Games had begun. It would wind its way across the state to Salt Lake City over several days. During that time, most of the athletes would have arrived at the Olympic Village, the media would have taken their positions at the main media center, and the IOC and other Olympic officials would be clenched in their respective meetings. There would still be time left for finishing touches, but we were on stage. The city and state, the nation, and the world audience would already be reading stories about the Games. Reality would begin to shape perception.

The torch had crossed during the night. The flame was "asleep" in its lantern, waiting to ignite the morning's first torch and begin its run. The lighting was planned for sunrise February 4, 2002, beneath the red rock of Delicate Arch in Moab, Utah. Standing under Utah's most famous landmark, a northern Ute named Frank Arrowchis brought the flame from the lantern to the torch held by his granddaughter Stephanie Laree Spann, and she in turn began the final three days run. As it passed by, Governor Leavitt predicted: "Utah will never be the same again."

Fraser and I were perched on an overlooking cliff for a bird's eye view. We had begun our hike up the Moab rocks well before 4:00 a.m. This was an event we were not going to miss. Kelly, Cindy, Scott, Don, Ed, Gordon—a whole host of us were there. It was bitterly cold and we were overheated from the climb. We chuckled that we were walking symbols of our "fire and ice" color scheme.

The flame having passed, we hiked back to our cars and drove to catch an aircraft back to Salt Lake. Lining the road, we saw all the people who had journeyed to see the coming torch. Children, flags, lawn chairs for weary grandparents: it was the same here as it had been over the 13,000 or so miles across the other 46 states it had traversed. A symbol of peace and civilization, to be seen and witnessed.

In December, I landed in Atlanta, Georgia, with a delegation of officials to receive the Olympic flame. Delta Airlines had provided an entire aircraft to bring the flame to the United States from Athens. The plane had been modified and certified to carry specially designed lanterns. In the three months since the attack, we had had just enough time to adjust the torch relay route to include visits to the sites of the September 11 disasters.

In the aftermath of 9/11, the Olympic torch seemed to represent more than just the Olympics. We staged several events in honor of those who were lost, in New York, Pennsylvania, and Washington, D.C. The torch seemed to give articulation to feelings that were still felt deeply since the stunning events of that September morning. Everywhere it traveled, cheering the torch seemed like a first opportunity for citizens along the route to respond to the attacks in a tangible way. Somehow the flames of Ground Zero and the patriotism they fanned, combined with the flame from Olympia, generated a great emotional response from people.

In New York, Mayor Rudy Giuliani held the torch along with members of the New York Fire Department, the New York Police Department, and the Port Authority. Many on New York streets held aloft pictures of friends and colleagues who had been killed. Elsewhere we gathered 100 family members of the victims of the attacks. We boarded a ferry with the torch and powered to the middle of New York harbor. With the Statue of Liberty as backdrop—holding her own flame of freedom aloft—each widow or widower or child who had lost a parent held the torch for a moment and spoke words in tribute to the one they had lost.

In Washington, D.C., after a torch ceremony at the Pentagon honoring victims and rescuers, we stood with the president on the White House lawn. The person chosen to run the torch through the Rose Garden and hand it to President Bush was Elizabeth Howell. A recent bride, her young husband had been a summer intern at the Pentagon. He had vanished in the attack on that fateful morning. After lighting the cauldron, Elizabeth stood on the dais with the torch and began to quietly cry. With the ceremony proceeding around them, the president put his arm around her, comforting this very young widow. He asked her how she was doing. "Before this morning," she replied through tears, "I've only been able to look back. Running the torch here today...it's led me to look forward. I'm ready to move forward now." It was a poignant moment, and only one of many.

All along the route there were tributes to the victims and heroes of September 11. There was a ceremony in Pennsylvania near the field where United Flight 84 went down. For 65 days, in small and large towns and cities, people poured out into the streets to witness the passing of the torch, sometimes in the freezing rain or snow, waving American flags and cheering on the heroes who were carrying the torch—often firemen and policemen chosen in honor of the sacrifices made by their colleagues in New York. Many times, fire trucks were stationed across the road, their ladders raised to form an arch under which our runner would pass. Firefighters stood in reverence, police officers and veterans saluted.

The torch arrived in Salt Lake a day before opening ceremonies, giving us time to wind it through the venue communities and major population centers along the Wasatch Range. Almost all of our

11,500 torchbearers had been selected because they had inspired another person or people. There were a few exceptions: we inserted praiseworthy individuals who were well known in their communities. We also let those who had contributed $1 million to the Olympics select one torchbearer. Among the former, we chose Stockton and Malone, both local NBA basketball heroes in the Salt Lake community. When Karl Malone's name had been announced, he said that he wanted to run the torch into the stadium or in some famous place, not in the desert somewhere. A storm erupted. To run the torch was an honor, wherever. Talk shows and letters to the editor fumed with outrage. I agreed with them; while Karl was a star, he had disqualified himself from running the torch, particularly in a place of honor or visibility. In contrast, John Stockton expressed honor and humility at being chosen: we selected him as the final runner to carry the torch to Salt Lake City Hall and recognized him on stage.

As Ann and I had donated to the Games, we could select one runner. It was Ann. After sunset, along a residential street east of Salt Lake City, my family and I waited for the flame to be passed to her. We cheered when she held it aloft; we ran alongside of her on the street and sidewalk as she jogged her 1/5th mile to the next person. It was a more emotional moment for us than was apparent to others.

It was in the fall of 1997 that Ann had been diagnosed with MS. Despite aggressive treatments with intravenous steroids, the disease had been destructive. By her arrival in Salt Lake City in 1999, she had lost a good deal of strength and mobility; we were planning to install an elevator in our mountain home. Three great things happened in Utah. She met Fritz Bleitshau, an 80-year-old, highly skilled reflexologist (someone who employs alternative medicine techniques to rebuild strength). Despite his age and retirement, he agreed to treat her; it was two hours, three days a week. Second, she fell in with several delightful women horseback riders in Heber, Utah. Margo Gogan became her best friend and her dressage instructor. The first time Ann rode, she was exhausted within a few minutes and too weak to do more than hang on. The third great thing was too personal to recount. But combined, they worked a miracle. Ann's strength slowly returned as did her feeling and mobility. We cancelled the elevator. In fact, she did so well that she was able to become quite an accomplished dressage rider, placing well in various competitions.

There was the love of my life running the Olympic torch down the street. We had wondered if she would be in a wheelchair by that time. Among my children and me, there was not a dry eye.

Fraser and his wife Jennifer also encountered a family challenge. Months before the Games were to begin, their 20-year-old son Michael was diagnosed with rapidly growing, potentially terminal cancer. Aggressive chemotherapy, again and again, guided by the team at the Huntsman Cancer Center stopped the cancer's growth. Ahead of them was the task or restoring health and the hope through prayer that remission would last.

Fraser and I were not alone among the SLOC team facing challenges at home. Alice Mahmood, our director of information systems, learned of her son's auto accident and paralyzed legs while working on our team. We stood together at his bed in a hospital in Wyoming. Ranch Kimball, our director of venue construction, was diagnosed with cancer. And we lost several good friends. Alan Barnes, our director of the Interfaith Council, died suddenly after many years of service to the SLOC team. Bruce Dworshak, our director of press center operations, died in early 2001. Randy Montgomery was killed in a motorcycle accident. Randy Moore and Matt Walters died in the spring of 2001. The trials of life don't stop, even for the Olympics.

Every one of the SLOC people wanted to run the torch, of course. But doing so would mean fewer community heroes would have that opportunity. Because it was not possible for all of us to run the torch, I decided that none of us would be torchbearers, myself included. But we wanted each of us to be able to hold the flame that had come to symbolize the purpose of our work together. Very early on February 8, the opening day, we brought the torch to the Gateway Olympic

Square where more than a thousand SLOC folks had gathered. We passed the torch to one another, capturing each of us by photo while holding it high. It was a morning of hugs and cheers.

The climax of the torch run was its entry into the opening ceremonies and lighting of the Olympic cauldron. The decision of who would be the final torchbearer to light the cauldron was traditionally one of the most secret and suspenseful responsibilities for the organizing committee. Atlanta chose Muhammad Ali, himself an Olympian, a champion, and a heroic fighter in life. For many like me, Ali's lighting of the cauldron was the high point of the Olympic opening. Other cities distinguished the moment less with the person who lit the cauldron and more with the way it was done. Lillehammer's torch was carried into the opening ceremonies by skier Stein Gruben on the 120-meter ski jump. Barcelona's cauldron was lit by a flaming arrow, shot from the floor of the stadium. All of these were "wow" moments. This was a decision I would make alone. To preserve the suspense, only four others would know my selection: Fraser, Don Mischer, Dick Ebersol of NBC, and Scott Givens. Of course, I got a good deal of solicited and unsolicited advice. From the very start, we knew who the logical and most meaningful person—team—would be to light the cauldron: Mike Eruzione, captain of the U.S. hockey gold medal winning team in the 1980 Miracle on Ice along with that entire Olympic men's hockey team. The more we talked about it, the more excited we got. Dick Ebersol sent us a video of the 1980 award ceremony in Lake Placid. I choked up. Mike stood on the podium to receive his gold, then waved to all his teammates to climb up there with him. Jammed together, they held hands high in celebration.

Dick's idea was to repeat the scene. We would have Mike get the torch, hold it, then motion to teammates hidden around him to gather and lift the torch to the cauldron. For this to work, we needed the entire team. Could we find them? Could we keep it a secret?

I had called Mike at least a year in advance and asked him to come to Salt Lake: "I want you to have a place of prominence with the torch, in the stadium." We began lining up the other teammates, promising only a prominent place. We didn't want the secret to get out. Only in the dark, early morning rehearsal of 1:00 a.m. February 8, opening ceremonies day, did they learn they had been selected.

Other Olympic heroes carried the flame. Dorothy Hamill and Dick Button gave the torch to Peggy Fleming and Scott Hamilton, all figure skating greats. Alpine skiers Phil Mahre and Bill Johnson, recovering from a serious injury, in turn gave the torch to speed skaters Bonnie Blair and Dan Jansen. From them, the torch passed to Jimmy Shea, the third-generation Shea to compete in the Olympics, and to his father. Grandfather Jack Shea, 91, had died the week before in a car accident. Jimmy remarked: "It was like all three of us were standing there together." The Sheas passed the flame to Picabo Street, alpine gold medalist, and Cammi Granato, captain of the gold medal women's hockey team of 1998. They ran the torch up the stairs to Mike Eruzione, waiting at the base of the cauldron.

This was the moment I had looked forward to. Fifty-five thousand others and I filled the stadium with cheers. And then the torch was lifted by the twenty-man team to the base of the cauldron. The flame traveled slowly up the 117-foot base tower, towards the glass bowl at the top. Gas was being fed to jets along the way. The flow was engineered to grow as the flame neared the top, but instead, the flame was growing smaller as it ascended. Strong gusts of wind were dispersing the gas faster than it could fuel the flame. Was it going out entirely? Oh my goodness, that delight I took in Sydney's problem with their cauldron! I didn't breathe. There were a few gasps from around me. And then, flash, the whole Cauldron bowl was swirling with flame, now shooting twenty-five feet into the air. Glorious, glorious, glorious!

THE WORLD TRADE CENTER FLAG

As the torch made its way across the country, we began to realize that we would have to do something in the opening ceremonies to recognize the wellspring of emotion and patriotism that the torch generated. The idea for bringing the tattered World Trade Center flag into the Olympic stadium came from USOC. Steve Bull had been negotiating with the Port Authority for use of the flag for months. It was the very flag that had flown over the North Tower the morning of the attacks and then had been recovered from the rubble at Ground Zero.

During the parade of nations in the opening ceremonies, the host country's delegation is always the last in line. The last eight American athletes in line would carry the 9/11 flag. The plan had been kept secret, but a few days before the opening ceremonies, the Port Authority leaked it. USOC President Sandy Baldwin was quoted as saying, "Many of (the athletes) had expressed they would like to do something, while showcasing America's best, to commemorate those who were lost."

Of course, the media loved it. The Ground Zero flag in the opening ceremonies would be a dramatic storyline. But the IOC was not enthusiastic.

The Olympic Charter that governed every aspect of Olympic protocol stipulated that displays of nationalistic sentiment were not permitted. The host country's flag could fly over the stadium, typically next to the cauldron. Its national anthem could be played while that flag was raised. Each nation participating in the Olympics could present its flag along with its delegation of coaches, judges, and athletes during the parade of nations. But the Olympics had a firm tradition of international impartiality. Hitler's efforts to use the Games in the 1930s to celebrate Aryan superiority had sent aftershocks that were still felt in Olympic circles. The formal presentation of colors with an honor guard and anthem was reserved for the Olympic flag—typically raised by former Olympians.

Caroline Shaw called two days before the ceremony with advance word of a firestorm about to hit in the press. The IOC, still broadly caricatured in the public view due to a bid scandal, had decided that the World Trade Center flag could not take a place in the ceremonies as planned by the USOC. I was sympathetic with the policy and history that prompted their decision, but I felt that it was wrong. They were miscalculating the depth of emotion involved. With all that we had done to restore the relevance and integrity of the Games, and with the way that our country had rallied around them, such an obvious miscue could be devastating.

We promptly issued our own statement "respectfully disagreeing" with the IOC decision. I said I would be contacting the IOC to see if we couldn't discover a different solution to the problem, one that would allow the flag to be included.

At that point I learned that the White House had also taken an interest in how things transpired. Nothing came through official channels, of course, but our White House liaisons let us know that emotions were high and that we had better be on the right side of the issue. By then I had already made our position public. It was a top story on the evening news and in newspapers around the country.

The IOC was understandably upset. My comments seemed to suggest that their decision was motivated by anti-American sentiment. Without an understanding of the historic roots of its prohibition against nationalism in the ceremonies, Americans would accuse the IOC of anti-American motives.

I requested an emergency meeting in advance of the games. President Rogge and Executive Director Carrard came, along with Gerhard Heiberg. It was a long and often passionate exchange. I argued that this flag represented much more than the American dead. It was a symbol of healing for all of those who lost loved ones in the attacks. The victims came from more than eightly different countries, including almost all of the seventy-seven countries that would be present at our Games.

"If you shut down this flag," I said at one point, "you run the risk of threatening the whole Olympics. The lion's share of sponsorship and broadcasting revenue comes from American companies and they are going to be offended by this. American consumers could boycott the products of sponsoring companies. This has the potential of unraveling all that we've done. You need to be thoughtful here," I warned. "You're making a mistake."

Carrard was clearly unmoved. "Expressions of nationalism would set a dangerous precedent for the Games." He then took us through the Olympic Charter and an historic tutorial about excessive nationalism. He made valid points, but I responded with indignation to his tone and unwillingness to differentiate the world tragedy of September 11 from national pride.

President Rogge listened intently. He said "Mitt, why don't you lay out what you think the options are and tell me what you think the advantages and disadvantages are of each."

I did just that. My preference was to have the team carry in the flag, in part because that was what had been announced in the media. I was concerned that anything less could lead to public backlash.

Rogge asked whether we couldn't just raise the World Trade Center flag up the flagpole during the anthem as already prescribed in the Olympic protocol. This wasn't a possibility: the flag was torn and fragile. It could not survive in a stiff breeze. Rogge pursued the idea. "Then how about just carrying the flag in during the playing of the national anthem?"

We discussed a wide range of options, but this idea of President Rogge's began to sound better and better. President Rogge further reasoned that carrying the flag in with the team, as had been originally planned, would not show proper respect. The parade of nations was a time of cheering and celebration; athletes mugged for camera shots. Somehow, the flag would not be properly recognized. Someone suggested having selected American athletes be the ones who would carry in the flag during the national anthem; this would placate the wishes of the USOC.

It was about 1:00 a.m. the next morning when we finally agreed. The World Trade Center flag would be brought into the stadium just before the anthem was played and held in front of the symphony and choir. A second American flag would be raised during the anthem. As we emerged from our conference room, NBC *Today* show producers were there, asking for an announcement to be taped for their morning news. Despite the late hour and lack of time to prepare a statement, I sat with David Bloom, the show's much-admired host who died later while covering the Iraq War, and responded to his questions. Yes, the Ground Zero flag would indeed be an integral part of the opening ceremonies.

There were some members of the IOC that were not at all happy with President Rogge's compromise. They felt that any concession on the issue of nationalism was a mistake. In fact, President Rogge took criticism from both sides: Americans felt he initially had been insensitive to the tragedy; IOC members felt he'd gone too far. My estimation of President Rogge had been raised immeasurably, not just by the creativity of his compromise, but by the quiet decisiveness and leadership he had demonstrated. Here was a new leader for the IOC; he would be a good one. Most important, our opening ceremonies would recognize the fallen and the brave.

POTUS

They really do call him that. The Secret Service calls the president "POTUS" for "President of the United States." POTUS was coming to Salt Lake City for the opening ceremonies and that meant we had some work to do. We would have a presidential box where he and his guests would sit. It would have special security requirements. And other requirements as well; the president's staff, during one of their many trips to advance the event, asked if we would build an apartment for the president and his family behind the box in what was then a large hallway. This he could use for interviews with the media and for relaxing: it was very unlikely that he would want to watch the entire ceremonies, they said. He'd want to duck into the apartment. So, we built the apartment.

The president's arrival was an event in and of itself. Helicopters search the field, all aircraft are diverted, the military base is at the ready, and all manner of dignitaries are lined up for the official welcome.

Multiple limos and caravans are staged on the runway, some as decoys. Then Air Force One appears. It's quite a sight; it represents our country. On some visits, I'm told that people just want to touch the airplane: one boy overseas said it was as close as he would ever come to touching America.

President Bush once invited me to join him in his limo. Cool. It's quite narrow inside; the thick protection panels, of course, make it smaller. People waved heartily when they saw him drive by. Here was the leader who had declared the War on Terror, who had invaded Afghanistan to root out the Taliban. This was more than your average president.

He spoke to the U.S. team at the Olympic Village. They swarmed him after his remarks; he shook everyone's hand. He told them to do their very best, to represent their country and their families well, and that he was proud of them.

At the beginning of the ceremonies, President Bush and President Rogge and I took to the field to be recognized and to honor the arrival of the World Trade Center flag. The President was cheered, not only as he entered, but as he walked the entire length of the field to return to the box.

During opening ceremonies, he never moved from his seat. The advance persons and security team were amazed. He loved the show. When each nation passed, we commented on their uniforms, their demeanor, the size of their delegation, and so forth. With the president in the center he was flanked on his right by the first lady, me, Ann, Fraser, Jennifer Bullock, Mayor Rocky Anderson and Rocky's date. On his left sat President Rogge, Mrs. Rogge, President Samaranch, Sandy Baldwin, then president of the USOC, and our SLOC chairman, Bob Garff and Mrs. Garff.

The artistic segments were extraordinary. Oohs and aahs were frequent. Ann and I teared up more than once. It was going better than we had ever seen it before. The artistic show would earn eight Emmys, a record for such an event. NBC reported that the ceremonies had the highest ratings of any in Olympic history. My favorite segment was the only one that didn't get rave reviews in the media: the train sequence. The music and dancing were wholly captivating. But when I watched it on TV later, I realized that it just couldn't be captured on a small screen. Most of the show was perfect for TV; some was even better than being there. The blue ice color, for example, was absolutely brilliant in broadcast, brighter even than in person. But the trains, they were best for the lucky ones in the stadium.

When it was time to officially open the Games, the president made another trip down the elevator to the field. He sat among the athletes. When the folks from the IOC saw him, some were irate. This was grandstanding. This did not fit protocol. But those were the exceptions; most IOC members told me they thought it was great. Then he stood at the appointed minute: "On behalf of a proud, determined, and grateful nation, I declare open the Games of Salt Lake City, celebrating the Olympic Winter Games." That first "on behalf of" sequence wasn't in the script; the president just adlibbed. Again, a few IOC folks were critical; most were not. It really would be difficult to function if you worried about getting criticism. President Bush didn't.

Perhaps the president's most charitable act, besides coming all the way to Salt Lake City in the first place, was agreeing to leave before the finale and the fireworks. Had he stayed, the rest of the audience would have been required to stay in their seats until he had left the area, about another ten minutes. And it was cold. So he left after declaring the Games open and watched the fireworks from his limo, down the street.

WHETHER WEATHER

On talk shows, on the street, the most frequently asked question was what kind of weather would be best—or worst—for the Games.

People assumed that snow was good. Wrong. Snow meant event delays, stuck cars, snowplows, avalanche danger, course grooming, and other bad and expensive things. Our manmade snow was superior for competitions: it withstood thirty runs rather than the ten preferred for natural snow. So snow was not good. Of course, we wanted a good base before the Games began, both for the slopes and to make the city look beautiful.

Warm was bad. It had been so warm during the first two weeks of Calgary that they had covered outdoor skating surfaces with straw to keep ice frozen. Slopes were soft and difficult to maintain. Warm was good for spectators but bad for sport.

Rain was a disaster. Rain terrorized the organizers in Nagano. Rain ruins slopes. It makes a mess of park-and-ride lots. It's ugly and uncomfortable.

Sun and cold are very good. The cold keeps ice surfaces hard and fast, critical for the sliding track at Olympic Park. Sun provides good slope definition for skiers. If it's overcast, it's very difficult to distinguish high and low points, to determine where the air ends and the ground begins. Sun is also beautiful and warm for the spectators. And as long as it's also cold, the sun won't hurt the snow or ice for competition.

No one wanted to speak the word we all feared: inversion. Salt Lake City is surrounded quite literally by mountains. Several times each winter, a malevolent pressure system locks atmosphere in the valley. It quickly becomes dense with fog. Then in a day or two, pollution begins to saturate the fog. If the inversion lasts many days, it can totally obscure vision. It is cold, damp, ugly, dark, and impenetrable. When in inversion, you can't see the mountains around the city; you just see fog. If we had inversion during the Games, Salt Lake City would not be pretty; our decorations would be invisible. And worst of all, inversion would mean that people in the stadium would not be able to see the ceremonies very well, if at all. Fireworks would be heard, not seen. Sport would be largely unaffected for inversion doesn't reach into the mountains or, of course, into the arenas. But for ceremonies, inversion was worst case.

February 7, the day before opening ceremonies, was the third day of a growing inversion in Salt Lake City. I was concerned.

Several days before, I had received a call from the First Presidency of my church. They had asked if they could see where they would be sitting for the opening ceremonies. Don Stirling and I met them at the stadium. As Don and I walked them to the elevator, President Hinckley smiled and asked, "and just what would be the best weather for opening ceremonies?" Don and I chuckled, but inside we were thinking the same thing: if anyone could get God's ear on a matter like the weather, it would be these men. I'm sure a good Catholic would feel the same about the Pope and so on for people of other faiths. But we'd been asked the question and I wasn't going to hold back: "the best would be cold and clear." He continued, "cold and clear, that's the best?" "Well, yes, cold and clear, and then maybe just a touch of snow, not too much for the ice skaters, but just enough for the TV cameras." We all chuckled again; he smiled, and then boarded the elevator.

It was Mayor Rocky Anderson who made the connection. Late during the night before opening ceremonies, a wind front moved through Salt Lake City. It was strong enough to blow some of the massive balloons we had planned to use in the ceremonies against posts and fencing. Even though they had been fastened with ropes, the wind was just too strong. The balloons were damaged, one or two beyond repair; we could not use the balloon feature in the opening. Perhaps by closing they could be rehabilitated. Banners and decorations at our venues and on our streets were blown away or torn beyond recognition. The crew that had spent days installing them had left Salt Lake; they returned by charter aircraft to hang replacement banners. To almost everyone, it looked like a bit of bad luck. Not to me. The wind also blew out the fog, the pollution and the high-pressure inversion. The 8th was as clear and sunny a day as I had seen in quite some time. Rocky called me in my office: "I'm almost persuaded to become a Mormon again," he said, "almost." We laughed heartily: I knew it would take a mighty miracle to do that! But it was indeed a fortunate turn of weather. And while I won't here ascribe heavenly intervention, if it were there, it surely did come just when we needed it most.

And that was just the start. The entire seventeen days were as good as I have ever seen in Utah, in February. Sun almost every day; we handed out cases of suntan lotion to the spectators. Light snow for beauty but not enough to seriously affect traffic or field of play. Clear skies so that visibility stretched to the highest peaks.

Our cauldron again caused a few hearts to falter just before closing ceremonies. It had worked beautifully for the seventeen days of the Games. Water had flowed flawlessly; the flame had been moderated to conserve fuel but was burning bright; and spectators came day and night to have their picture taken with it in the background. But just before closing ceremonies were to begin, the needle on the cooling water dial began to rise, first past yellow, then into the red. Jim Doyle, the project engineer from Wet Design, was near fibrillation. He checked every valve, every meter. For some reason, the cooling water was rising in temperature. At some point, the flame would have to be shut off before the glass blew. Then it hit him. Spectators had arrived in the stadium and they were flushing the toilets in the bathrooms. That had lowered water pressure. Whatever *can't* go wrong, will. As the ceremonies inched toward start time, people stopped visiting the bathrooms and the water pressure gave him what he needed for cooling. Saved.

But wind was the biggest issue we faced for closing. During rehearsals, we had clocked the winds in the stadium as parameters for closing ceremony. At anything near 20 MPH, the skaters and the props went airborne. And at that speed, fireworks were impossible; safety became a factor. The day had been beautiful: sunny with light breezes. But late in the afternoon, Fraser called with alarm. There was a severe front with heavy winds, gusting well above 35 MPH, heading our way from the West. Our weather tracking stations were recording its movement. If we were lucky, it would not hit until 9:00 p.m., the official ending time of our ceremonies. It could arrive as much as twenty minutes earlier, however.

By the time ceremonies approached, the forecast arrival was just before 9:00 p.m. I met with Don Mischer to see if we could begin ten minutes early. No way: TV time. I wondered if we could move a little more quickly through the program. Again, no way, music was pre-recorded, other than for voice, and it was just as closely timed. We would just have to hope. Don had a hotline phone wired next to my seat; I would have to make the call whether or not to start the fireworks. If the wind hit as hard as expected, I would have no choice at all.

Don's people and Fraser's weather team called throughout the show with weather updates. The front would hit before the end of ceremonies. The show had gone on longer than planned and the front was moving more quickly. About 8:30 p.m., I got another update. The front was about twenty miles away, over the Great Salt Lake. It had encountered a stiff breeze from the east that was now holding it up. It would be delayed for an indefinite time.

The show went on as planned. The balloons from opening that had been repaired were brought in as part of the last sequence over the ice. And then came the fireworks. Ann and I climbed to the top row of the stadium to see the whole valley. In sequence with the music, in a scale I had never imagined, synchronized fireworks were launched from five sites across the valley. The colored mushroom cap from each stretched almost one mile in diameter. Dazzling. Lighting the fire within and without. When the show ended, I made my way to the press conference room in the press tower. The creative team was there; we celebrated and hugged. What a finish!

I had forgotten entirely about the storm. Caroline said to look outside. Our flags were flat out vertical, snapping in the sustained wind. White ponchos we had passed out to spectators were rushing in a mass to the south end of the stadium along with all manner of trash and paper. Our balloons were destroyed. The few people who remained in the stadium were holding on, quite literally.

Yes, the weather had been very good to us, right up until the last minutes of the closing ceremonies. As much as anything we had planned, good weather had helped create fabulous Olympic Winter Games.

GAMES-TIME CEO

Fraser and I had prepared for long days and nights at the main operations center (MOC). We planned on taking shifts there, probably four hours each, then rotating to the other. We had heard of Olympic managers spending the night nearby at prior Games; we had hotel rooms just down the street. The COO of the Games in Atlanta spent that last one hundred days before the Games began as well as the Games nights on a bed he put in his office. So we were ready.

After seventeen days of the Olympics, I had spent about one hour in the MOC, maybe a little more, but you get the point. Decisions were being made at the venues by trained and capable venue managers. Fraser and I weren't needed for decisions. Our work on that front was over.

Every morning, there was a scheduled meeting with the IOC leadership to review the prior day's events, receive criticism, and prepare for corrective action. After a few days, the meetings were cancelled. There were no criticisms. We were needed at the venues to say thank you. Twenty-three thousand people were going to work seventeen days in some cases and without pay of any kind. These were heroes to me and to Fraser. And we wanted to see every person we could and tell them thank you. We also wanted to see the athletes and the venues and hear the bands we had hired. We wanted to walk around Olympic Square and attend the medals awards and concerts. So we went to work to enjoy the Games. And it was the easiest job ever.

THOSE MAGNIFICENT VOLUNTEERS

My days were booked with visits to the venues. Steve Young, our volunteer chairman, Fraser, and I hit as many venues as possible every day. Often, I took in a good portion of an Olympic competition. More of my time, however, was devoted to walking the venue, finding each volunteer and personally thanking them for their contribution and work. I asked how they were doing and how they were enjoying what they were doing; I got uniformly positive responses. I saw one of my nieces at Deer Valley, ushering spectators to the grandstand. She said she was having the most fun she'd had; she never wanted the Games to end. Sometimes, I would encounter volunteers who were temporarily overwhelmed. As a venue was loading, for example, we had long lines, even though we would have pulled all our volunteers from other assignments to help at the gate security area. I regularly joined in, looking through bags and purses, working to speed the entry.

Food tents were the best place to see the largest number of volunteers. People from shifts that were ending were there as well as those just coming on the job. I'd walk from table to table, hugging and mugging for photos. I ruined what I thought were perfectly good volunteer uniforms by autographing parkas. The warmth with which they greeted Fraser and me wasn't because we were famous; it was because we were visible tokens of their Olympic family. During the Games and since, I have not met a single volunteer who had a bad experience. Many have said it was the experience of a lifetime.

I have thought about that. The volunteers' work was not glamorous. The food was warm and hearty, but not more than adequate. The jobs were not mentally challenging, particularly given the level of capability of the volunteers: ticket taking, ushering, serving, parking, driving, security, snow shoveling, slope grooming, directing traffic, etc. But they loved it. Spectators regularly said that our volunteers were the best part of our Games. They were friendly, accommodating and clearly having a great time. Their laughter and smiles elicited the same kind of feelings in our guests.

What accounted for the volunteer experience? Of course, the people of Utah are friendly to begin with and the folks who signed up to be volunteers were self-selected sorts of giving people. But that was also true in other Olympic cities. The volunteers in Salt Lake didn't drop out or drop their smiles. I attribute two other factors. They fully understood the greater purpose of what they were accomplishing. Our volunteer training meetings had two distinct parts, one for job training, the other for sharing our vision. They knew as well as any in our management team that the Games were about sharing the great human qualities of the athletes with the citizens of the world; about affirming peace and civilization. And the second factor was that they were asked to work hard, to stretch. Many had to leave their homes well before 4:00 a.m. to reach remote park-and-ride lots, get shuttled to their venue, and prepare for the competitors and spectators. It was cold, dark, hard work that didn't let up for seventeen straight days.

People in the community recognized the Games as an act of service, rather than just a job. I remember learning about the driver of an Olympic van that took curling athletes to and from their venue. On her own initiative, she took her van home the night of February 13 to decorate it for the Valentine's Day holiday. She pasted paper hearts and heart candies all over the interior upholstery and strung streamers across the seats. She did it so that the foreign athletes in her car would feel special and recognize Valentine's Day as a charming American holiday. She did it to contribute in her own quiet way to the spirit of the Games.

On a grander scale, I think of the volunteer spirit shown by the people of Orem, a city south of Salt Lake City. A group of citizens in Orem took it upon themselves to make the women's hockey team from Kazakhstan feel the spirit of hospitality. When they saw how poorly dressed and poorly equipped the women were from Kazakhstan, a group of volunteers raised money and bought them better equipment. They bought them new coats, hats, gloves, even fancy new sweat-suits that they started wearing everywhere they went. People from Orem made it a point to show up whenever the women from

Kazakhstan had a match to cheer them on. The team did not advance, but they won the affection and admiration of an entire community thousands of miles from their own.

Dan Gardner, the brother of my friend Kem Gardner, was asked if he could house some athletes prior to the Olympic Village being open. As luck would have it, he was assigned the Paralympic Ski Team from Armenia. There were five or six athletes in all. One of them had no arms. The others were also severely handicapped. When they arrived at Dan's home, they didn't all have modern skis. They had wooden skis and limited cold weather gear. Dan went to work raising money. He didn't stop until he could purchase state-of-the-art gear for "his" team. Dan called ski companies directly and arranged for discounts on the equipment. He drove the Armenian Paralympians to all of their practices and orientation sessions and other events personally. It became his life to take care of these Paralympic athletes.

Volunteer by volunteer, they made a remarkable difference. Every one you talked to, whether the athletes, foreign dignitaries, the press, when asked about what made Salt Lake stand out, they would mention the cheerful attitude and helpfulness of our volunteers. "What's hot in Salt Lake City?" *Sports Illustrated* asked. They gave their own answer, "Volunteers. They're affable, helpful and seemingly always there when needed." Everyone from Juan Antonio Samaranch and Jacques Rogge to Dick Ebersol of NBC hailed the Utah volunteers as the best in the business. The community was just outstanding. Everyone was anxious to pitch in and help.

We even had one of our volunteers jump into the luge track to stop a runaway sled that was going beyond where it would normally stop. He was concerned for the safety of the athlete and reached out to stop him. He lost his fingertip under one of the razor sharp runners but he never complained. This man was an upholsterer by trade, so losing a fingertip was a significant thing for him. But not only did he not file suit, he considered it a badge of honor from his service to the Games.

THE ONE GOOF

I wanted to attend men's downhill on the morning of the first day. The event was to be held at Snowbasin, about an hour from my home in Park City. We left three hours before the event.

A Utah state trooper drove my car. I was accompanied by a former Secret Service agent, Dennis Crandall, and by Spencer Zwick, my Games-time assistant. About three miles from the highway exit, all traffic stopped. After a long delay, we drove in the breakdown lane to see what was causing the delay. Virtually all the traffic was exiting the highway, heading for our park-and-ride lot at the base of the mountain. But at the bottom of the exit ramp, a single state trooper stood, talking through the window of each exiting vehicle. Her message was that this park-and-ride was full and that they should get back on the highway and go to the next park-and-ride lot. Now this made no sense for all the cars to exit in order to be told to get back on, especially when it was causing everyone about a thirty-minute delay. So I donned a reflective jacket and went to the mouth of the exit and began to wave the cars on. After about twenty minutes, we were joined by law enforcement. The traffic quickly cleared.

We passed the park-and-ride lots where all spectators would leave their cars, board one of a few hundred busses, and start the twenty-minute ride up the mountain. As a big cheese, I got to stay in my car, following the busses. With only four miles to go, the busses stopped. And they didn't move. At all. We waited twenty minutes. No movement. The trooper passed the busses one by one, but with real difficulty. The road had two narrow lanes and occasionally a bus came down the other direction, requiring him to stop and causing us to fight our way between tight and angry busses on our side of the road. We passed literally hundreds of stopped busses stretched two to three miles. What could possibly be the delay? I had called ahead to Fraser who was at the venue; he said there was no backup there at the unloading area. We had no helicopter to survey the road; that would change the next day.

Finally, I came to the end of the bus line. Standing in the middle of the road was a police officer. He had stopped the first bus and told the driver the bus did not have proper credentials to proceed. Every person in the bus was with the Olympic Family having full credentials, but the bus had the wrong color sticker. The bus was too large to turn around in the narrow mountain road, so it was just stopped there. And the police officer wouldn't let any other bus pass.

I was not happy. The event started in twenty minutes. People had been waiting here for over thirty minutes. Many would inevitably miss the first, and best competitor, races. The policeman was not from Utah; he had come up from Colorado. He was not one of our volunteers who had been trained in adaptability, that was for sure. I expressed my frustration, including a jab or two of un-Mormon-like language. I told him to immediately release the bus and get all the busses out of there. What was he thinking?!

Throughout the Games, I encountered people who had been on that bus. One actually snapped a picture of me as I was walking up to it. The expression is one only familiar to my boys after a serious youthful infraction. The people on the bus had gotten out after it had been stopped for several minutes, to walk the last mile to the event; he had ordered them back aboard. Reportedly, his language had a color all its own. It was the one and only dumb thing I saw during the entire seventeen days. I was glad he was not one of our volunteers or our own law enforcement. But nothing like it ever happened again, so far as I know. Anywhere.

TRANSITION COMPLETE

The Main Media Center bustled with activity throughout the Games. It occupied the entire expanded Salt Palace, Utah's cavernous convention center. Print media from around the world had each ordered office space, which our venues construction team had constructed in a massive open area. Smaller media outlets shared a room that looked like NASA Mission Control, except it was ten times larger. Broadcasters had even more space. Manolo Romero's team was dispersed throughout the Olympic venues, shooting every event with hundreds of video cameras. Manolo's live feed from all four hundred camera operators converged on the MMC control room, a spider web of hundreds of miles of cable and hundreds of TV monitors. Each broadcaster, like NBC for the U.S., selected camera shots for their own broadcast, over which they added their commentary. Because there were seventy or so different country broadcasters, the studio build-outs encompassed acres.

Days before the Games began, I went to the MMC to see how Beth White had it running. It was abuzz; it didn't slow for weeks. My favorite spot was the NBC section. NBC had built two stage-studios as large as any permanent ones I had ever seen. Near the center of it all was the office of Dick Ebersol, NBC's master Olympic producer. Dick is a man who lives for the Olympics. He is a master at bringing the athlete, the story, and the competition to the viewer. He knew how to touch the hearts of the viewers. From Dick, I had gained invaluable advice on matters from opening ceremonies artistic elements to city decoration. Dick's office was classic Ebersol. He's a health nut who insists that his hotel room have a treadmill installed in his room. But he also smokes cigars, regularly. The Salt Palace is a no-smoking building. So Dick worked out a compromise: his office had its own vent system installed with a specially built chimney through the roof. I could see it from the balcony. There was Dick's office below with a tin chimney reaching to the top of the convention center. "I did it my way."

A day or so before our opening, Dick invited Fraser, me, and a few others to his "office" to watch the introductory video they had produced to open their Olympic coverage. Some of the text, spoken by Bob Costas and Jim McKay, opens this book. It touched our hearts profoundly. Even Caroline Shaw was moved. We were remarkably fortunate that they were the ones who took the Games to the American public.

On the second day of the Games, I returned to the media center. Beth met me at the door. Everything was working as planned. Caroline accompanied me to a press conference to give an assessment of the Games so far. I had become used to these by then. Large crowds of reporters, rows of TV cameras, assertive questioners. I sat at the press table and looked out beyond the lights. There were not many people. Some looked like they were in the room just to find a place to eat a sandwich. There were a few polite questions, but not much energy.

It had happened just like we hoped—we knew—it would. The managers, the guys in suits were no longer the story. The athletes had taken center stage. Finally. Three years under the microscope looking for every angle, every flaw, every decision that could be dissected relating to the Games preparations. And now with the Games actually underway, we were next to irrelevant. Yes! As we had receded, the heroics of athletes had ascended. The story of the Games was finally about the people and the qualities that make the Olympics so compelling to the world.

ATHLETES LIGHT THE FIRE WITHIN

The Olympics makes heroes. Young men and women who, for the right reasons, at the right time, step up and do something breathtaking. They capture our hearts and stir the imagination, and they often come to represent some aspect of human courage.

When I think about the Salt Lake City 2002 Winter Games, I first think of a trio of women whose remarkable stories captured the spirit of our Games: Stefania Belmondo, Janica Kostelic, and Vonetta Flowers.

When she arrived in Salt Lake City for her fourth Olympics, Stefania Belmondo of Italy was already among the most decorated winter Olympians in history. A diminutive 5 feet 2 inches tall, weighing in at 105 pounds, cross-country skier Belmondo had lungs of iron and legs of steel that had propelled her to a gold and a bronze in Albertville, a silver and two bronzes in Lillehammer, and a silver and a bronze in Nagano. The lone gold medal came in the grueling women's 15-kilometer cross-country and an ill-fated trip to a small village in the Italian alps had cost her her medal when the pressure of the high altitude shattered the French crystal that filled the center of medals awarded at the Albertville Games. When her medal broke, Belmondo told herself she was just going to have to win herself another gold to go with all of her bronze and silver medals. That was, of course, easier said than done. Belmondo was an "elderly" 33 years old in Salt Lake City. And adversity seemed to be courting her.

Several weeks before the Games, while she was training in Sun Valley, Idaho, with the rest of the Italian team, someone stole her skis right out of the team trailer. It was something of a tragedy. Cross-country skiers spend months, even years finding just the right pair of skis. Stefania was inconsolable. She then recovered, and on a relatively new pair of skis, was something of a dark horse on the morning of February 9 at Soldier Hollow as the racers neared the starting line for the 15-kilometer race.

The favorites were the Russian women, Julija Tchepalova and Larissa Lazutina, wearing bib numbers one and two, respectively. In fact, Lazutina had beaten Belmondo in four of five races at Nagano. Belmondo, with bib number three, kept up with the fearsome Russian pair for most of the race, even moving into the lead in the eleventh kilometer. But then disaster struck. Just before an incline, Belmondo's left pole had become tangled between the legs of another skier and her pole had snapped. Stunned, Belmondo came to a standstill and sobbed bitterly as half a dozen other skiers sprinted past. An alert French coach on the side of the track spotted Belmondo and rushed to her aid. He handed her his own pole and told her to take it. Belmondo took the pole but, as by far the smallest racer of the entire field of 60, the man's pole was much to big for her and she essentially pulled herself with one pole for 700 meters or so. By that time her coach, alerted to her plight by radio, found a way to where she was on the course and handed her an extra pole just her size.

By that point, of course, nearly a dozen skiers had passed the Italian. She was thirteen seconds off the lead with only two or three kilometers to go—a seemingly insurmountable lead. Belmondo began skiing again with strength, but her confidence was shaken and she was tired. She admitted later to having been fearful that she would not be able to keep up the pace. But that's when she focused. She felt a surge of intensity and power well up inside her and, one by one, she started chasing down and passing the skiers in front of her. With half a kilometer to go, she and Lazutina broke away from the pack and on the final hairpin turn rounding into the home stretch and the grandstands packed with thousands of people, Belmondo started to put distance between herself and the powerful Russian. It was a stunning victory. She let out a scream, more like a roar, as she crossed the finish line. She had won her eighth Olympic medal (she would win her ninth, a silver, before the Games were over). She had become the first person in Olympic history to become an Olympic champion and then to win the same event ten years later. Her victory was so clearly due only to sheer determination and super-human effort. Yet when asked how she wanted to be remembered, Belmondo paused and carefully replied, "I would like to be remembered as someone, win or lose, who always tried to do my best. That is how I want to be remembered. I always tried to do my best."

Janica Kostelic also made history at the Salt Lake Winter Games. A young phenom from, of all places, war-torn Croatia, Kostelic had torn up the junior World Cup circuit at age fourteen, winning twenty-two races in a row. At great personal sacrifice, Janica's father had taken her and her brother, Ivica—also an Olympian, to the Austrian alps to train, scrounging together money for lift tickets and sleeping in their car. Janica's victories were so unexpected at international events that she often had to provide her own flag for the medals ceremony and sing her own anthem.

But in 1999, Janica had fallen and blown out her knee. Two years later she severely injured her other knee and in 2002 she had had the last of three corrective surgeries to fix the problem. Winner of the World Cup in 2001, she had yet to win a race in 2002. And her training regimen leading up the Olympics included time off on the Adriatic Coast to recuperate from surgery and only a few short weeks in the mountains.

When Janica was in the lead after two legs of the women's Alpine combined, it was something of a shocker. Janica and her brother literally trained running mountain paths and using logs from the woodpile as weights. Before she was done she would win all but one of the four races she entered in Salt Lake, and that one brought her a silver. It would be the most dominant performance for a female athlete in Olympic history. She would win the giant slalom, the slalom, and the combined and would take second in the super-G. She would be hailed as a conquering hero back in Zagreb where 200,000 fans would come out to greet her arrival. And yet she somehow remained starry-eyed and unassuming through it all.

When she won her first gold, topping her two pace-setting slalom runs with an absolutely fearless dash down the mountain in the downhill portion, her mother and brother were still on the plane over from Croatia. They learned about her win by phone. Other passengers on the plane heard them exclaim that their daughter and sister had won a gold medal. They started chanting, "Bravo." Janica's mom and brother arrived in downtown Salt Lake just in time to sprint to the medals plaza and see her receive her medal. It was a family effort to get her there, so it was fitting to have them together in her first moment of celebration.

Vonetta Flowers, of course, made history by becoming the first African-American in history to win Winter Olympic gold. And she did it in a new Olympic sport, women's bobsled, in the sled that was supposed to be the United States' second fastest.

I first became quite intimately aware of the discipline of women's bobsled through Jen Davidson, a local Utah athlete who singled me out and began lobbying me at every turn to bring women's bobsled to the Olympic stage. I met Jen while I was out at the bobsled track looking over the shading system that was giving us some trouble. She walked up and introduced herself and made a pitch for how important it was to include women in bobsled competition. I asked a lot of questions and she had the info. I went to various events with the USOC and she would be there and would button hole me in a corner and lobby: "What have you done for the women? You could really make a difference if you got behind this Mitt. They will listen to you." I became convinced that it made sense to get men and women in both bobsled and skeleton.

Jen was the brakewoman for the best bobsled pilot in the business, Jean Racine. Racine and Davidson were supposed to win it all. But, with only weeks to go till the Games, Racine dumped her partner (with whom she had won the World Cup) and opted for the brawnier rookie, Gea Johnson. It proved to be a fatal decision. Johnson was hampered by a pulled hamstring.

On the eve of competition, Racine called Vonetta Flowers, Jill Bakken's brakewoman in sled USA 2. She asked Flowers to ditch Bakken, as she had left Davidson, and join Racine on sled one. By joining Racine, Flowers was virtually guaranteed to win a gold medal. But Flowers refused. And her loyalty to Bakken, the second-ranked pilot on the U.S. team, paid off. The two of them had a spectacular first run, launching themselves a full .30 seconds ahead of the nearest competition. Thirty hundredths is just eons of time in bobsled. Nothing short of a crash in heat two was going to keep the duo off the podium. And nothing did.

Flowers, who had always thought her track-and-field successes in college would land her in the Summer Olympics, wept openly at the medals ceremony. She felt the full weight of history as the first African-American to win Winter Olympic gold. Months later she even revealed that she and Jill Bakken were not alone in that USA 2 sled. There was another little someone tucked away inside of Vonetta where no one could see. She became a mom just six months after winning Olympic gold.

Other golden moments came from Apollo Anton Ohno, Derek Parra, Mario Lemieux, and the Canadian hockey team that broke the fifty-year medal drought by besting the Americans on the final day of competition. Sarah Hughes exuberantly skating the program of her lifetime when she had nothing to lose and everything to gain. There was the French judge controversy and the awarding of twin golds to Jamie Salé and David Pelletier of Canada and Elena Berezhnaya and Anton Sikharulidze of Russia in the pairs figure skating competition. There were many, many moments of exquisite drama and intrigue in our 2002 Games. But perhaps the most moving story belonged to Jimmy Shea.

Jimmy was a third-generation Olympian. His father, Jim Shea, Sr., had competed in Nordic skiing in the 1964 Innsbruck Games and his grandfather, Jack Shea, had won two gold medals as a speed skater in the original Lake Placid Winter Games back in 1932.

Jimmy had been one of those who made it his business to know me and to lobby for classification of his sport as an official Olympic discipline some twenty years after it had been excluded from the Games. Of course, we had prevailed with the IOC to make skeleton a sport again, and we had big plans for making Jimmy Shea and his father and grandfather a part of our opening ceremonies. Jack Shea had delivered the oath of the athletes in the Lake Placid Games and we would have Jimmy do it for ours. The three of them would help carry the torch to its final appointment with the cauldron as America's only three-generational family of Olympians. Tragically, Jack Shea was killed by a drunk driver just seventeen days before the opening ceremonies.

Jimmy himself said it seemed like such a wasted opportunity not to have him in Salt Lake. The irony was somewhat cruel. But both Sheas carried the torch in Rice Eccles stadium in memory of their father and grandfather. Jim Shea, Sr.'s daughter called afterwards to say she had seen "grandpa" with them on TV, in spirit.

After all the hoopla of the ceremonies, it was time for Jimmy to focus in on his sport. He was a World Cup champion, but a circulation problem in his left leg had led to slower start times and in 2002 he had placed a disappointing fifth in the world rankings with only one second place finish to call his own.

The favorites that snowy afternoon in Olympic Winter Park were Martin Rettl of Austria, reigning world champion, and Gergor Staehli of Switzerland. And after the first run, Rettl was in second place, just .14 seconds out of the lead. Staehli was .27 seconds off the pace and Jimmy Shea was somehow atop the leader board.

Mr. Shea is a very affable fellow. But come race time he is remarkably focused and intense. Skeleton athletes race down the bobsled track at speeds reaching 80 miles per hour on a small metal sled. They do it face first with their chin literally inches off the ice.

To prepare himself for his run, Jimmy typically lets out a primal scream and then sprints across the starting platform and back. His father swears he has seen his son knock officials over without really noticing he gets so focused before a race.

It had started snowing the afternoon of the skeleton competition, a marked disadvantage for the leaders. Accumulating snow slows a track down and no one would face the reality of that fact more than Jimmy since the leader after the first run always sleds last on the second. Staehli and Rettl both had fantastic runs. Shea had only .13 seconds to flirt with on his second run if he were going to beat defending champion Rettle to the top of the podium.

Predictably, he had a slow start. Before he even got to his first split time, Jimmy had lost .09 seconds and would soon give away the other .04 before stabilizing. Halfway down he trailed Rettl for the lead by one one hundredth of a second. He stayed there, virtually even with Rettl all the way through the last split only to reclaim the lead and win the gold in the final few hundred yards of the track.

The scene at the bottom of that track when Jimmy won was near pandemonium. The fans were absolutely ecstatic and Jimmy was jumping around like a wild man. He tore off his helmet and reached in with his hand and seemed to be digging around inside for something. What seemed like a full minute later he pulled out a small photograph. It was a picture of his grandfather, Jack. Jimmy held it up for everyone to see, pointing at the photograph. He dedicated his victory to him.

I happened to be lucky enough to be there with Jimmy and with his family at the end of that race and it was a real thrill. It was as close to athletic glory as I'm likely to ever come. The spirit of joy and affection that flowed freely through the crowd that day was electric.

THE PARALYMPIC REDUX

For most of us at SLOC, the Olympics and Paralympics were all one experience. Ours was the first Olympic organizing committee in history to organize both events. It proved successful, but overwhelming. Scott Givens oversaw Olympic opening and closing ceremonies but he also guided the same for the Paralympics. And just as the Olympic opening would receive Emmys, so too would the Paralympic opening ceremonies. Amazing feat.

The same was true for virtually every SLOC function and manager: each made preparations for both events. There was also a team fully dedicated to the Paralympics, driving us all to keep the "next Games" from dropping out of our consciousness. Xavier Gonzales had run the Paralympics in Sydney and brought SLOC a wealth of know-how and perspective. When the Paralympics began only ten days after the Olympics, we were glad that we had made preparations well in advance: they came so quickly, there was hardly a chance to catch one's breath.

Once again, the volunteers were the face of the event. Even though these competitions didn't get the media play, they got the heart and soul of the people of Utah. The excellence of these athletes in performing each sport was eye opening. I remember watching a father sitting with his wheelchair-bound son, watching the hockey competition at the Paralympics. No words needed to pass between them for a great deal to be understood. Men, grown boys like him, competed at world-class levels to stadiums filled with spectators.

Youth from all over the state attended Paralympic events. Often, they had selected a country to cheer other than our own. One side of the arena would be cheering one country, the other side for the other. The athletes loved it: filled seats and cheering crowds, cheering for every team. I loved it too. People who could probably not find a way to attend the pricey Olympics were inspired by athletes who were just as accomplished.

One Paralympian stood out. He promoted the event from the beginning, making appearances anywhere we asked. He helped raise donations. He took days to shoot images for our Paralympic videos. Chris Waddell, a gold medal athlete from prior Paralympics, would not only compete in our Paralympics, he would help us carry them to the public. Chris had been injured in a skiing accident years before; now paraplegic, he skied the mono-ski that is a familiar feature at Utah ski resorts. And he skied very well. He explained that his greatest compliment had come from an able-bodied competitor who had seen him training on the slopes; he simply had said: "nice turns." Paralympians don't want congratulations for their "courage" or for how well they do "given their disability." They want to be recognized for their ability, not their disability.

WHAT ABOUT THE MONEY?

At the start of the Games, we had nearly $50 million in funds for contingencies. Prior organizers and the IOC staff confirmed that a figure below that would not be prudent. Contingencies were by definition unforeseen. But we had planned so thoroughly, taking measures to protect from every risk we could imagine, that we really wondered if we would need the prescribed amount. Nevertheless, extreme weather conditions, lawsuits, uncollectible payments from bankrupt sponsors or broadcasters, major security issues, or other surprises had the potential to consume cash. We were committed to make sure we did not leave debts for taxpayers in the event something went wrong.

But nothing went wrong. Nothing. Every aspect of the Games occurred as well or better than we planned. The weather was perfect. Transportation worked. Information technology performed virtually flawlessly. Security was comprehensive. Sponsors were pleased. Broadcasters were pleased. The IOC and USOC were delighted. We used almost no contingency funds.

In fact, there were some positive economic developments. We not only met our $180 million ticket target, we beat it by $3 million. With 95 percent of our tickets sold, we established a new Olympic record. Our sponsor program, shared with the USOC, achieved $876 million in revenues, roughly 80 percent more than the prior sponsorship record set by Atlanta! Our donor program provided almost $50 million. Our Olympic superstore did so well that we had to close it before the Games were over: we simply ran out of all merchandise. It had 320,000 customers who purchased an average of $87.80 each. We collected nearly $36 million in licensing fees and other revenues.

The better than expected contingency results and the better than expected revenues meant that we finished the Olympic Winter Games of 2002 with a much better than expected $56 million surplus. We surprised the federal government by returning $10.5 million in undrawn funds. It may have been the first time that has ever happened. The remaining surplus was provided to a foundation that will preserve Olympic venues for athletic training and youth sport, and to the IOC and USOC.

LEGACY OF THE GAMES

Some folks in Utah felt that a Games legacy meant money and venues. Those folks were surely satisfied. In addition to the financial contribution, the Games helped build multiple ice skating rinks, multiple ski jumps, a bobsleigh track, a speed skating track, married student housing, community parks and roads and bridges, all costing hundreds of millions.

Many more of us were interested in the legacy we left to the world, in the legacy we left for Utah and America, and legacy of memories in those who touched the Games in some way. Had we "lit the fire within?" Dick Ebersol concluded: "These Games surpassed my wildest expectations. Far and away the best Games I have ever been involved in." Dan Covey, a torchbearer from Ohio said: "While my involvement only lasted a few moments, the experience will be etched in my memory forever." Mike Eruzione, captain of the 1980 men's hockey team: "the excitement that was generated from the opening ceremony carried on throughout the Games to the closing ceremony. . . . This, to me, was the perfect Olympic Winter Games." The perspectives were superlative, time and again. The words of IOC President Rogge: "People of America, Utah, and Salt Lake City, you have given the world superb Games. You have reassured us that people from all countries can live peacefully together."

To all those who came together to host the world, the Games fulfilled our vision. "We leave this place as dreamers because we know that the dream we share can come true."

EPILOGUE

Monday March 18, the Paralympics closing ceremonies had closed the Friday before. The cauldron had been extinguished. Twenty-three thousand volunteers were all back to work, with little time to decompress. The SLOC team showed up at headquarters, I am told. Exhilaration, celebration, satisfaction, emptiness, uncertainty, and dread all showed up as well. After accomplishing so much together, we would part ways to an indefinite future.

Ann and I were on a jet headed to Boston. No time for us either to decompress. No moment to savor the success of the Games. No time for good-byes.

In the days leading up to opening ceremony, I began to get calls from Massachusetts. Jim Rappaport, former GOP party head, had decided to run for lieutenant governor. The then GOP governor, Jane Swift, had selected a running mate not to Jim's liking and he was going to try to beat him in the primary. But he also wanted me to come back to run for governor myself. That made about as much sense to me as the logic Ann and Kem Gardner had used when they asked me to think about going to Utah to run the Olympics: none. I didn't want to run against an incumbent in my own party.

More calls came. Party activists almost plead with me to give it serious thought. Two people I had never heard of or met began draft movements, collecting delegate commitments to vote for me at the upcoming Republican convention. A state representative endorsed me for governor. Most of the attention I was getting stemmed from the apparent electoral weakness of the incumbent. She had taken over for the elected governor when he became Ambassador to Canada. Her first months had been a public relations disaster; from high approval ratings, she dropped to below 20 percent approvals. A poll I would commission showed such poor ratings that the pollster, a longtime Massachusetts pro, said she was unelectable. If I didn't run, he concluded, the GOP would lose the office and probably disappear altogether as a viable political party in Massachusetts: the legislature had dropped to 15 percent Republican. Democracy needs two parties; if I didn't run.... If not me, who?

For three years, Ann and I had tried to think about what we would do after the Olympics. We made no headway at all. We decided it might be easier to list what we knew we *wouldn't do*. At the top of that list was "run for Governor of Massachusetts." And here we were, with days to go before opening ceremonies, and we were thinking about it.

Coca-Cola had a board of directors meeting while in Salt Lake City for the Olympics. I was invited. I sat with Peter Uberroth, CEO of the Los Angeles Games of 1984. He had considered running for governor of California after their Games, but decided that he needed a bit of a break, a time for transition. Then U.S. Senator Pete Wilson ran and won. And the window never really opened again. "If the window is open, go through it; it may never be open again."

I called Charlie Manning, my communications director from 1994. He was encouraging. He had been sending articles about Governor Swift all along. I knew where he had come out. Then I called my "wing man," Bob White. He was there at the founding of Bain Capital, there during the last weeks of my run against Senator Kennedy, there at the beginning of my Olympics job. Bob is true blue, through and through. Bob got on a plane and flew to Utah. He arranged for a few top political consultants to give me the lay of the land.

Cindy Gillespie joined us for the meetings with the consultants. Watching her interact with Washington officials, I had come to highly regard her political savvy. While she was a longtime Democrat, she hailed from the Scoop Jackson wing of her party, closer to many Republicans than to the Ted Kennedy extremity. We chose Mike Murphy as our lead strategist. He turned out to be sheer brilliance and just as important, hilarious.

The campaign was a good deal like a turnaround. First rule, the vision: know why you're running. Very simply, I was running to help people. Massachusetts had been burdened too long by waste, abuse, inefficiency, and patronage. Government needed to be more about public service and less about self-service.

Second rule: assemble the right people for the team. Bob White and I brought in top quality people who were all in better jobs already. That meant they were there for the right reason. I endorsed Kerry Healey as my lieutenant governor; she had been party chair. Ben Coes, campaign manager, had run a Maine railroad, literally. Eric Kriss and Kelt Kindick, policy heads, both were former colleagues of mine from Bain & Company and Bain Capital; both agreed to work for free. Eric Fehrnstrom, communications director, was top media person at the leading ad firm in Boston. Martha Chayet, finance, had retired after top honors with prior governors. Alex Dunn, field and volunteers, was founder and CEO of an Internet company. Tagg Romney, campaign manager for my lieutenant governor candidate and my oldest son, had Harvard Business credentials and management experience. Cindy Gillespie, debate prep, had joined a high-paying Washington contractor but left to help, as did Spencer Zwick, who had also been an advisor in the Olympics. Charlie Manning and Rob Gray were Massachusetts political whizzes. Bob White was "FOC," friend of candidate, and Mike Murphy was strategy.

Third rule: carry out a strategic audit. We analyzed the state and its problems. We considered the obstacles we faced in the campaign. It was a little daunting. Thirteen percent of the registered voters in Massachusetts are Republican. The major paper is decidedly liberal: it would surely endorse my opponent, both in editorial and in daily coverage. My insistence that we not raise taxes would be unpopular with municipal, state, and teachers' unions; combined, their membership and spouses would number in the hundreds of thousands. Add to that the inherent Democratic base of minorities and the poor and it looked almost impossible to overcome. Our strategy would not segment and appeal to distinct voter groups and bases; instead, I would sell my vision straight to the electorate, unvarnished. I was running to help people, not to find a job. If I were elected, great. If I were to lose, so be it.

Fourth rule: communicate the vision and challenge the team to stretch. We would focus every effort on matters that count the most and make every decision in a way that is consistent with the vision. The vision of a campaign expands as issues are addressed on a wide front of topics. Before the campaign was over, I had taken positions on scores of matters. I believed that they were all consistent with our vision: helping people. My team exceeded expectations. I have never seen a more innovative team, taking more initiative on so many fronts. They simply out-worked and out-thought the competition.

And so, on January 2, 2003, I was inaugurated governor of Massachusetts. The cycle began again: another turnaround, in worse shape than I had imagined.

The first challenge was budgetary. I had not run for governor to manage numbers, but numbers were what stood out in our triage. During the campaign, the debate moderators and the media reporters were unrelenting with questions about the budget: how would I fill a $1 billion budget gap in the next year's budget? I had answers, but I knew that we would never have the best and final numbers until we got inside the books and did the kind of bottom-up analysis Fraser had led in the Olympics. Shortly after the election, Eric Kriss and Kelt Kindick got access to government people and figures and went to work. A few weeks into their analysis, Eric came with somber news. The budget gap for the next year, which began in July, was closer to $3 billion. Further, there was a shortfall for the last six months of the current year as well. We were about $600 million short. Immediate cuts were necessary to prevent a possible cash crunch. The budget for next year would test the entire administration team: finding $3 billion would be a real stretch.

The vision had already been set: it was the heart of the last year's campaign. I was determined not only to adhere to our themes, but also to fight for every single promise I had made. Spencer Zwick had been daily strategist and advisor during the campaign; we traveled together virtually every day. I asked him and Cindy Gillespie who had prepared me for debates to collect every single position and promise I had made during the campaign. These I organized by cabinet post and time frame: each secretary would have a specific blueprint that would stretch our mission, far.

Assembling the team was the most important thing I would do. I asked Bob White, of course, to head my transition effort. For two months, Bob worked ceaselessly with the staff he organized to search for top people. We wanted men and women who were not looking for a paycheck but rather for a mission to accomplish. Eric Kriss agreed to be secretary of administration and finance. Kelt Kindick would agree to leave his senior position at Bain & Company to be my top financial officer. Beth Myers came back into the workforce after years away raising her two children. She was an experienced political person with chief of staff experience; she'd do the same for me. Cindy Gillespie left her job in Washington to lead federal relations and policy.

We recruited other extraordinary people to serve, people who gave up a good deal to make a difference, to help people. My senior team was half men and half women, just as I had promised I would try to achieve during the campaign; that result ranked my administration as first in the nation among all fifty states for women in senior state leadership positions.

The team went to work with bold ideas and resolve. We knew that with 85 percent of each house of the legislature in the opposition party, it would be impossible to achieve any victory unless one of two things occurred. First, either we were able to build so much public support that we effectively forced an outcome. Or second, there was common perspective and collaboration possible. The normal giving and getting through compromise and coalition building just wasn't an option in Massachusetts politics given the overwhelming power of the opposition party. I had no veto threat at all. So we wouldn't worry about our win-loss ratio: I didn't care how many battles we lost. I cared only about how many battles we won.

We were fortunate that the Democratic leaders were good people; we often didn't agree—but we got along. I respected their views. They often respected those of my administration as well. In truth, we were working for the same things, but sometimes with different viewpoints.

There is not one day when I have regretted making a full commitment to public service. The battles, the triumphs, the personal associations are more rewarding than I could have ever imagined. I could have made a good deal more money over the last five years had I stayed at my investment job. It would mostly have gone to the taxman or to kids who are better off earning their own. Instead, I have come to know many more people and to help many more people I do not know. It's a currency of an entirely different denomination: it can't be taxed, stolen, or depleted. The more I have of it, the richer I feel.

INDEX

A

ABC, 24, 118
Abrahamson, Alan, 178, 304
Achieve Global, 201
Acker, Ron, 240–41
ACPA. *See* Anti-Cybersquatting Consumer Protection Act of 1999
ACS. *See* Affiliated Computer Services
Adams, Abigail, xv
Adams scholarship, x
Affiliated Computer Services (ACS), 82
Africa, 24, 28
African Americans, 259–60
Albertville Olympics, 47
Alcohol Policy Coalition, 173
ALEM, 79
Ali, Mohammed, 330, 348
Alta Club, 17
American Association of Retired Persons, 261
American Express, 48
American Motors, 10–13
Americans with Disabilities Act, 44
American University, 24
Anderson, Jerry, 66
Anderson, Rocky, 221, 294, 354; alcohol debate and, 277–79; weather and, 357
Anheuser-Busch, 219, 276
Anthony, Marc, 254

Anti-Cybersquatting Consumer Protection Act of 1999 (ACPA), 214
Arcelareta, Jorge, 260
Armenia, 265
Armitage, Dick, 241, 311
Arnot, Doug, 71, 295
Arrowchis, Frank, 343
Arthur Andersen, 42
Ashcroft, John, 236, 308
Ashton, Alan, 264–65
AT&T, 64, 113, 129, 219
Atlanta Olympics: federal funding and, 43-44, 225–26; Justice Department and, 43–44; security and, 50–51, 286; sponsorships and, 131–34, 210

B

Bach, Thomas, 151
Badami, Craig, 33
Badami, Nick: conflicts of interest and, 30, 31, 33; resignation of, 34; SLOC board structure and, 30, 31, 33
Bain, Bill, 54, 57, 63
Bain & Company, 13, 53, 59–60
Bain Capital, 1, 6, 13; culture at, 83–84; Romney's decision to be SLOC head and, 19; success of, 7, 15–16; turnaround of, 53
Bakken, Jill, 371
Baldwin, Sandy, 197, 350, 354
Bank of America, 49–50, 141–43

Barenaked Ladies (BNL), 254, 283
Barnes, Alan, 347
BASF, 36
Bausch & Lomb, 213
Beau-Rivage, 55
Bechtel, 48, 65–66; SLOC budget and, 46, 51, 105, 113, 115
Bell South, 121
Belmondo, Stefania, 367–69
Belmont, Mass., 52
Bennett, Bob, 5, 228, 229, 307
Bennett, Geoff, 330–31
Bennion, John, 71, 176
Berezhnaya, Elena, 372
Bettman, Gary, 310–11
Bills, Bob, 197, 252
bin Laden, Osama, 286, 307
Black, Roger, 245–46
Blackmun, Scott, 200
Blair, Bonnie, 349
Blake, Norm, 199–200
Blazey, John, 234–35, 241
Bleitshau, Fritz, 346
Bloom, David, 353
BMW, 210–11
BNL. *See* Barenaked Ladies
Bombardier Snow Cats, 212–13
Borncamp, Ginny, 97–98
Boston Globe, 40, 106, 178
Bowen, Gordon, 315
Boyer, Roger, 90
branding, 128–31
Brandweek magazine, 123
Bremmer, Kristine, 178
Brigham Young University, 2, 13, 271
Brighton Ski Resort, 216
British Petroleum, 36
Brooks and Dunn, 254
Brophy, John, 82
Brown, Jim, 71
budget. *See* SLOC budget
Budweiser, 45–46, 129, 173, 219
Bull, Steve, 350
Bullock, Fraser, x; alcohol debate and, 277; communication and, 97–98;

community support and, 245; culture and, 88; family challenges of, 347; security and, 93, 295; SLOC budget and, 111–12, 113; SLOC staff and, 67–70; SLOC structure and, 75–77; volunteers and, 360–61
Bullock, Jennifer, 347, 354
Bullock, Michael, 347
Burton, H. David, 274
Busch, Auggie, 176
Bush, George W., xxv, 235, 299–300, 345, 353–55
Business Week, 201
Busser, Dave, 64, 203
Button, Dick, 349

C

Calgary Olympics, 61
California, Los Angeles, University of, 161–62
Cameroon, 24, 25
Camillo, Mark, 288, 292, 308, 309–10
Campbell's Soup, 92
Canada, 61
Cannon, Chris, 228
The Canopy Group, 263
Card, Andy, 235
Carrard, François, 150, 165, 166, 187, 189, 190, 351–52
Cash, Don, 17
Catholic Charities, xii
Catlin, Don, 161
CDC. *See* Center for Disease Control
Center for Disease Control (CDC), 235–36
Certified Angus Beef, 91, 129, 201
Chayet, Martha, 381
Chevrolet, 210
Chicago Tribune, 179
Christian Science Monitor, 172, 281
Church of Jesus Christ of Latter-day Saints (LDS). *See* Mormon Church
Citizens Against Olympic Waste, 257

Clark, Steve, 260
Cleveland, Grover, 9
Clinton, Bill, 100, 233, 240, 288
CNN, 179, 180
Coca-Cola, 120, 127, 129, 210, 219–20, 253, 279, 380
Coes, Ben, 381
Coles, Phillip, 154
Coltrin, Steve: media relations and, 173, 176–81; Romney's decision to be SLOC head and, 4–5; SLOC bid scandal and, 36–37; SLOC media strategy and, 36
Coltrin & Associates, 36
Compaq, 203–4
Congo, 26
Conrad, Diane, 88
Cook, Merrill, 228
Corradini, Deedee, 237, 245
Costas, Bob, xx, 366
Council on Disability, 261
Couric, Katie, 191–93
Cousteau, Jean-Jacques, 334
Cousteau, Jean-Michel, 334
Covey, Dan, 377
Crabtree, Gordon, 105
Crandall, Dennis, 364
creative features: cauldron, 323–26, 348; ceremonies, 329–35; colors, 326–27; fireworks, 338; music, 335–38; opening ceremonies, 327–29; rings, 322–23; success of, 339–40; Sydney Olympics and, 317–20; theme and, 315–17; wow moments, 333–35
Crittenden, Gary, 134
Crow, Sheryl, 254
culture: communication and, 96–100; donor program and, 89–91; food services and, 91–92; fun and celebration and, 100; mission and, 83–87; passion and pride and, 87–88, 103–4; SLOC budget and, 114; SLOC Guiding Principles and, 86–87; SLOC structure and, 95–96;

sponsorships and, 88–89; teamwork and, 92–94, 101–2; vision and, 83
Curry, Ann, 252

D

d'Alessandro, David, 124–26, 199, 202, 212, 223
Dave Matthews Band, 254
Davidson, Jen, 370–71
Dearden, Commissioner, 292–93, 295–96
DEC. *See* Digital Equipment Corporation
Deer Valley, Utah, 2, 7
Defense Department (DoD), 295, 296
DeFrantz, Anita, 146, 147
Del Monte, 36
Dell, Michael, 203
Delta Airlines, 129, 253
Denton, Jean, 234
Deseret Morning News, 170–73, 175, 182, 189
Digital Equipment Corporation (DEC), 203
Dingell, John, 227
Dion, Celine, 330
Disney, 328
Dixie Chicks, 337
Dizdarevic, Sead, 220
Dobbs, Lou, 180
DoD. *See* Defense Department
Don Mischer Productions, 329
doping, 160–63
Dowley, Mark, 123, 205, 206
Doyle, Jim, 325, 358
Dunn, Alex, 381
Dworshak, Bruce, 347

E

Ebersol, Dick, 124, 199, 223, 327, 366, 377
Eccles, Lisa, 340–41
Eccles, Spence, 17, 90, 340–41
Education Department, 251

Eisner, Michael, 176
environment, 35, 246
Eruzione, Mike, xxi–xxii, xxiv, 327, 334, 348–49, 377
Erwin, Sam, 171
ESPN, 179
Essomba, Rene, 24, 26
Essomba, Sonia, 24
Eynon, Ed, xviii, 56; community support and, 255; culture and, 101, 103; minority outreach program and, 260; SLOC culture and, 84, 85; SLOC staff and, 62–63, 67, 70; SLOC structure and, 76, 78, 95; sponsorships and, 138; volunteers and, 267
Eyring, Henry B., 272–73, 274

F

Fantin, Linda, 172–73
Faust, James E., 273
Federal Bureau of Investigation (FBI): security and, 258–59, 288–89, 295; SLOC bid scandal and, 25
Federal Emergency Management Agency (FEMA), 288–89
Fehrnstrom, Eric, 381
FEMA. *See* Federal Emergency Management Agency
Finley, Bob, 101, 114, 326
Finneran, Tom, xiv
First Security Bank, 17
Fleming, Peggy, 349
Flint, Kelly, xviii, 80; culture and, 103; marketing and, 71–72; resignation of, 56–58; SLOC budget and, 47–48; SLOC culture and, 84; sponsorships and, 126–27, 134
Flowers, Bob, 296, 308, 312
Flowers, Vonetta, 20, 367, 370–72
Foo Fighters, 254
Forbes magazine, 67
Ford, Bill, 176
Foster, David, 316, 336
Fowler, John, 32

France, 47
Franklin Covey, 316
Freeh, Louis, 285, 289
Freeman, Cathy, 318, 334
Froderberg, Wayne, 257
Fuji, 119
Funaki, Kazuyoshi, 334

G

Ganga, Jean-Claude, 26
Gardner, Dan, 363
Gardner, Kem: communication and, 97; donor program and, 89–90, 262; Romney's decision to be SLOC head and, 3-5, 16-17; Mormon Church and, 272, 273
Garff, Robert, 354; donor program and, 263, 265; Mormon Church and, 273; public relations and, 73–74; Romney as SLOC head and, 4–5, 17, 34
Gateway, 204–7, 219
Gateway Mall, 89
Gay and Lesbian Alliance (GLA), 261
GELD memo, 155–59
General Accounting Office, 43
General Mills, 92
General Motors, 130, 210–11
George S. and Dolores Dore Eccles Foundation, 90, 340
Germany, 285–86
Geronimo, 8
Gerstner, Lou, 176
Gillespie, Cindy, xviii, 82, 301–2, 381; community support and, 251; culture and, 88, 103; federal funding and, 44, 63–64, 227, 231–35, 240; Interstate reconstruction and, 44; SLOC staff and, 63–64
Giuliani, Rudy, 344
Givens, Scott, 73, 101, 163, 240, 283; creative features and, 316, 320–24, 328–29, 334, 336
GLA. *See* Gay and Lesbian Alliance
Glenn, John, 334

Gogan, Margo, 346
Goldberg, David, 330
Gonzales, Xavier, 374
Google, 175
Gore, Al, 231, 286
Gorrell, Mike, 170–71
Gosper, Kevin, 146–47, 154–55
Granato, Cammi, 349
Grand America Hotel, 113, 266
Grant, Ray, 88, 340
Gray, Rob, 381–82
Grennes, Ina, 188
Gruben, Stein, 348

H

Häggman, Bjarne, 26
Häggman, Pirjo, 26
Hagin, Joe, 235, 299, 308
Hales, Robert D., 272–76, 279, 282
Halleran, Tom, 81, 239
Hallmark, 254
Hamill, Dorothy, 333, 349
Hamilton, Scott, 349
Hamson, Rod, 56
Hanson, Congressman, 228
Hastert, Dennis, 308
Hatch, Orrin, 5, 228, 306, 308–9
Healey, Kerry, 381
Health and Human Services (HHS),
    235–36
Heber City, Utah, 246–47
Heber Creeper, 249
Heiberg, Gerhard, 188–90, 276–77,
    351
Hellenic Society, 80
Herman Miller Corporation, 201
HHS. See Health and Human Services
Hill, Hannah Hood, 8–9
Hinckley, Gordon B., 282, 284;
    authority of, 273; Mormon Church
    financial commitment and, 272–76;
    SLOC bid scandal and, 271;
    weather and, 357
Hitler, Adolf, 350
Hoagland, John, 241–42
Hodler, Marc, 25, 149, 150, 151, 190

Holding, Earl: conflicts of interest
    and, 30, 31, 33; donor program
    and, 266–67; resignation of, 34;
    SLOC board structure and, 30, 31,
    33
homeless, 256–57
Homestead Resort, 248
Hopkins, Brett, 70–71
Howell, Elizabeth, 345
Huerta, Mike, 82, 233–34
Hughes, John, 173
Hughes, Sarah, 372
Human Factors, 83–84
Huntsman Cancer Center, 74, 347
Huntsman, Jon and Karen, 90,
    265–66, 272–73
Hybyl, Bill, 121, 135, 196, 197, 199,
    200
Hyland, Libby, 114

I

Ibarra, Mike, 231–32, 298–99
IBM, 51, 65, 124, 129–30, 202, 255
IFs. See International Federations
IHC. See Intermountain Health Care
IMG. See International Management
    Group
Indiana, University of, 160
Interfaith Council, 261, 282
Intermountain Health Care (IHC), 90,
    97–98, 220
International Federations (IFs), 61, 62
International Management Group
    (IMG), 135–36, 201
International Olympic Committee
    (IOC): document disclosure and,
    153–59; doping laboratory and,
    160–63; GELD memo and, 155–59;
    reforms within, 35; SLOC bid scan-
    dal and, 24–25, 42, 145–47; SLOC
    budget and, 113; SLOC relations
    with, 141–67; sponsorships and,
    119–21, 163–64
IOC. See International Olympic Com-
    mittee
Iowa Beef Corporation, 91

Ireland, 25
Irish, Carolyn Tanner, 139

J

Jackson, Michael, 330
Jackson, Scoop, 381
Jansen, Dan, xxii–xxiii, 273, 349
Jansen, Jane, xxiii
Jardine, Jim, 42, 57, 63–64
Jeffries, Will, 238
Jet Set Sports, 220, 251
John Hancock Company, 120, 124,
    125–26, 129, 202, 212
Johnson, Bill, 349
Johnson, Dave, 340; media relations
    and, 190–91; SLOC bid scandal
    and, 23, 24, 26–29, 156; Utah
    Olympic bid and, 3
Johnson, Don, 289, 296, 308
Johnson, Gea, 371
Johnson, J.D., 296–97, 309–10
Johnson & Johnson, 123–24, 127
Joklik, Frank: Bechtel and, 65; public
    relations and, 73–74; religion and,
    270; Romney as SLOC head and,
    17–18; SLOC bid scandal and, 27,
    36–37; SLOC budget and, 46–47,
    51, 52, 105; SLOC staff and, 60–61,
    64, 75, 77
Jones, Brad, xiv
Justice Department, 101; Atlanta
    Olympics and, 43–44; SLOC bid
    scandal and, 25, 42, 157–58

K

Katz, Brian, xviii, 42, 158, 174
Kazakhstan, 362–63
Kellogg's, 201
Kelson, Valerie, 248
Kennard, Aaron, 187
Kennedy, Joe, 232
Kennedy, Ted, xi, 13–15, 125, 169,
    176, 230–31, 381
Kerry, John, xi
Killy, Jean-Claude, 267, 334

Kim, Jung Hoon "John", 26
Kim, Un Young, 26, 147
Kimball, Ranch, 66, 347
Kindick, Kelt, 381, 383
King & Spaulding, 72
Kingman, Sharon, 64–65
Kissinger, Henry, xxiii
Knight, Michael, xxv, 62
Kodak, 119, 120, 124, 201–2, 219,
    253
Korea, 37
Kostelic, Janica, 20, 367, 369–70
Krimsky, John: culture and, 88; SLOC
    budget and, 109–10; sponsorships
    and, 121–23, 126, 127–28, 131,
    134–36; USOC problems and, 196
Kriss, Eric, 381, 383
KSL, 91, 196, 201, 260
KTVX Channel 4, 24, 155, 157

L

Ladies Professional Golf Association,
    71
Landels, Bill, 220–21
Latham & Watkins, 42
Latinos, 260
Latter-day Saints (LDS) Church. *See*
    Mormon Church
Lausanne, Switzerland, 24–25, 55,
    113, 145
Layton, Alan, 30–33, 34
Lazutina, Larissa, 368–69
LDS. *See* Mormon Church
Leavitt, Mike: Romney as SLOC head
    and, 18–19; security and, 290;
    SLOC bid scandal and, 25, 26–29;
    SLOC board structure and, 29, 30,
    32; SLOC budget and, 108–9
Lehman, Matt, 82
Lemieux, Mario, 372
Leno, Jay, 26
Lewis, Mark, xviii, 71–72, 202; com-
    munity support and, 251; donor
    program and, 263; media relations
    and, 176; sponsorships and, 131,

134–36, 138, 205, 206, 208–10;
torch relay and, 79
LexisNexis, 175
Libya, 25
"Light the Fire Within," 315–17;
SLOC vision and, xxii
Lillehammer Olympics, 244
Long, Joyce, 101
Los Angeles Olympics: federal funding
and, 227; financial troubles of,
118–19; security and, 286
Los Angeles Times, 178, 304
Lucent Technologies, 64, 130
Lund, Steve, 90, 201

M

Ma, Yo-Yo, 337
Madonna, 330
Mahmood, Alice, 65, 263, 347
Mahre, Phil, 349
Malaysia, 325
Mali, 25
Manning, Charlie, 14, 31–32, 178,
380, 381–82
The Map, 41
Marker, 91, 138, 139, 195–96
marketing: donor program, 89–91,
262–67; licensing, 71; parasite,
214–15; revenues and, 48–49;
SLOC bid scandal and, 196; SLOC
staff and, 71–73; sponsorships, 71,
88–89, 118–19, 119–21, 201–24;
successes in, 201–2; USOC and, 71,
196–201
Marriott, Bill, Jr., 54–55
Marriott Corp., 36, 54, 201
Marshall, Thurgood, Jr., 231–32,
298–99
Mason, George, 11
Massachusetts, 15
Massachusetts Supreme Judicial Court,
xii
Mattell Toys, 217
Maytag Corp., 201
Mbaye, Keba, 158

McCain, John, 198, 308–9; federal
funding and, 227–28, 229–30;
Olympic military support and, 43,
298
McCann, Pat, 235
McCarthy, Steve, 79–80
McDonald's, 44–45, 106, 120, 124,
129, 201, 202, 219
McGarry Bowen, 315
McKay, Jim, xx, 366
McKinsey & Company, 199
McNeil, Jim, 279
McVeigh, Timothy, 42, 286
media: community support and, 244;
relations with, 74, 169–93; security
and, 187–90, 292–93; September 11
and, 187–88; SLOC bid scandal
and, 25, 190–91; SLOC budget and,
106, 109–10; SLOC staff and, 74
Mercedes, 210
Meridian Management, 71-72, 125
Merode, Prince de, 161, 166
Mexico, 8–9
Mey, Ray, 289
Myers, Beth, 383
Michaelis, Vicki, 178
Michigan, 9
Midway, Utah, 247, 248–49
military: Olympic support of, 43; secu-
rity and, 297–98, 309–10
Miller, Larry, 268
Minority Outreach Council, 260–61
Miracle on Ice hockey team, xxi–xxii,
334, 348–49
Mischer, Don, 329–33, 336, 341, 359
Mitchell, George, 25, 146
Monsanto, 134
Monson, Thomas S., 273
Monster.com, 201, 209–10, 282
Moore, Randy, 347
Morgan Stanley, 211–12
Mormon Church: alcohol debate and,
276–80; financial commitment of,
272–76; history of, 269; media
relations and, 172, 173, 180;

(cont'd from 391) Quorum of the Twelve Apostles of, 273, 284; SLOC bid scandal and, 4, 271, 280–81; SLOC and, 269–84; volunteers and, 282–84

Mormon Tabernacle Choir, 271, 336, 337

Movenpick Hotel, 55

MSNBC, 203

Mukora, Charles, 26

Munich, Germany, 285–86

Murdock, Kent, 136, 137

Murphy, Mike, 381, 382

N

Nagano Olympics: ticket sales for, 117–18; torch relay and, 79

Nash, Jim, 49, 141–43

National Basketball Association (NBA), 71

National Governing Bodies (NGBs), 62

National Guard, 43, 239, 296

National Hockey League (NHL), 310–11

National Olympic Committee Assistance Program, 24

National Olympic Committee, Cameroon, 24

National Olympic Committees (NOCs), 119–20, 197

Native Americans, 260

Nauvoo, Ill., 8

NBA. *See* National Basketball Association

NBC, xx, 78, 118, 124, 153, 163, 179, 228, 271

Nelson, Lyle, 262

New Orleans, La., 8

Newsweek, 179, 281

New York, 8

New Yorker magazine, 281

New York Times, 124, 179, 281

NGBs. *See* National Governing Bodies

NHL. *See* National Hockey League

NOCs. *See* National Olympic Committees

Noorda, Ray, 263–64

NSYNC, 254

Nu Skin, 90, 91, 130, 201

O

O. C. Tanner, 91, 136–37, 139, 196

Office Depot, 208–9

OfficeMax, 208

Ogden, Utah, 250

Ohno, Apollo Anton, 372

Oklahoma City bombing, 42, 286

Olympic Cauldron, 323–26

Olympic Medals Plaza, 275; alcohol debate and, 277–79; community support and, 253–54

Olympics: athletes and, xxiii–xxiv, 34; athletics and, xxi–xxii; essence of, xxv; functions of, 41; meaningful moments of, xxi–xxii; military support of, 43; opening ceremonies of, xxi–xxii, xxiv–xxv; sport and, 34

Olympic Square, 253–54

Olympic Village, 239–40

One Country, One Town, 251–52

Ortega, Kenny, 330

P

Pace, Steve, 257–58

Pacificorp, 220

Pacific Rim, 28

Paine, Billy, 129

Palm, 36

Panasonic, 120, 124, 129, 130

Paralympic Games: community support and, 251; donor program and, 90, 265–66; federal funding and, 238; opening ceremonies of, 374–75

Park City, Utah, 2, 29

Park City Mountain Resort, 30, 33, 101, 253

Parra, Derek, xv–xvi, xxiv–xxv, 372

Payne, Michael, 150, 165, 166

Pelletier, David, 372

Petersen, Chase, 137
Pfizer, 219, 253
Pontiac, Mich., 9
Ponturo, Tony, 277
Pound, Dick, 25, 27, 145–46, 147, 150
PowerBar, 92
Powers, John, 178
Pratt, Parley P., 2
Prazmark, Rob, 135, 208, 209, 211, 223–24
Presidential Decision Directive 62, 288
Price, John, 90
Priestner-Allinger, Cathy, 61–62, 213, 259
Pritchard, Don, 91–92, 277
Promus Hotel, 199
Provo, Utah, 250, 276

Q

Questar, 17, 91, 137–38, 139, 196, 324
Quorum of the Twelve Apostles, 273, 284
Qwest, 64

R

Racine, Jean, 371
Rappaport, Jim, 379
Ray, Quinney & Nebeker, 57
Reagan, Ronald, xv, 72, 274
Reno, Janet, 230, 232
Rettl, Martin, 373
revenues: broadcasting rights and, 117, 118; donor program and, 117; marketing and, 48–49; sales and, 48–49; SLOC budget and, 109, 117–39; sponsorships and, 48–49, 117, 118–19; ticket sales and, 117–18
Rich, Charles, 97–98
Rimes, LeAnn, 337
Robbins, Jeff, 264
Roche, Lisa Riley, 170–71, 172, 173, 189
Rogge, Jacques, 151, 167, 188, 189, 335, 351–53

Rollins, Kevin, 90
Romero, Manolo, 78–79, 366
Romney, Ann, ix, xviii; as advisor, 52–53; health of, 104, 346–47; Mitt Romney's car accident and, 39; Romney as SLOC head and, 1, 5–6, 16; September 11 and, 302
Romney, Craig, 52
Romney, Gaskell, 8
Romney, George, 8, 10–13
Romney, Laurie, 52
Romney, Marion G., 12
Romney, Matt, 52
Romney, Miles, 7–8
Romney, Miles Park, 8–9
Romney, Mitt: background of, 7–13; car accident of, 39–40; education of, 13; family life of, 13; as Mormon, 15; Olympic vision of, 34–36; in politics, 13–15, 19–20, 379–84; as SLOC head, 1–21
Romney, Tagg, 381
Roney, Blake, 90, 201
Roosevelt, Franklin D., 190
Roosevelt, Teddy, xv
Rose, Nick, 138, 139
Rupert, Jamie, 191, 334

S

safety. *See* security
Salé, Jamie, 372
Salt Lake Olympics: closing ceremonies of, 72–73; community and, 35, 50, 243–68; creative features of, 315–41; federal funding and, 225–42; opening ceremonies of, xxiv–xxv, 72–73, 162–63, 327–29, 349–55; security and, 285–300; September 11 and, 20, 301–13; theme of, 315–17; torch relay of, 79–80, 343–49; traffic and, 364–65; vision of, xxii, 34–36, 60; volunteers and, 259–62, 267–68, 282–84, 360–63; weather and, 355–60

Salt Lake Organizing Committee (SLOC): accounting in, 46; budget of, 42–43, 44–50, 51–53; community and, 50; conflicts of interest and, 29, 30–31; culture at, 63, 83–104; federal relations and, 42–44, 63–64; Guiding Principles of, 86–87; investigation of, 41–42; IOC and, 141–67; management at, 52, 62–63; media relations and, 36, 169–93; Mormon Church and, 269–84; Romney as head of, 1–21; staff of, 59–82; strategic audit of, 39–58; structure of, 29, 30–34, 75–77, 95–96; turnaround of, 53–55. See also Salt Lake Olympics; SLOC budget; SLOC staff

SLOC bid scandal: assistance program expenditures and, 24–25, 28–29; causes of, 35; community support and, 244; FBI and, 25; federal funding and, 42, 225, 227–28; impact of, xxi, xxiii, 23; investigation of, 23, 24–25, 25–26, 41–42; IOC and, 24–25, 42, 145–47; Justice Department and, 25, 42, 157–58; marketing and, 196; media and, 25, 190–91; Mormon Church and, 4, 271, 280–81; tuition payments and, 24–25; USOC and, 25. See also Salt Lake Olympics; Salt Lake Organizing Committee

SLOC budget: bank loans and, 49–50, 141–43; cost cutting and, 48, 54–55, 109, 111–15; culture and, 114; decoration and, 114; entertainment and, 113–14; media and, 106, 109–10; problems with, 44–48; publicizing, 109–10; revenues and, 48, 109, 117–39; review of, 105–9; security and, 294–97; travel and, 113; turnaround and, 54. See also Salt Lake Olympics; Salt Lake Organizing Committee

SLOC staff: communications and, 73–74; core group of, 60–66; importance of, 59–60, 61; management and, 66–71; marketing and, 71–73; media relations and, 74; outside contractors and, 78–80; pulling together of, 60, 74–78; SLOC vision and, 60; team weaknesses and, 80–82; torch relay and, 79–80. See also Salt Lake Olympics; Salt Lake Organizing Committee

Salt Lake Tribune, 57, 58,161, 170, 172, 173, 175, 186, 278, 280

Salvation Army, 257

Samaranch, Juan Antonio, 354; community support and, 243; GELD memo and, 158; IOC and, 144–45; leadership of, 35; SLOC bid scandal and, 24–25, 37, 146; SLOC budget and, 113, 150; SLOC-IOC relations and, 158–59, 164–66

Samsung, 64, 120, 124, 130, 219, 253

Sanders, Barry, 42

Santos, Daryl, 138, 139

scandal. See SLOC bid scandal

Schamasch, Patrick, 161

Schlumberger, Sema, 65, 120, 124, 202, 255

Schultz, Dick, 121, 135, 196, 197, 198

Scottish Power, 222, 323

Sears, 46, 201

Secret Service, 287–89; security and, 293, 295, 297

security: Atlanta Olympics and, 50–51, 286; community support and, 246, 258–59; FBI and, 295; federal funding and, 43, 225, 299–300; Los Angeles Olympics and, 286; manpower and, 297–99; media and, 187–90, 292–93; military and, 297–98, 309–10; rehearsals for, 92–93; Secret Service and, 287–89, 293, 295, 297; September 11 and, 305–13; SLOC bud-

get and, 294–97; UOPSC and, 289–92, 293–94, 294–95, 306–7
Seiko, 202
Senate Appropriations Committee, 228
Senegal, 158
Seoul, Korea, 37, 149–50
September 11: impact of, 302–3; international reaction to, 304–5; media and, 187–88; Salt Lake Olympics and, 20, 301–13; Salt Lake opening ceremonies and, xxiv–xxv; security and, 305–13; world after, 305–8
Shalala, Donna, 235–36
Shaw, Bill, 143, 255
Shaw, Caroline, xviii, 161, 280, 350; media relations and, 74, 170, 173, 175, 177–78, 180, 183–84, 366–67; September 11 and, 303
Shaw, Robert, xxv
Shea, Jack, 349, 372
Shea, Jim, Sr., 372
Shea, Jimmy, 20, 192, 349, 372–74
Shelby, Richard, 44
Shelledy, Jay, 57, 173, 278, 280
Shriver, Sargent, 39–40
Sikharulidze, Anton, 372
60 Minutes, 190–91
SLOC. *See* Salt Lake Organizing Committee
Smith, Joseph, 8
Smith's Food and Drug Stores, 91, 130, 219
Snowbasin Resort, 30, 33, 227, 290
Soldier Hollow, Utah, 247
Sorensen, Mr. and Mrs. Jim, 262–63
South America, 28
South Korea, 26
Spann, Stephanie Laree, 343
Spielberg, Steven, 334, 335
sponsorships: Atlanta Olympics and, 131–34, 210; automotive, 210–11; benefits of, 128–31; brand enforcement and, 213–18; branding and, 128–31; commercialism and, 222–24; culture and, 88–89; federal

funding and, 227; financial services, 211–12; hall of fame, 218–20; history of, 118–19; IOC and, 119–21, 163–64; office materials and, 207–9; ongoing efforts for, 201–24; renewal program for, 123–27; revenues and, 48–49, 117, 118–19; technology, 202–7; TOP, 120, 124, 151; USOC and, 119, 120–22
Sports Illustrated, 120, 152, 179, 214–15, 363
Sprunger, Thierry, 166
St. Johns, Az., 8
Staehli, Gergor, 373
staff. *See* SLOC staff
Stafford, Brian, 309
Stanfield, Judy, 251
Staples, 207–9
State Department, 43
Stemberg, Tom, 81, 207
Stevens, Ted, 227–29, 308, 309
Sting, 337
Stirling, Don, xviii, 340; donor program and, 88–91, 263, 264; marketing and, 71, 72; SLOC culture and, 85; sponsorships and, 131, 134–36, 136–39, 202, 208; weather and, 357
Street, Picabo, 349
Strug, Carrie, 273
Studebaker-Packard, 10–11
Suburu, 211
Sullivan, Chris, 134
Sun Valley Resort, 266
Supreme Court, U. S., 240
Swartz, Jim, 90
Swaziland, 25
Swift, Jane, 379
Sydney Olympics: community support and, 256–57; creative successes in, 317–20

T

Taylor, Lillian, 261–62
Tchepalova, Julija, 368
Telemundo, 260

Texaco, 45

Thatcher, Margaret, xvi

Thomas, Grant, 65–66, 99–100

Thomas, Shelley: community support and, 245, 252; media relations and, 170, 171, 173, 187; pulling together of, 73–74; SLOC budget and, 106; SLOC media strategy and, 36; torch relay and, 79

Thompson, Tommy, 235–36

3Com, 36

3M, 36

Tickets.com, 201

Tillery, Donna, 52, 258

Time magazine, 152, 179

Today show, 191–93, 252, 302, 352–53

Tonight Show, 26

Topham, Verl, 17

transportation: demand management plan for, 82; federal funding and, 43, 225–26, 234–35, 237–39; Interstate reconstruction and, 43, 44

Transportation Department, 226, 239

Trapasso, Jody, 233

Travaglini, Robert, xiv

Tubbs, Dave, 289, 296, 308

Tutu, Desmond, 334, 335

U

Ueberroth, Peter, xxv, 28, 380; marketing and, 118–19; SLOC bid scandal and, 37; sport department and, 62

United Airlines, 135

United States Anti-Doping Agency, 161

UOPSC. *See* Utah Olympic Public Safety Command

UPS, 124

U.S. Amateur Sports Act, 228

U.S. Figure Skating Federation, 62

U.S. Forest Service, 227, 241, 290

United States Olympic Committee (USOC): creation of, 228; marketing and, 71, 196–201; SLOC bid scandal and, 25; sponsorships and, 119, 120–22

U.S. Robotics, 36

U.S. West, 126

USA Today, 178, 179, 281

USF&G, 199

USOC. *See* United States Olympic Committee

UTA. *See* Utah Transit Authority

Utah, University of, 239, 262, 318

Utah Olympic Public Safety Command (UOPSC), 289–92, 293–94, 294–95, 306–7

Utah Power, 17, 91, 201, 220–22, 323

Utah Symphony, 336

Utah Transit Authority (UTA), 237

V

Valez, Richard, 261–62

Value in Kind (VIK): phantom, 163–64, 165; sponsorships and, 44–46

Van Komen, George, 173

VIK. *See* Value in Kind

Visa, 48, 120, 124, 130, 201, 211–12, 220

W

Waddell, Chris, 273, 375

Wahoo! snack chips, 92

Walesa, Lech, 334, 335

Walker, Mike, 240

Wall, Ann, 216–17

Wallace, Mike, 190–91

Wall Street Journal, 125, 292–93

Walters, Matt, 347

Ward, Lloyd, 201

Wasatch Front Regional Council, 235, 238

Wasatch Mountains, 2–3

Washington Post, 179, 228, 240

Watters, Mark, 330

Weitzen, Jeff, 205–7

Welch, Dominick, 280

Welch, Jack, 176

Welch, Tom, 154, 340; media relations and, 190–91; Mitt Romney's decision to be SLOC head and, 3–4; severance package of, 55; SLOC bid scandal and, 23, 24, 26–27, 28–29; SLOC budget and, 52, 55; as SLOC head, 3; sponsorships and, 133; Utah Olympic bid and, 3

Weld, William, 14

West, Togo, 240

Wet Design, 323–25, 341, 358

Whitaker, Tom, 248

White, Beth, 78, 366

White, Bob, 381, 382, 383; culture and, 100; SLOC budget and, 54, 106; SLOC staff and, 66–68

White, Thomas, 308

White House Task Force on the Olympic and Paralympic Games, 231

Wilkinson, Beth, 42

Williams, John, 335, 336, 337

World Cup Soccer Games (1994), 229–30

World Trade Center attack (1993), 286

X

Xerox, 120, 124, 129, 201, 202

Y

Yamaguchi, Kristi, 192

Yarrow, Ralph, 263

Young, Brigham, 8, 269, 284

Young, Steve, 267, 360

youth, 251–53

Youth Sports Program, 252

Z

Zweifel, Madame, 145

Zwick, Spencer, 364, 381, 38